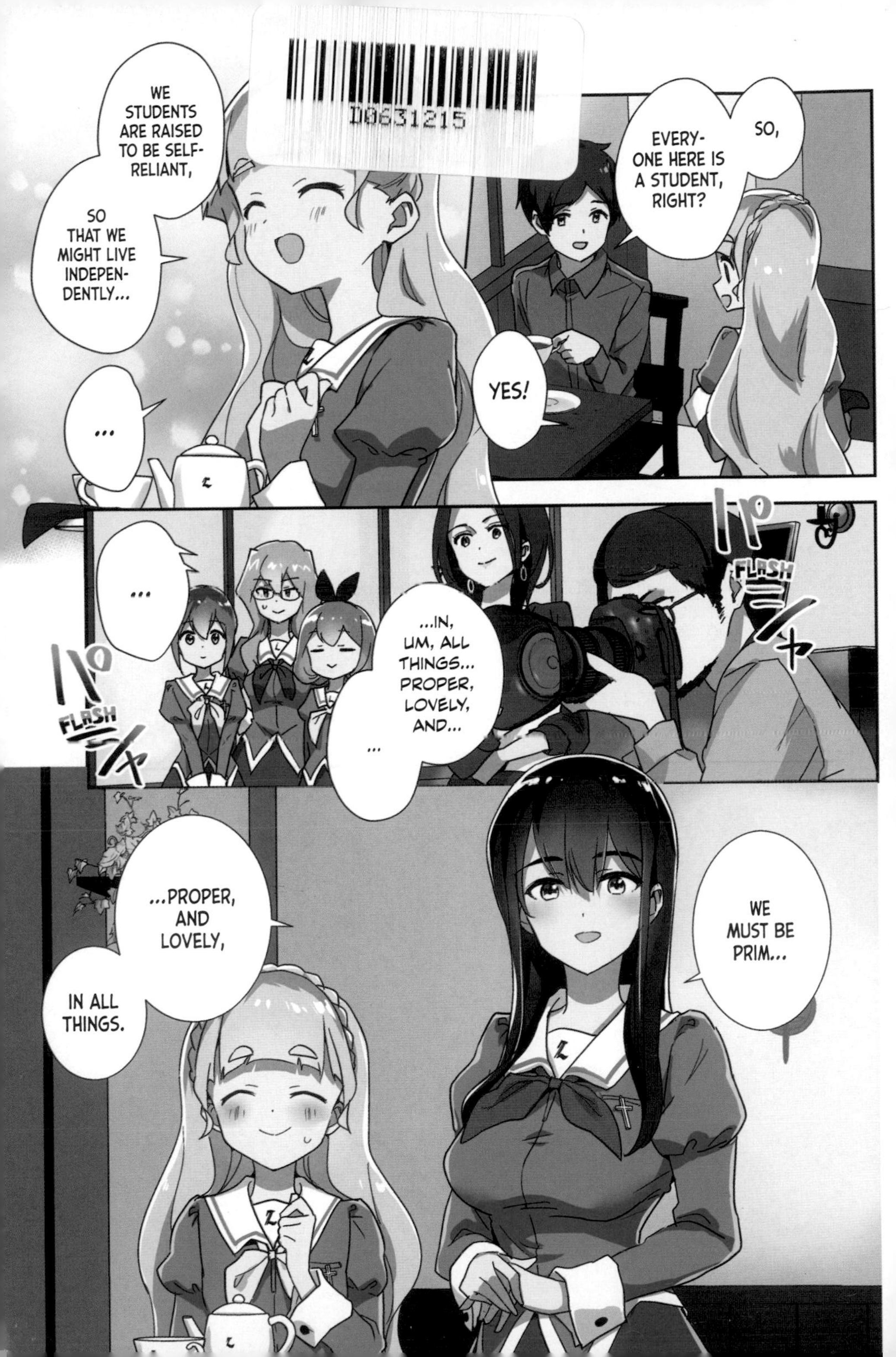
SO,
EVERY-ONE HERE IS A STUDENT, RIGHT?
YES!
WE STUDENTS ARE RAISED TO BE SELF-RELIANT,
SO THAT WE MIGHT LIVE INDEPEN-DENTLY...
...
パ
FLASH
シャ
...IN, UM, ALL THINGS... PROPER, LOVELY, AND...
...
...
パ
FLASH
シャ
WE MUST BE PRIM...
...PROPER, AND LOVELY,
IN ALL THINGS.

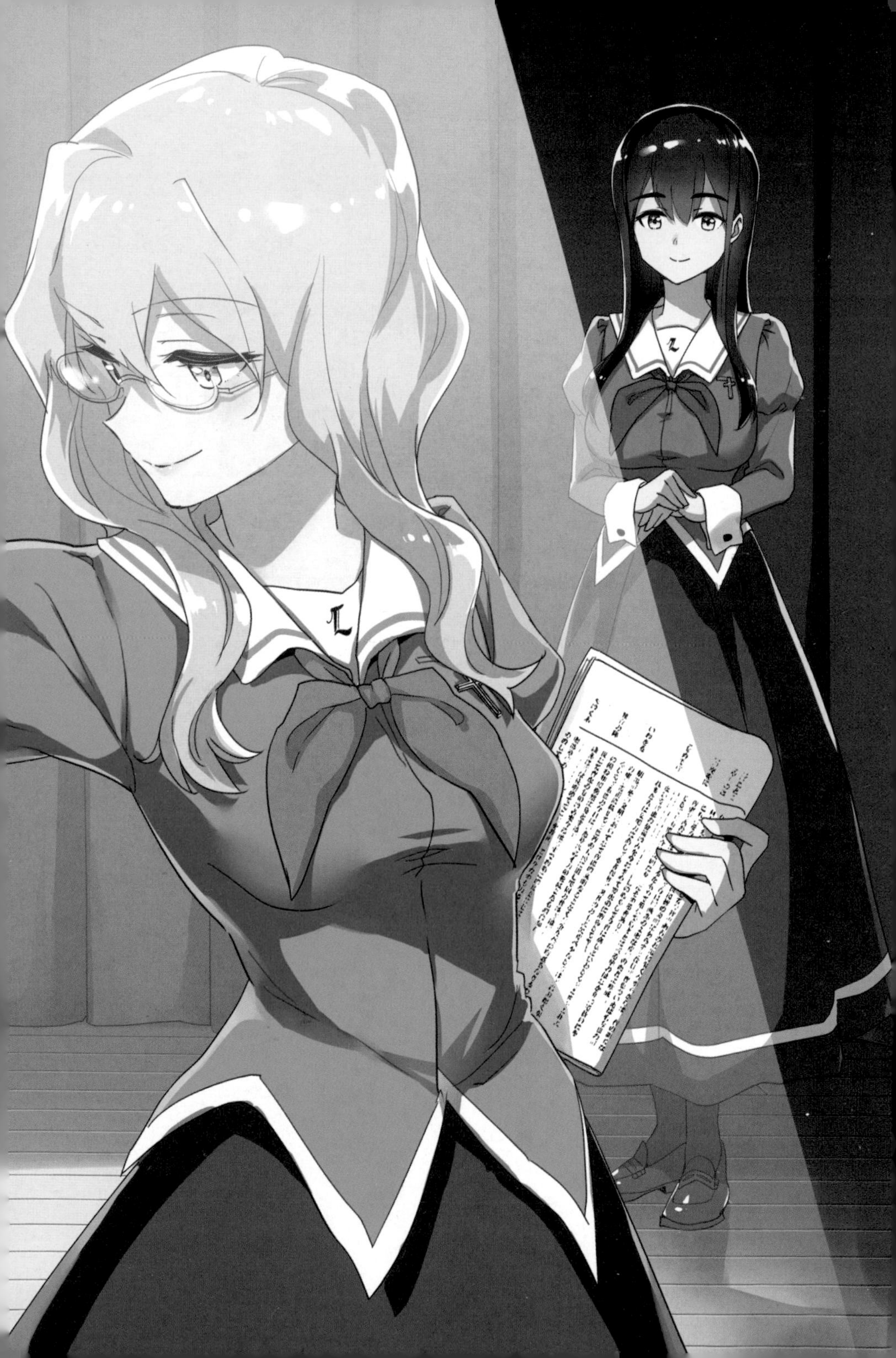

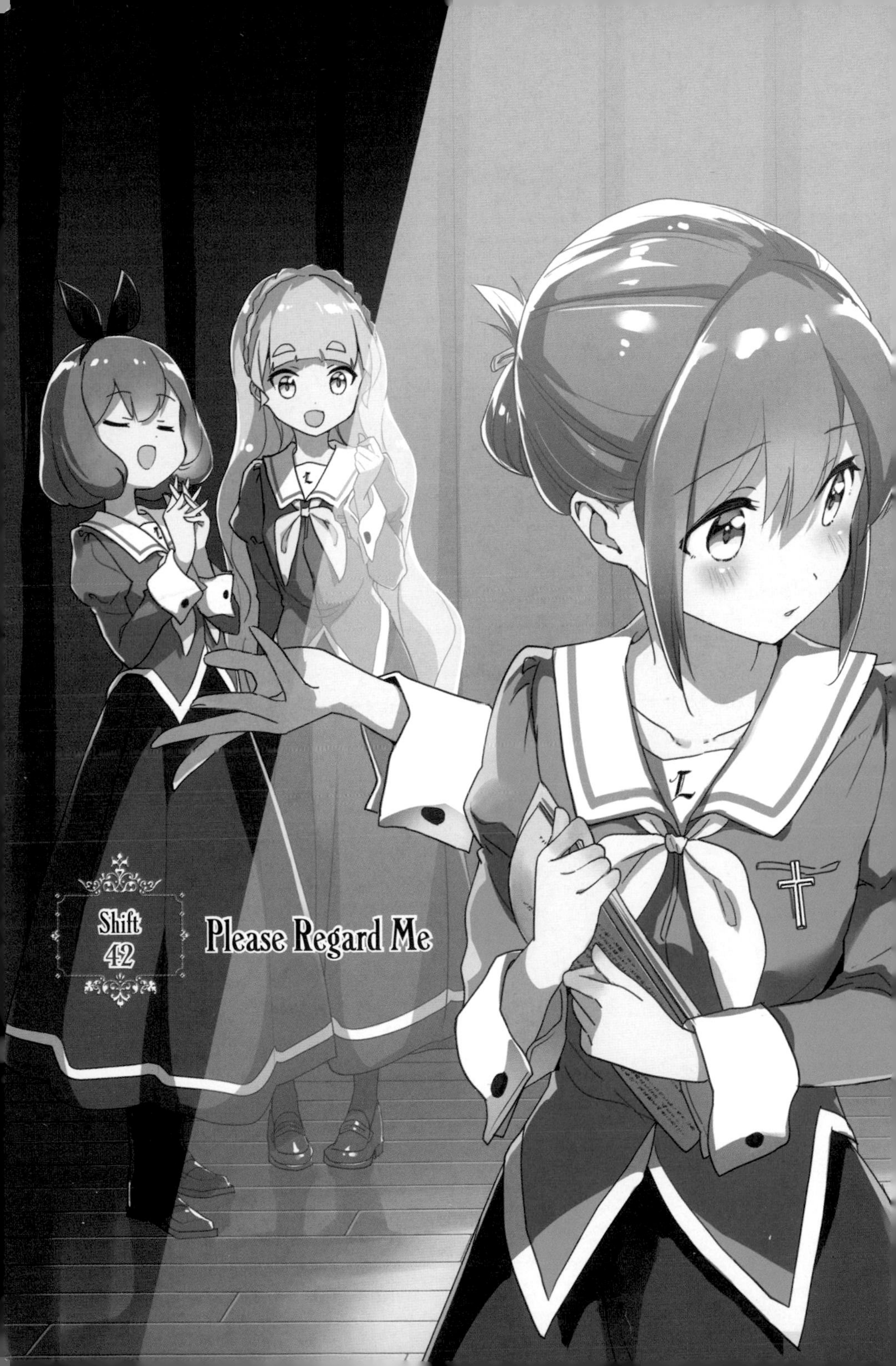
Shift 42
Please Regard Me

CONTENTS

9

Schwestern
in
Liebe!

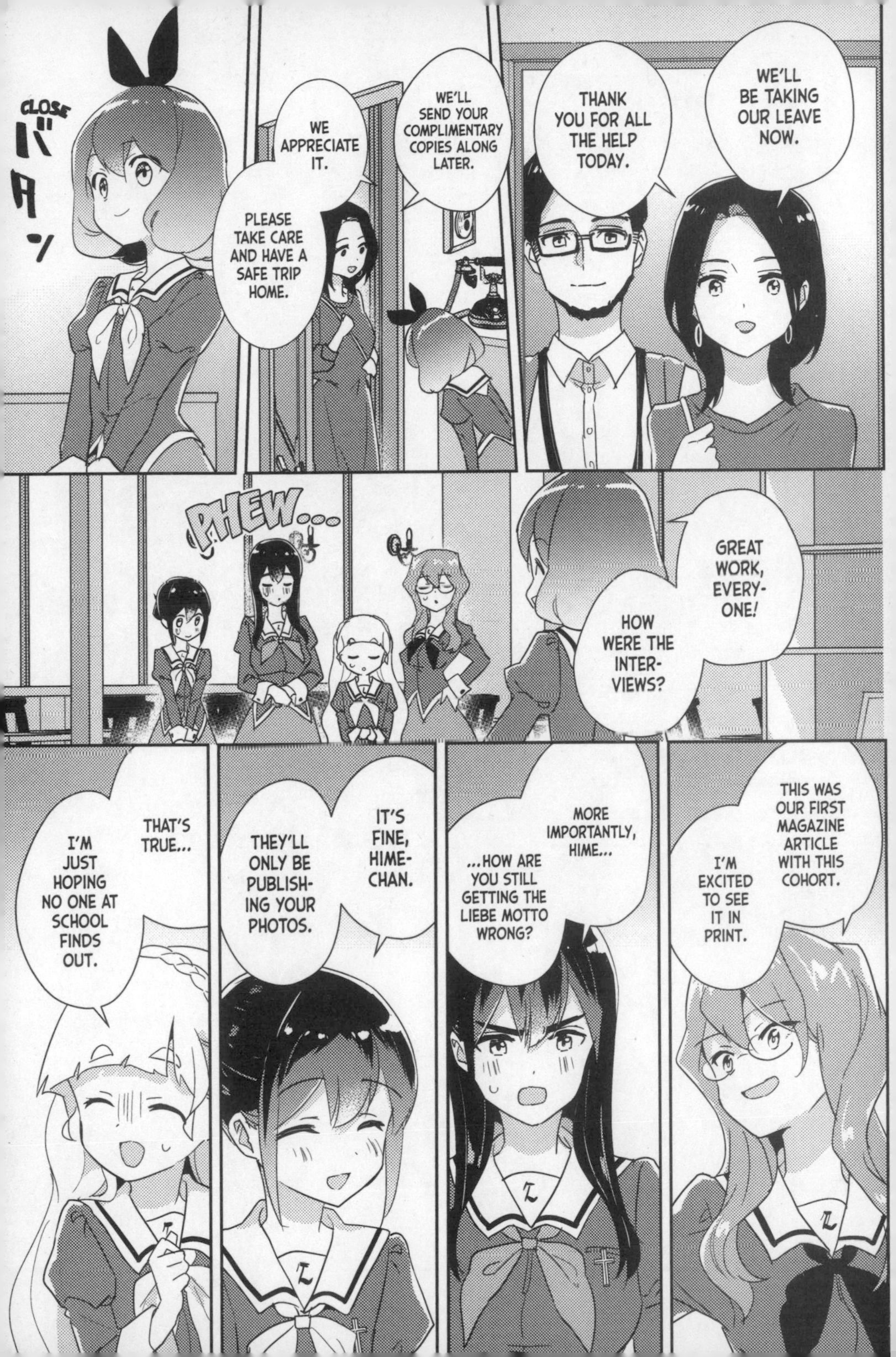
WE'LL BE TAKING OUR LEAVE NOW.
THANK YOU FOR ALL THE HELP TODAY.
WE'LL SEND YOUR COMPLIMENTARY COPIES ALONG LATER.
WE APPRECIATE IT.
PLEASE TAKE CARE AND HAVE A SAFE TRIP HOME.
CLOSE
バタン
GREAT WORK, EVERY-ONE!
HOW WERE THE INTER-VIEWS?
PHEW...
THIS WAS OUR FIRST MAGAZINE ARTICLE WITH THIS COHORT.
I'M EXCITED TO SEE IT IN PRINT.
MORE IMPORTANTLY, HIME...
...HOW ARE YOU STILL GETTING THE LIEBE MOTTO WRONG?
IT'S FINE, HIME-CHAN.
THEY'LL ONLY BE PUBLISH-ING YOUR PHOTOS.
THAT'S TRUE...
I'M JUST HOPING NO ONE AT SCHOOL FINDS OUT.

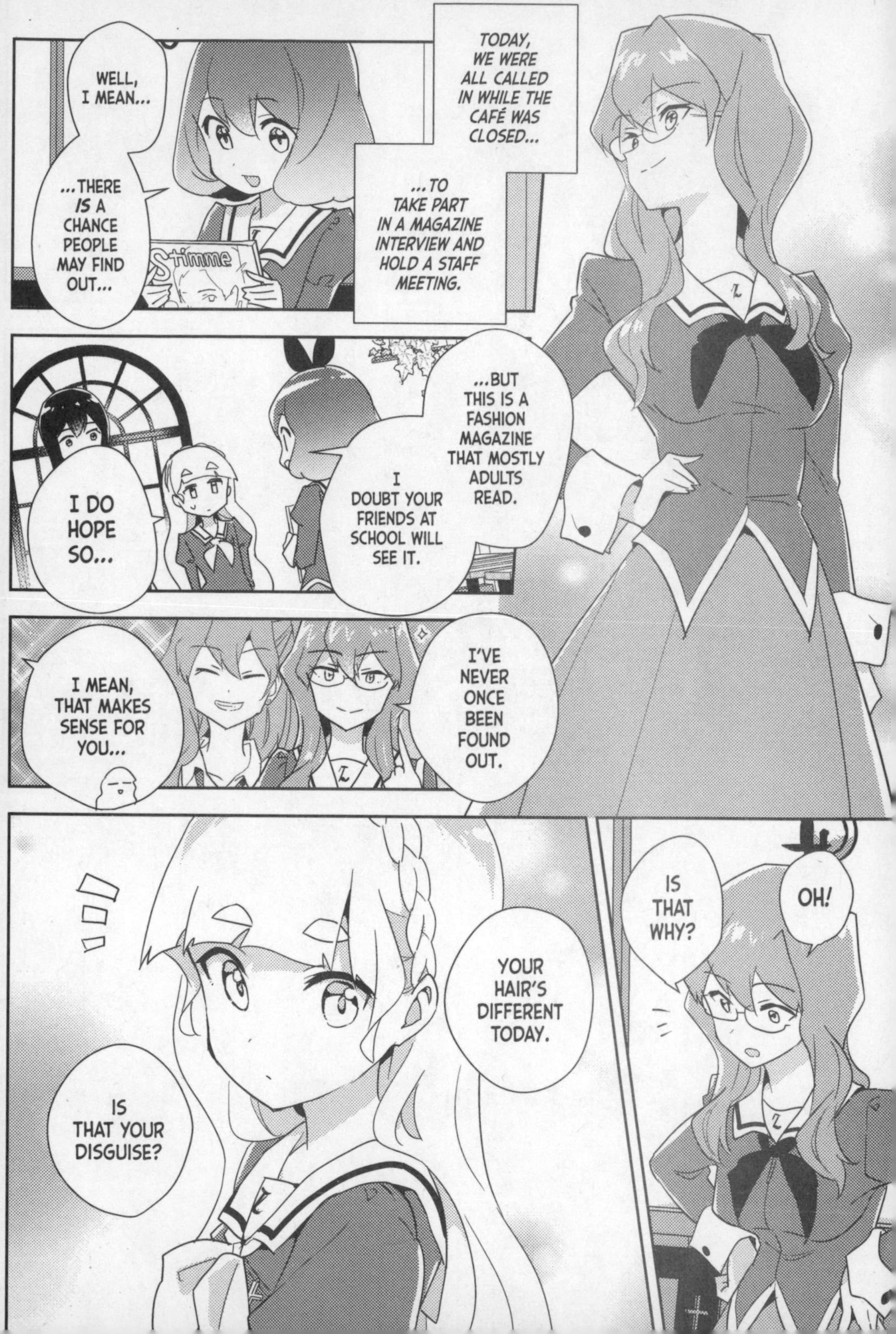
TODAY, WE WERE ALL CALLED IN WHILE THE CAFÉ WAS CLOSED...
...TO TAKE PART IN A MAGAZINE INTERVIEW AND HOLD A STAFF MEETING.
WELL, I MEAN...
...THERE *IS* A CHANCE PEOPLE MAY FIND OUT...
Stimme
...BUT THIS IS A FASHION MAGAZINE THAT MOSTLY ADULTS READ.
I DOUBT YOUR FRIENDS AT SCHOOL WILL SEE IT.
I DO HOPE SO...
I'VE NEVER ONCE BEEN FOUND OUT.
I MEAN, THAT MAKES SENSE FOR YOU...
OH!
IS THAT WHY?
YOUR HAIR'S DIFFERENT TODAY.
IS THAT YOUR DISGUISE?

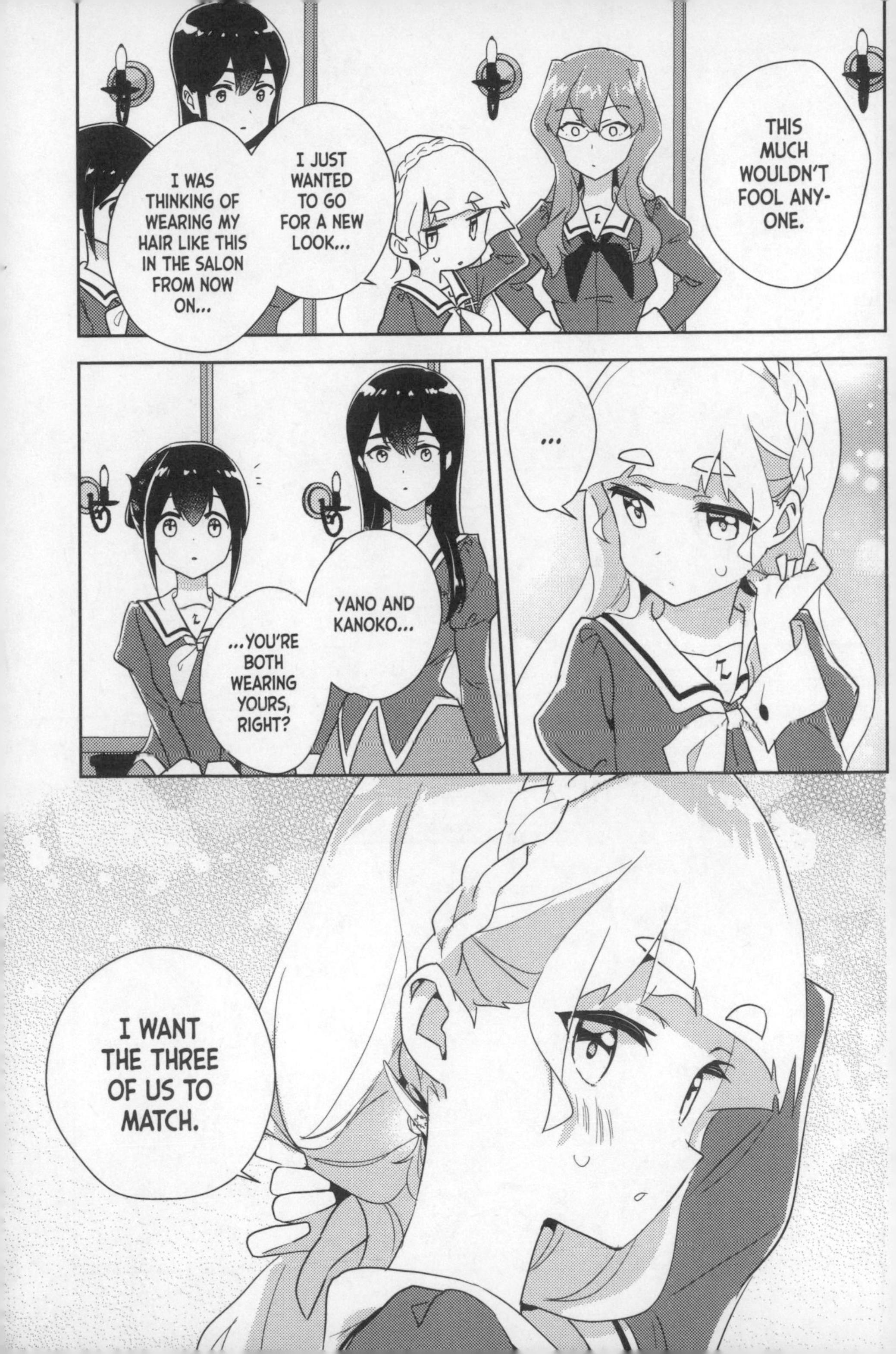
THIS MUCH WOULDN'T FOOL ANY-ONE.
I JUST WANTED TO GO FOR A NEW LOOK...
I WAS THINKING OF WEARING MY HAIR LIKE THIS IN THE SALON FROM NOW ON...
...
YANO AND KANOKO...
...YOU'RE BOTH WEARING YOURS, RIGHT?
I WANT THE THREE OF US TO MATCH.

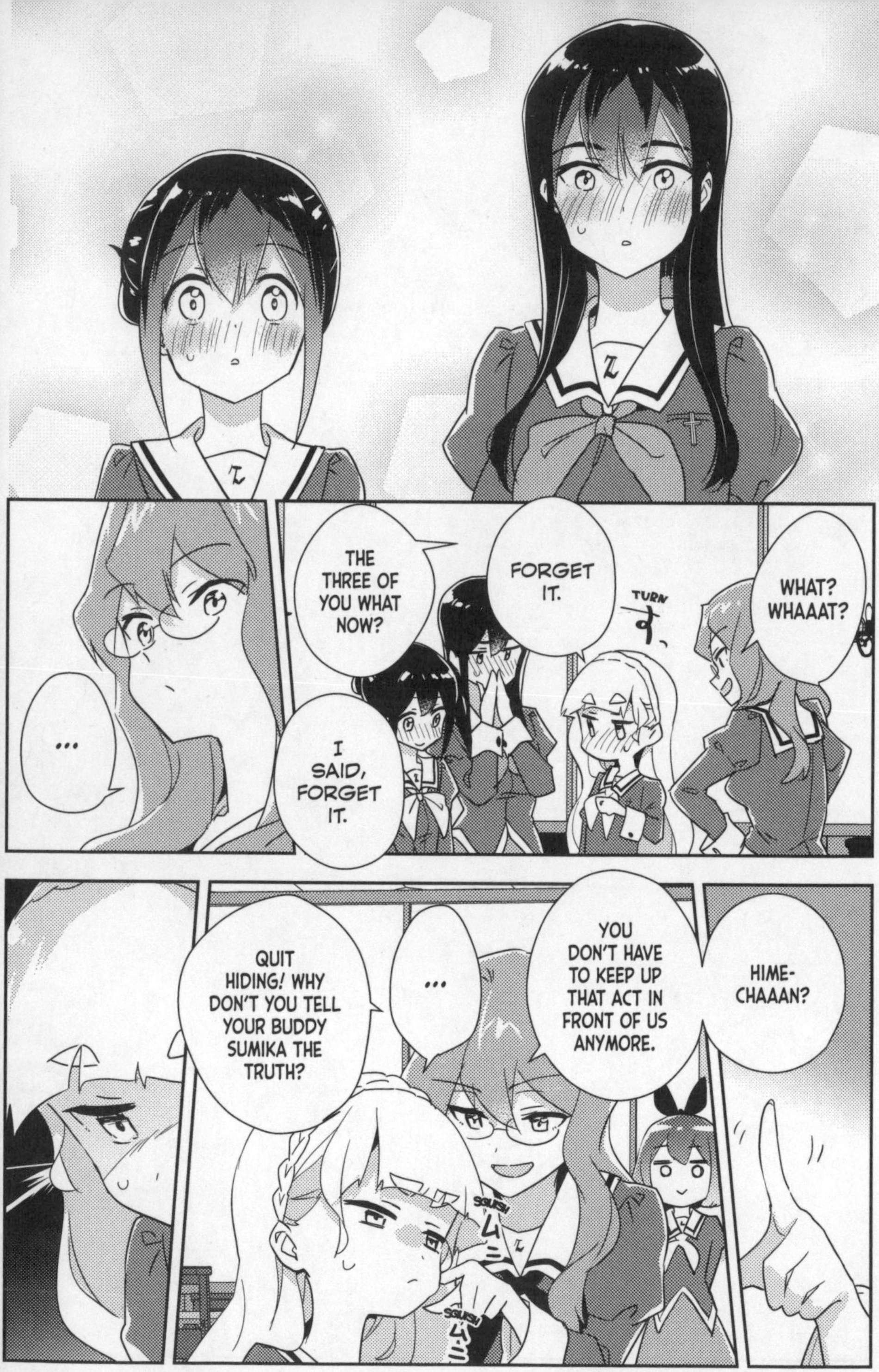
WHAT? WHAAAT?
TURN
FORGET IT.
THE THREE OF YOU WHAT NOW?
I SAID, FORGET IT.
...
HIME-CHAAAN?
YOU DON'T HAVE TO KEEP UP THAT ACT IN FRONT OF US ANYMORE.
...
QUIT HIDING! WHY DON'T YOU TELL YOUR BUDDY SUMIKA THE TRUTH?
SQUISH
SQUISH

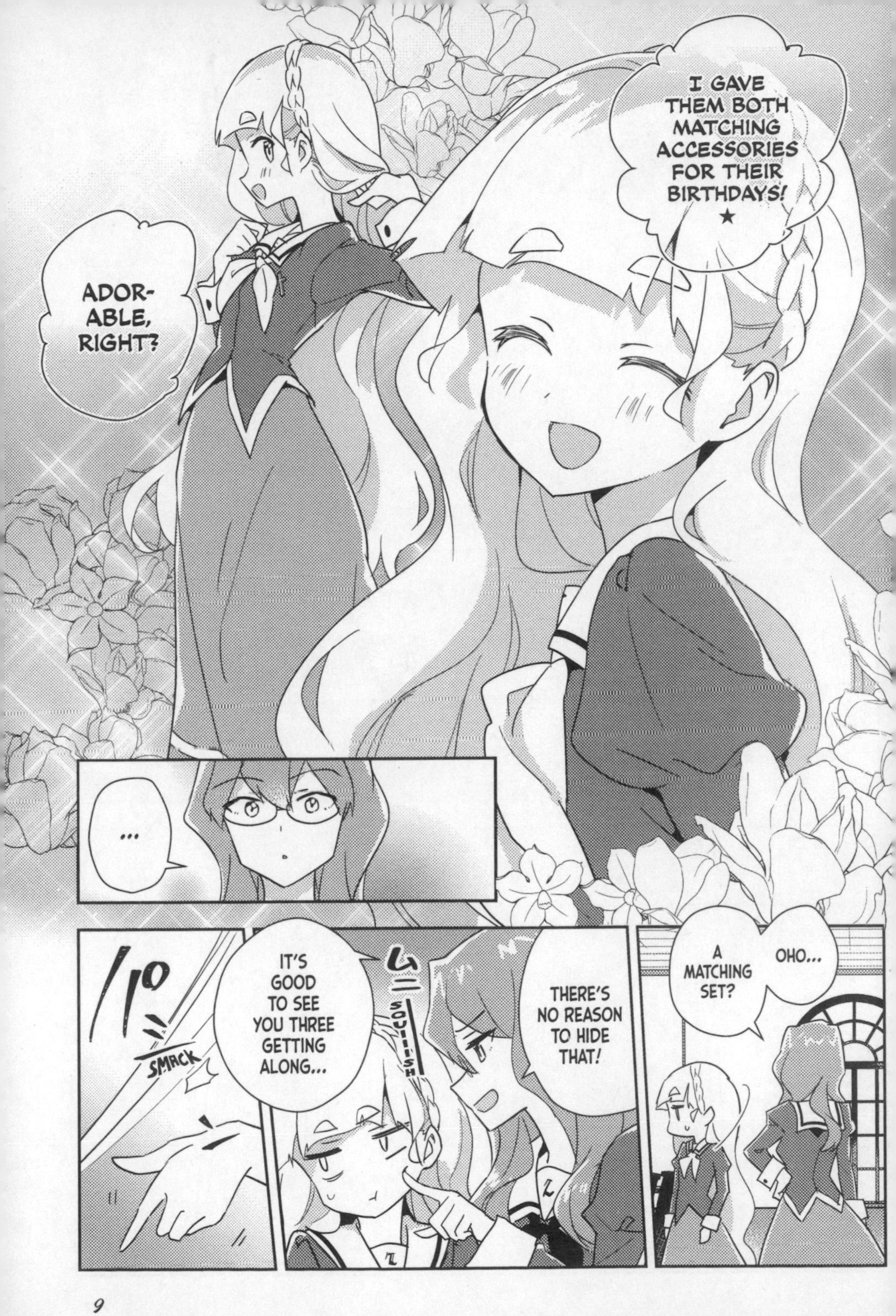
I GAVE THEM BOTH MATCHING ACCESSORIES FOR THEIR BIRTHDAYS! ★
ADOR-ABLE, RIGHT?
...
OHO...
A MATCHING SET?
THERE'S NO REASON TO HIDE THAT!
SQUIIISH
IT'S GOOD TO SEE YOU THREE GETTING ALONG...
SMACK

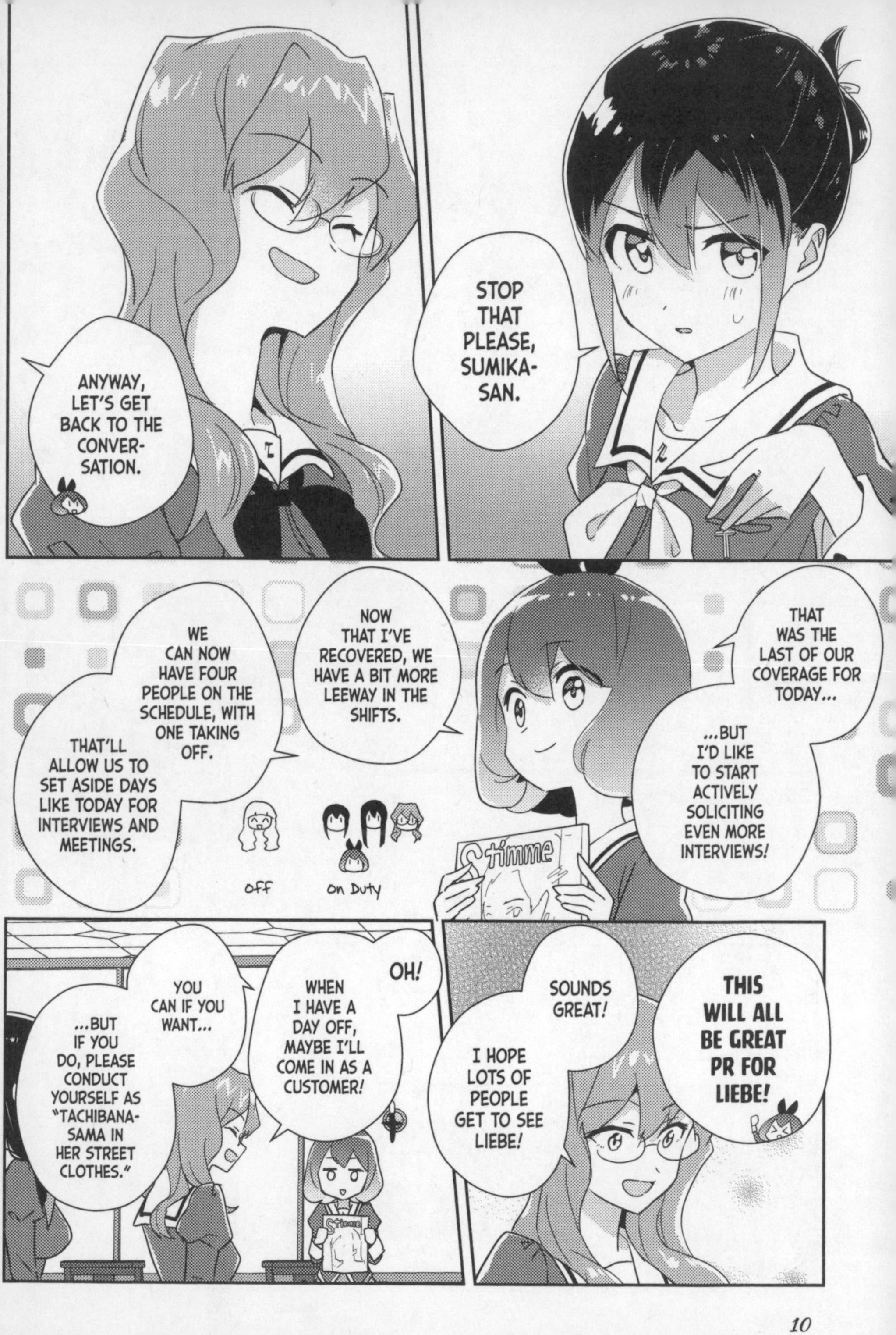
STOP THAT PLEASE, SUMIKA-SAN.
ANYWAY, LET'S GET BACK TO THE CONVER-SATION.
THAT WAS THE LAST OF OUR COVERAGE FOR TODAY...
...BUT I'D LIKE TO START ACTIVELY SOLICITING EVEN MORE INTERVIEWS!
Stimme
NOW THAT I'VE RECOVERED, WE HAVE A BIT MORE LEEWAY IN THE SHIFTS.
WE CAN NOW HAVE FOUR PEOPLE ON THE SCHEDULE, WITH ONE TAKING OFF.
THAT'LL ALLOW US TO SET ASIDE DAYS LIKE TODAY FOR INTERVIEWS AND MEETINGS.
On Duty
Off
THIS WILL ALL BE GREAT PR FOR LIEBE!
SOUNDS GREAT!
I HOPE LOTS OF PEOPLE GET TO SEE LIEBE!
OH!
WHEN I HAVE A DAY OFF, MAYBE I'LL COME IN AS A CUSTOMER!
YOU CAN IF YOU WANT...
...BUT IF YOU DO, PLEASE CONDUCT YOURSELF AS "TACHIBANA-SAMA IN HER STREET CLOTHES."

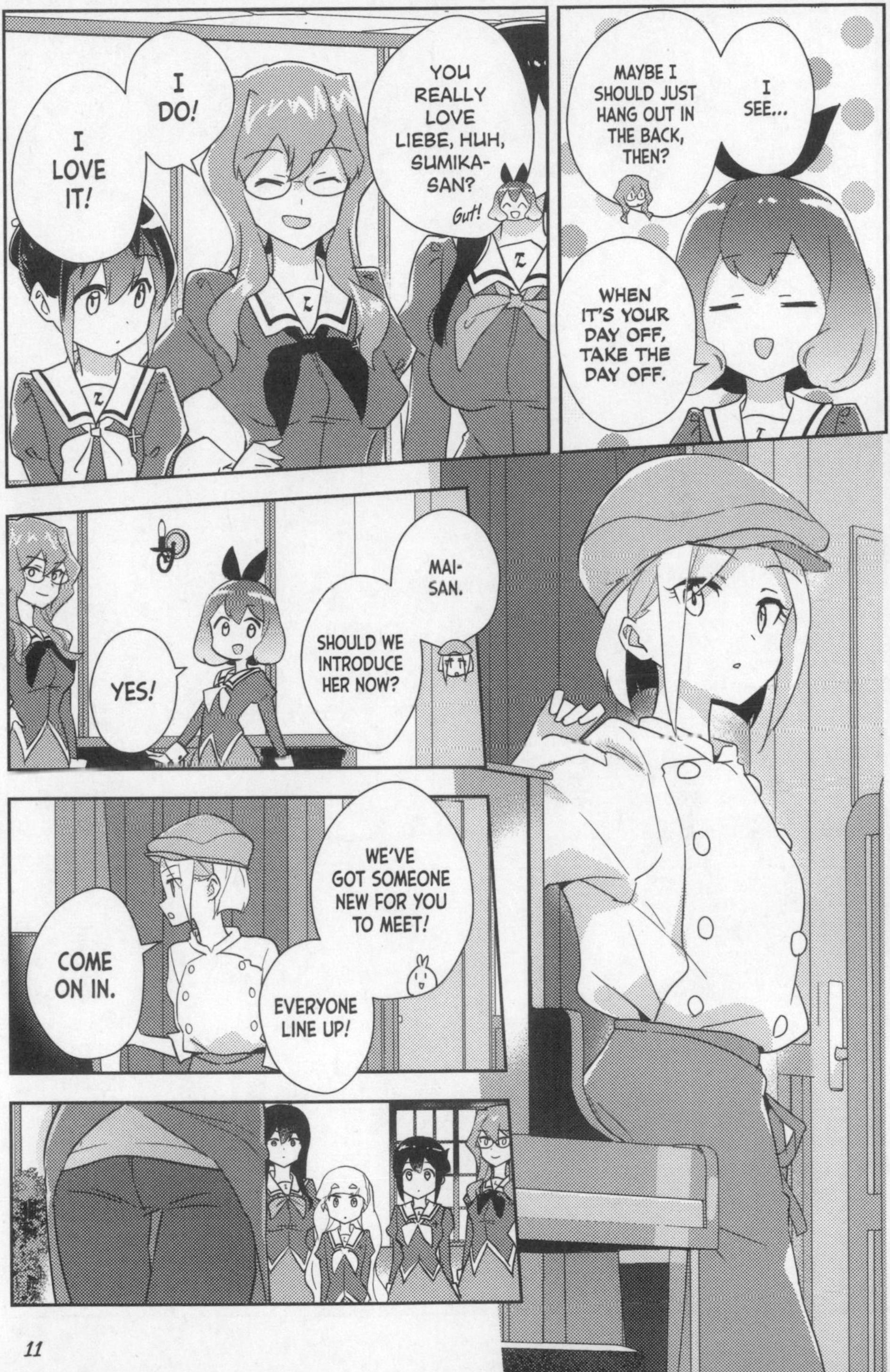
I SEE...
MAYBE I SHOULD JUST HANG OUT IN THE BACK, THEN?
WHEN IT'S YOUR DAY OFF, TAKE THE DAY OFF.
YOU REALLY LOVE LIEBE, HUH, SUMIKA-SAN?
Gut!
I DO!
I LOVE IT!
MAI-SAN.
SHOULD WE INTRODUCE HER NOW?
YES!
WE'VE GOT SOMEONE NEW FOR YOU TO MEET!
EVERYONE LINE UP!
COME ON IN.

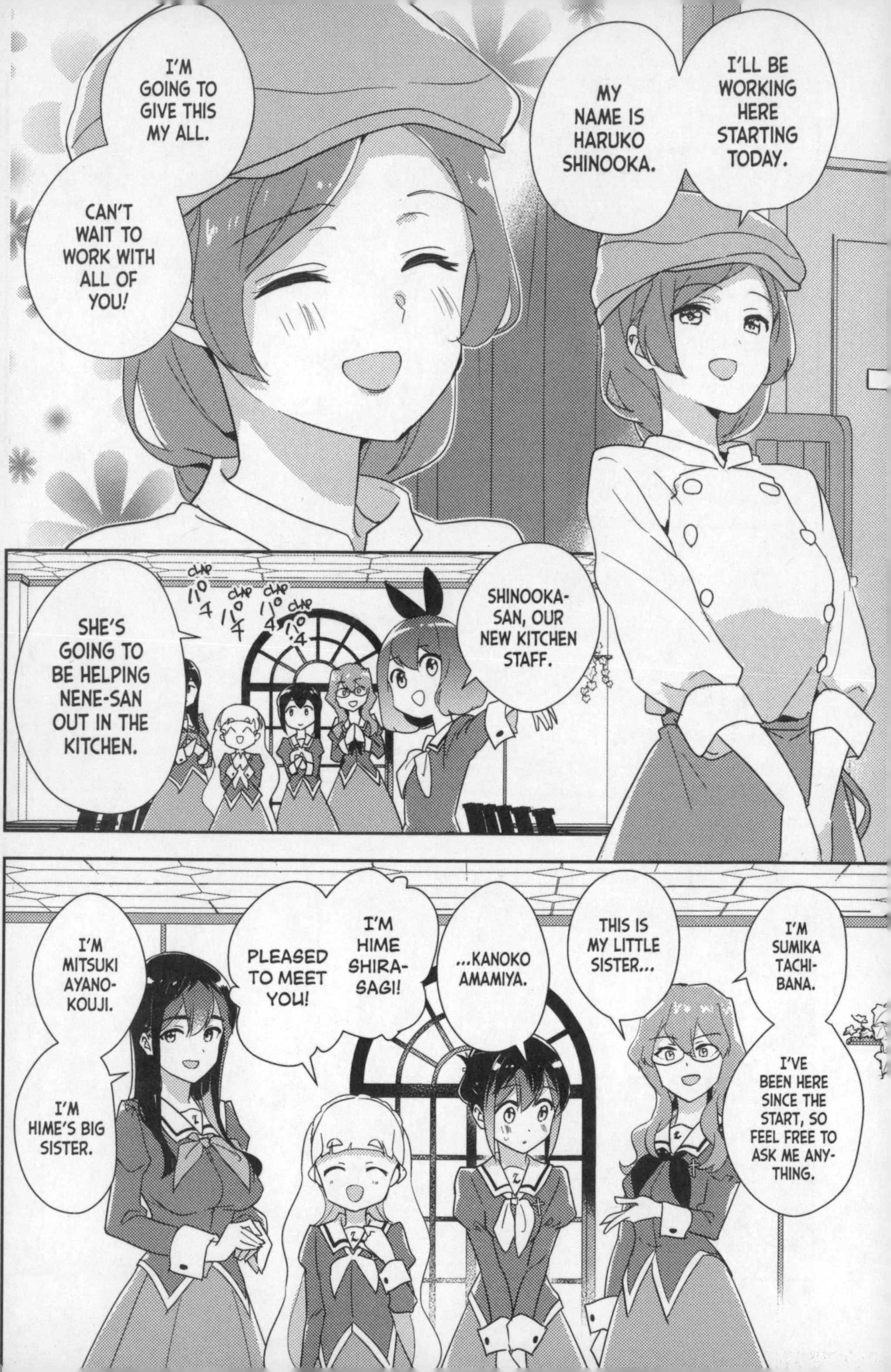
I'LL BE WORKING HERE STARTING TODAY.
MY NAME IS HARUKO SHINOOKA.
I'M GOING TO GIVE THIS MY ALL.
CAN'T WAIT TO WORK WITH ALL OF YOU!
SHINOOKA-SAN, OUR NEW KITCHEN STAFF.
CLAP
CLAP
CLAP
CLAP
SHE'S GOING TO BE HELPING NENE-SAN OUT IN THE KITCHEN.
I'M SUMIKA TACHIBANA.
I'VE BEEN HERE SINCE THE START, SO FEEL FREE TO ASK ME ANYTHING.
THIS IS MY LITTLE SISTER...
...KANOKO AMAMIYA.
I'M HIME SHIRASAGI!
PLEASED TO MEET YOU!
I'M MITSUKI AYANOKOUJI.
I'M HIME'S BIG SISTER.

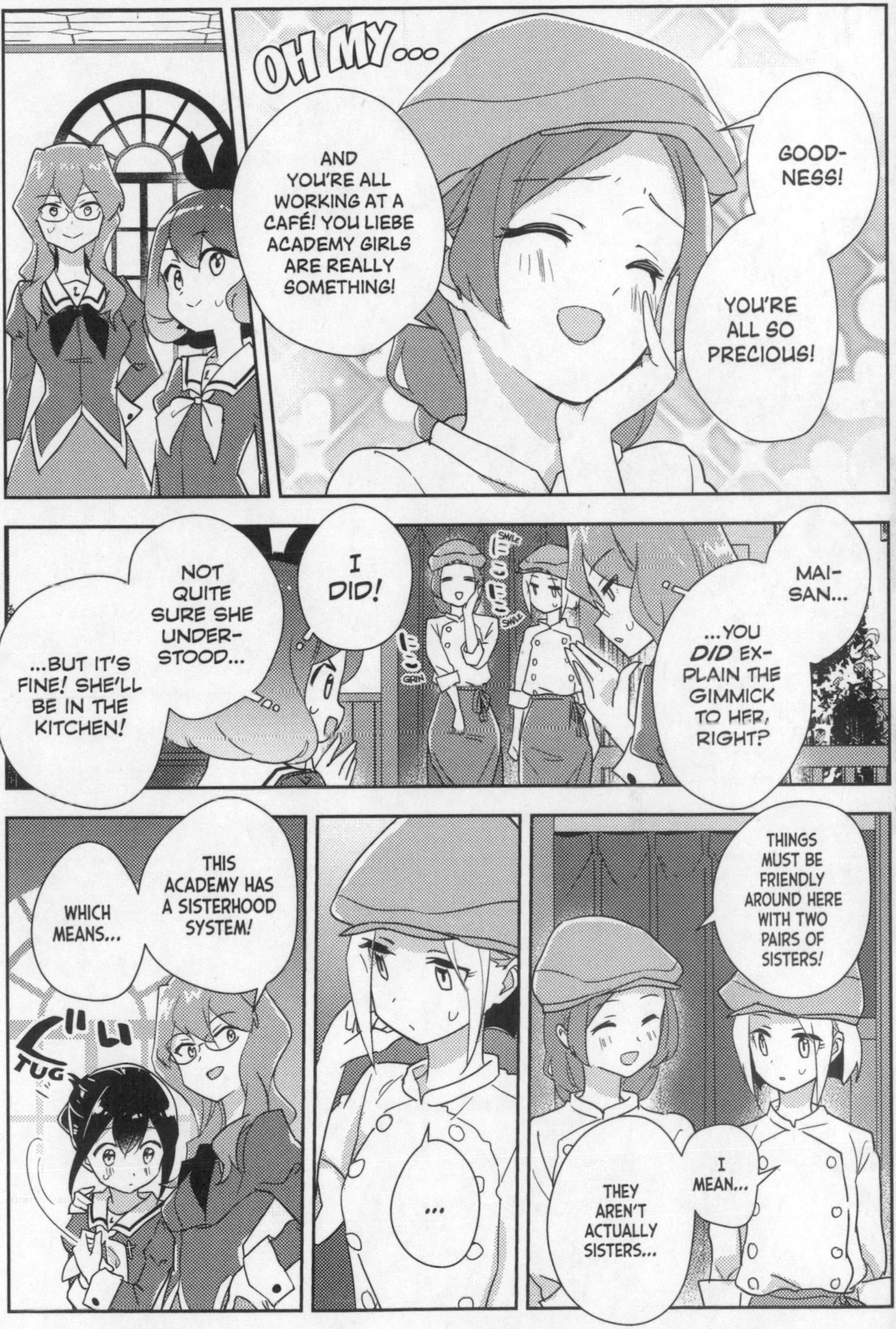
GOOD-NESS!
YOU'RE ALL SO PRECIOUS!
OH MY...
AND YOU'RE ALL WORKING AT A CAFÉ! YOU LIEBE ACADEMY GIRLS ARE REALLY SOMETHING!
MAI-SAN...
...YOU *DID* EX-PLAIN THE GIMMICK TO HER, RIGHT?
SMILE
SMILE
I DID!
GRIN
NOT QUITE SURE SHE UNDER-STOOD...
...BUT IT'S FINE! SHE'LL BE IN THE KITCHEN!
THINGS MUST BE FRIENDLY AROUND HERE WITH TWO PAIRS OF SISTERS!
I MEAN...
THEY AREN'T ACTUALLY SISTERS...
...
THIS ACADEMY HAS A SISTERHOOD SYSTEM!
WHICH MEANS...
TUG

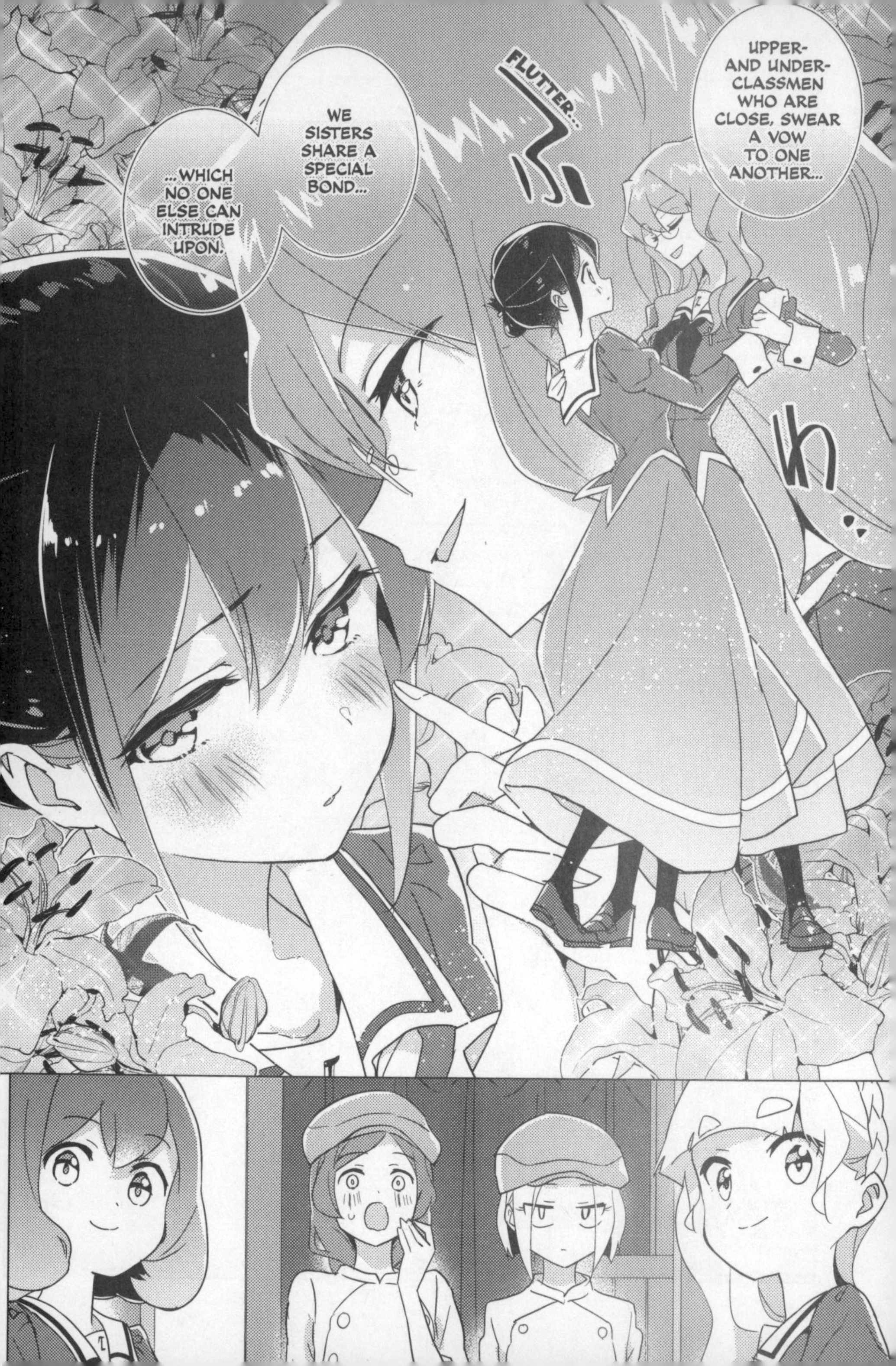
UPPER- AND UNDER-CLASSMEN WHO ARE CLOSE, SWEAR A VOW TO ONE ANOTHER...
FLUTTER...
WE SISTERS SHARE A SPECIAL BOND...
...WHICH NO ONE ELSE CAN INTRUDE UPON.

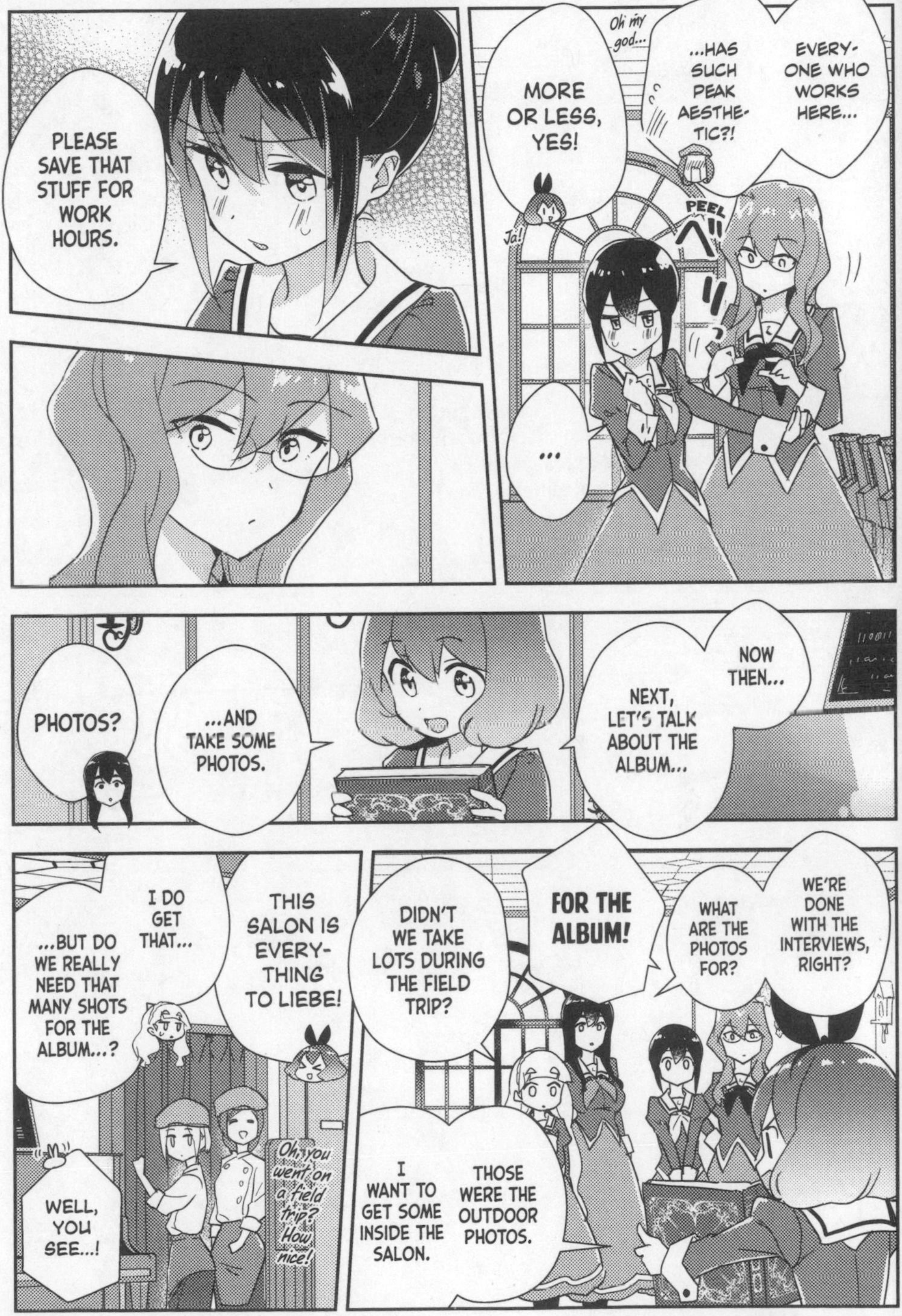
EVERY-ONE WHO WORKS HERE...
...HAS SUCH PEAK AESTHE-TIC?!
Oh my god...
MORE OR LESS, YES!
PEEL
Ja!
...
PLEASE SAVE THAT STUFF FOR WORK HOURS.
NOW THEN...
NEXT, LET'S TALK ABOUT THE ALBUM...
...AND TAKE SOME PHOTOS.
PHOTOS?
WE'RE DONE WITH THE INTERVIEWS, RIGHT?
WHAT ARE THE PHOTOS FOR?
FOR THE ALBUM!
DIDN'T WE TAKE LOTS DURING THE FIELD TRIP?
THOSE WERE THE OUTDOOR PHOTOS.
I WANT TO GET SOME INSIDE THE SALON.
THIS SALON IS EVERY-THING TO LIEBE!
I DO GET THAT...
...BUT DO WE REALLY NEED THAT MANY SHOTS FOR THE ALBUM...?
Oh, you went on a field trip? How nice!
WELL, YOU SEE...!

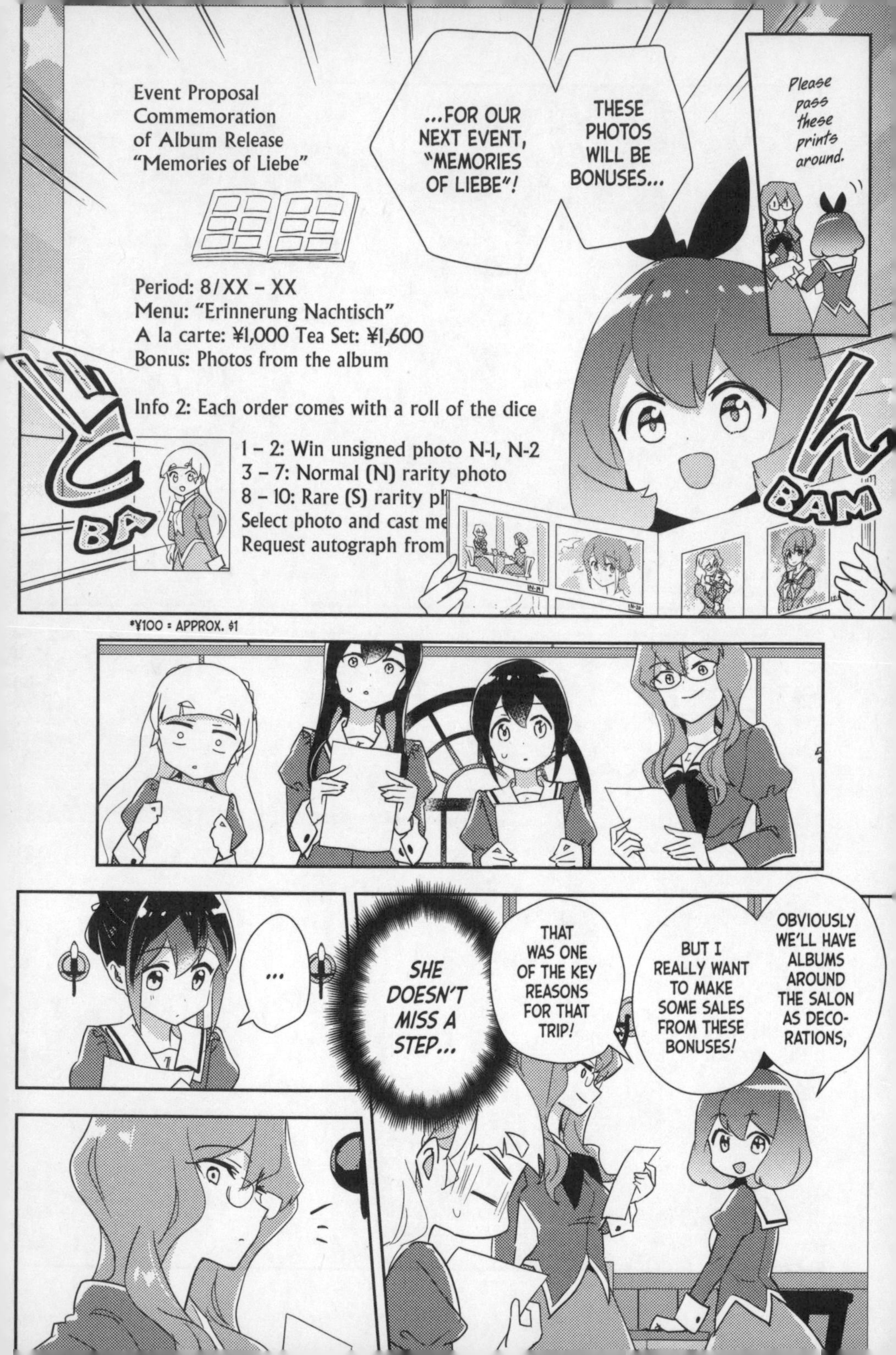
Please pass these prints around.
THESE PHOTOS WILL BE BONUSES...
...FOR OUR NEXT EVENT, "MEMORIES OF LIEBE"!
Event Proposal
Commemoration of Album Release
"Memories of Liebe"
Period: 8/XX – XX
Menu: "Erinnerung Nachtisch"
A la carte: ¥1,000 Tea Set: ¥1,600
Bonus: Photos from the album
Info 2: Each order comes with a roll of the dice
1 – 2: Win unsigned photo N-1, N-2
3 – 7: Normal (N) rarity photo
8 – 10: Rare (S) rarity ph
Select photo and cast me
Request autograph from
BAM
BA
*¥100 = APPROX. $1
OBVIOUSLY WE'LL HAVE ALBUMS AROUND THE SALON AS DECORATIONS,
BUT I REALLY WANT TO MAKE SOME SALES FROM THESE BONUSES!
THAT WAS ONE OF THE KEY REASONS FOR THAT TRIP!
SHE DOESN'T MISS A STEP...
...

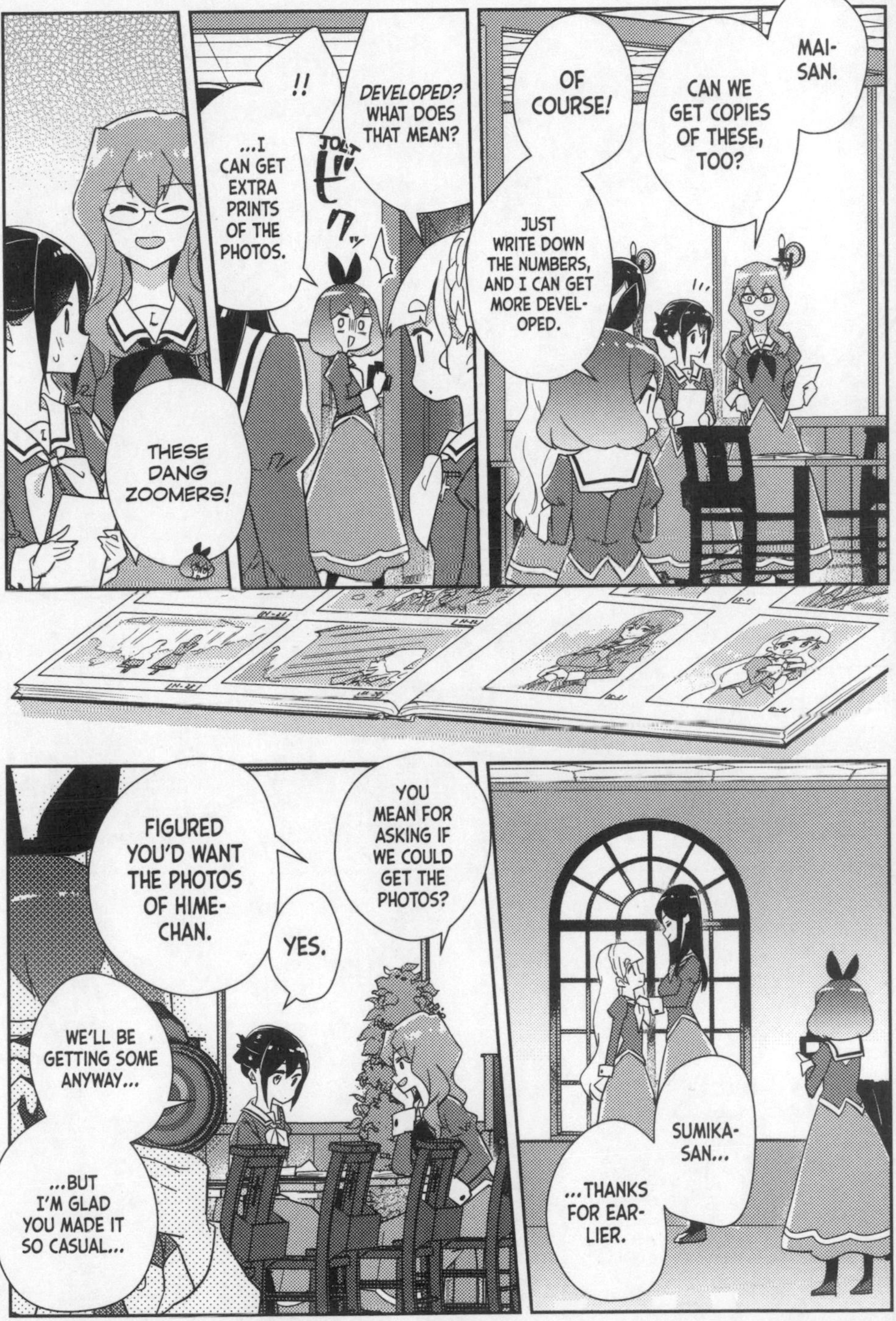
MAI-SAN.
CAN WE GET COPIES OF THESE, TOO?
OF COURSE!
JUST WRITE DOWN THE NUMBERS, AND I CAN GET MORE DEVEL-OPED.
DEVELOPED? WHAT DOES THAT MEAN?
JOLT
!!
...I CAN GET EXTRA PRINTS OF THE PHOTOS.
THESE DANG ZOOMERS!
SUMIKA-SAN...
...THANKS FOR EAR-LIER.
YOU MEAN FOR ASKING IF WE COULD GET THE PHOTOS?
FIGURED YOU'D WANT THE PHOTOS OF HIME-CHAN.
YES.
WE'LL BE GETTING SOME ANYWAY...
...BUT I'M GLAD YOU MADE IT SO CASUAL...

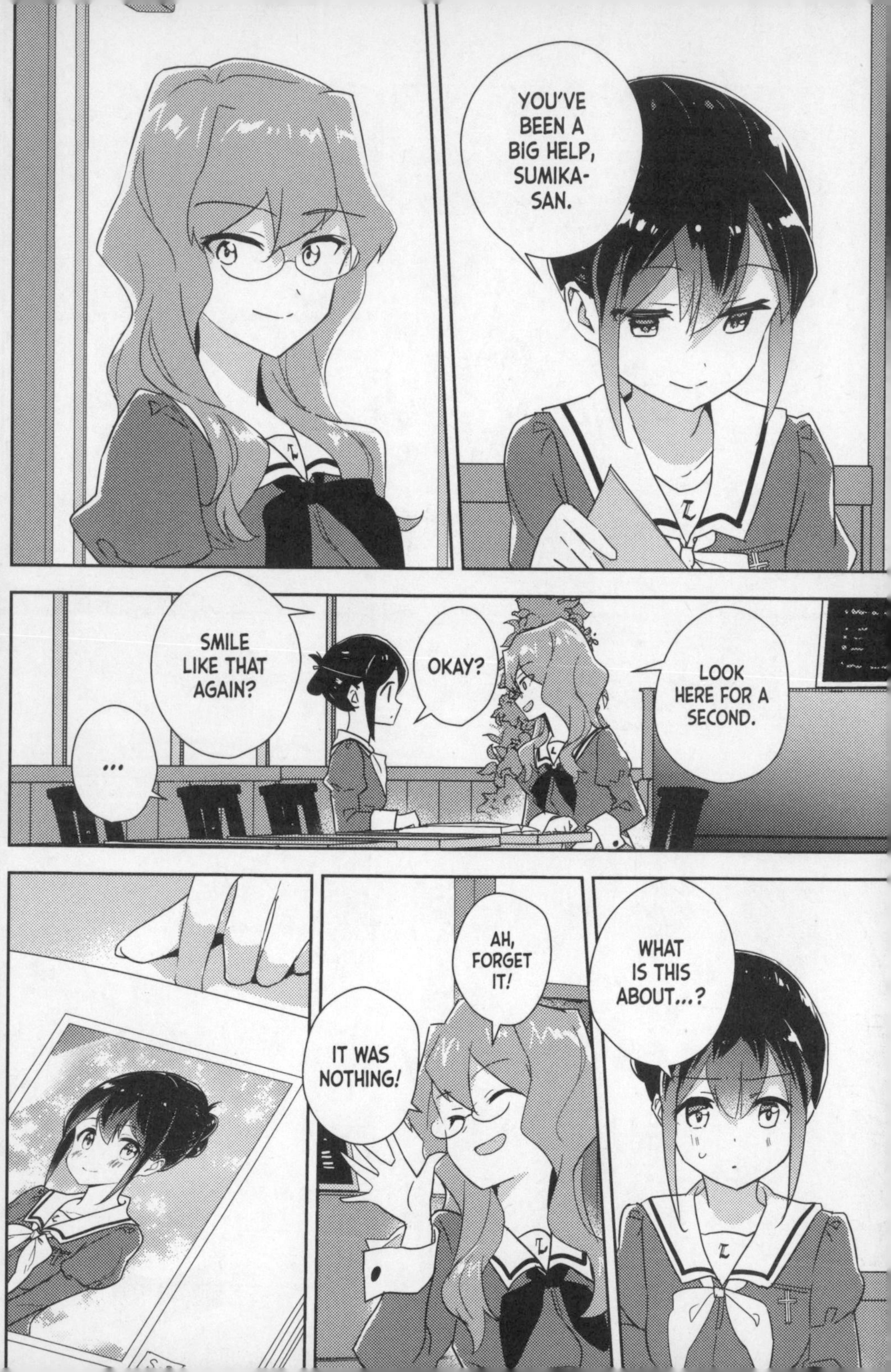
YOU'VE BEEN A BIG HELP, SUMIKA-SAN.
LOOK HERE FOR A SECOND.
OKAY?
SMILE LIKE THAT AGAIN?
...
WHAT IS THIS ABOUT...?
AH, FORGET IT!
IT WAS NOTHING!

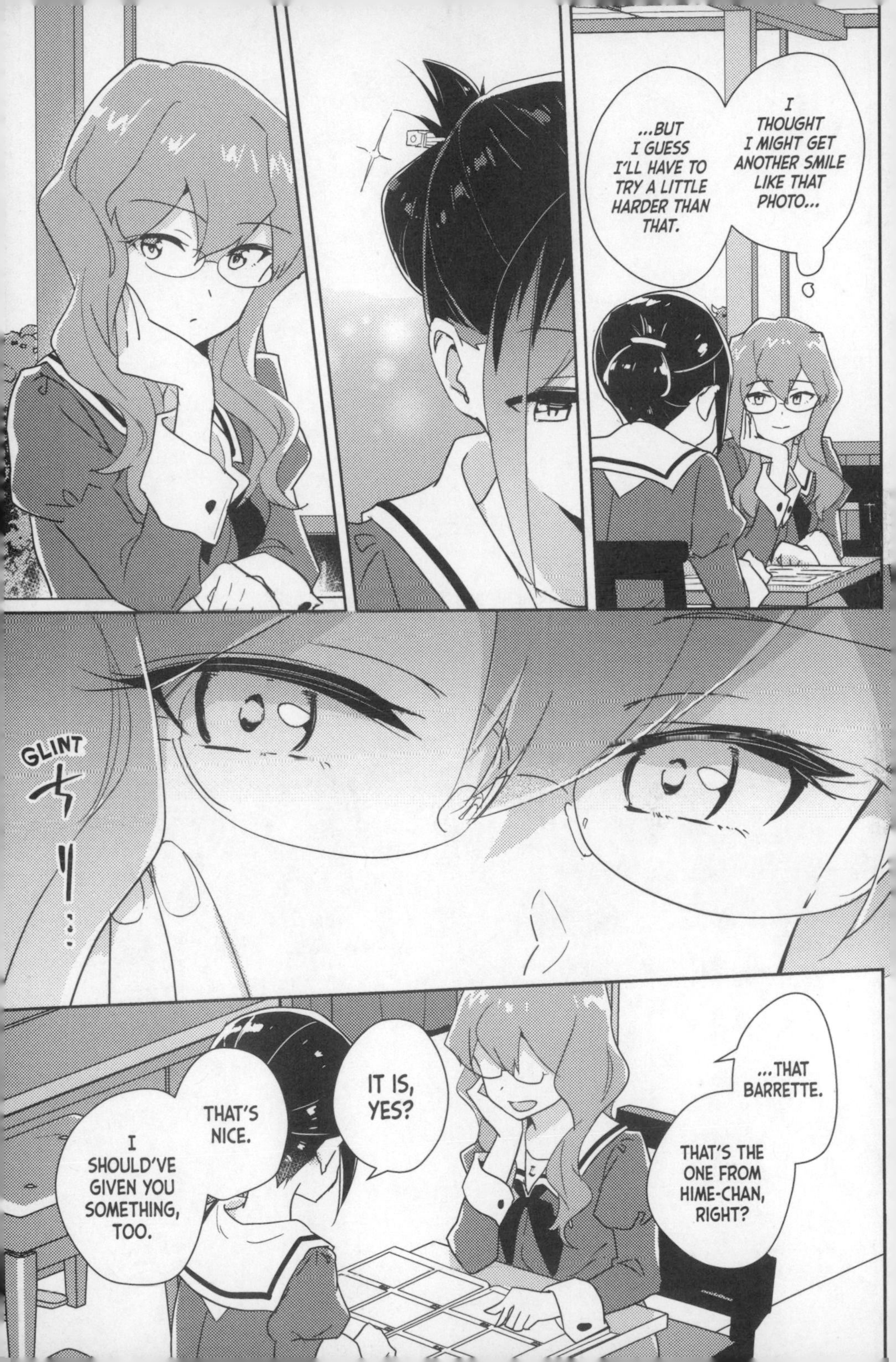
I THOUGHT I MIGHT GET ANOTHER SMILE LIKE THAT PHOTO...
...BUT I GUESS I'LL HAVE TO TRY A LITTLE HARDER THAN THAT.
GLINT
...THAT BARRETTE.
THAT'S THE ONE FROM HIME-CHAN, RIGHT?
IT IS, YES?
THAT'S NICE.
I SHOULD'VE GIVEN YOU SOMETHING, TOO.

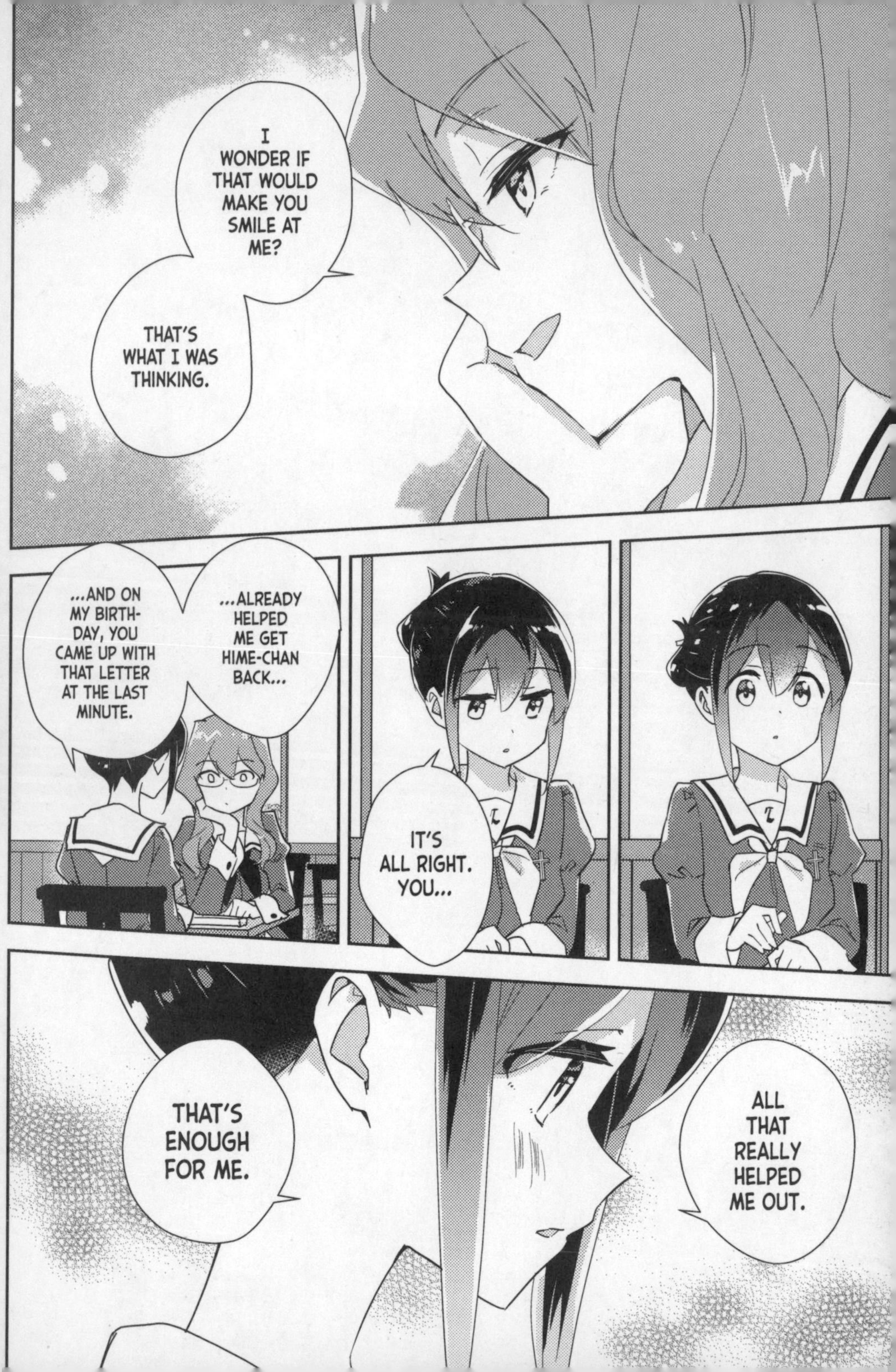
I WONDER IF THAT WOULD MAKE YOU SMILE AT ME?
THAT'S WHAT I WAS THINKING.
IT'S ALL RIGHT. YOU...
...ALREADY HELPED ME GET HIME-CHAN BACK...
...AND ON MY BIRTHDAY, YOU CAME UP WITH THAT LETTER AT THE LAST MINUTE.
ALL THAT REALLY HELPED ME OUT.
THAT'S ENOUGH FOR ME.

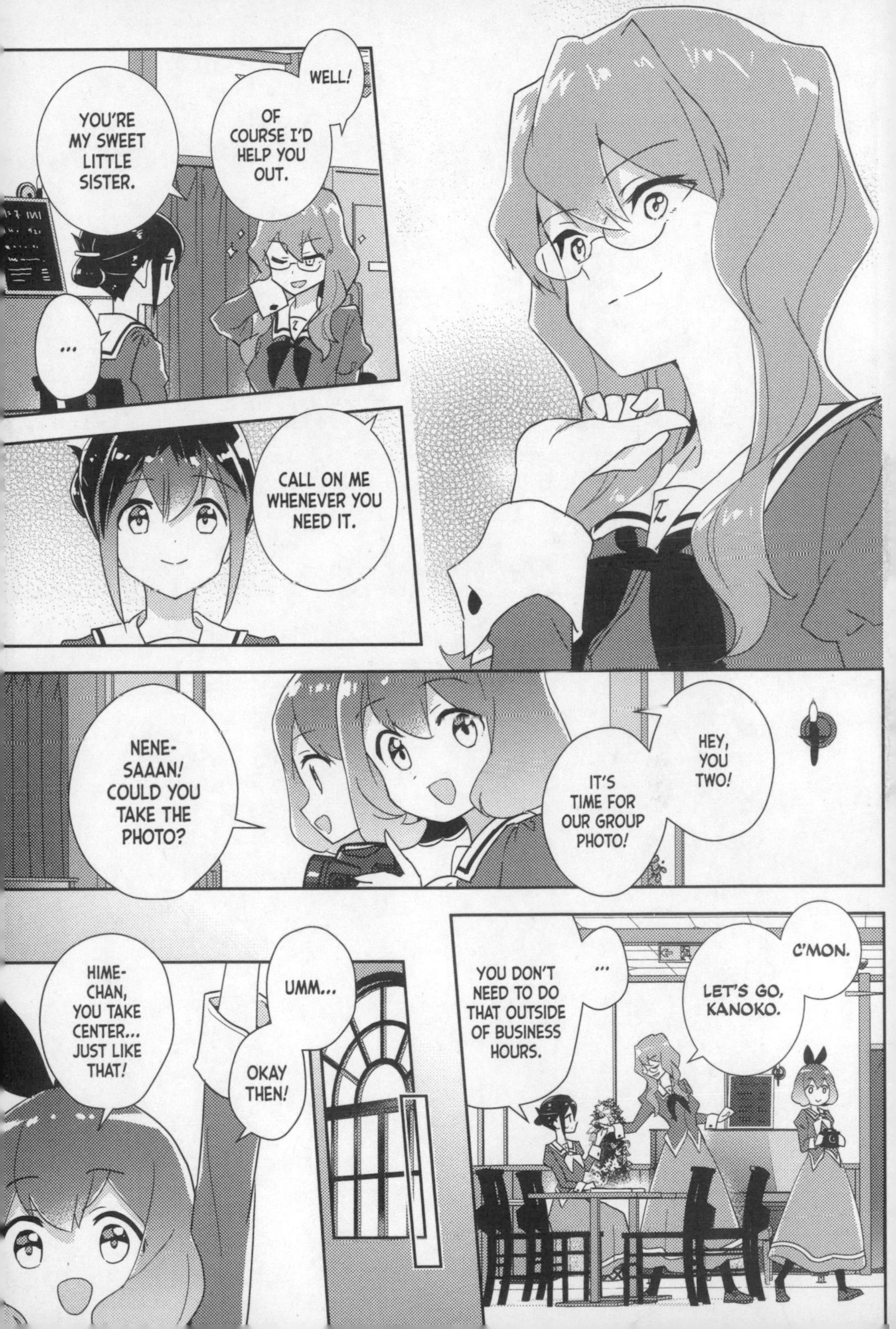

WELL!
OF COURSE I'D HELP YOU OUT.
YOU'RE MY SWEET LITTLE SISTER.
...
CALL ON ME WHENEVER YOU NEED IT.
HEY, YOU TWO!
IT'S TIME FOR OUR GROUP PHOTO!
NENE-SAAAN! COULD YOU TAKE THE PHOTO?
C'MON.
LET'S GO, KANOKO.
...
YOU DON'T NEED TO DO THAT OUTSIDE OF BUSINESS HOURS.
UMM...
OKAY THEN!
HIME-CHAN, YOU TAKE CENTER... JUST LIKE THAT!

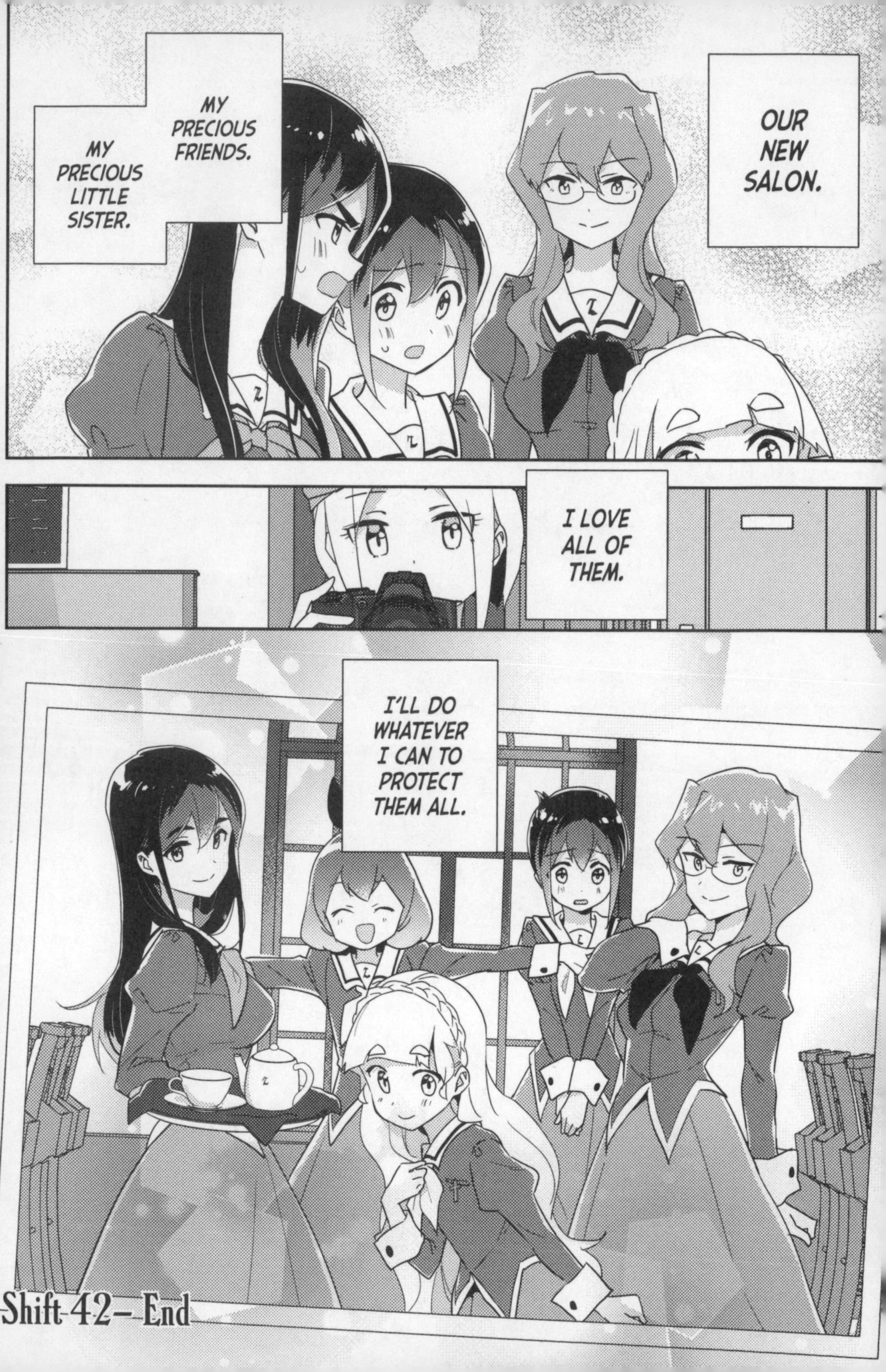
OUR NEW SALON.
MY PRECIOUS FRIENDS.
MY PRECIOUS LITTLE SISTER.
I LOVE ALL OF THEM.
I'LL DO WHATEVER I CAN TO PROTECT THEM ALL.

Shift 42 – End

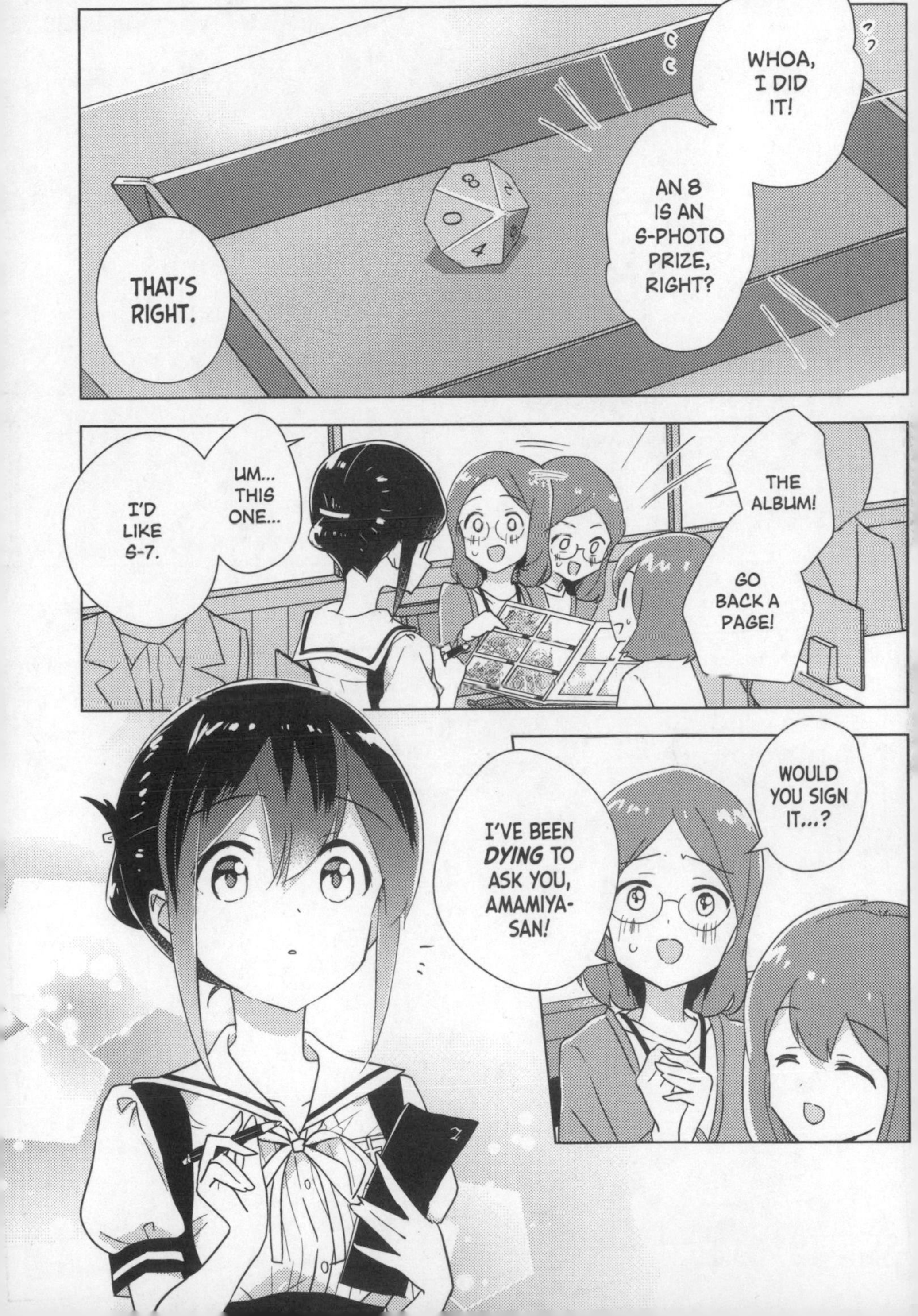
WHOA, I DID IT!
AN 8 IS AN S-PHOTO PRIZE, RIGHT?
THAT'S RIGHT.
THE ALBUM!
GO BACK A PAGE!
UM... THIS ONE...
I'D LIKE S-7.
WOULD YOU SIGN IT...?
I'VE BEEN *DYING* TO ASK YOU, AMAMIYA-SAN!

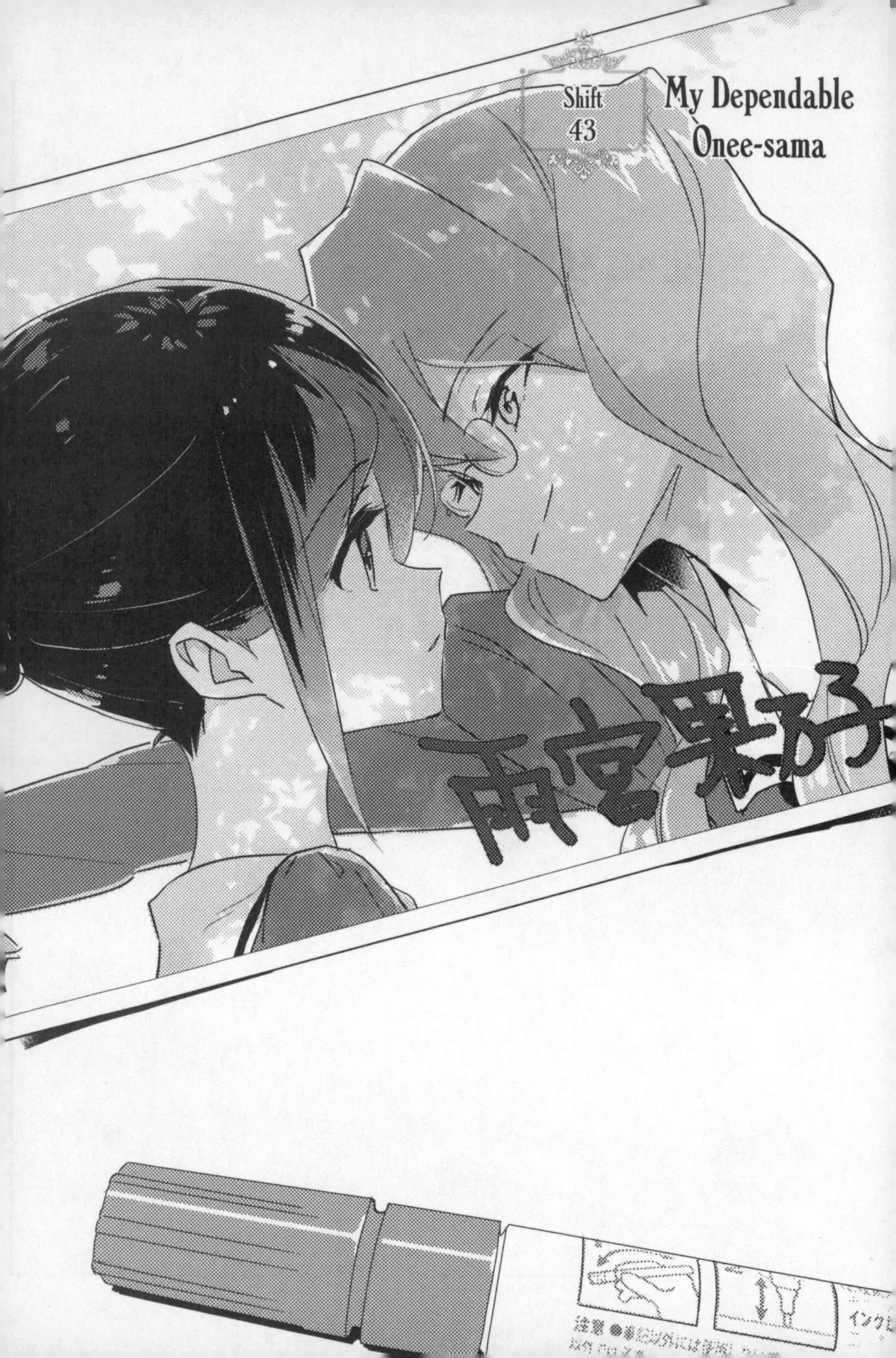
Shift
43
My Dependable
Onee-sama

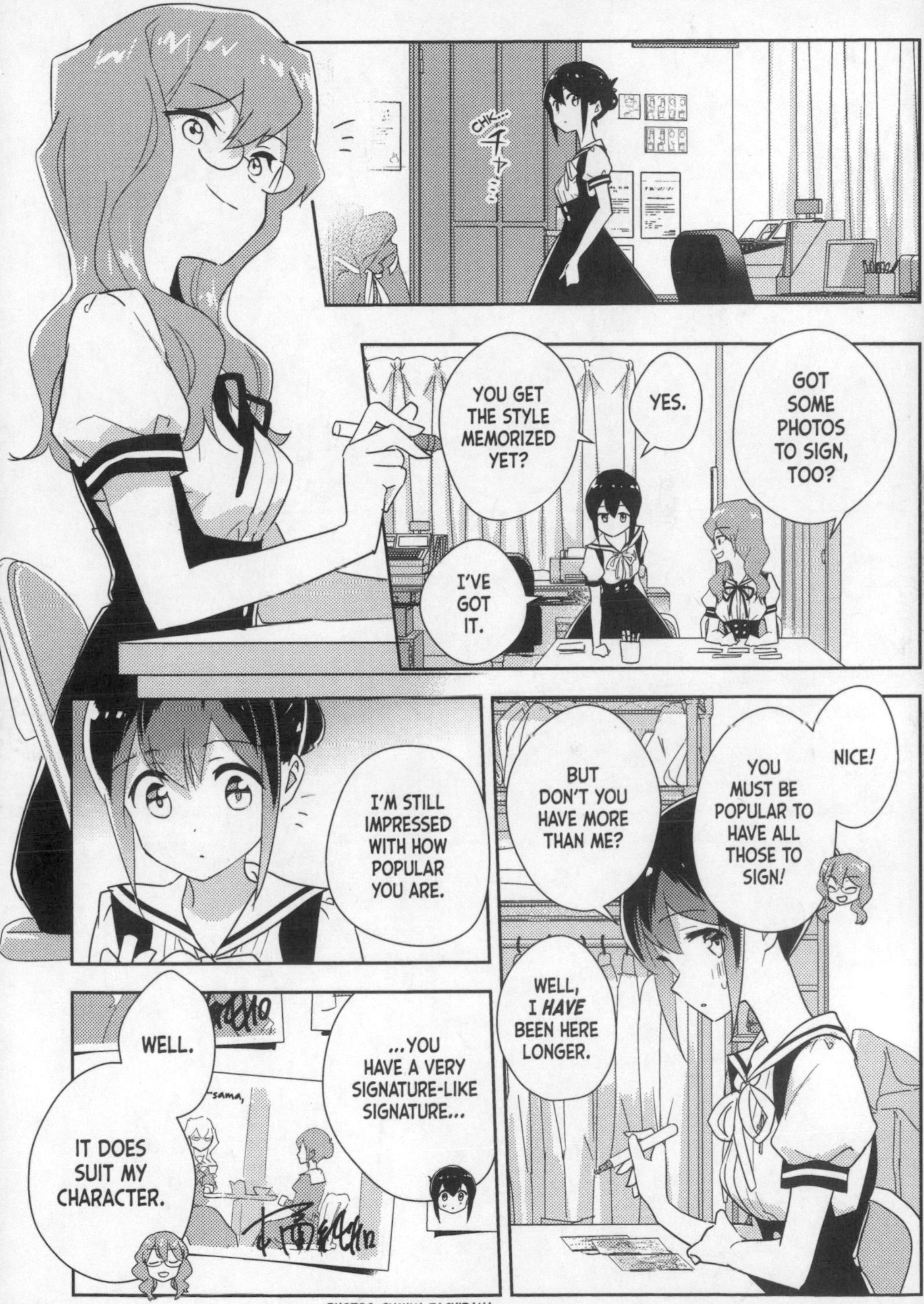
CHK...
チャ…
GOT SOME PHOTOS TO SIGN, TOO?
YES.
YOU GET THE STYLE MEMORIZED YET?
I'VE GOT IT.
NICE!
YOU MUST BE POPULAR TO HAVE ALL THOSE TO SIGN!
BUT DON'T YOU HAVE MORE THAN ME?
WELL, I *HAVE* BEEN HERE LONGER.
I'M STILL IMPRESSED WITH HOW POPULAR YOU ARE.
...YOU HAVE A VERY SIGNATURE-LIKE SIGNATURE...
WELL.
IT DOES SUIT MY CHARACTER.
-sama,

PHOTOS: SUMIKA TACHIBANA

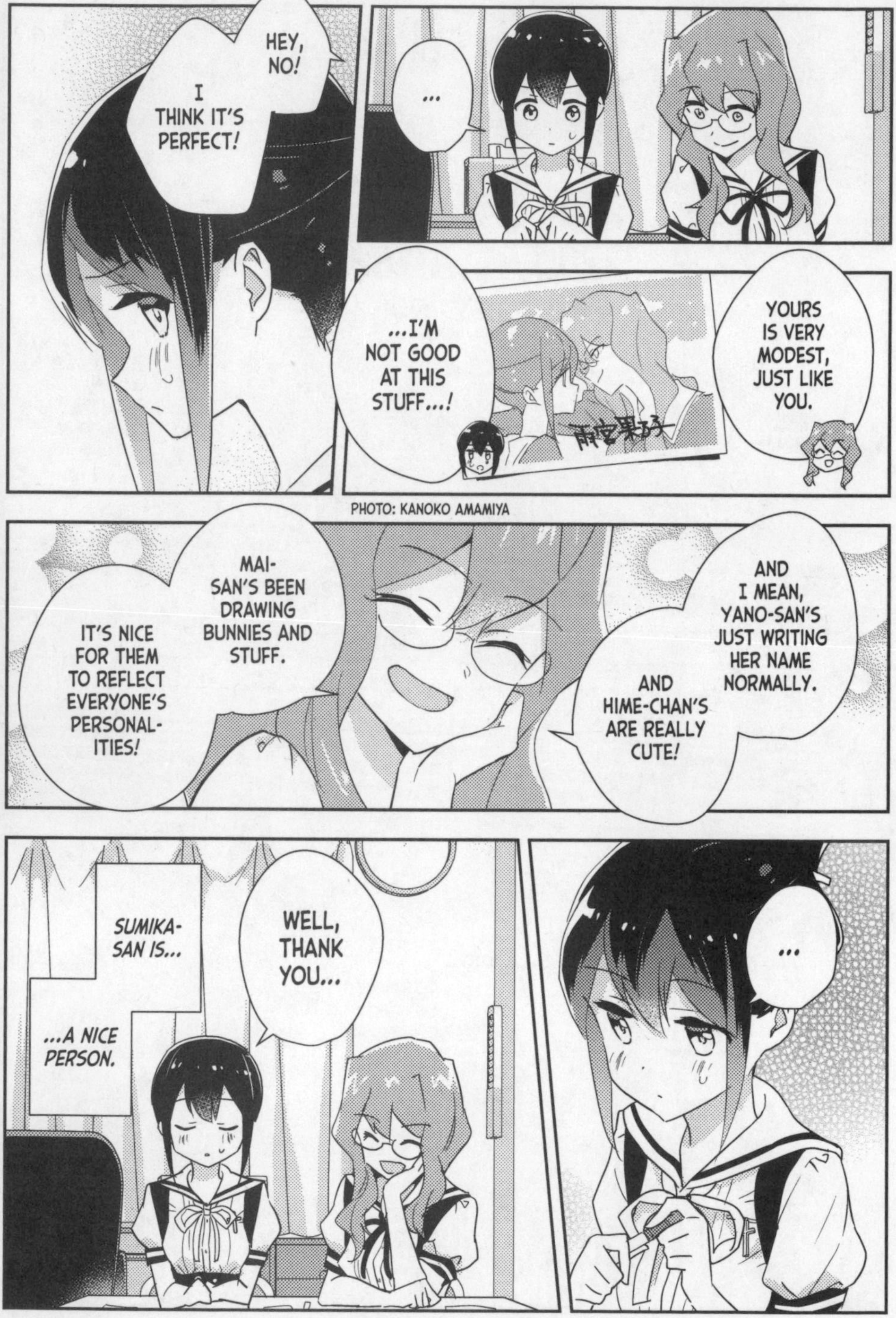
...
YOURS IS VERY MODEST, JUST LIKE YOU.
...I'M NOT GOOD AT THIS STUFF...!
PHOTO: KANOKO AMAMIYA
HEY, NO!
I THINK IT'S PERFECT!
AND I MEAN, YANO-SAN'S JUST WRITING HER NAME NORMALLY.
AND HIME-CHAN'S ARE REALLY CUTE!
MAI-SAN'S BEEN DRAWING BUNNIES AND STUFF.
IT'S NICE FOR THEM TO REFLECT EVERYONE'S PERSONAL-ITIES!
...
WELL, THANK YOU...
SUMIKA-SAN IS...
...A NICE PERSON.

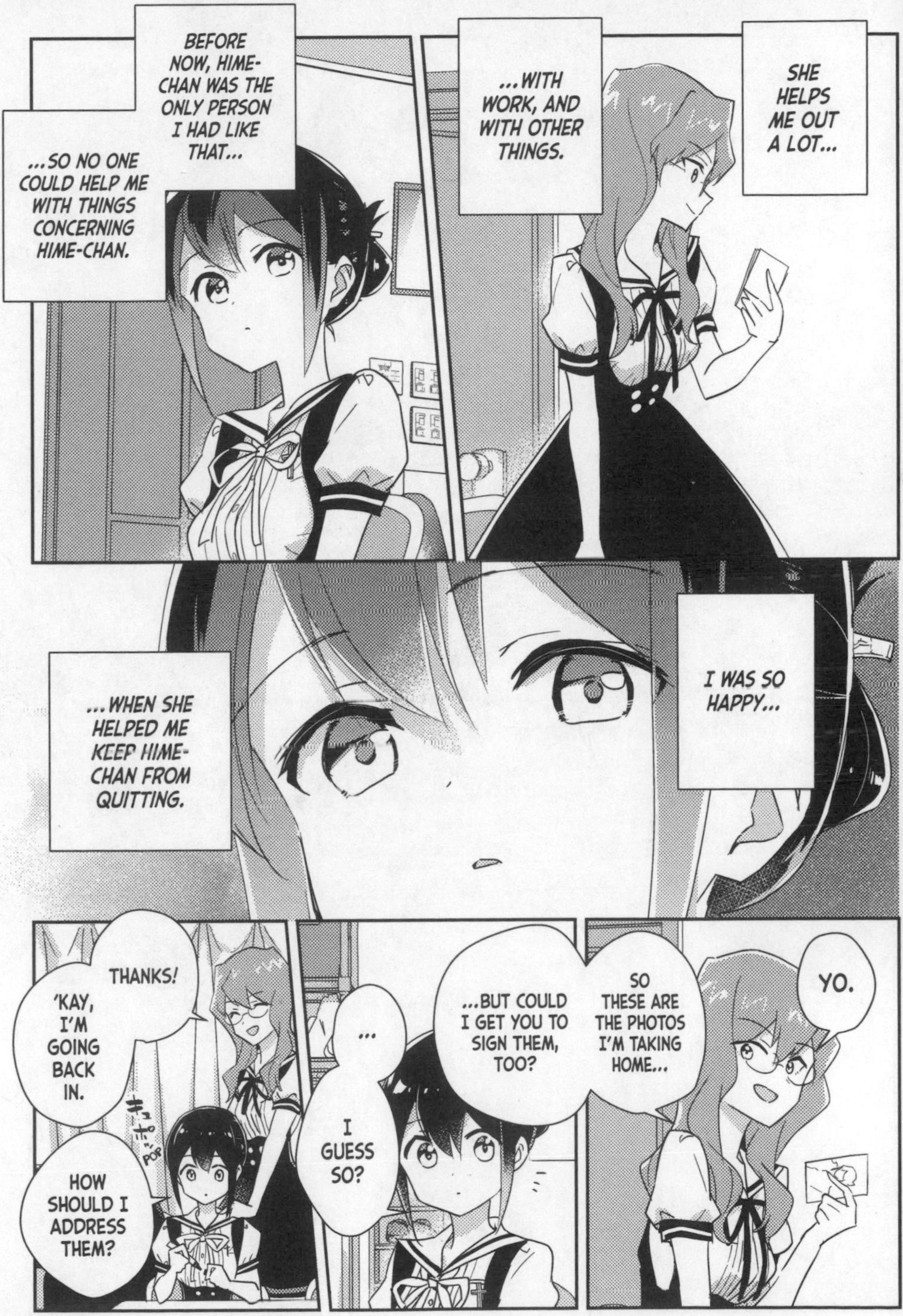
SHE HELPS ME OUT A LOT...
...WITH WORK, AND WITH OTHER THINGS.
BEFORE NOW, HIME-CHAN WAS THE ONLY PERSON I HAD LIKE THAT...
...SO NO ONE COULD HELP ME WITH THINGS CONCERNING HIME-CHAN.
I WAS SO HAPPY...
...WHEN SHE HELPED ME KEEP HIME-CHAN FROM QUITTING.
YO.
SO THESE ARE THE PHOTOS I'M TAKING HOME...
...BUT COULD I GET YOU TO SIGN THEM, TOO?
...
I GUESS SO?
THANKS! 'KAY, I'M GOING BACK IN.
POP
HOW SHOULD I ADDRESS THEM?

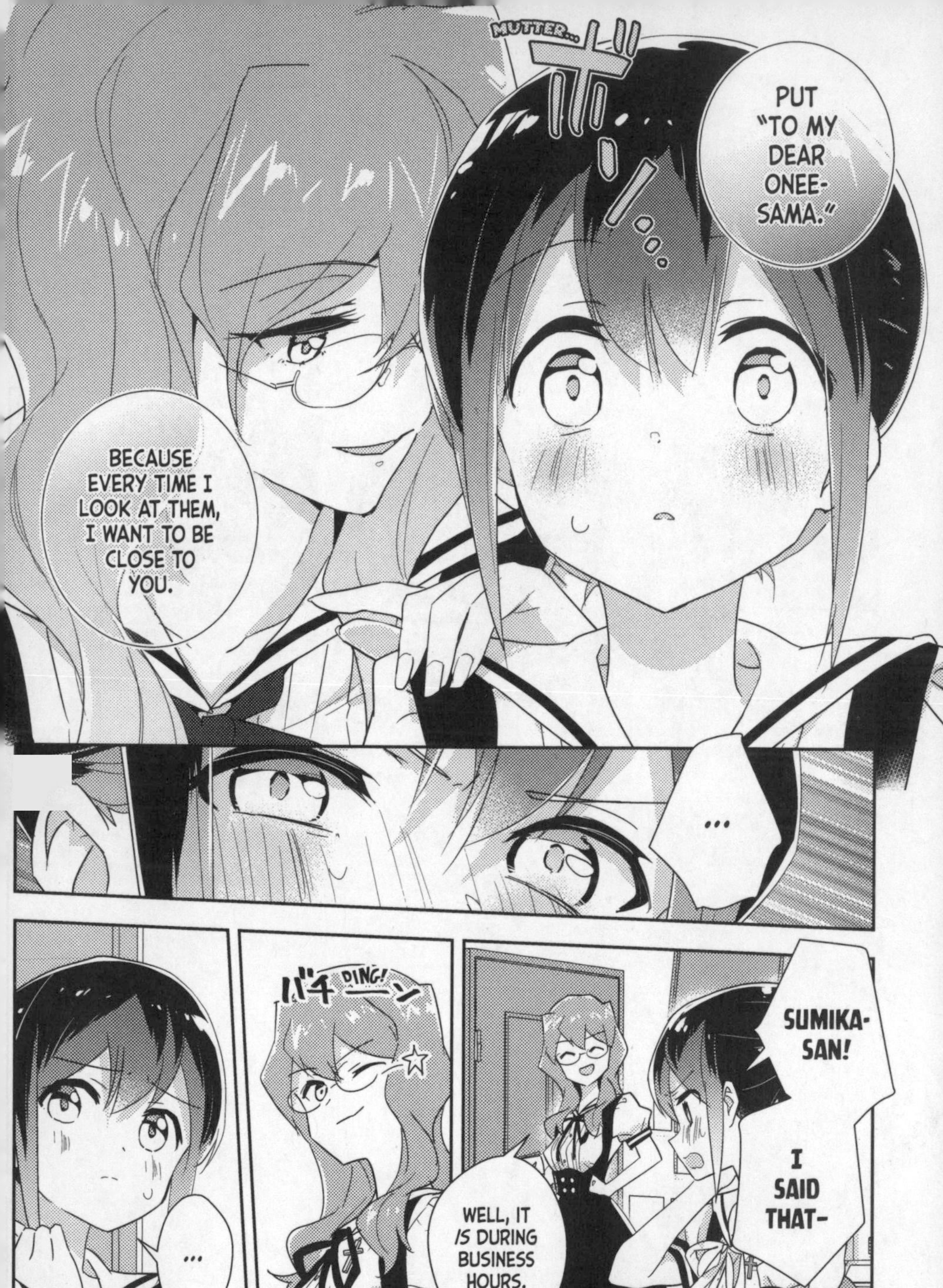
MUTTER...
PUT "TO MY DEAR ONEE-SAMA."
BECAUSE EVERY TIME I LOOK AT THEM, I WANT TO BE CLOSE TO YOU.
...
SUMIKA-SAN!
I SAID THAT-
DING!
WELL, IT *IS* DURING BUSINESS HOURS.
...

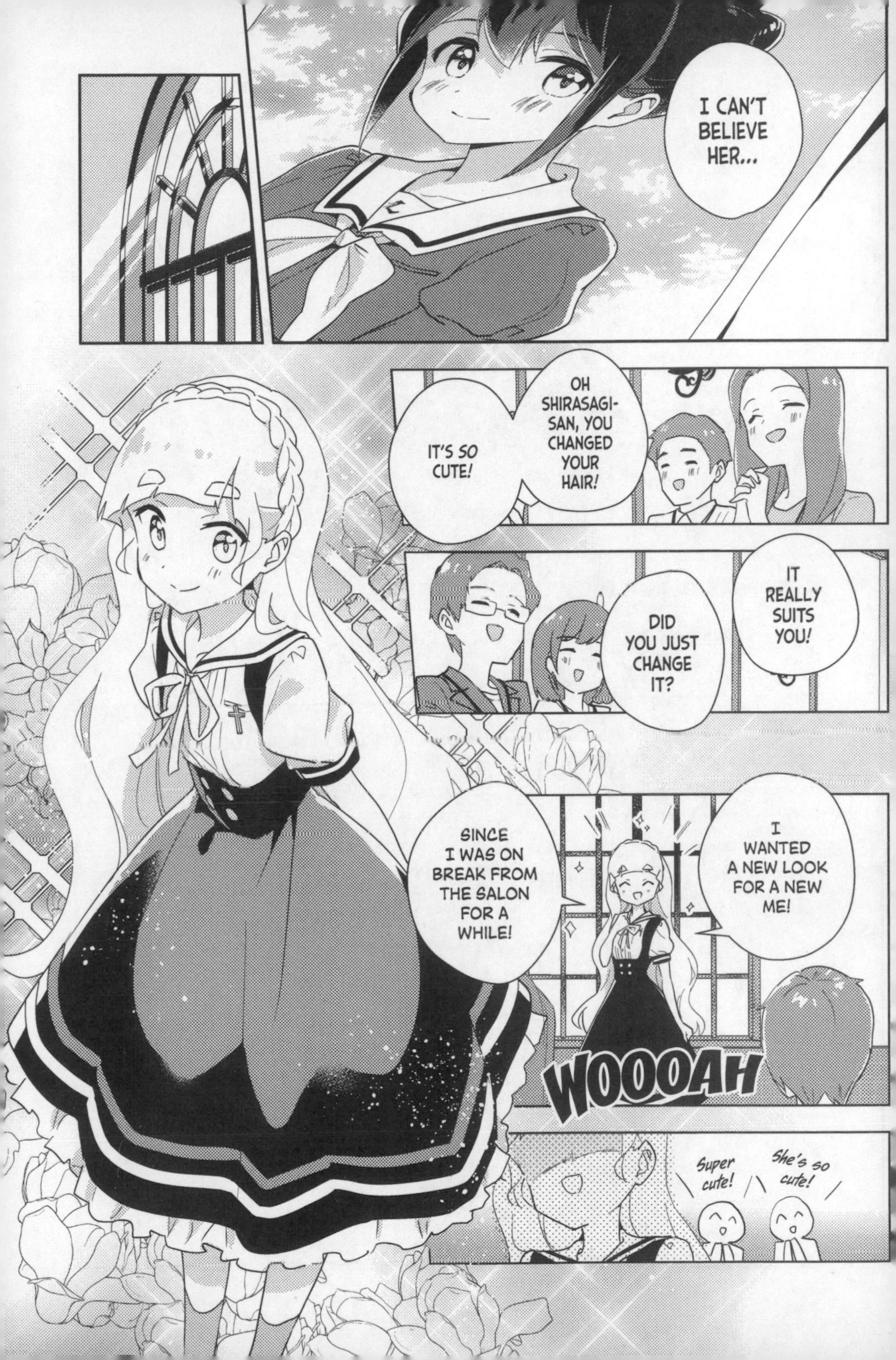
I CAN'T BELIEVE HER...
OH SHIRASAGI-SAN, YOU CHANGED YOUR HAIR!
IT'S SO CUTE!
IT REALLY SUITS YOU!
DID YOU JUST CHANGE IT?
I WANTED A NEW LOOK FOR A NEW ME!
SINCE I WAS ON BREAK FROM THE SALON FOR A WHILE!
WOOOAH
She's so cute!
Super cute!

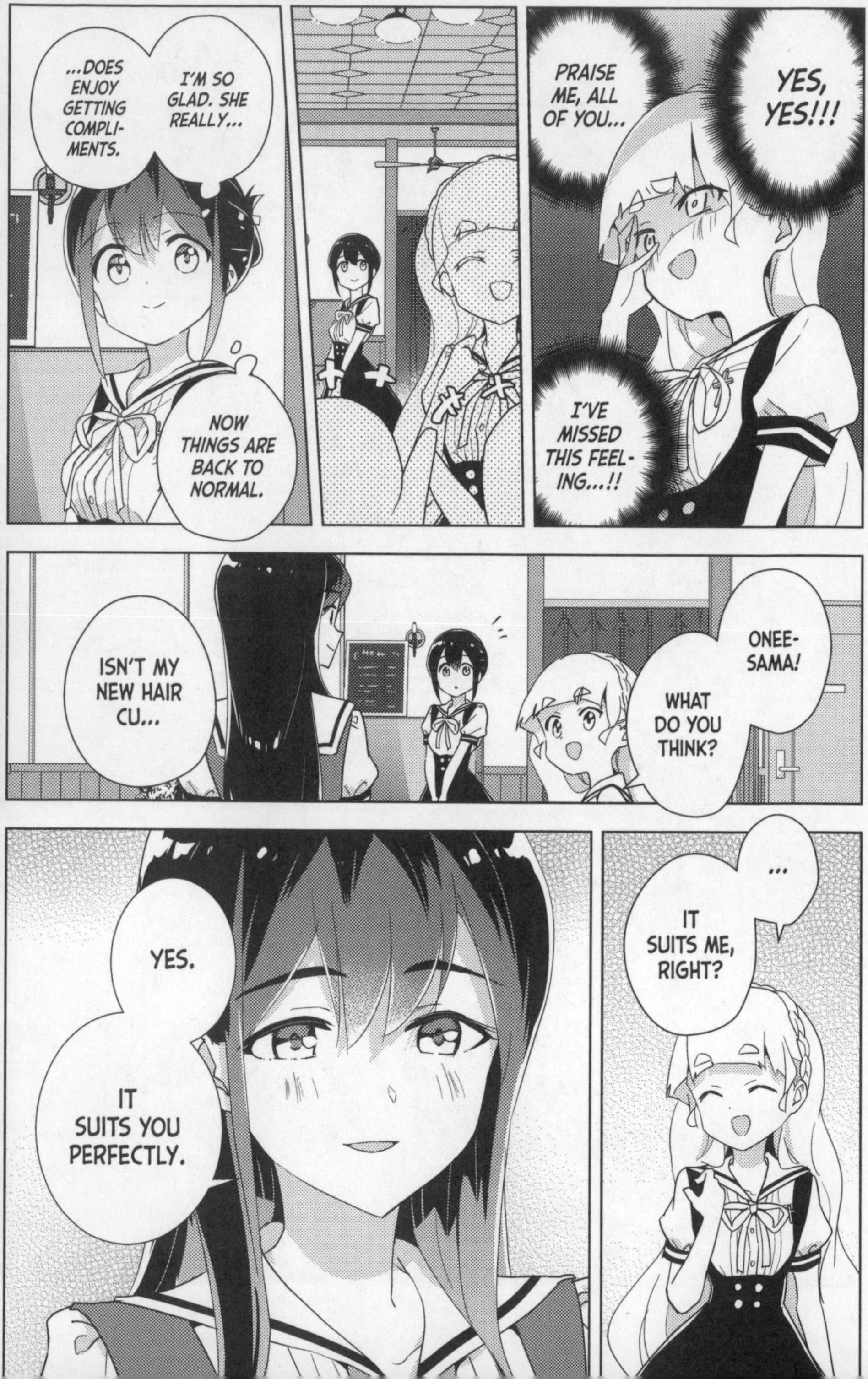
YES, YES!!!
PRAISE ME, ALL OF YOU...
I'VE MISSED THIS FEELING...!!
I'M SO GLAD. SHE REALLY...
...DOES ENJOY GETTING COMPLIMENTS.
NOW THINGS ARE BACK TO NORMAL.
ONEE-SAMA!
WHAT DO YOU THINK?
ISN'T MY NEW HAIR CU...
...
IT SUITS ME, RIGHT?
YES.
IT SUITS YOU PERFECTLY.

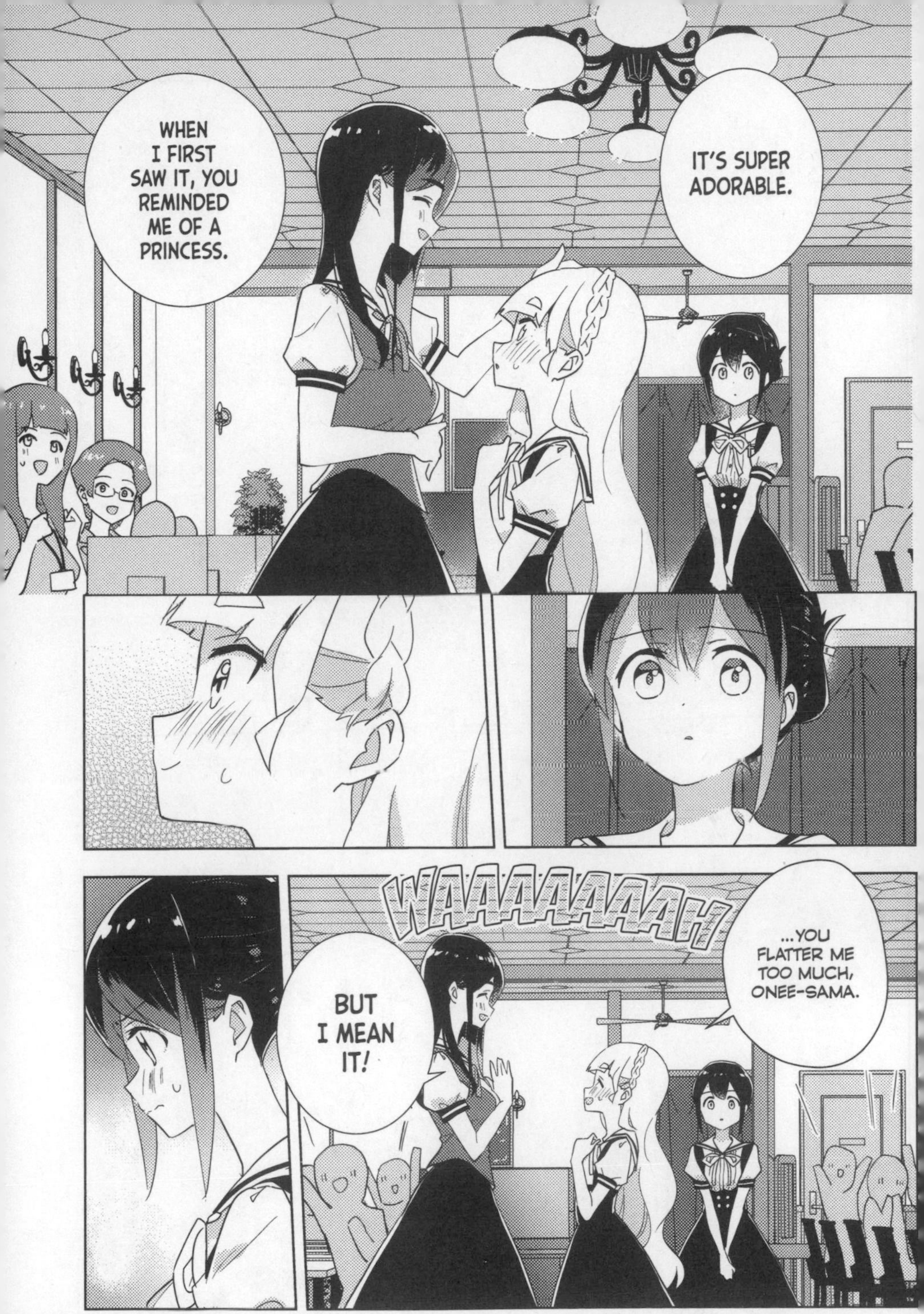

IT'S SUPER ADORABLE.
WHEN I FIRST SAW IT, YOU REMINDED ME OF A PRINCESS.
WAAAAAAAAAH
...YOU FLATTER ME TOO MUCH, ONEE-SAMA.
BUT I MEAN IT!

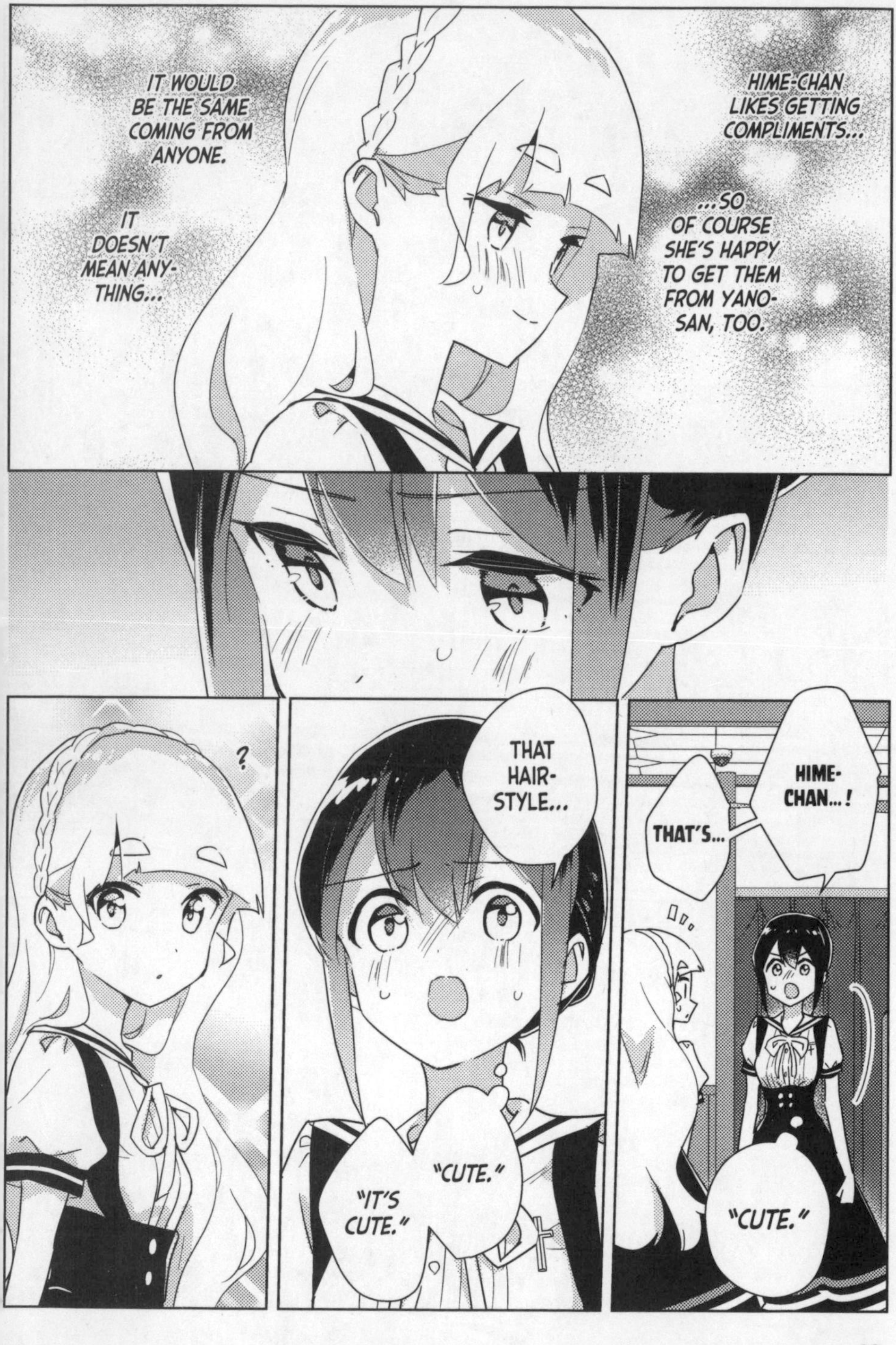
HIME-CHAN LIKES GETTING COMPLIMENTS...
...SO OF COURSE SHE'S HAPPY TO GET THEM FROM YANO-SAN, TOO.
IT WOULD BE THE SAME COMING FROM ANYONE.
IT DOESN'T MEAN ANY-THING...
HIME-CHAN...!
THAT'S...
"CUTE."
THAT HAIR-STYLE...
"CUTE."
"IT'S CUTE."
?

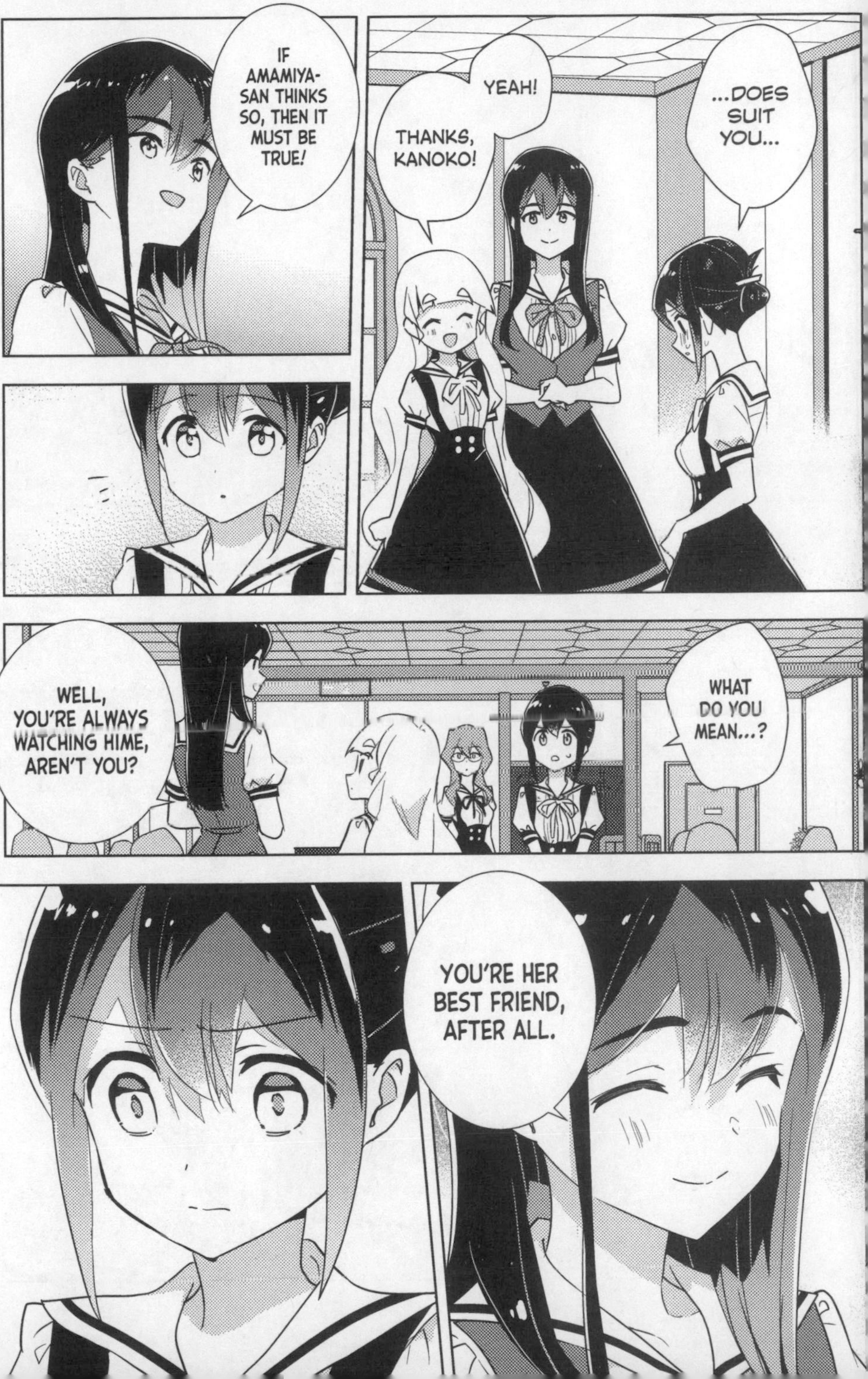
...DOES SUIT YOU...
YEAH!
THANKS, KANOKO!
IF AMAMIYA-SAN THINKS SO, THEN IT MUST BE TRUE!
WHAT DO YOU MEAN...?
WELL, YOU'RE ALWAYS WATCHING HIME, AREN'T YOU?
YOU'RE HER BEST FRIEND, AFTER ALL.

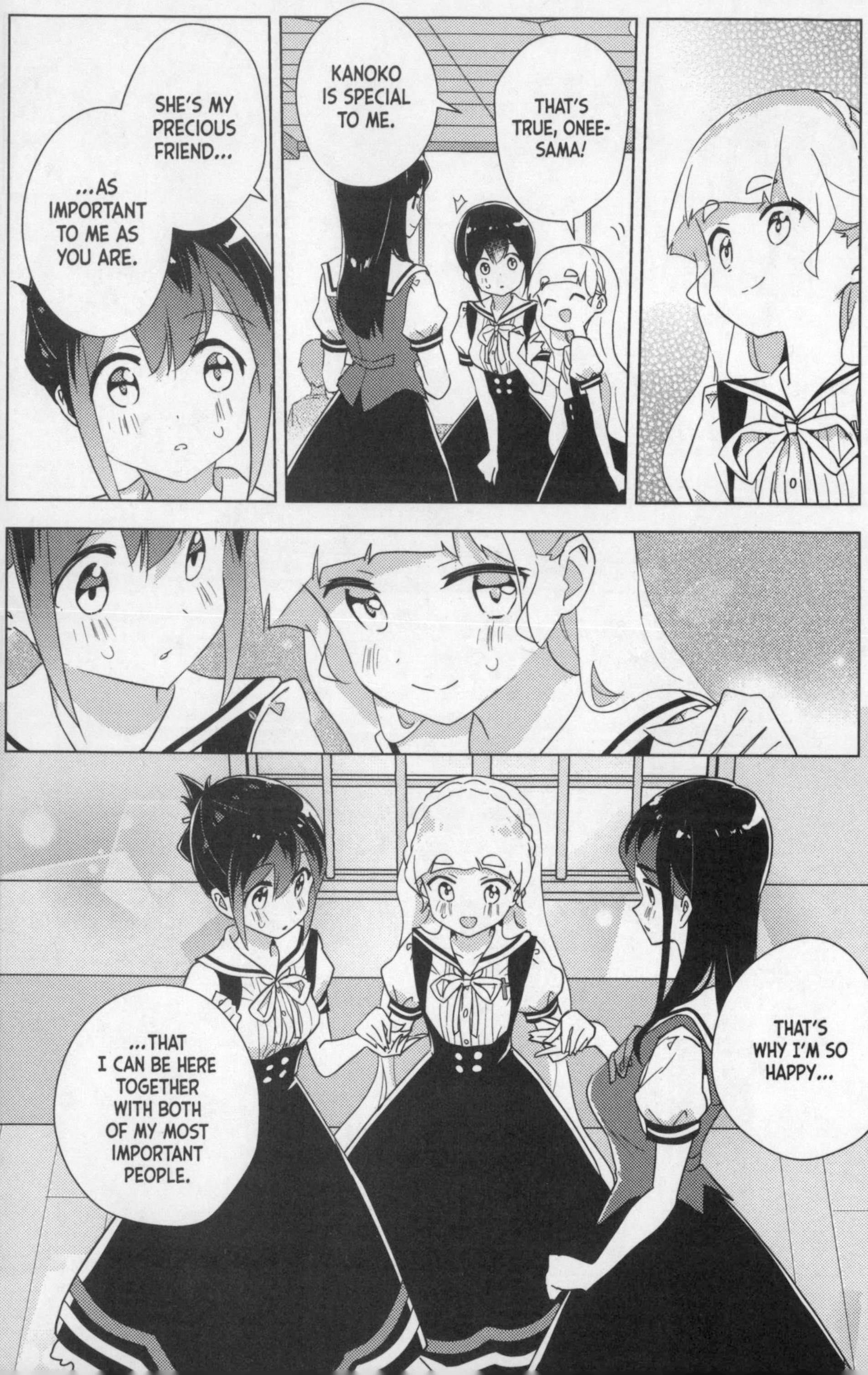
KANOKO IS SPECIAL TO ME.
THAT'S TRUE, ONEE-SAMA!
SHE'S MY PRECIOUS FRIEND...
...AS IMPORTANT TO ME AS YOU ARE.
THAT'S WHY I'M SO HAPPY...
...THAT I CAN BE HERE TOGETHER WITH BOTH OF MY MOST IMPORTANT PEOPLE.

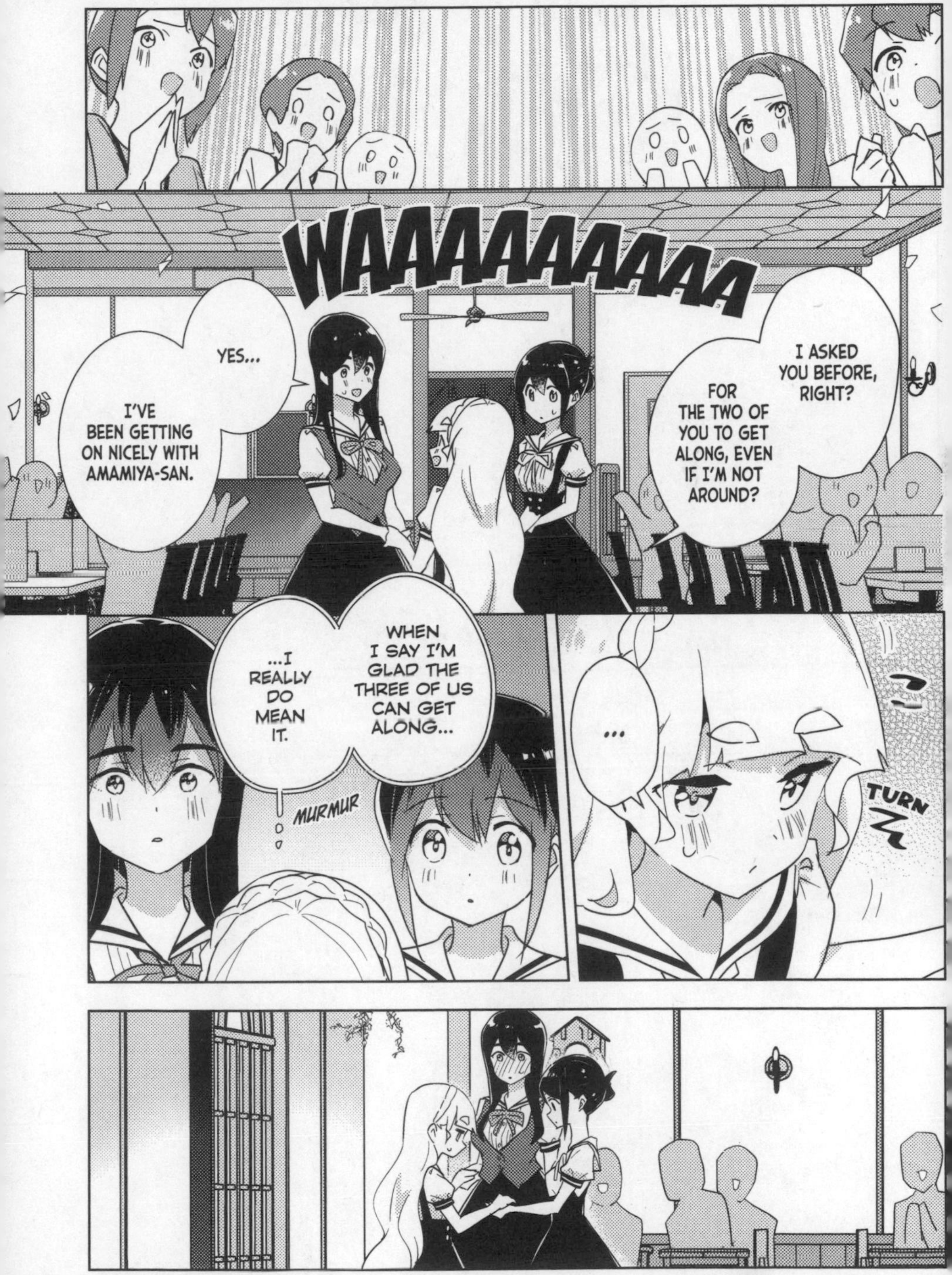
WAAAAAAAAA
I ASKED YOU BEFORE, RIGHT?
FOR THE TWO OF YOU TO GET ALONG, EVEN IF I'M NOT AROUND?
YES...
I'VE BEEN GETTING ON NICELY WITH AMAMIYA-SAN.
...
TURN
WHEN I SAY I'M GLAD THE THREE OF US CAN GET ALONG...
...I REALLY DO MEAN IT.
MURMUR

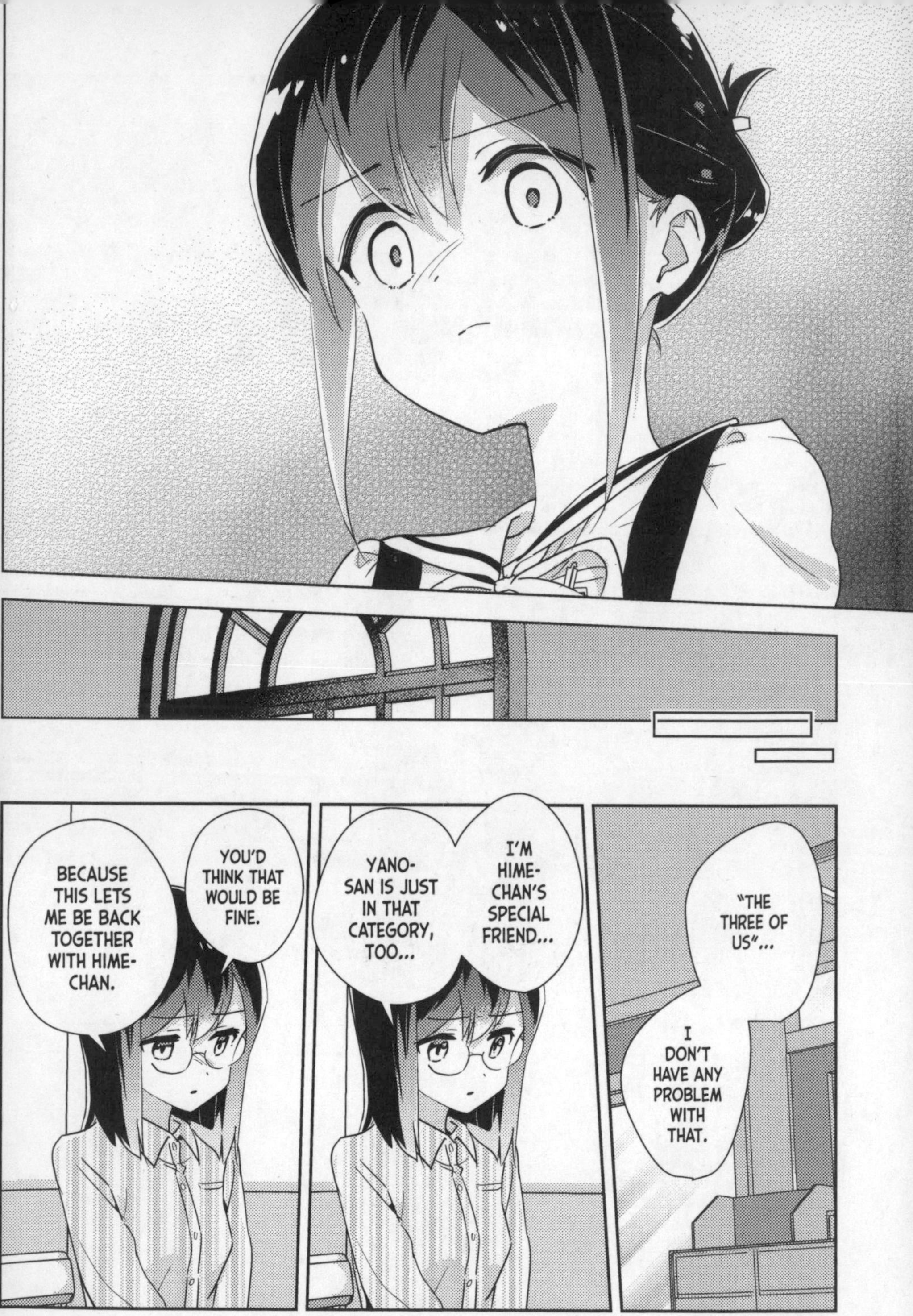
"THE THREE OF US"...
I DON'T HAVE ANY PROBLEM WITH THAT.
I'M HIME-CHAN'S SPECIAL FRIEND...
YANO-SAN IS JUST IN THAT CATEGORY, TOO...
YOU'D THINK THAT WOULD BE FINE.
BECAUSE THIS LETS ME BE BACK TOGETHER WITH HIME-CHAN.

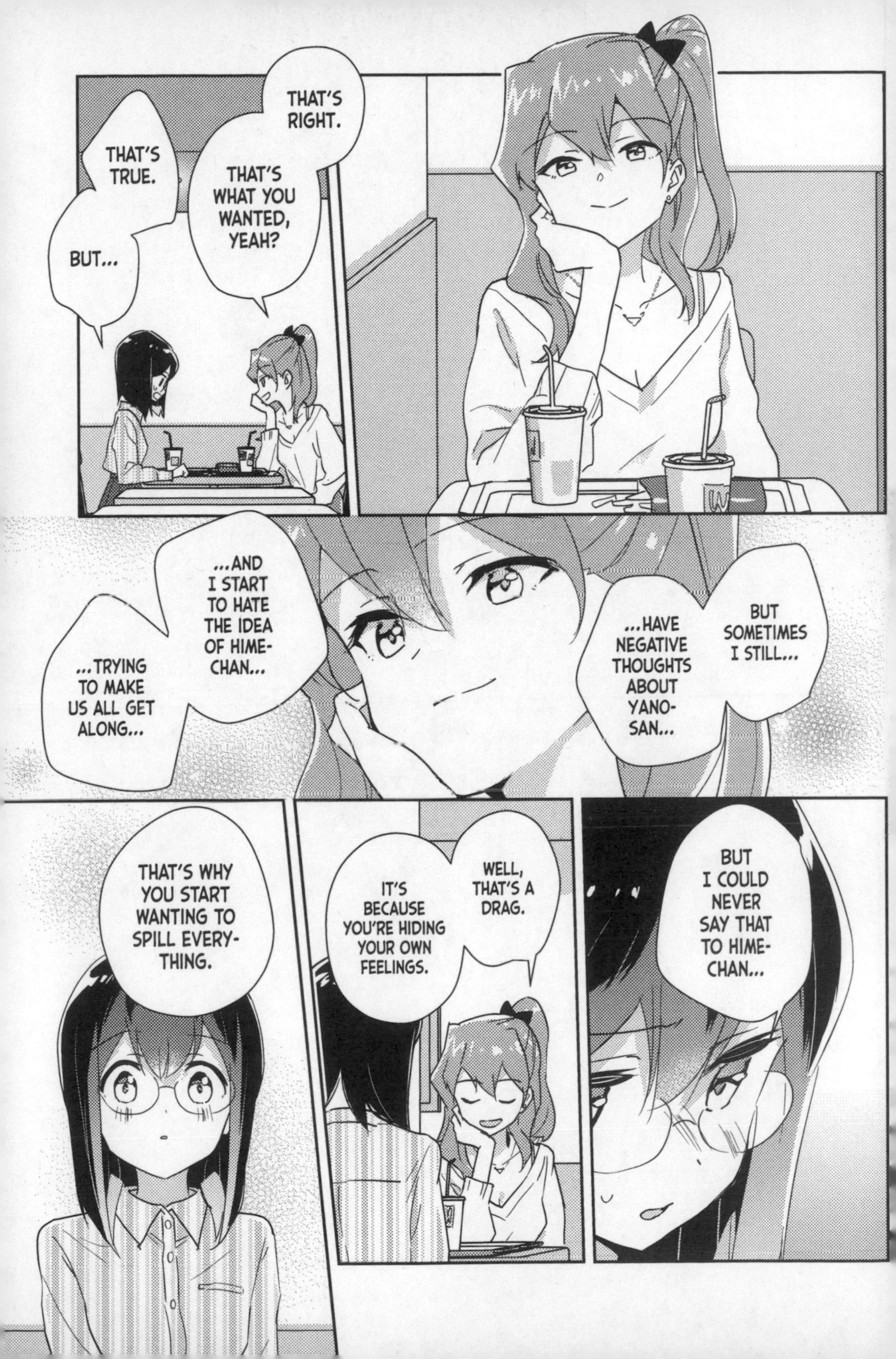
THAT'S RIGHT.
THAT'S WHAT YOU WANTED, YEAH?
THAT'S TRUE.
BUT...
BUT SOMETIMES I STILL...
...HAVE NEGATIVE THOUGHTS ABOUT YANO-SAN...
...AND I START TO HATE THE IDEA OF HIME-CHAN...
...TRYING TO MAKE US ALL GET ALONG...
BUT I COULD NEVER SAY THAT TO HIME-CHAN...
WELL, THAT'S A DRAG.
IT'S BECAUSE YOU'RE HIDING YOUR OWN FEELINGS.
THAT'S WHY YOU START WANTING TO SPILL EVERY-THING.

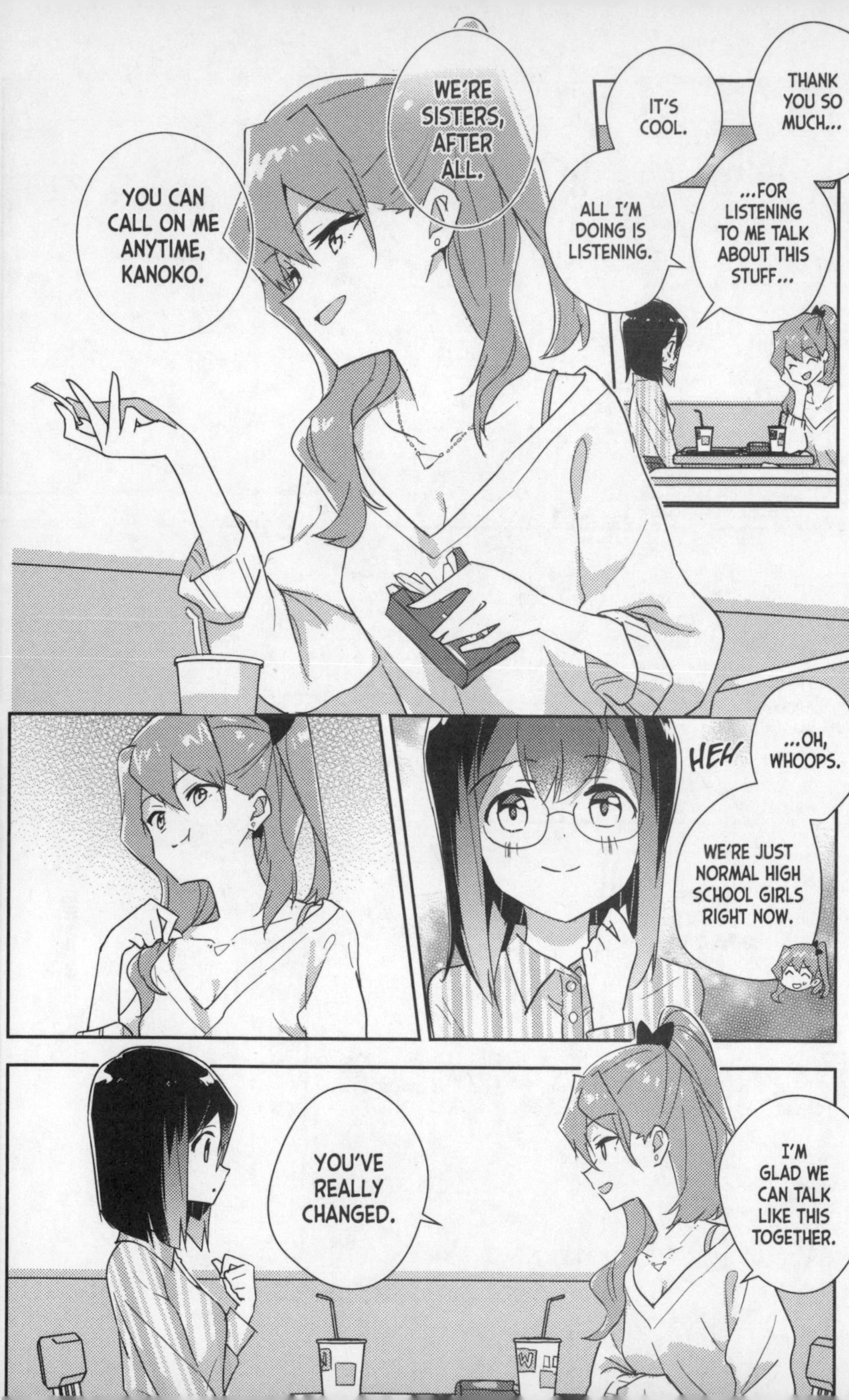

THANK YOU SO MUCH...
...FOR LISTENING TO ME TALK ABOUT THIS STUFF...
IT'S COOL.
ALL I'M DOING IS LISTENING.
WE'RE SISTERS, AFTER ALL.
YOU CAN CALL ON ME ANYTIME, KANOKO.
HEH
...OH, WHOOPS.
WE'RE JUST NORMAL HIGH SCHOOL GIRLS RIGHT NOW.
I'M GLAD WE CAN TALK LIKE THIS TOGETHER.
YOU'VE REALLY CHANGED.

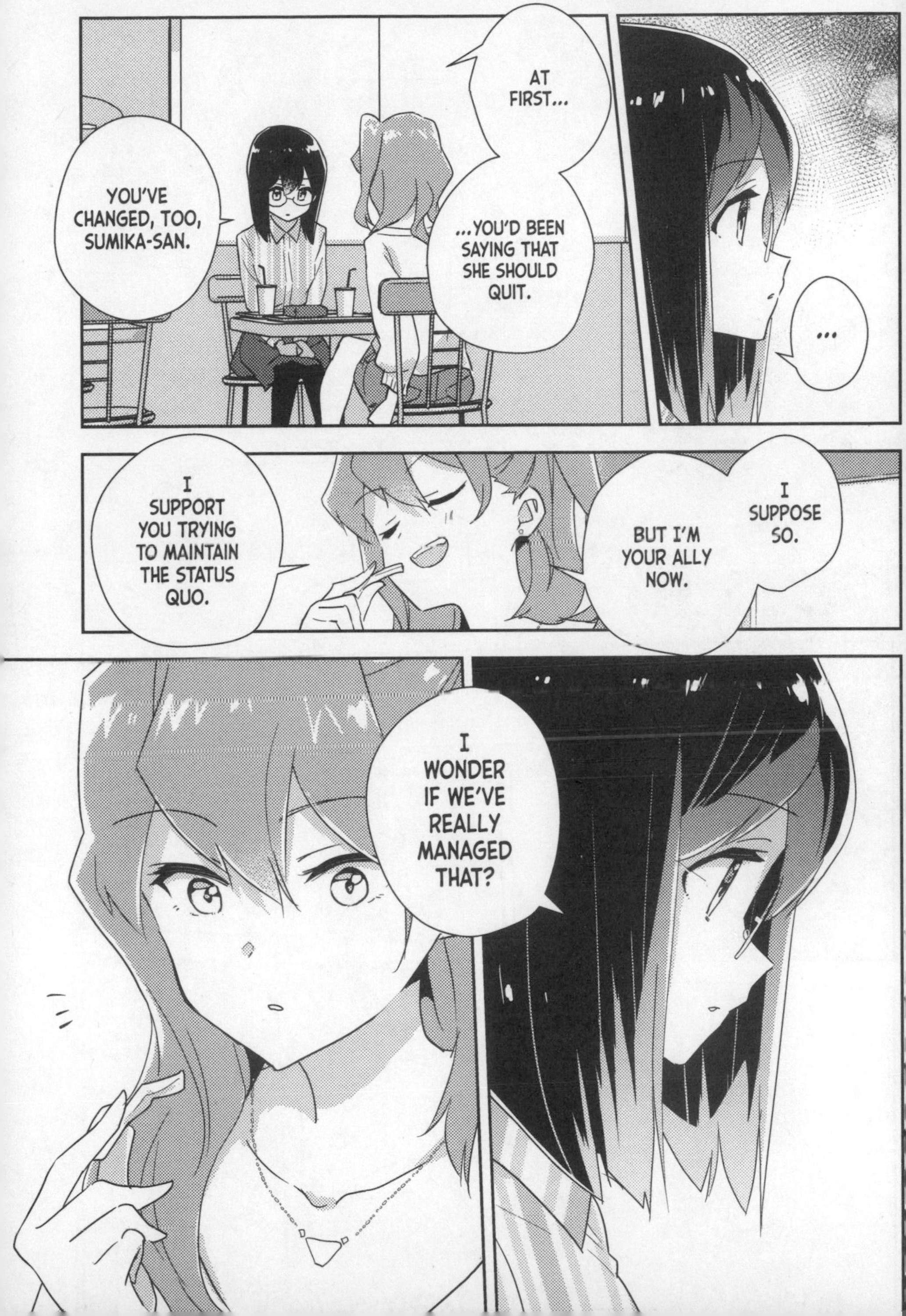
...
AT FIRST...
...YOU'D BEEN SAYING THAT SHE SHOULD QUIT.
YOU'VE CHANGED, TOO, SUMIKA-SAN.
I SUPPOSE SO.
BUT I'M YOUR ALLY NOW.
I SUPPORT YOU TRYING TO MAINTAIN THE STATUS QUO.
I WONDER IF WE'VE REALLY MANAGED THAT?

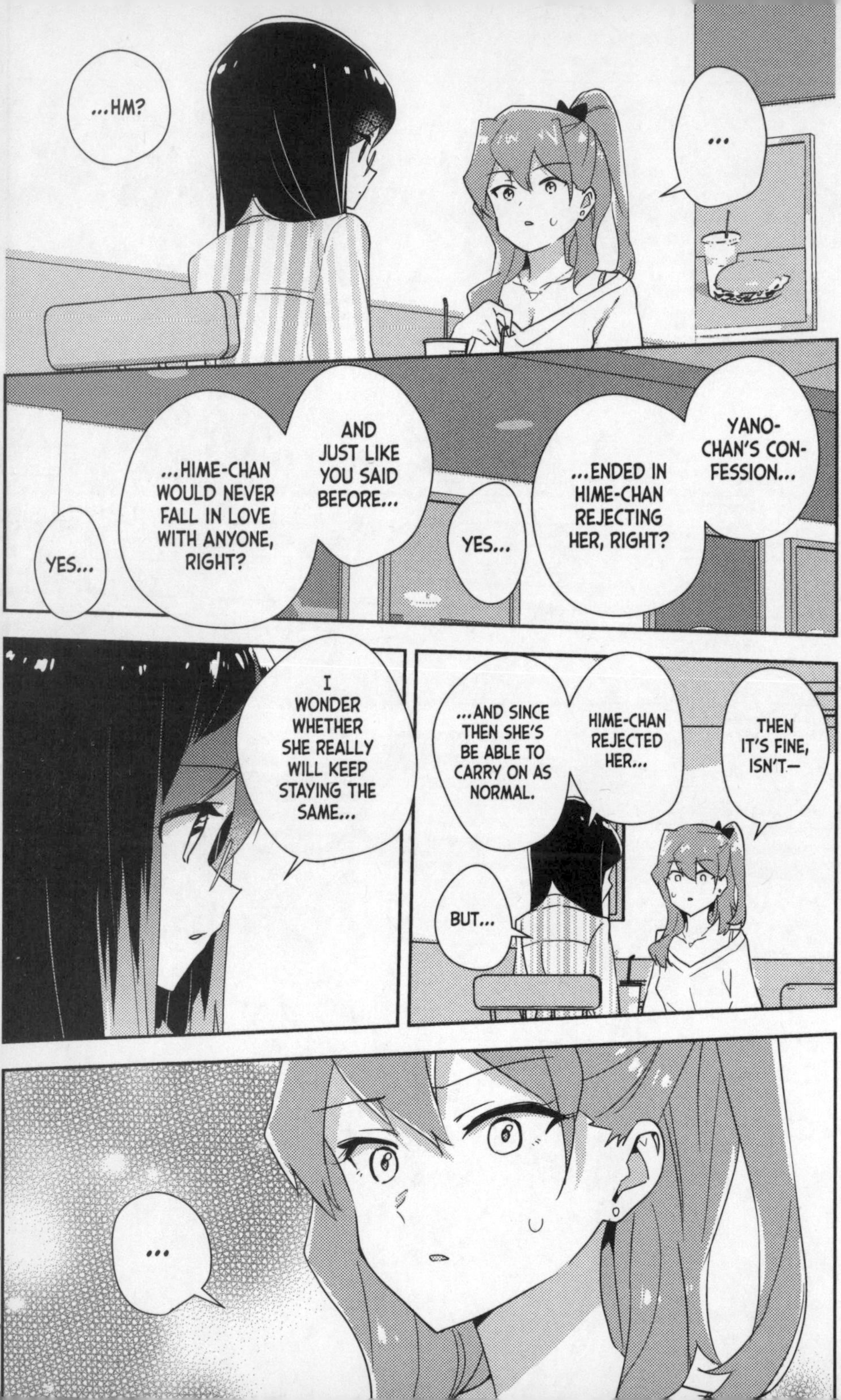
...
...HM?
YANO-CHAN'S CONFESSION...
...ENDED IN HIME-CHAN REJECTING HER, RIGHT?
YES...
AND JUST LIKE YOU SAID BEFORE...
...HIME-CHAN WOULD NEVER FALL IN LOVE WITH ANYONE, RIGHT?
YES...
THEN IT'S FINE, ISN'T—
HIME-CHAN REJECTED HER...
...AND SINCE THEN SHE'S BE ABLE TO CARRY ON AS NORMAL.
BUT...
I WONDER WHETHER SHE REALLY WILL KEEP STAYING THE SAME...
...

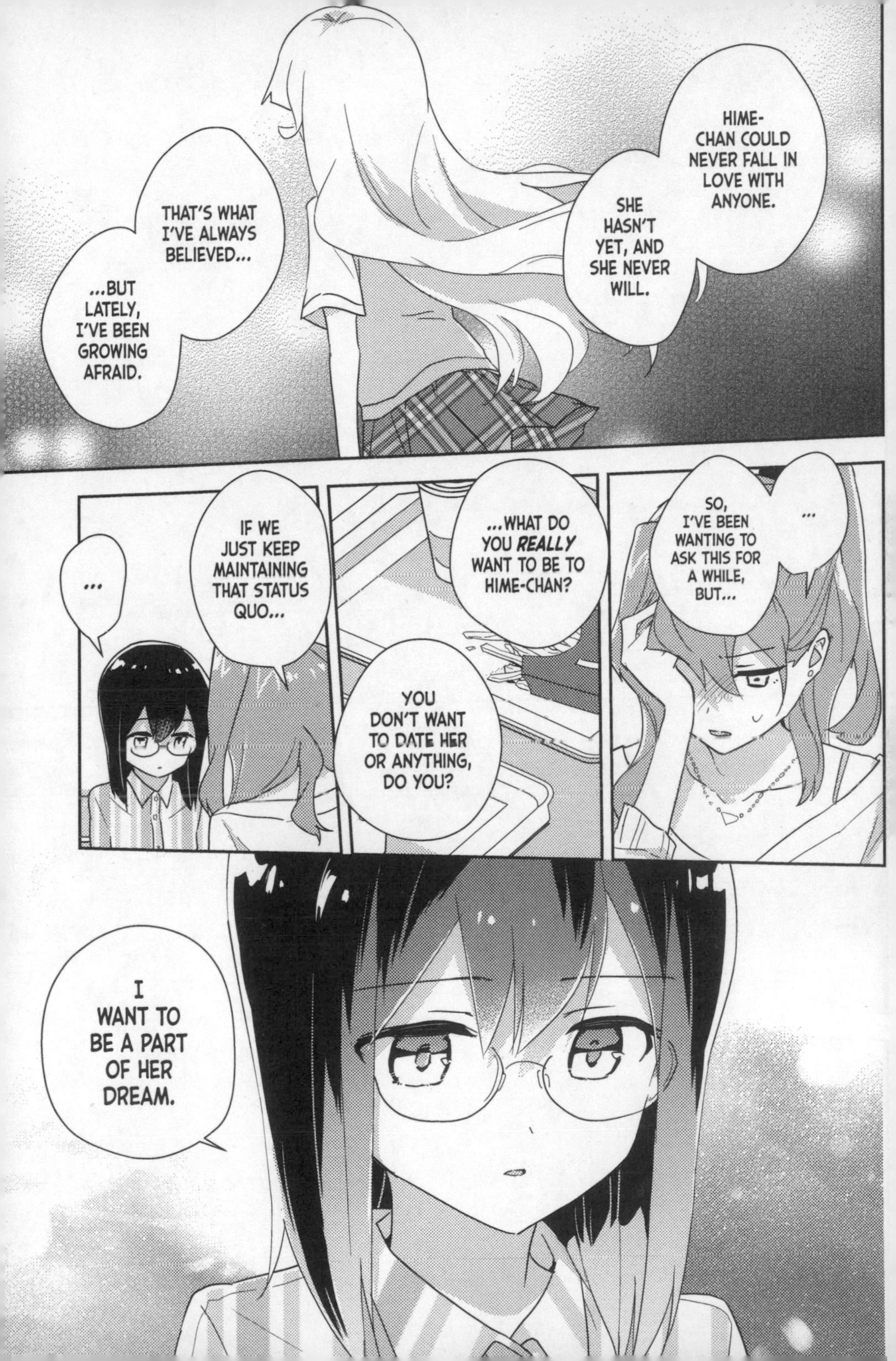
HIME-CHAN COULD NEVER FALL IN LOVE WITH ANYONE.
SHE HASN'T YET, AND SHE NEVER WILL.
THAT'S WHAT I'VE ALWAYS BELIEVED...
...BUT LATELY, I'VE BEEN GROWING AFRAID.
...
SO, I'VE BEEN WANTING TO ASK THIS FOR A WHILE, BUT...
...WHAT DO YOU *REALLY* WANT TO BE TO HIME-CHAN?
YOU DON'T WANT TO DATE HER OR ANYTHING, DO YOU?
IF WE JUST KEEP MAINTAINING THAT STATUS QUO...
...
I WANT TO BE A PART OF HER DREAM.

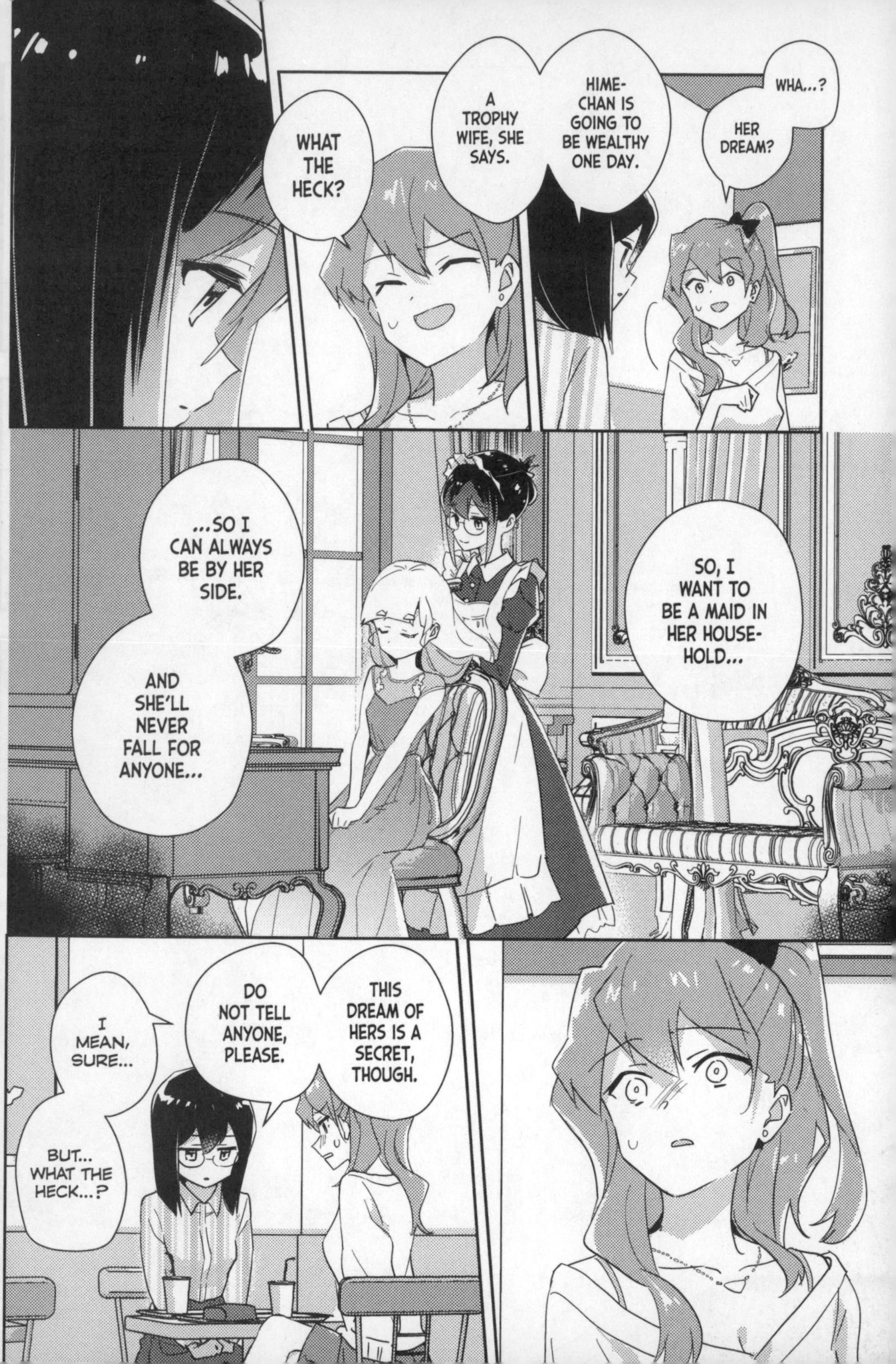
WHA...?
HER DREAM?
HIME-CHAN IS GOING TO BE WEALTHY ONE DAY.
A TROPHY WIFE, SHE SAYS.
WHAT THE HECK?
SO, I WANT TO BE A MAID IN HER HOUSE-HOLD...
...SO I CAN ALWAYS BE BY HER SIDE.
AND SHE'LL NEVER FALL FOR ANYONE...
THIS DREAM OF HERS IS A SECRET, THOUGH.
DO NOT TELL ANYONE, PLEASE.
I MEAN, SURE...
BUT... WHAT THE HECK...?

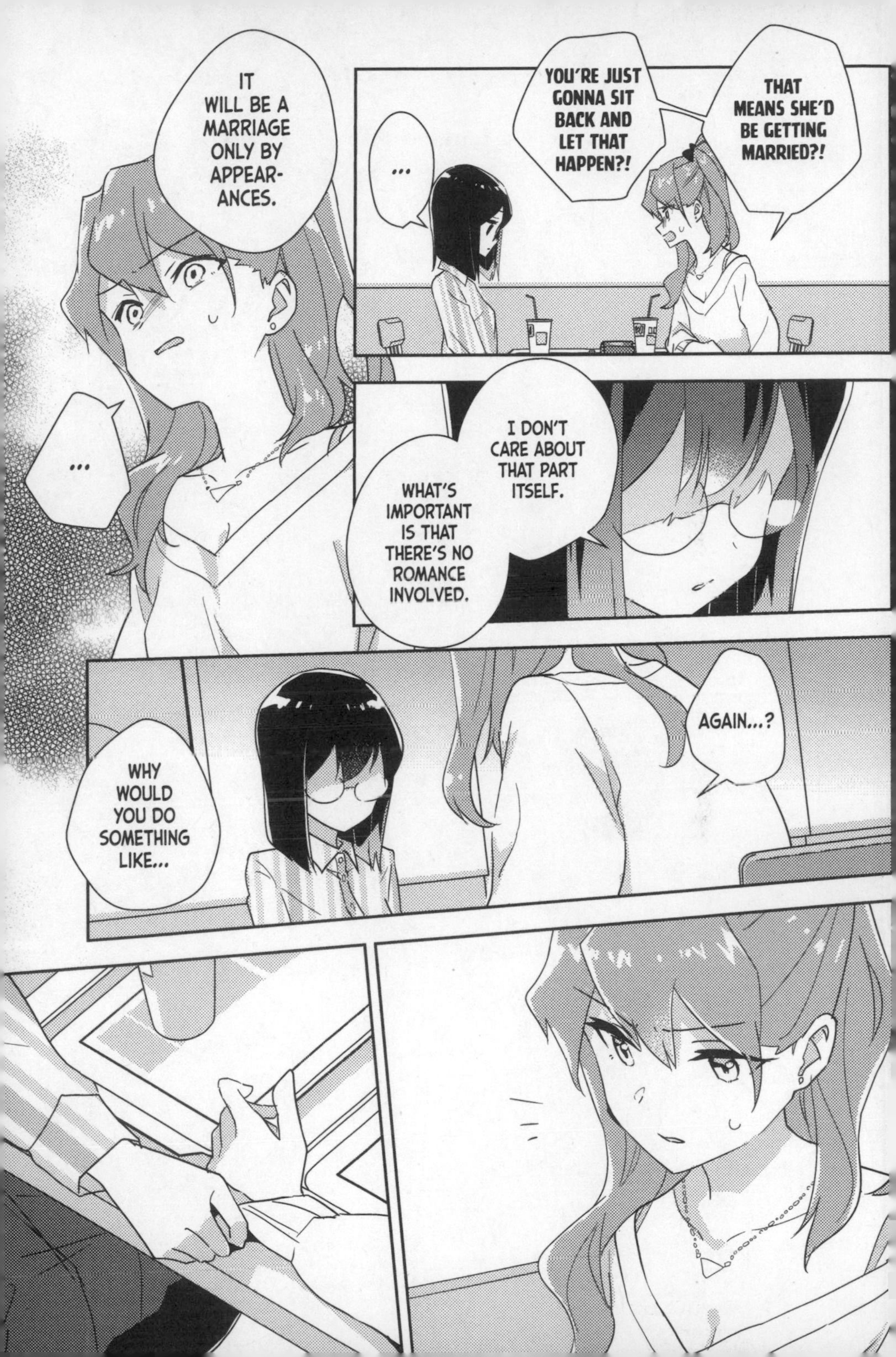
THAT MEANS SHE'D BE GETTING MARRIED?!
YOU'RE JUST GONNA SIT BACK AND LET THAT HAPPEN?!
...
I DON'T CARE ABOUT THAT PART ITSELF.
WHAT'S IMPORTANT IS THAT THERE'S NO ROMANCE INVOLVED.
IT WILL BE A MARRIAGE ONLY BY APPEARANCES.
...
AGAIN...?
WHY WOULD YOU DO SOMETHING LIKE...

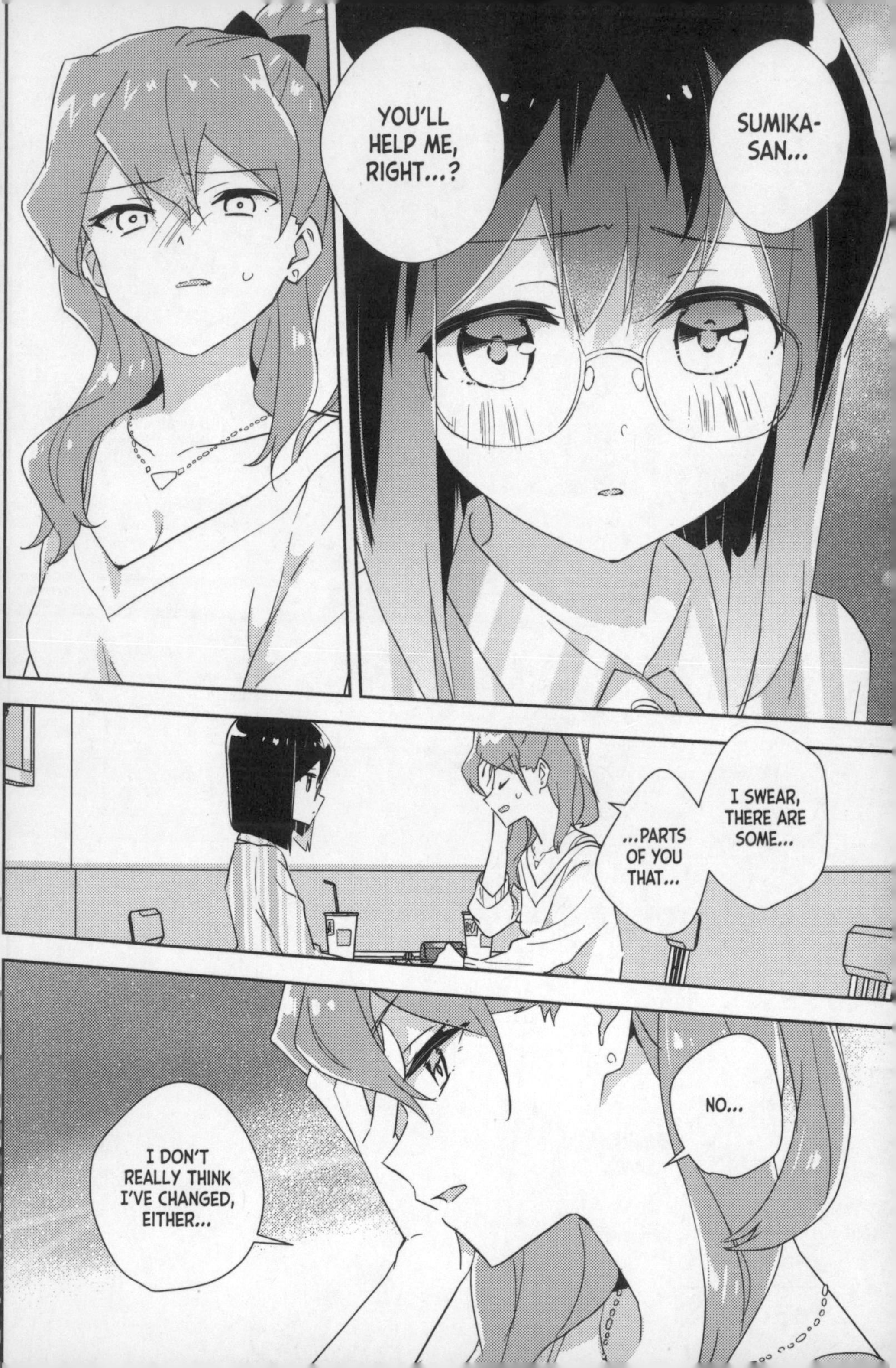
SUMIKA-SAN...
YOU'LL HELP ME, RIGHT...?
I SWEAR, THERE ARE SOME...
...PARTS OF YOU THAT...
NO...
I DON'T REALLY THINK I'VE CHANGED, EITHER...

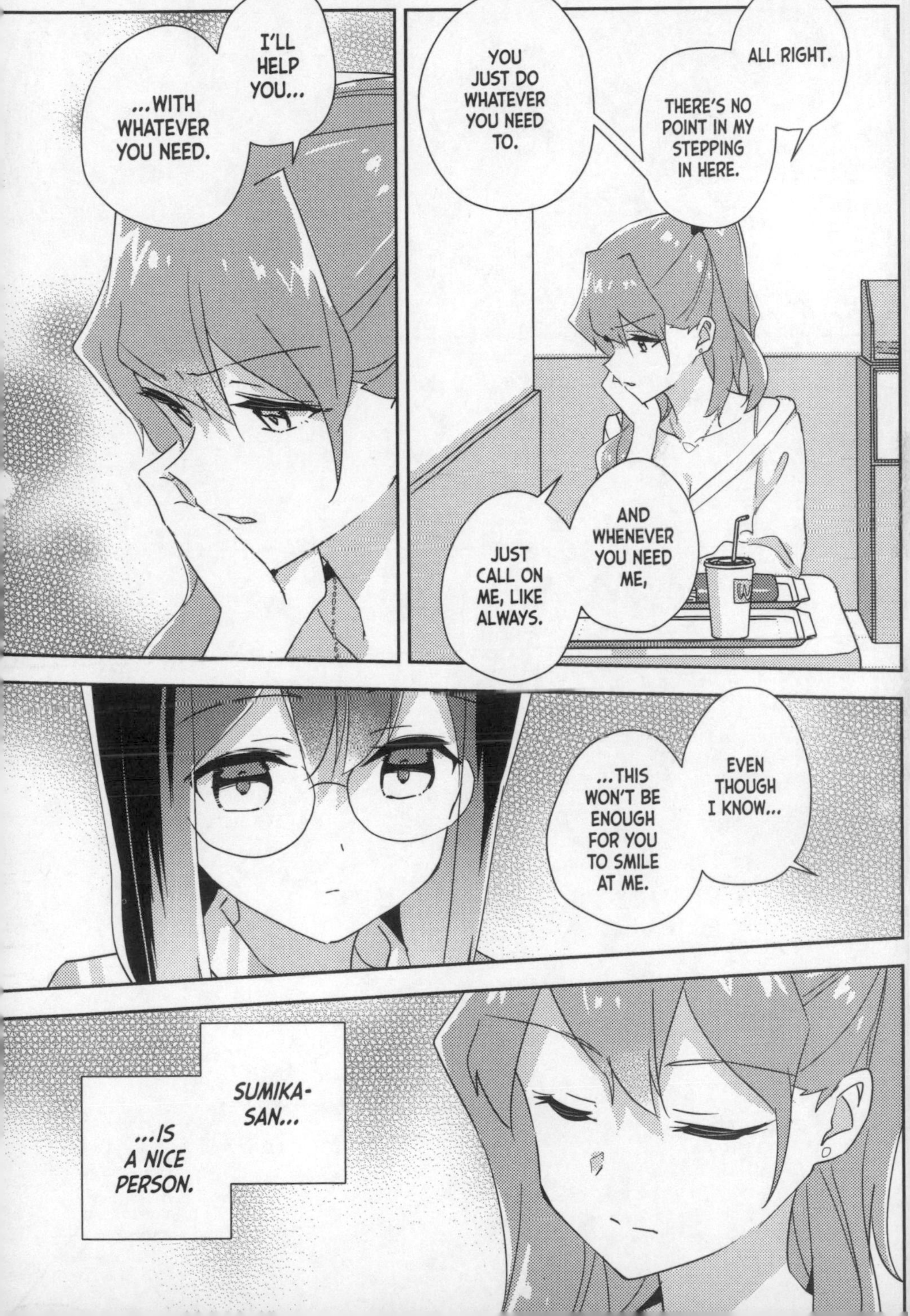
ALL RIGHT.
THERE'S NO POINT IN MY STEPPING IN HERE.
YOU JUST DO WHATEVER YOU NEED TO.
AND WHENEVER YOU NEED ME,
JUST CALL ON ME, LIKE ALWAYS.
I'LL HELP YOU...
...WITH WHATEVER YOU NEED.
EVEN THOUGH I KNOW...
...THIS WON'T BE ENOUGH FOR YOU TO SMILE AT ME.
SUMIKA-SAN...
...IS A NICE PERSON.

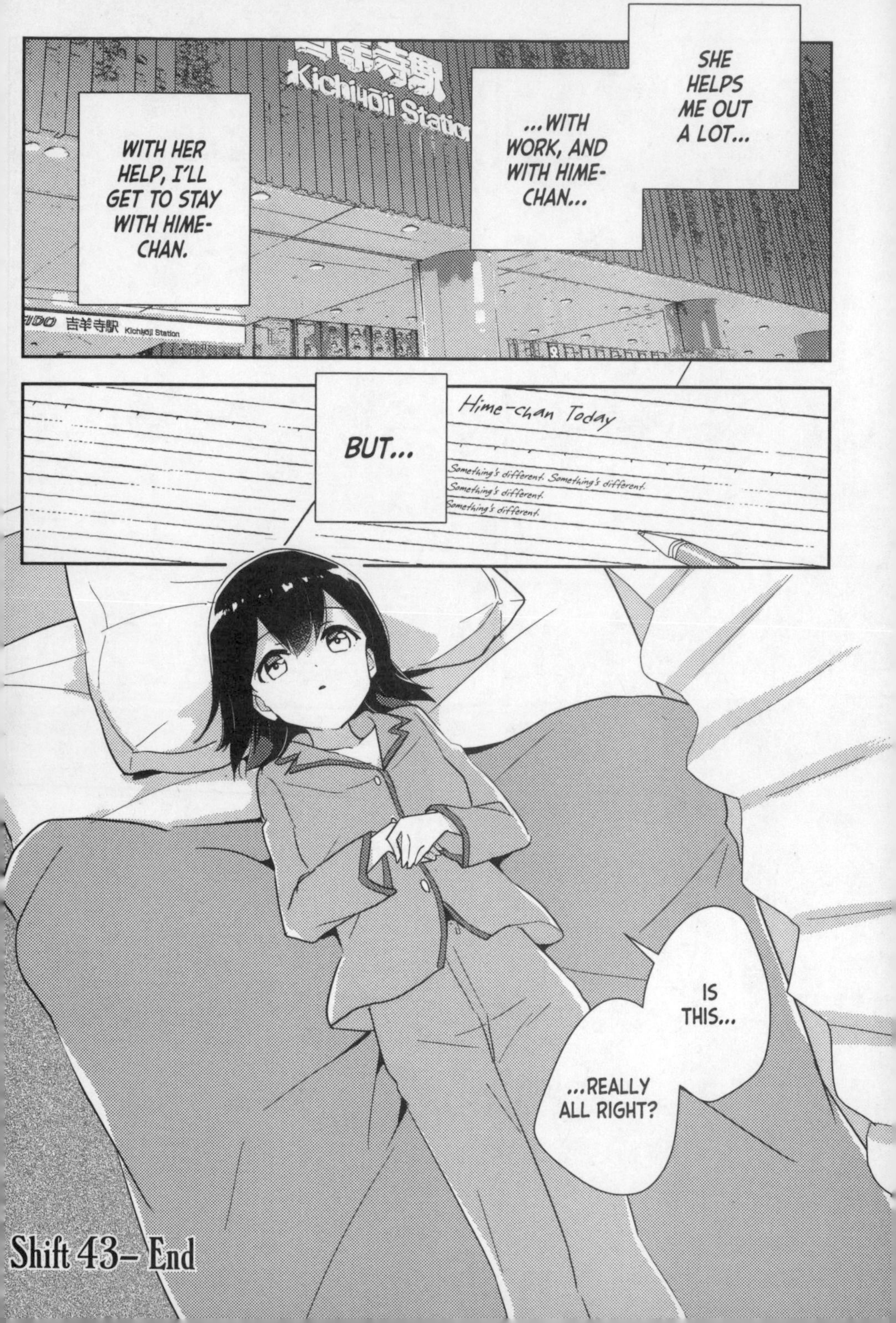
SHE HELPS ME OUT A LOT...
...WITH WORK, AND WITH HIME-CHAN...
WITH HER HELP, I'LL GET TO STAY WITH HIME-CHAN.
吉祥寺駅 Kichijōji Station
Hime-chan Today
Something's different. Something's different.
Something's different.
Something's different.
BUT...
IS THIS...
...REALLY ALL RIGHT?

Shift 43– End

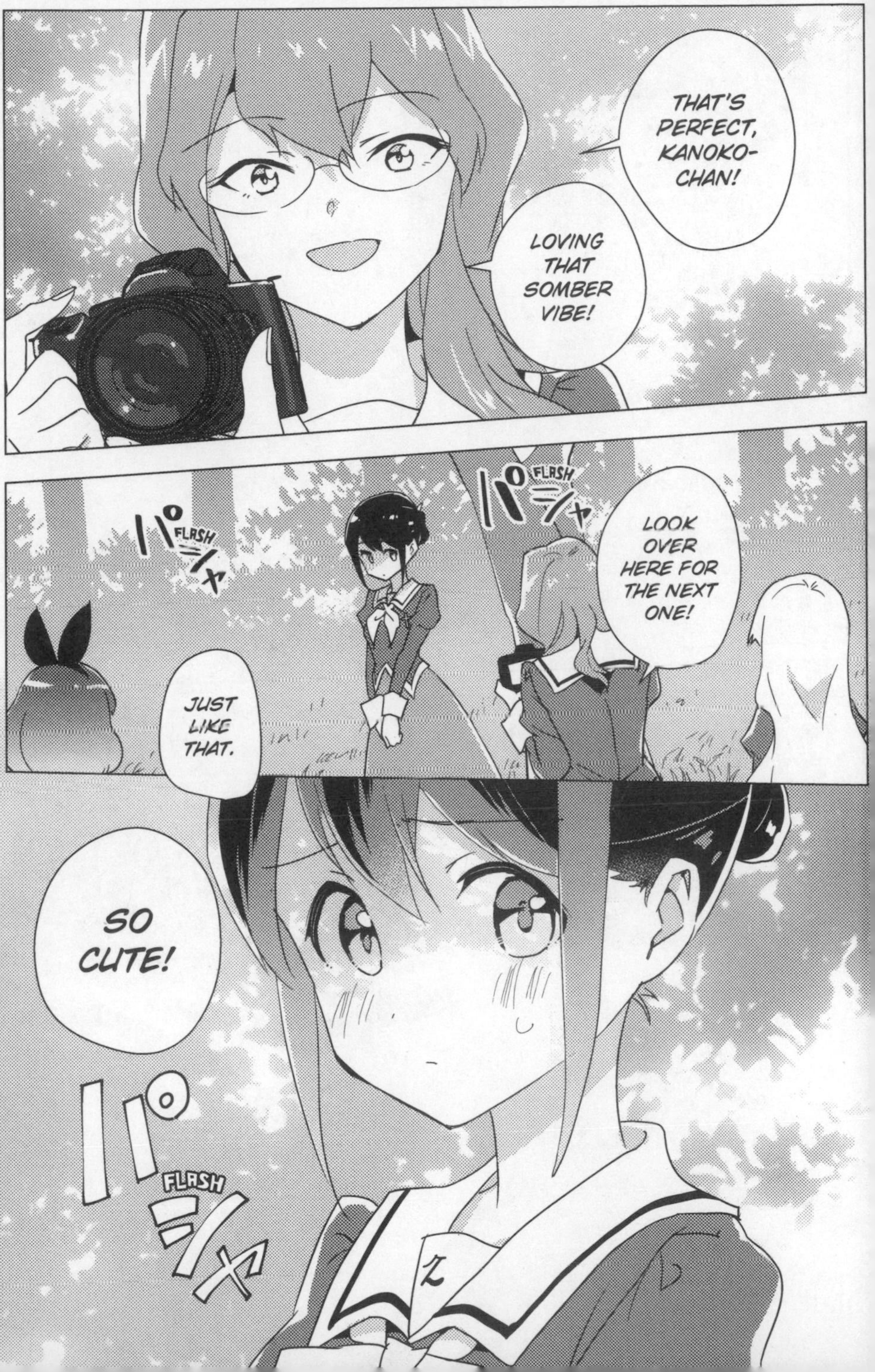
THAT'S PERFECT, KANOKO-CHAN!
LOVING THAT SOMBER VIBE!
パシャ FLASH
LOOK OVER HERE FOR THE NEXT ONE!
パシャ FLASH
JUST LIKE THAT.
SO CUTE!
パシャ FLASH

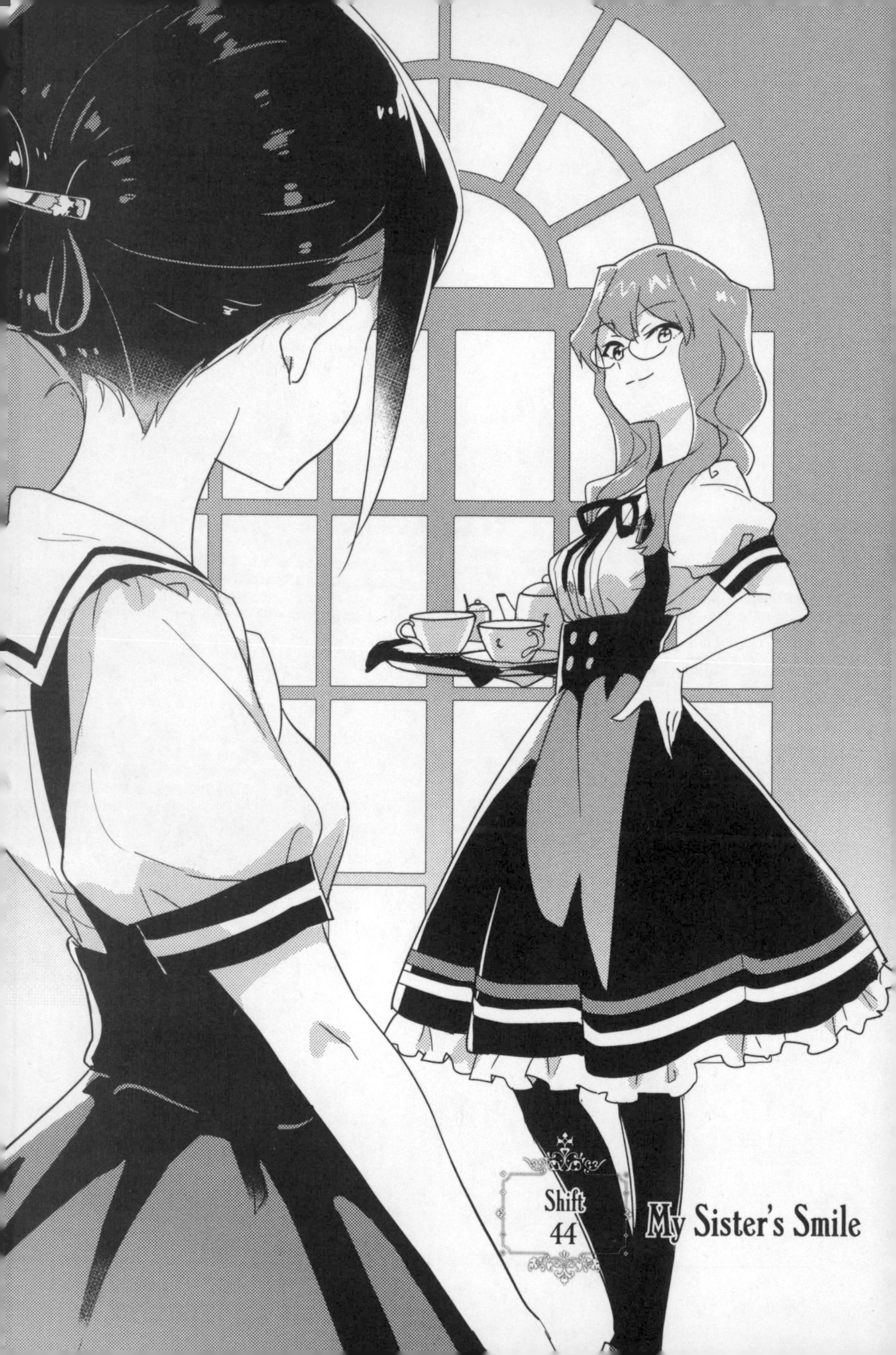
Shift
44
My Sister's Smile

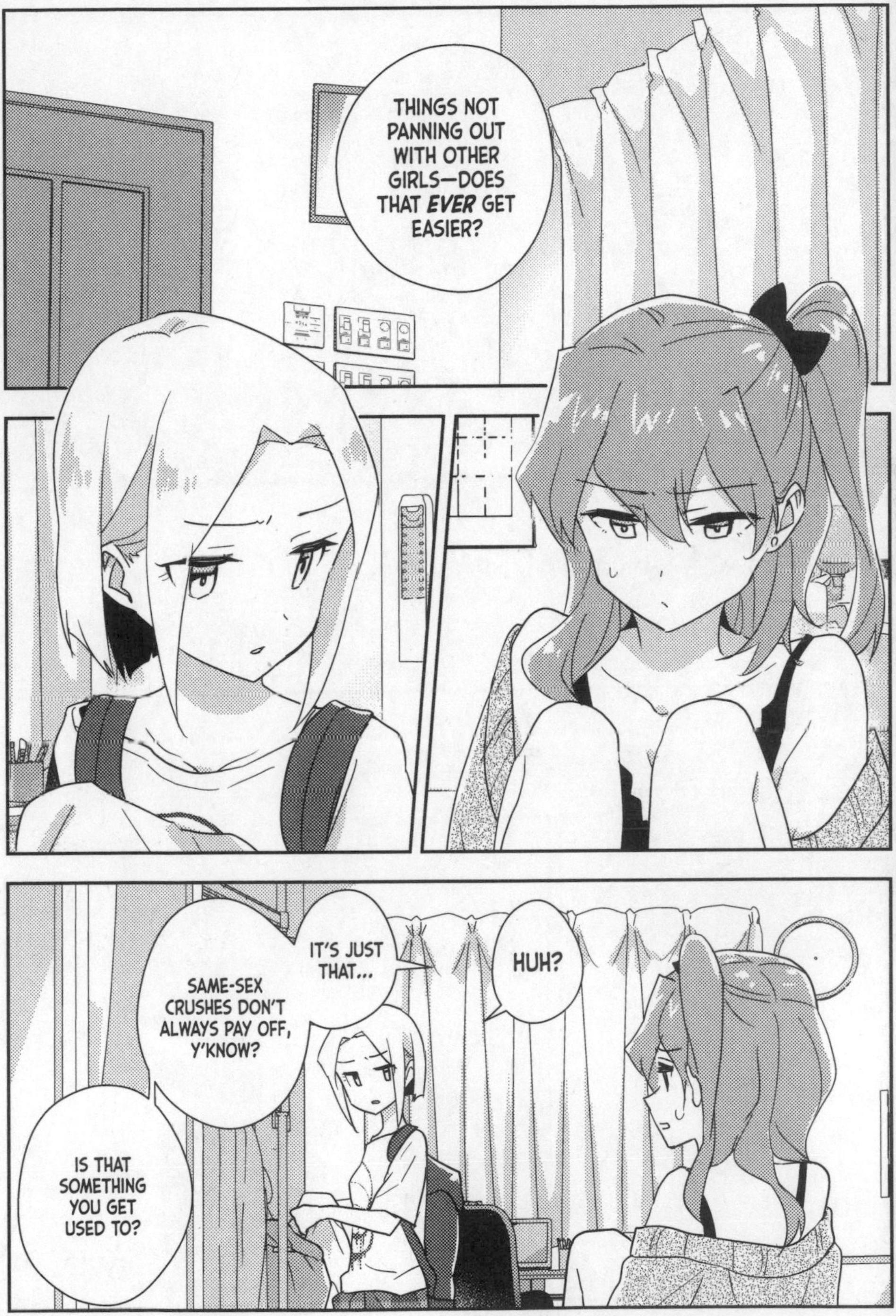
THINGS NOT PANNING OUT WITH OTHER GIRLS—DOES THAT *EVER* GET EASIER?
HUH?
IT'S JUST THAT...
SAME-SEX CRUSHES DON'T ALWAYS PAY OFF, Y'KNOW?
IS THAT SOMETHING YOU GET USED TO?

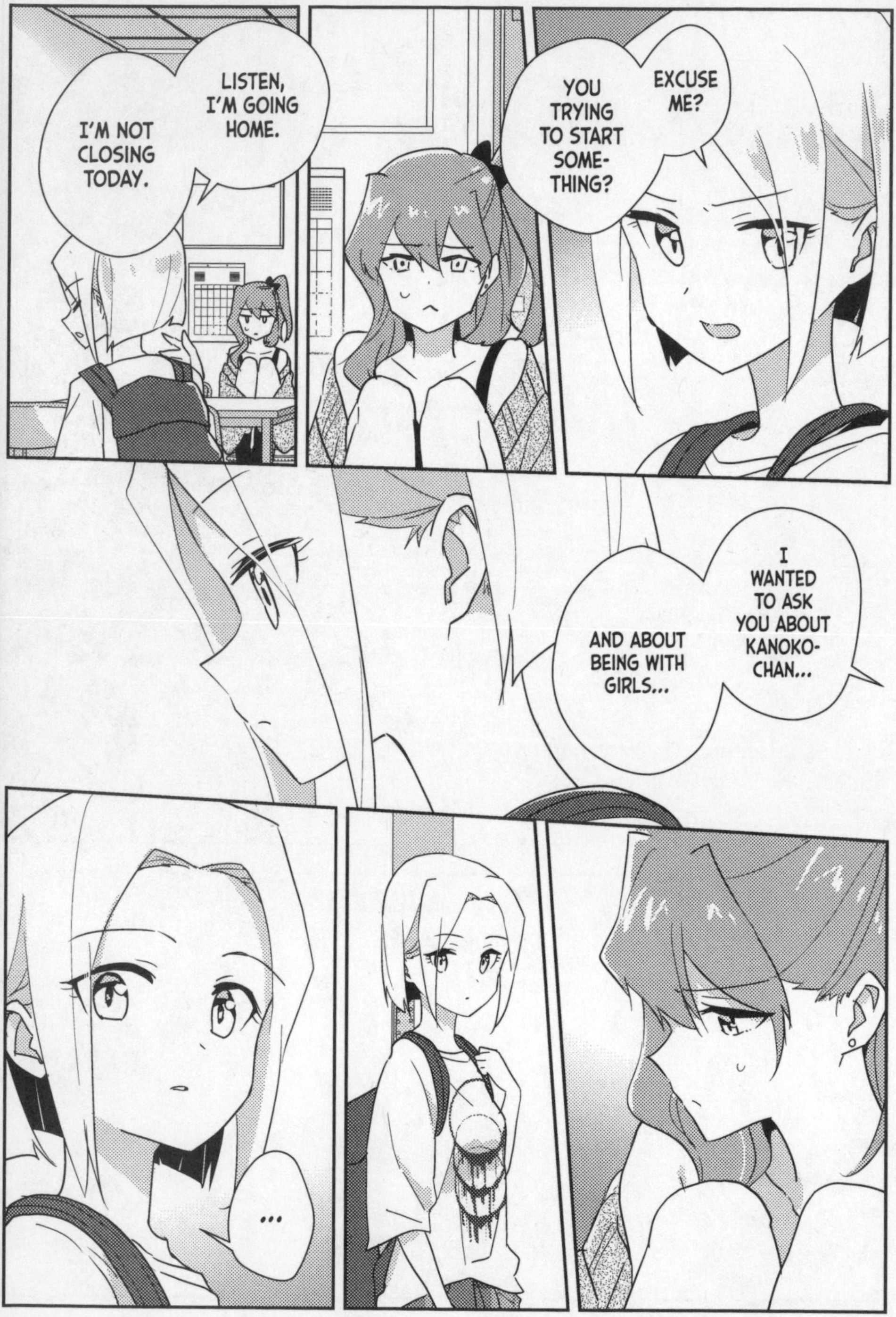
EXCUSE ME?
YOU TRYING TO START SOME-THING?
LISTEN, I'M GOING HOME.
I'M NOT CLOSING TODAY.
I WANTED TO ASK YOU ABOUT KANOKO-CHAN...
AND ABOUT BEING WITH GIRLS...
...

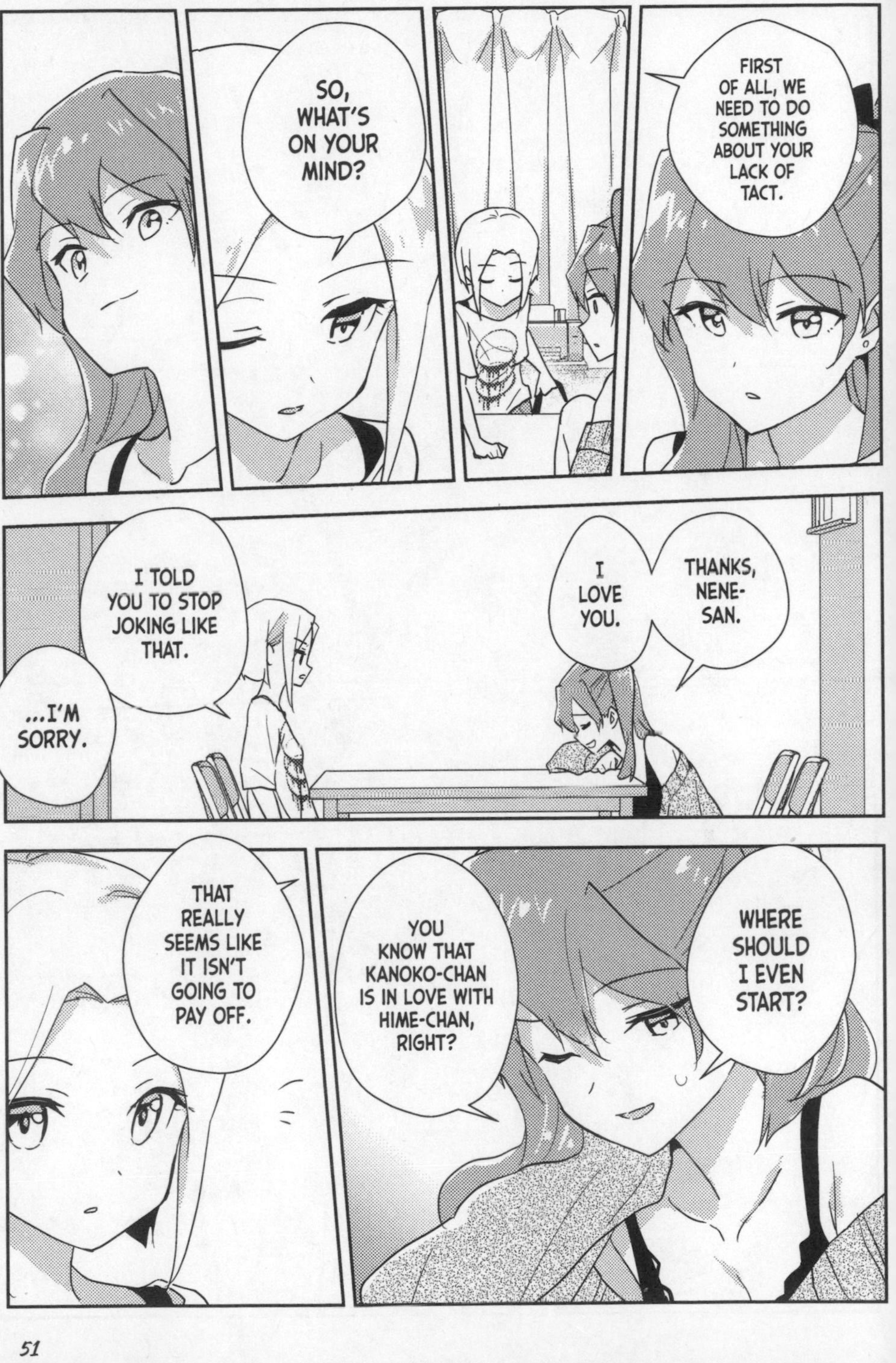
FIRST OF ALL, WE NEED TO DO SOMETHING ABOUT YOUR LACK OF TACT.
SO, WHAT'S ON YOUR MIND?
THANKS, NENE-SAN.
I LOVE YOU.
I TOLD YOU TO STOP JOKING LIKE THAT.
...I'M SORRY.
WHERE SHOULD I EVEN START?
YOU KNOW THAT KANOKO-CHAN IS IN LOVE WITH HIME-CHAN, RIGHT?
THAT REALLY SEEMS LIKE IT ISN'T GOING TO PAY OFF.

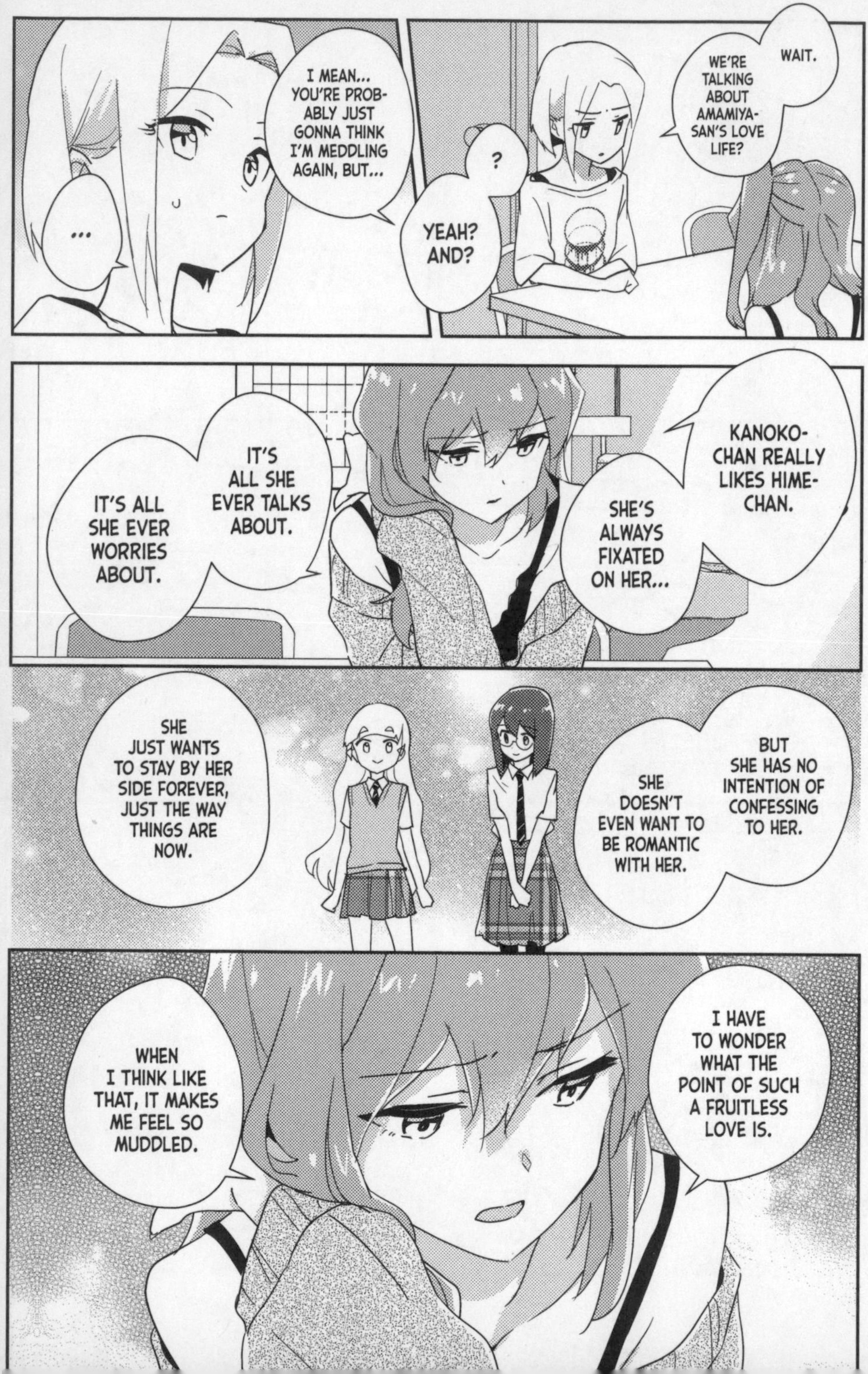
WAIT.
WE'RE TALKING ABOUT AMAMIYA-SAN'S LOVE LIFE?
?
YEAH? AND?
I MEAN... YOU'RE PROBABLY JUST GONNA THINK I'M MEDDLING AGAIN, BUT...
...
KANOKO-CHAN REALLY LIKES HIME-CHAN.
SHE'S ALWAYS FIXATED ON HER...
IT'S ALL SHE EVER TALKS ABOUT.
IT'S ALL SHE EVER WORRIES ABOUT.
BUT SHE HAS NO INTENTION OF CONFESSING TO HER.
SHE DOESN'T EVEN WANT TO BE ROMANTIC WITH HER.
SHE JUST WANTS TO STAY BY HER SIDE FOREVER, JUST THE WAY THINGS ARE NOW.
I HAVE TO WONDER WHAT THE POINT OF SUCH A FRUITLESS LOVE IS.
WHEN I THINK LIKE THAT, IT MAKES ME FEEL SO MUDDLED.

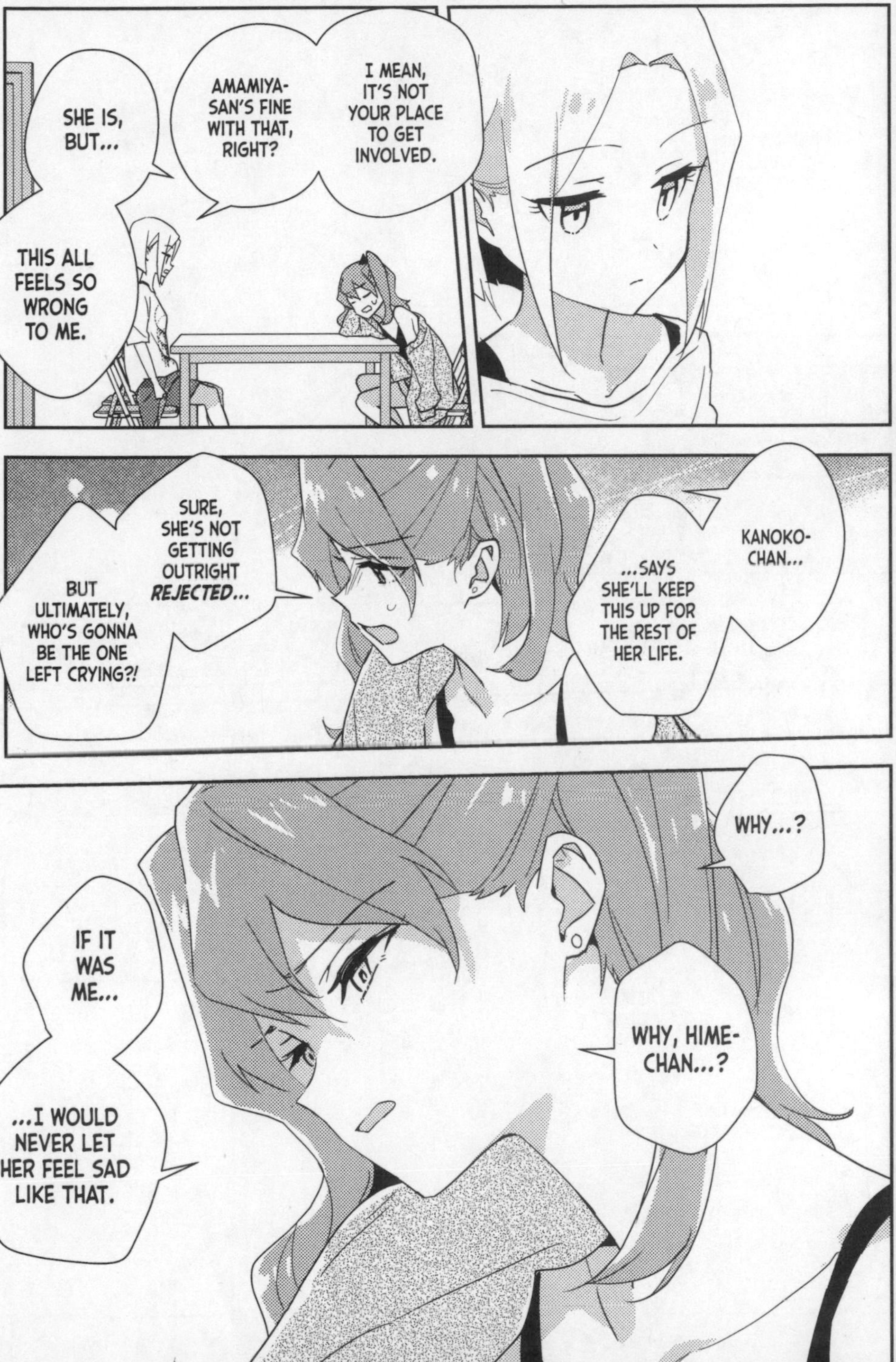
I MEAN, IT'S NOT YOUR PLACE TO GET INVOLVED.
AMAMIYA-SAN'S FINE WITH THAT, RIGHT?
SHE IS, BUT...
THIS ALL FEELS SO WRONG TO ME.
KANOKO-CHAN...
...SAYS SHE'LL KEEP THIS UP FOR THE REST OF HER LIFE.
SURE, SHE'S NOT GETTING OUTRIGHT *REJECTED*...
BUT ULTIMATELY, WHO'S GONNA BE THE ONE LEFT CRYING?!
WHY...?
WHY, HIME-CHAN...?
IF IT WAS ME...
...I WOULD NEVER LET HER FEEL SAD LIKE THAT.

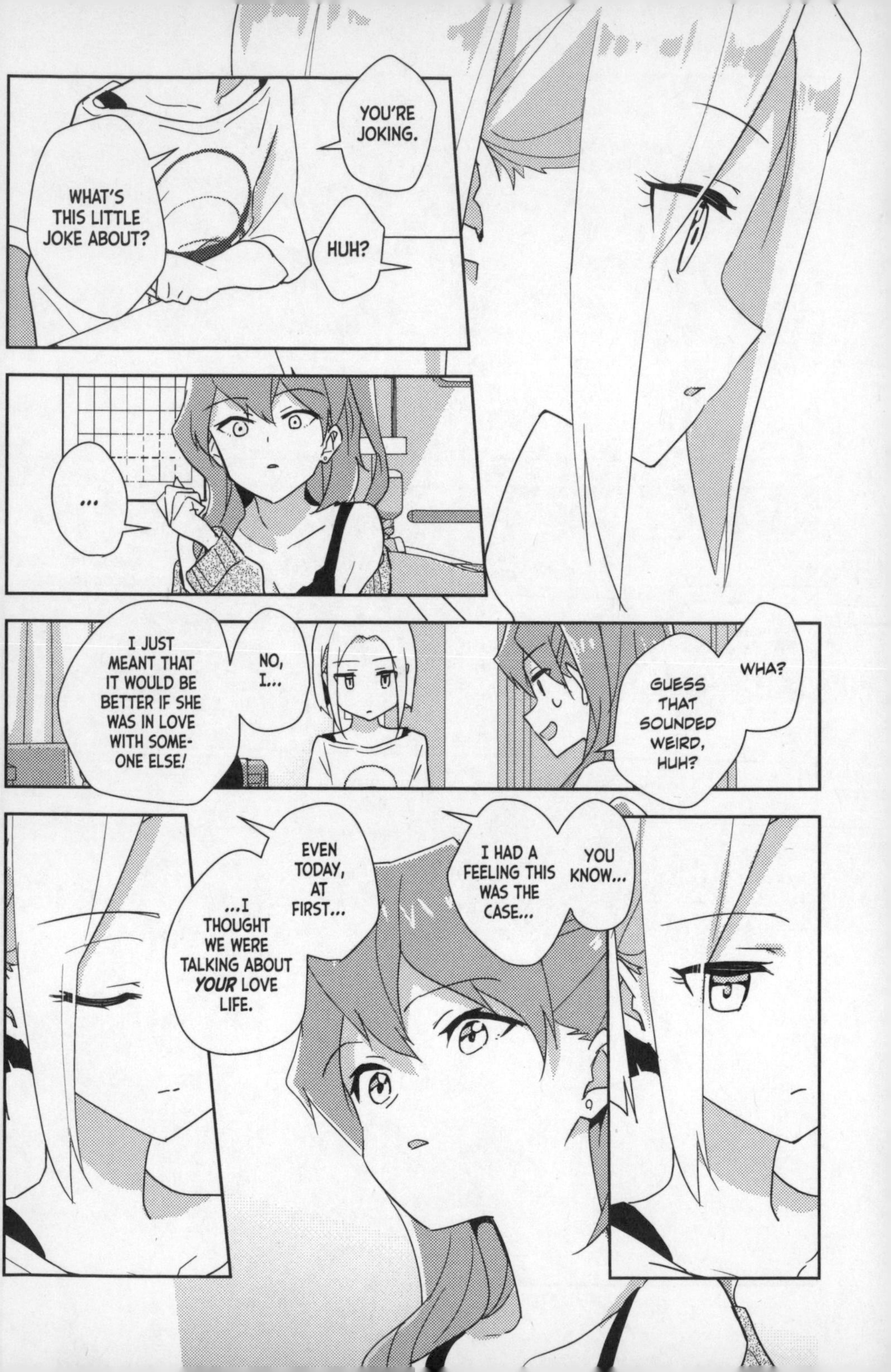
YOU'RE JOKING.
HUH?
WHAT'S THIS LITTLE JOKE ABOUT?
...
WHA?
GUESS THAT SOUNDED WEIRD, HUH?
NO, I...
I JUST MEANT THAT IT WOULD BE BETTER IF SHE WAS IN LOVE WITH SOME-ONE ELSE!
YOU KNOW...
I HAD A FEELING THIS WAS THE CASE...
EVEN TODAY, AT FIRST...
...I THOUGHT WE WERE TALKING ABOUT *YOUR* LOVE LIFE.

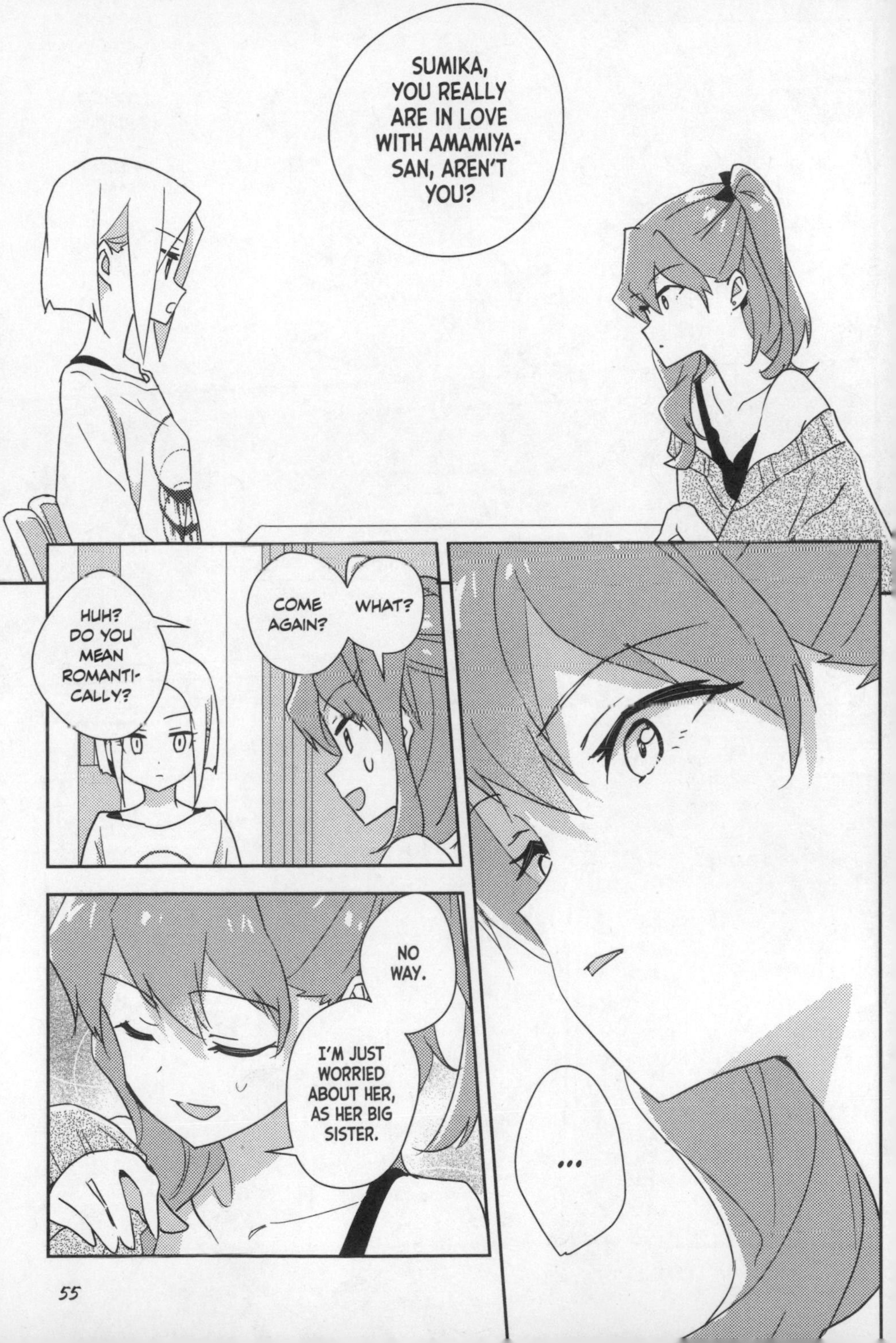
SUMIKA, YOU REALLY ARE IN LOVE WITH AMAMIYA-SAN, AREN'T YOU?
...
WHAT?
COME AGAIN?
HUH? DO YOU MEAN ROMANTI-CALLY?
NO WAY.
I'M JUST WORRIED ABOUT HER, AS HER BIG SISTER.

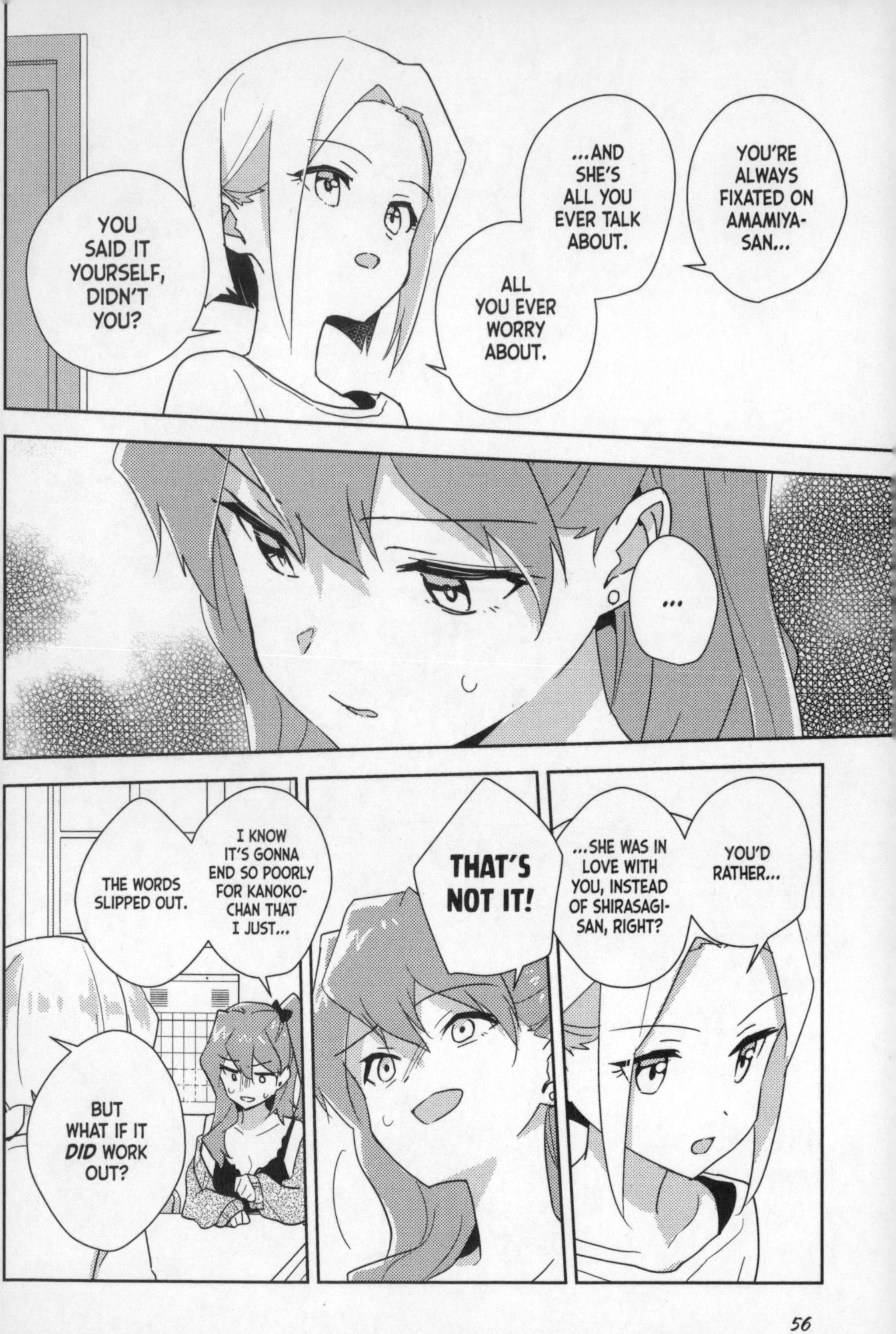
YOU'RE ALWAYS FIXATED ON AMAMIYA-SAN...
...AND SHE'S ALL YOU EVER TALK ABOUT.
ALL YOU EVER WORRY ABOUT.
YOU SAID IT YOURSELF, DIDN'T YOU?
...
YOU'D RATHER...
...SHE WAS IN LOVE WITH YOU, INSTEAD OF SHIRASAGI-SAN, RIGHT?
THAT'S NOT IT!
I KNOW IT'S GONNA END SO POORLY FOR KANOKO-CHAN THAT I JUST...
THE WORDS SLIPPED OUT.
BUT WHAT IF IT *DID* WORK OUT?

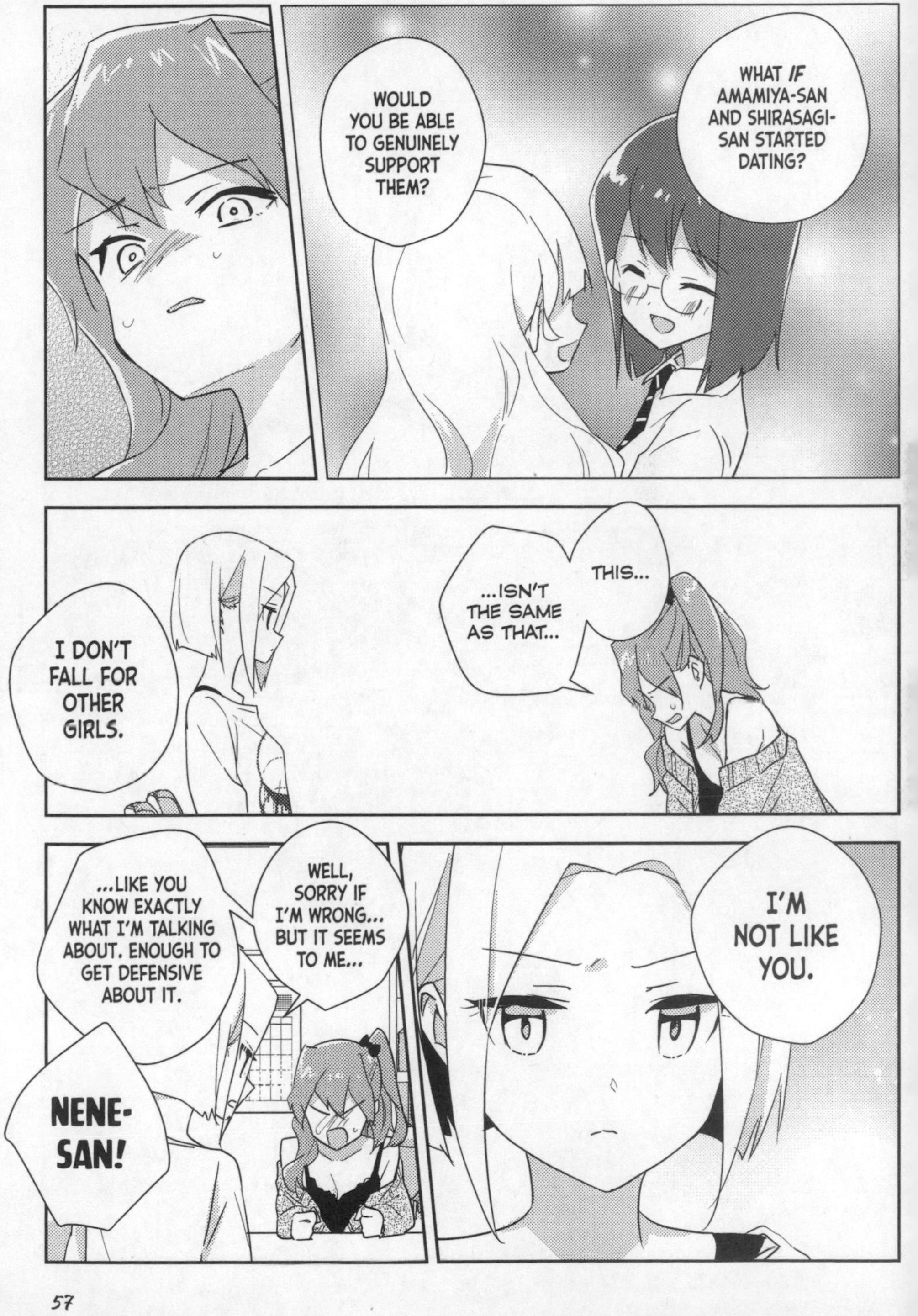
WHAT *IF* AMAMIYA-SAN AND SHIRASAGI-SAN STARTED DATING?
WOULD YOU BE ABLE TO GENUINELY SUPPORT THEM?
THIS...
...ISN'T THE SAME AS THAT...
I DON'T FALL FOR OTHER GIRLS.
I'M NOT LIKE YOU.
WELL, SORRY IF I'M WRONG... BUT IT SEEMS TO ME...
...LIKE YOU KNOW EXACTLY WHAT I'M TALKING ABOUT. ENOUGH TO GET DEFENSIVE ABOUT IT.
NENE-SAN!

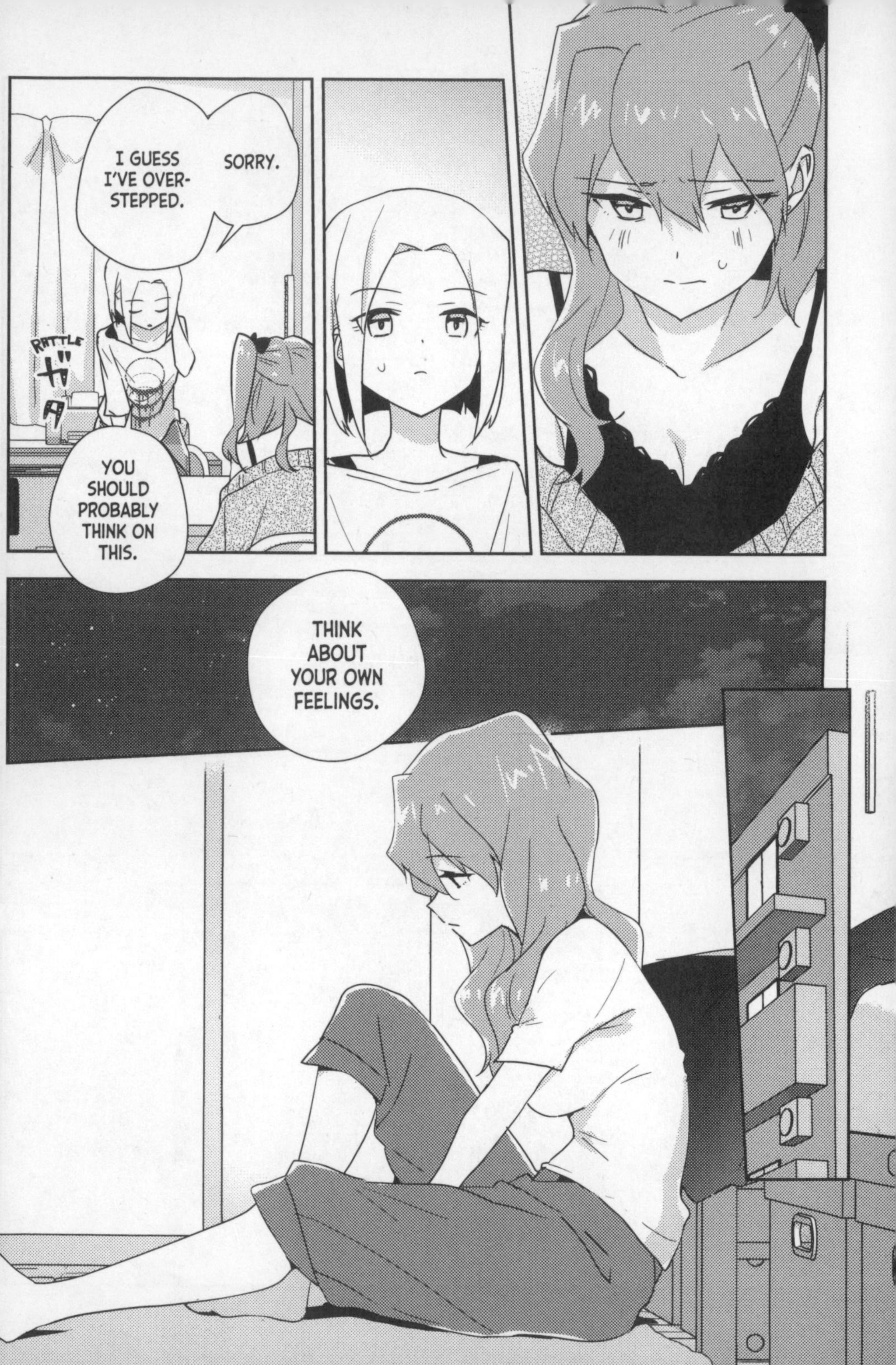
SORRY.
I GUESS I'VE OVER-STEPPED.
RATTLE
YOU SHOULD PROBABLY THINK ON THIS.
THINK ABOUT YOUR OWN FEELINGS.

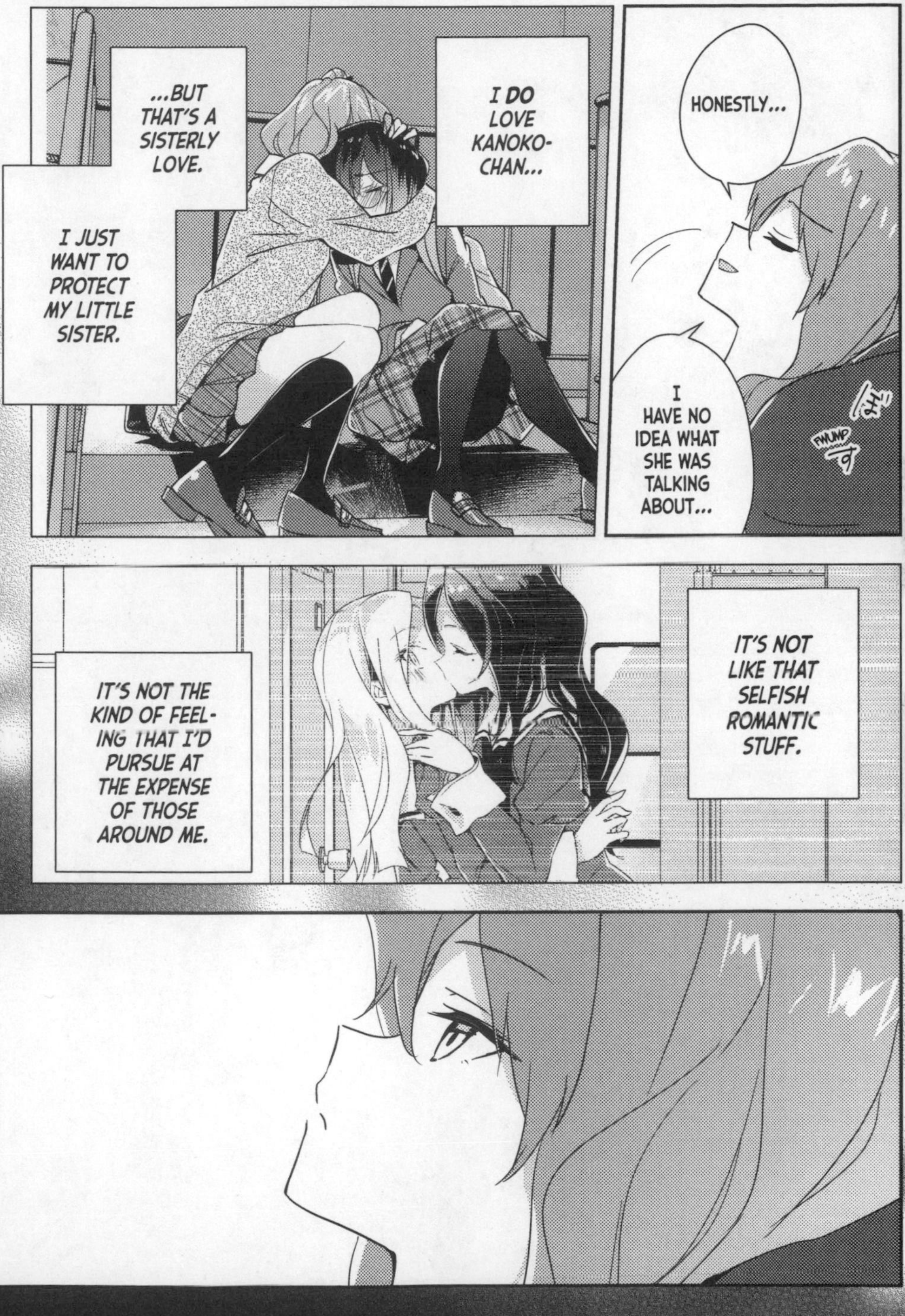
HONESTLY...
I HAVE NO IDEA WHAT SHE WAS TALKING ABOUT...
FWUMP
I DO LOVE KANOKO-CHAN...
...BUT THAT'S A SISTERLY LOVE.
I JUST WANT TO PROTECT MY LITTLE SISTER.
IT'S NOT LIKE THAT SELFISH ROMANTIC STUFF.
IT'S NOT THE KIND OF FEELING THAT I'D PURSUE AT THE EXPENSE OF THOSE AROUND ME.

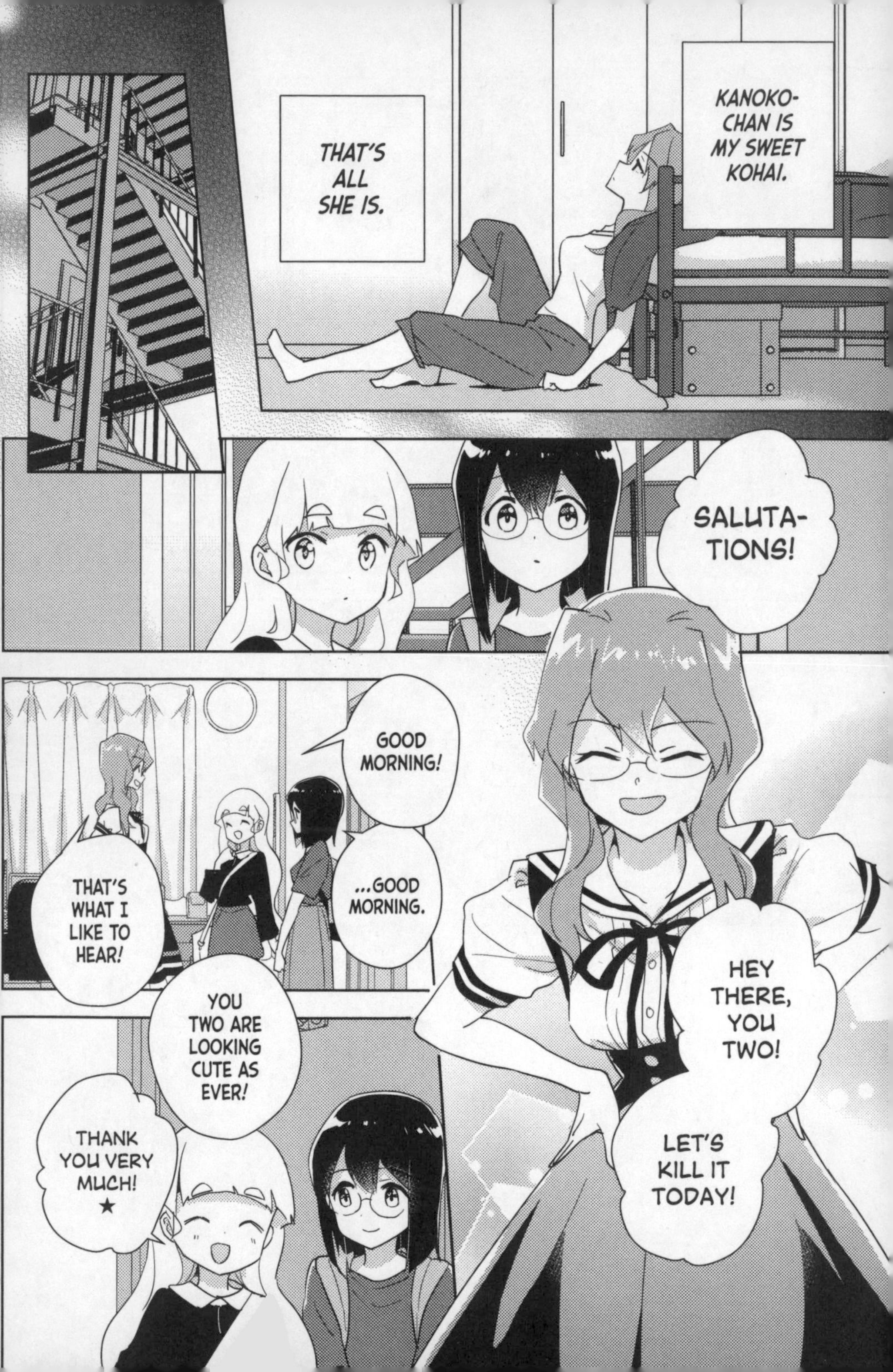
KANOKO-CHAN IS MY SWEET KOHAI.
THAT'S ALL SHE IS.
SALUTATIONS!
GOOD MORNING!
...GOOD MORNING.
THAT'S WHAT I LIKE TO HEAR!
HEY THERE, YOU TWO!
LET'S KILL IT TODAY!
YOU TWO ARE LOOKING CUTE AS EVER!
THANK YOU VERY MUCH! ★

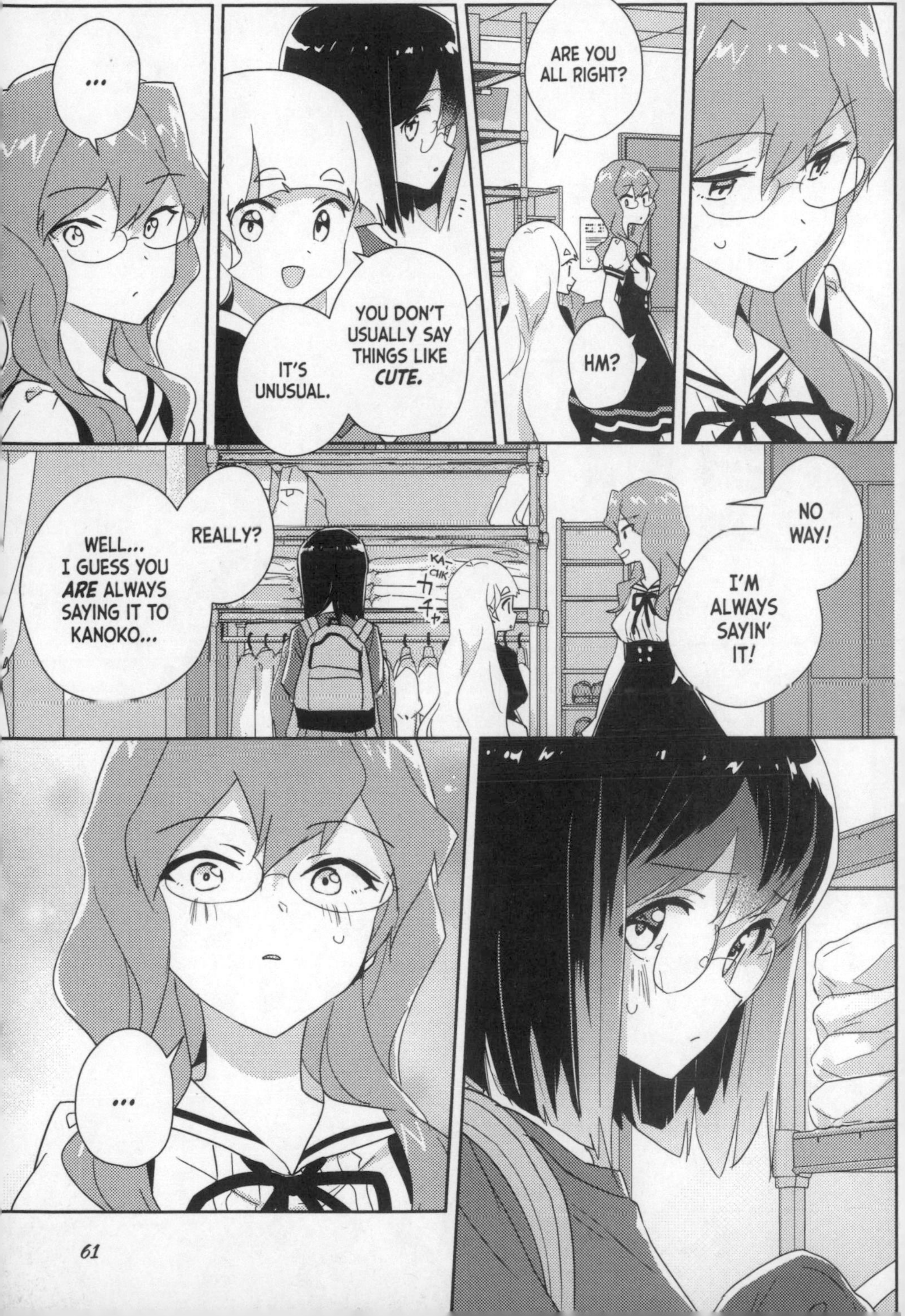

ARE YOU ALL RIGHT?
HM?
YOU DON'T USUALLY SAY THINGS LIKE *CUTE.*
IT'S UNUSUAL.
...
NO WAY!
I'M ALWAYS SAYIN' IT!
KA-CHIK
カチャ
REALLY?
WELL... I GUESS YOU *ARE* ALWAYS SAYING IT TO KANOKO...
...

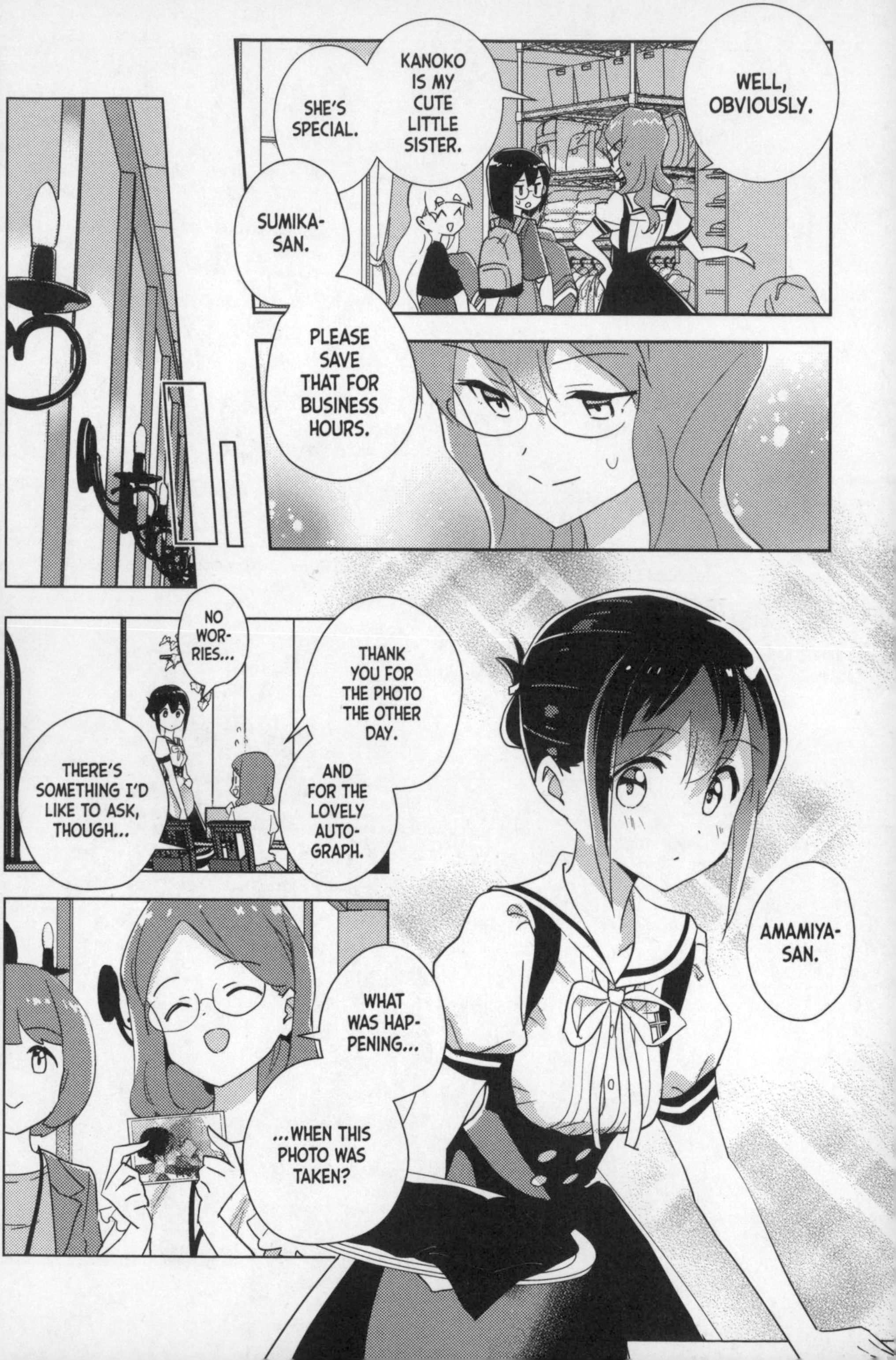
WELL, OBVIOUSLY.
KANOKO IS MY CUTE LITTLE SISTER.
SHE'S SPECIAL.
SUMIKA-SAN.
PLEASE SAVE THAT FOR BUSINESS HOURS.
AMAMIYA-SAN.
THANK YOU FOR THE PHOTO THE OTHER DAY.
AND FOR THE LOVELY AUTO-GRAPH.
NO WOR-RIES...
THERE'S SOMETHING I'D LIKE TO ASK, THOUGH...
WHAT WAS HAP-PENING...
...WHEN THIS PHOTO WAS TAKEN?

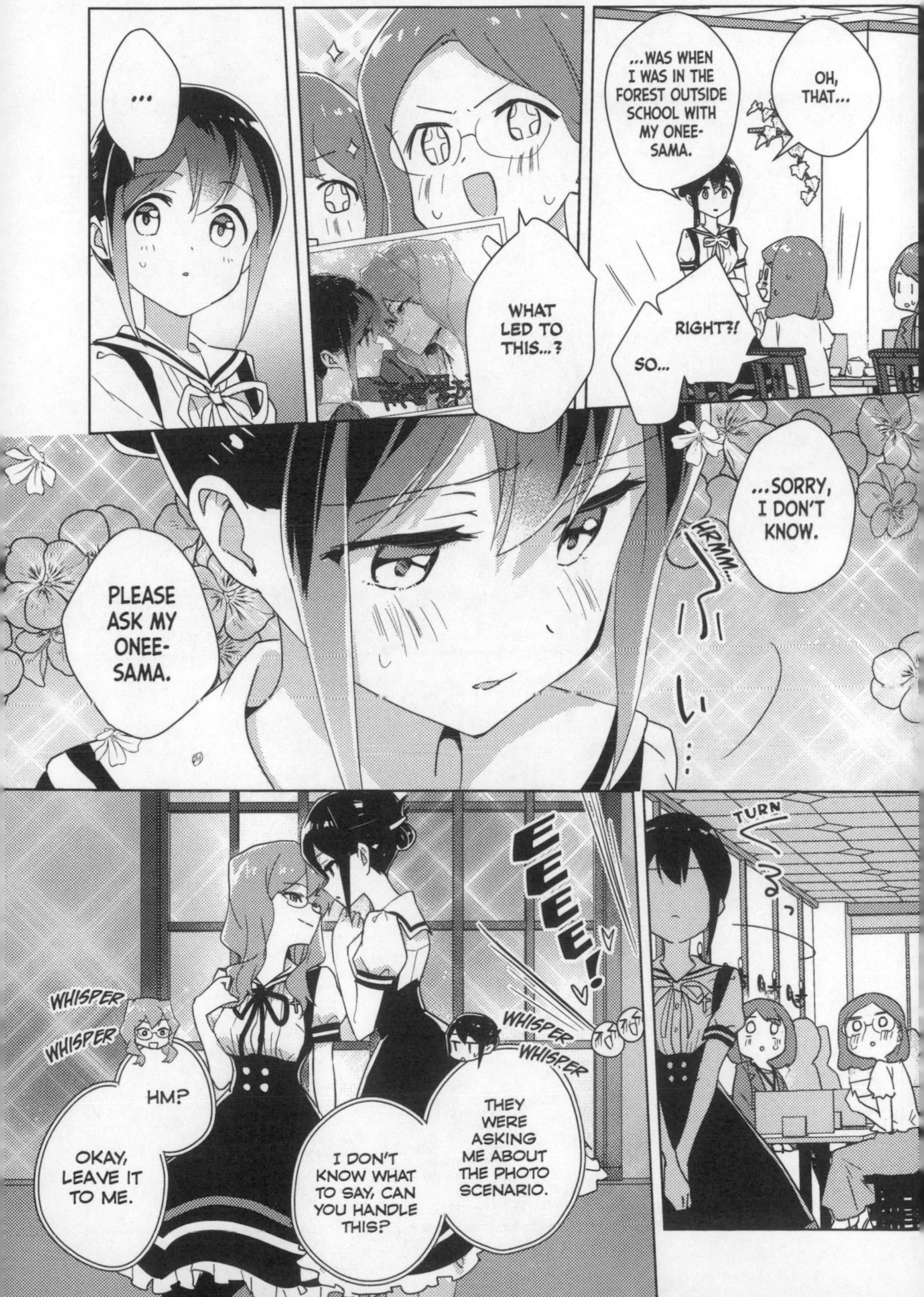
OH, THAT...
...WAS WHEN I WAS IN THE FOREST OUTSIDE SCHOOL WITH MY ONEE-SAMA.
RIGHT?!
SO...
WHAT LED TO THIS...?
...
...SORRY, I DON'T KNOW.
HRMMM...
PLEASE ASK MY ONEE-SAMA.
TURN
EEEE!
WHISPER
WHISPER
THEY WERE ASKING ME ABOUT THE PHOTO SCENARIO.
I DON'T KNOW WHAT TO SAY, CAN YOU HANDLE THIS?
WHISPER
WHISPER
HM?
OKAY, LEAVE IT TO ME.

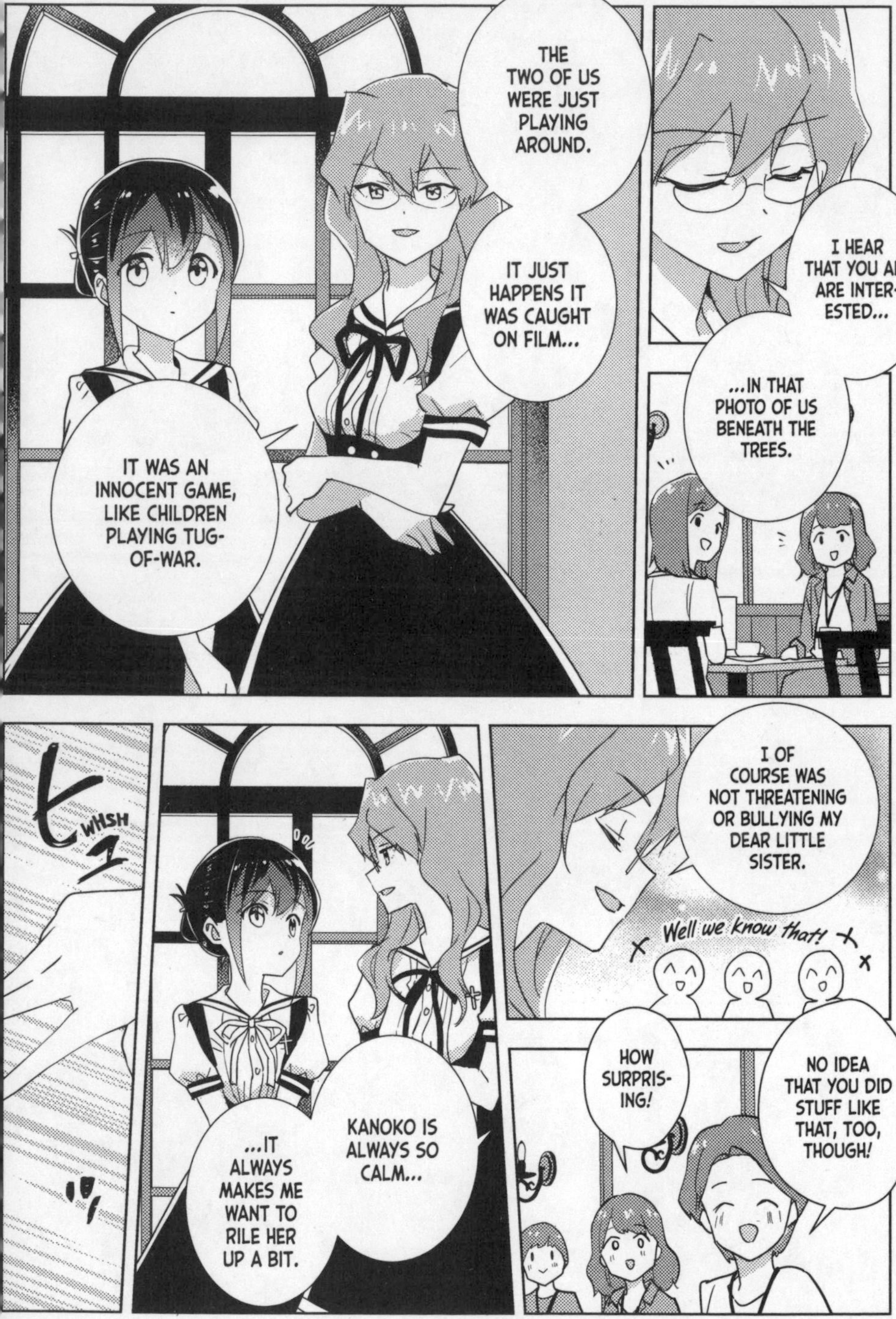
I HEAR THAT YOU ALL ARE INTER-ESTED...
...IN THAT PHOTO OF US BENEATH THE TREES.
THE TWO OF US WERE JUST PLAYING AROUND.
IT JUST HAPPENS IT WAS CAUGHT ON FILM...
IT WAS AN INNOCENT GAME, LIKE CHILDREN PLAYING TUG-OF-WAR.
I OF COURSE WAS NOT THREATENING OR BULLYING MY DEAR LITTLE SISTER.
Well we know that!
NO IDEA THAT YOU DID STUFF LIKE THAT, TOO, THOUGH!
HOW SURPRIS-ING!
KANOKO IS ALWAYS SO CALM...
...IT ALWAYS MAKES ME WANT TO RILE HER UP A BIT.
WHSH

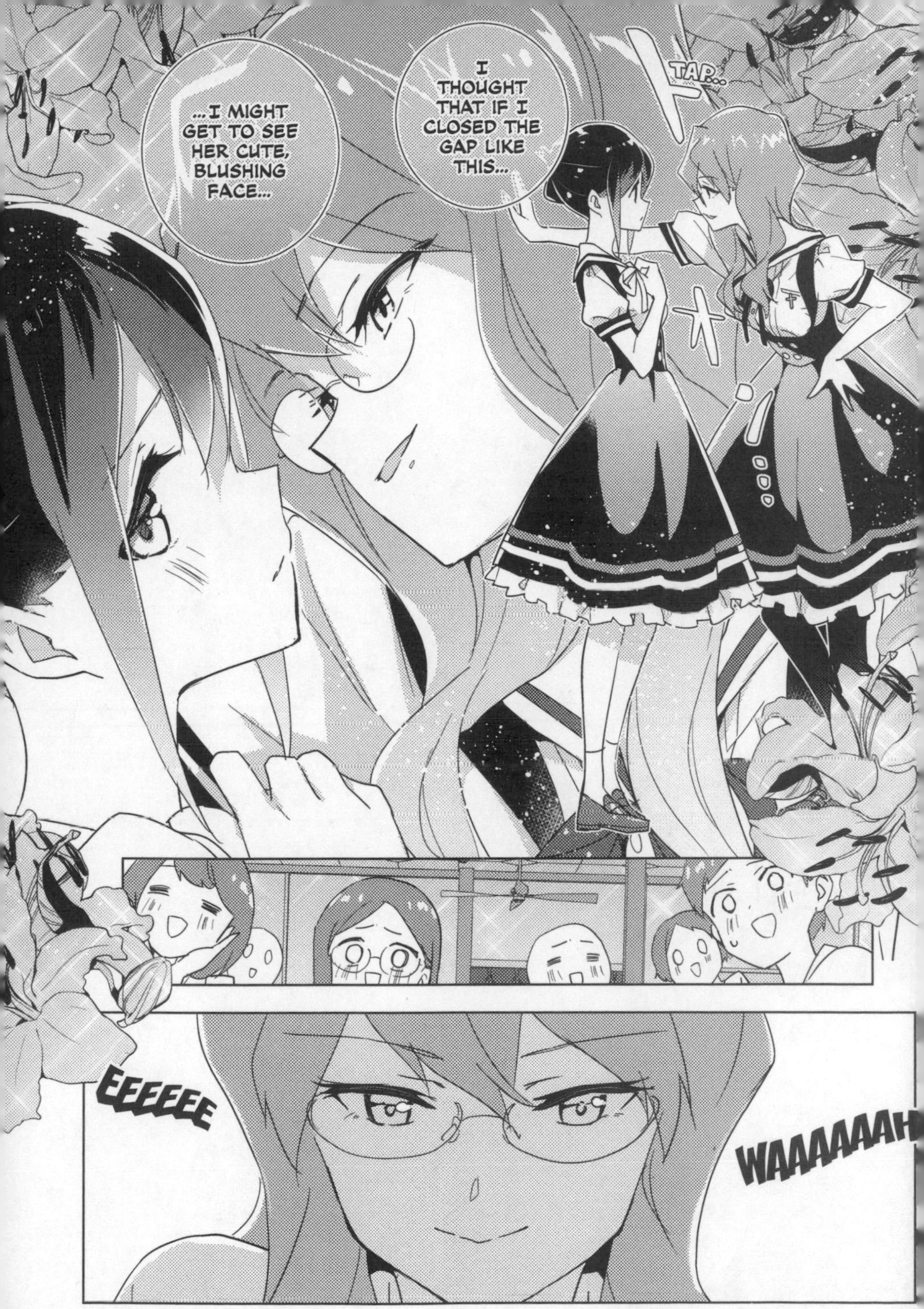
TAP...
I THOUGHT THAT IF I CLOSED THE GAP LIKE THIS...
...I MIGHT GET TO SEE HER CUTE, BLUSHING FACE...
EEEEEE
WAAAAAAH

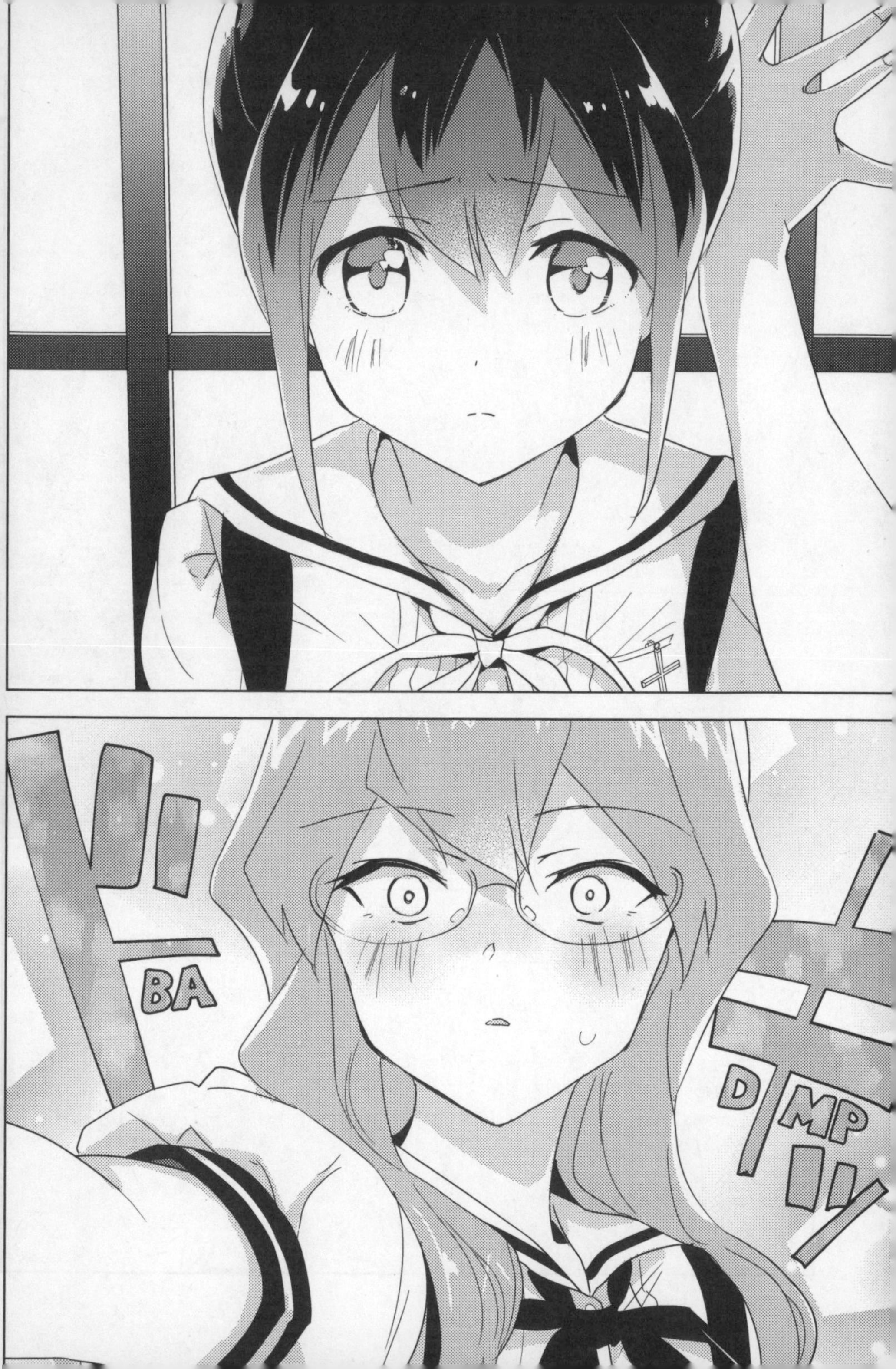
D MP
BA

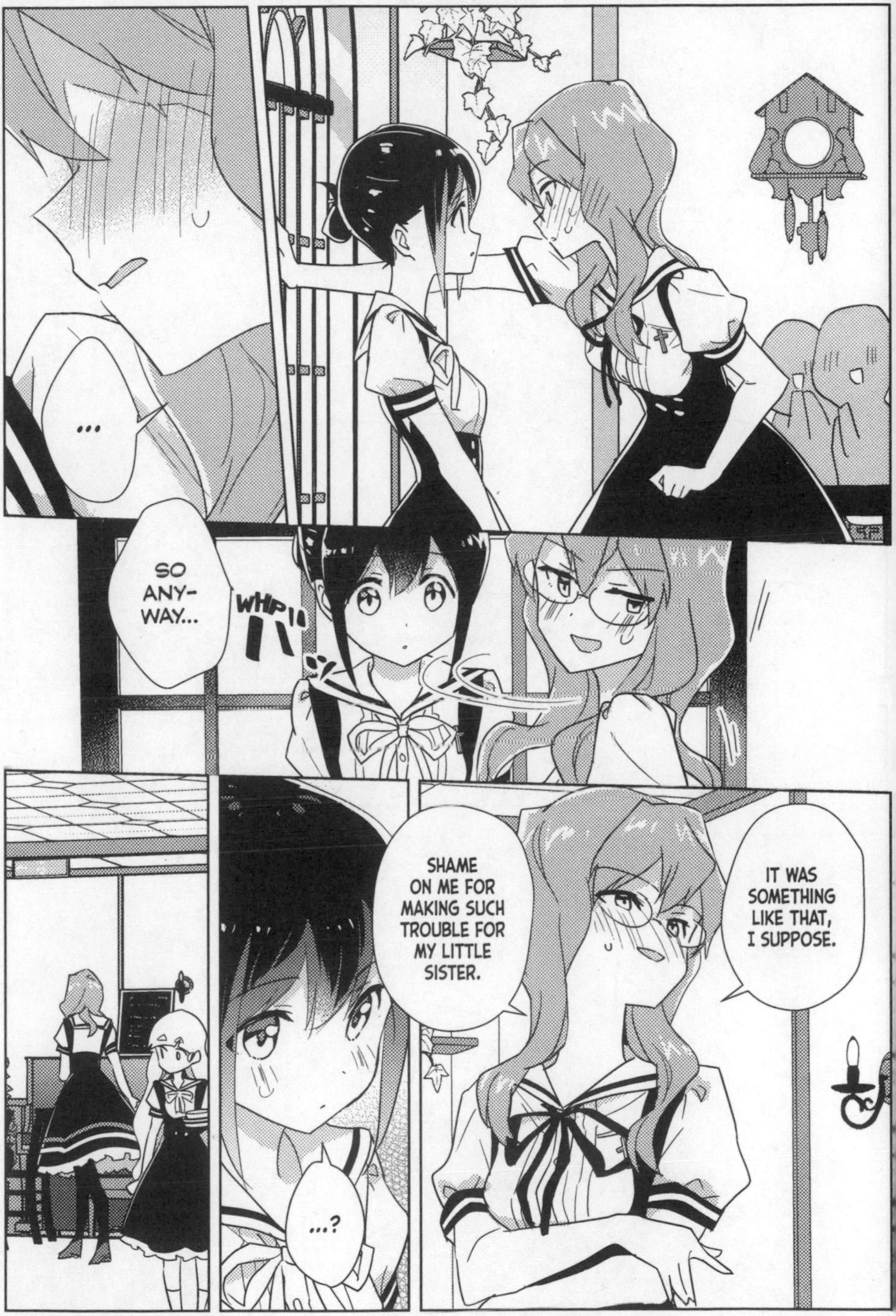
...
SO ANYWAY...
WHP
IT WAS SOMETHING LIKE THAT, I SUPPOSE.
SHAME ON ME FOR MAKING SUCH TROUBLE FOR MY LITTLE SISTER.
...?

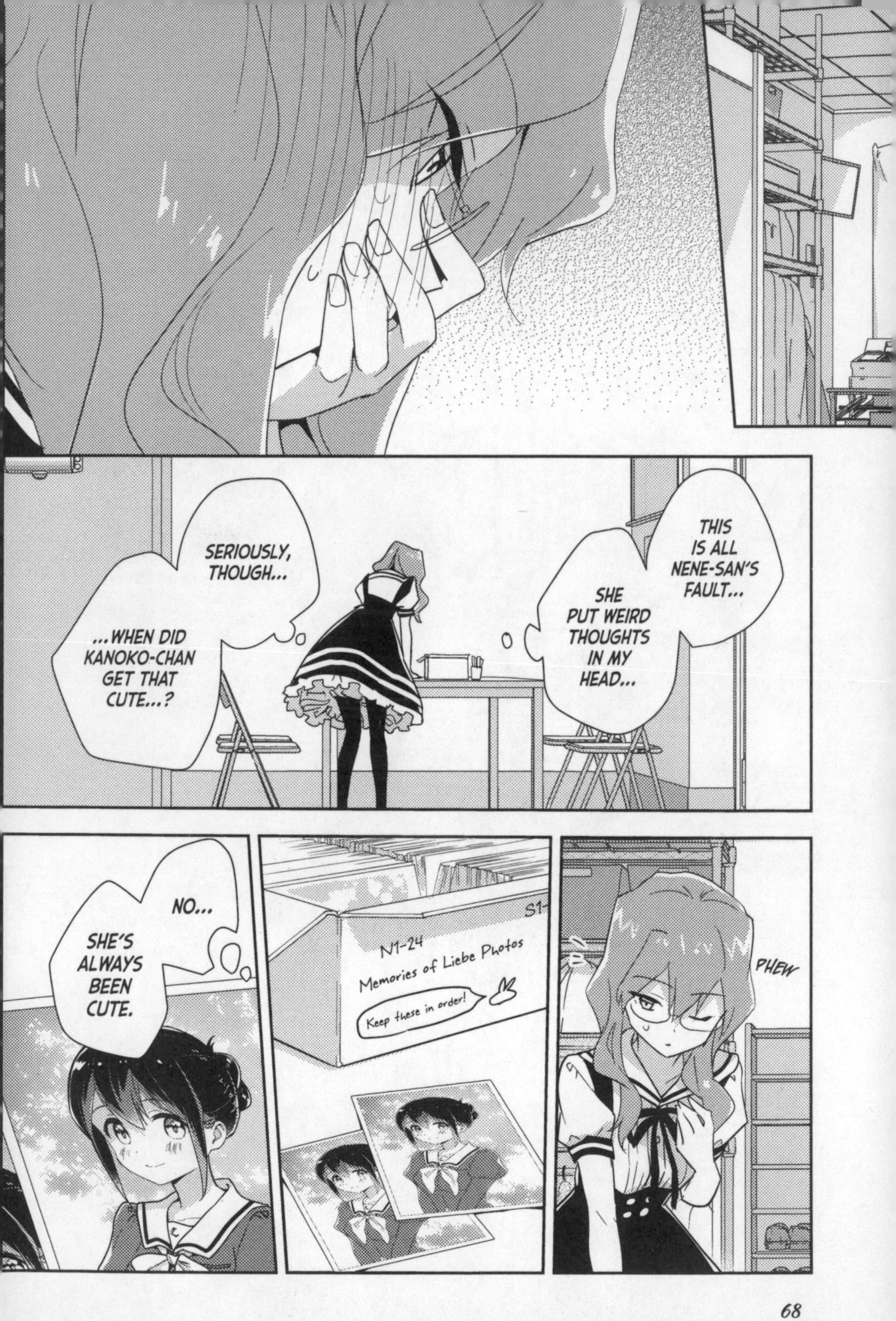
THIS IS ALL NENE-SAN'S FAULT...
SHE PUT WEIRD THOUGHTS IN MY HEAD...
SERIOUSLY, THOUGH...
...WHEN DID KANOKO-CHAN GET THAT CUTE...?
PHEW
N1-24
Memories of Liebe Photos
Keep these in order!
NO...
SHE'S ALWAYS BEEN CUTE.

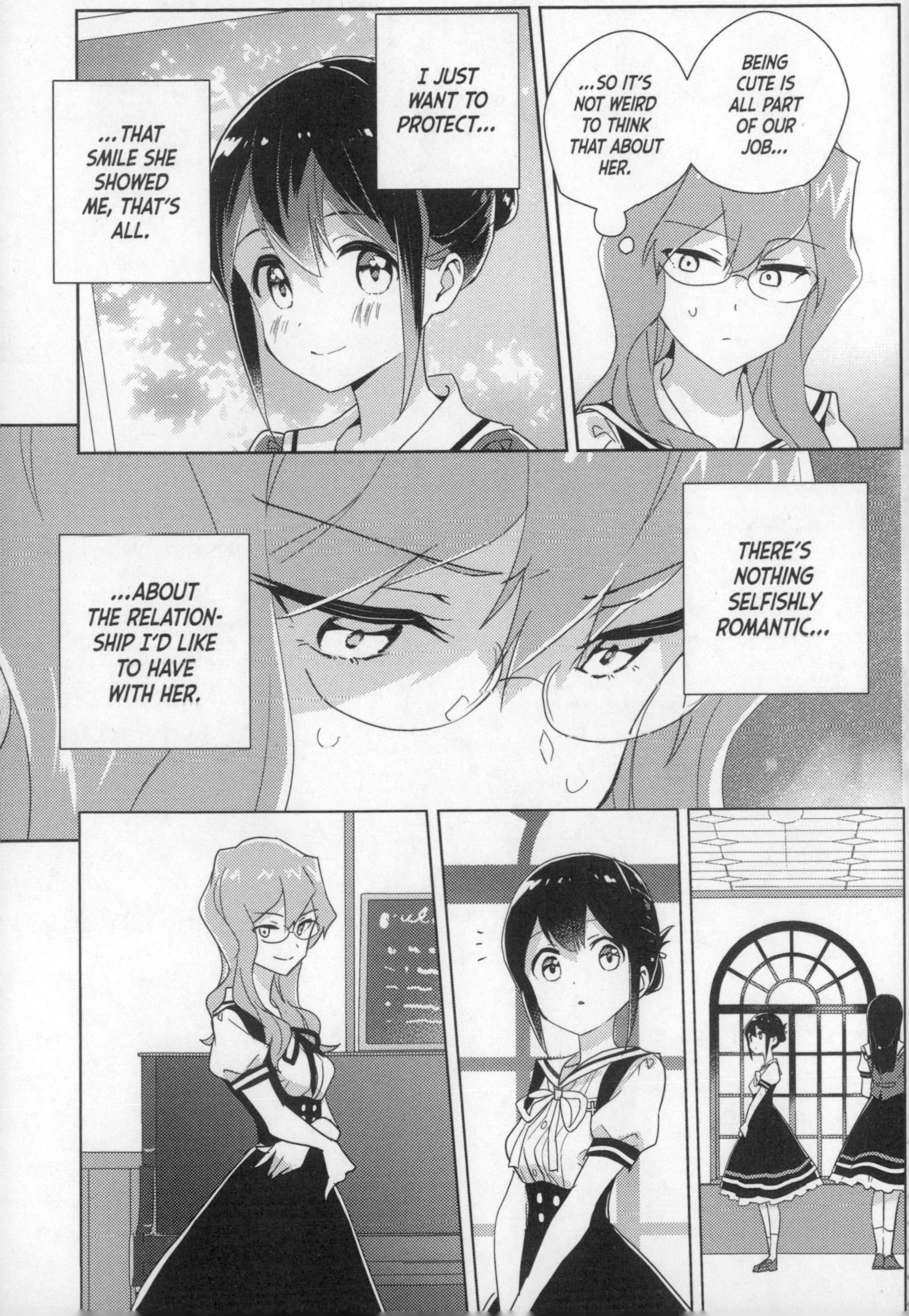
BEING CUTE IS ALL PART OF OUR JOB...
...SO IT'S NOT WEIRD TO THINK THAT ABOUT HER.
I JUST WANT TO PROTECT...
...THAT SMILE SHE SHOWED ME, THAT'S ALL.
THERE'S NOTHING SELFISHLY ROMANTIC...
...ABOUT THE RELATIONSHIP I'D LIKE TO HAVE WITH HER.

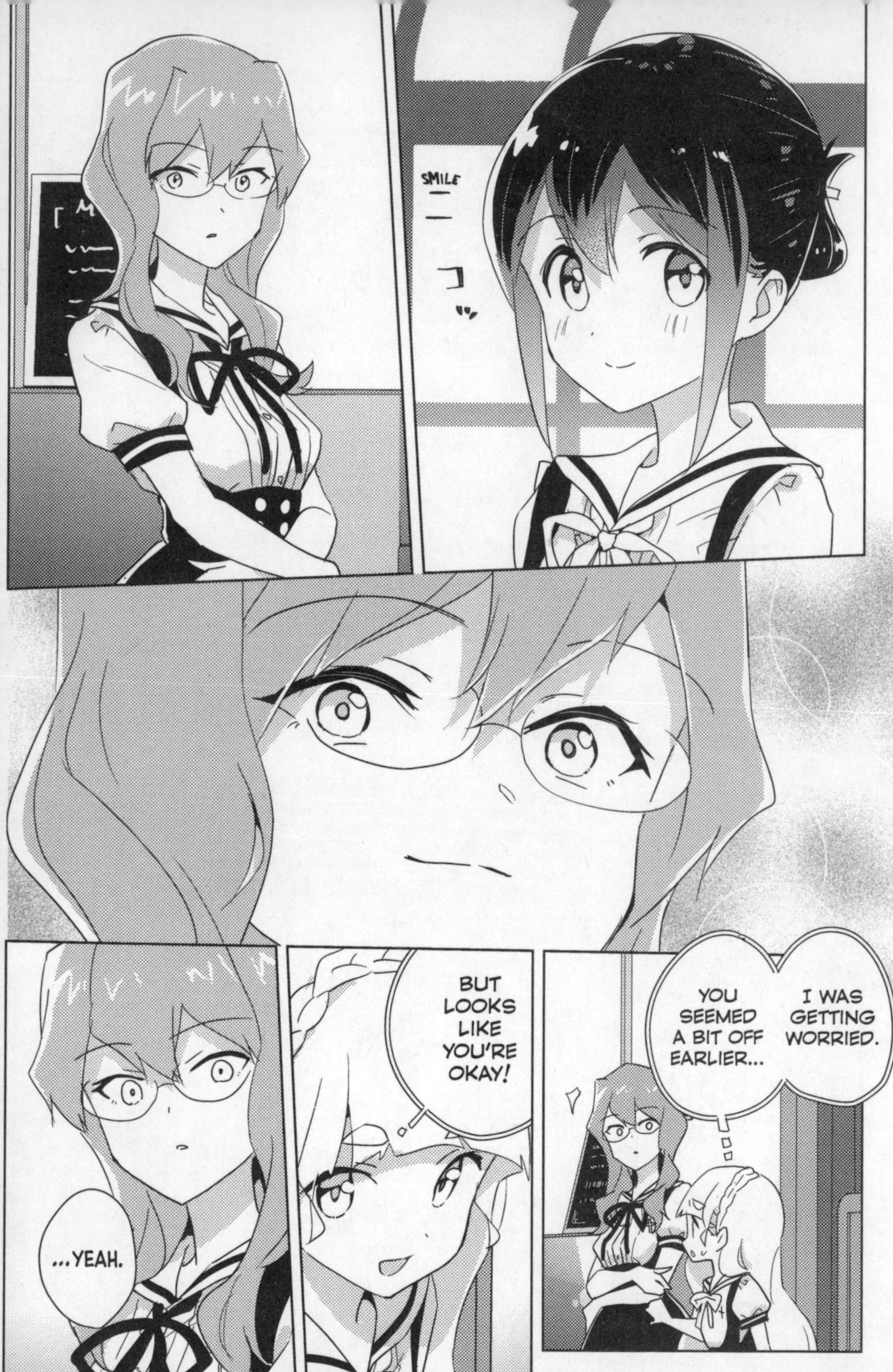
SMILE
YOU SEEMED A BIT OFF EARLIER...
I WAS GETTING WORRIED.
BUT LOOKS LIKE YOU'RE OKAY!
...YEAH.

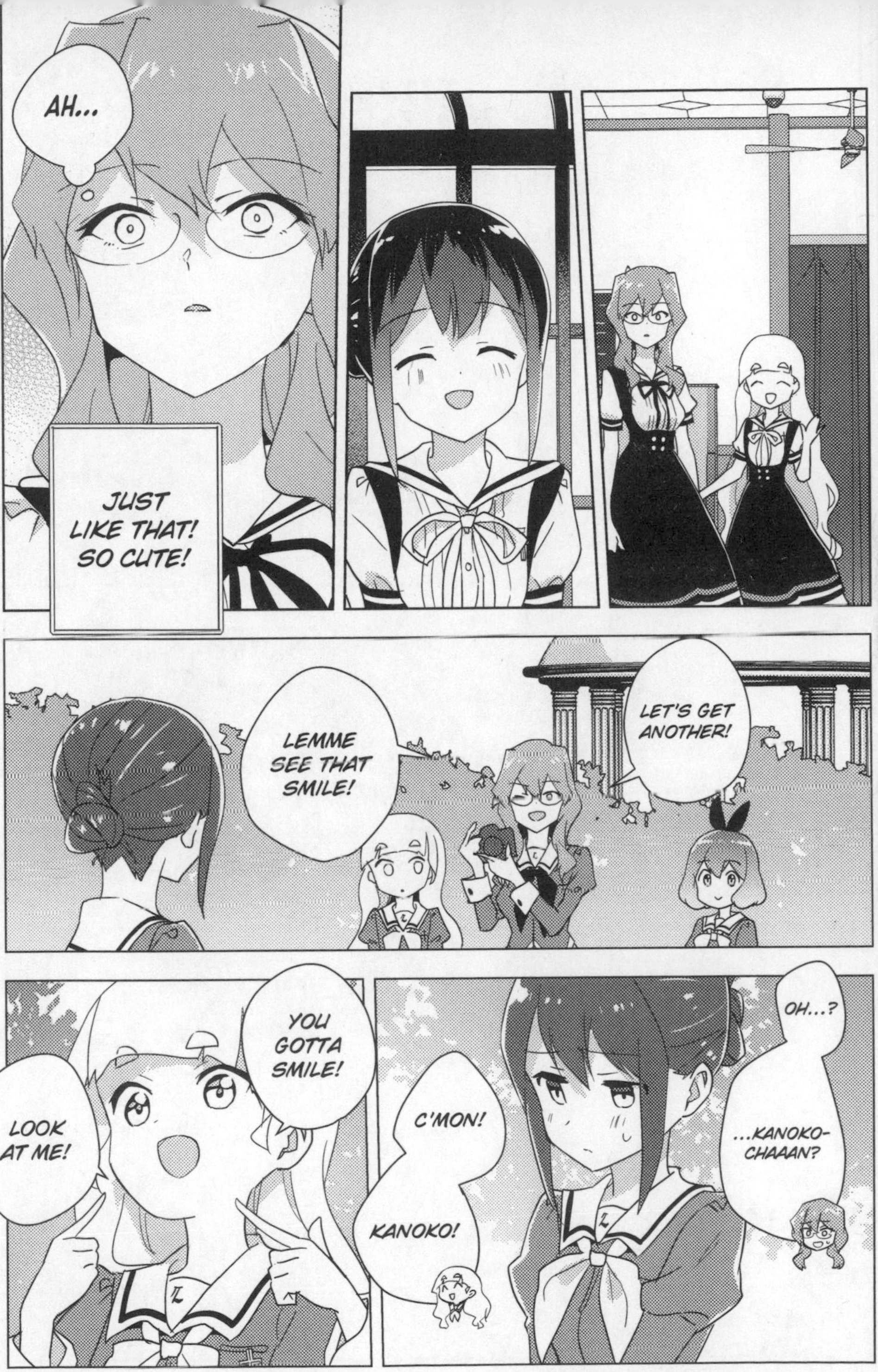
AH...
JUST LIKE THAT! SO CUTE!
LET'S GET ANOTHER!
LEMME SEE THAT SMILE!
OH...?
...KANOKO-CHAAAN?
C'MON!
KANOKO!
YOU GOTTA SMILE!
LOOK AT ME!

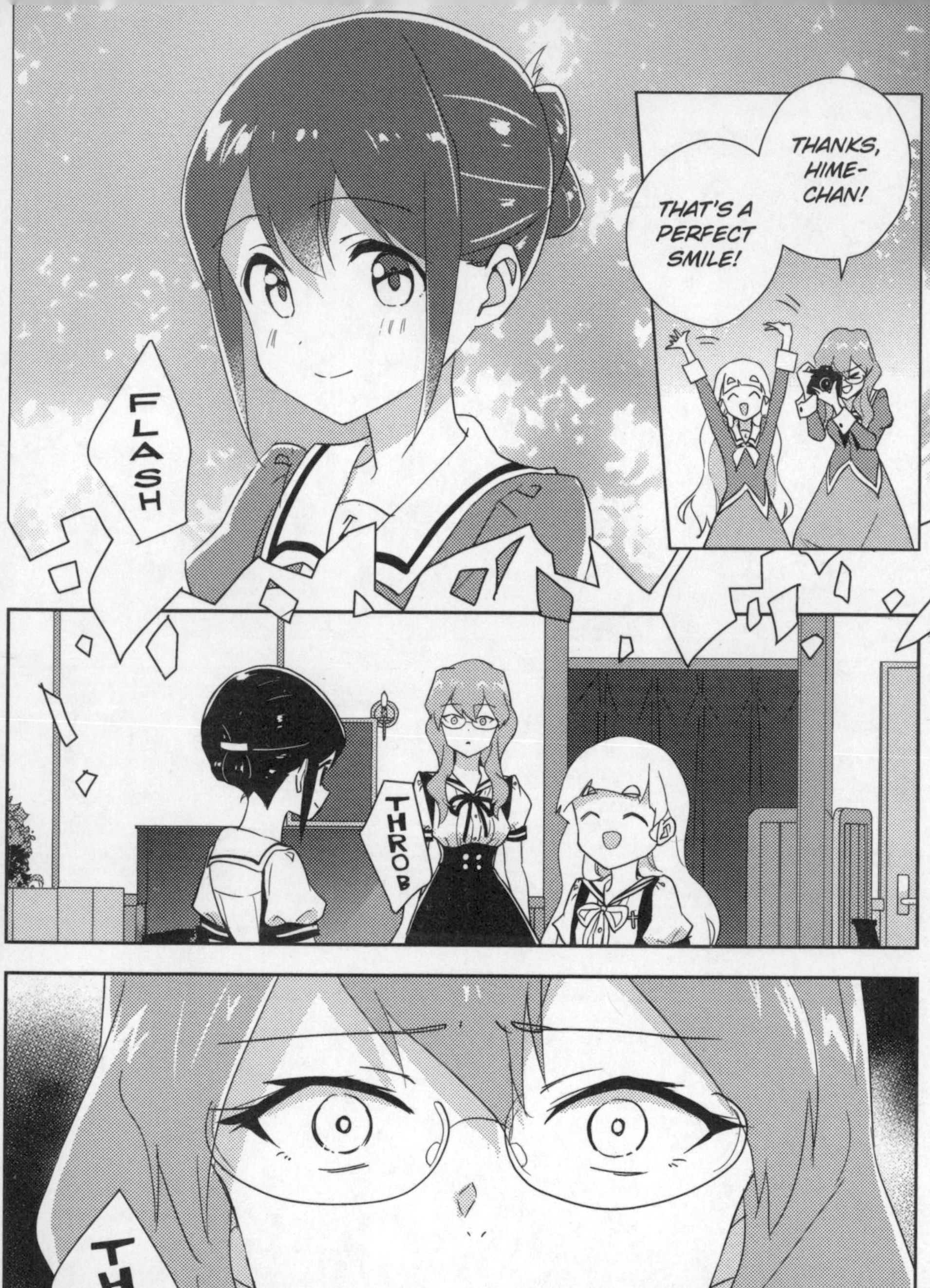
THANKS, HIME-CHAN!
THAT'S A PERFECT SMILE!
FLASH
THROB
THROB

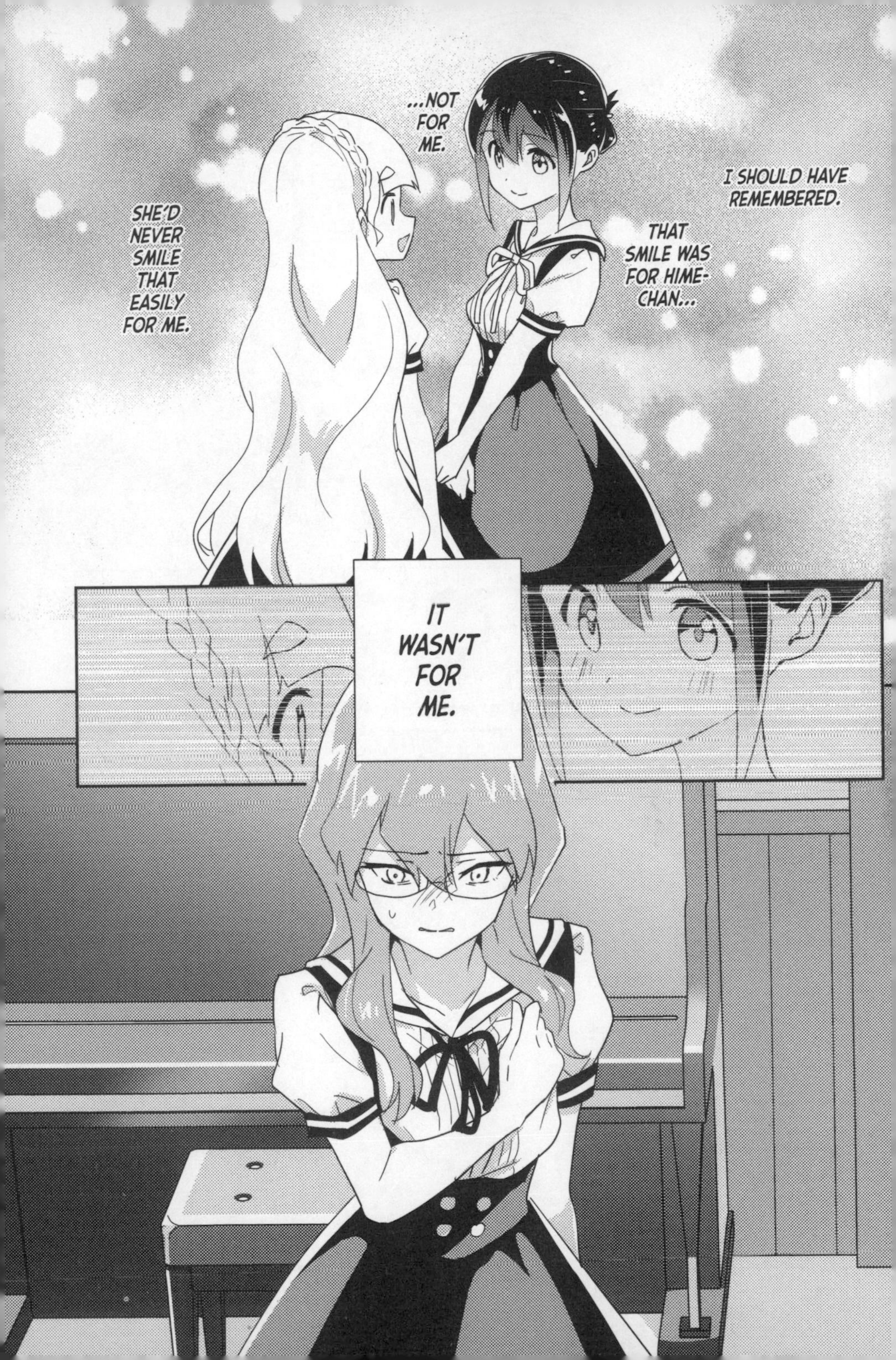
I SHOULD HAVE REMEMBERED.
THAT SMILE WAS FOR HIME-CHAN...
...NOT FOR ME.
SHE'D NEVER SMILE THAT EASILY FOR ME.
IT WASN'T FOR ME.

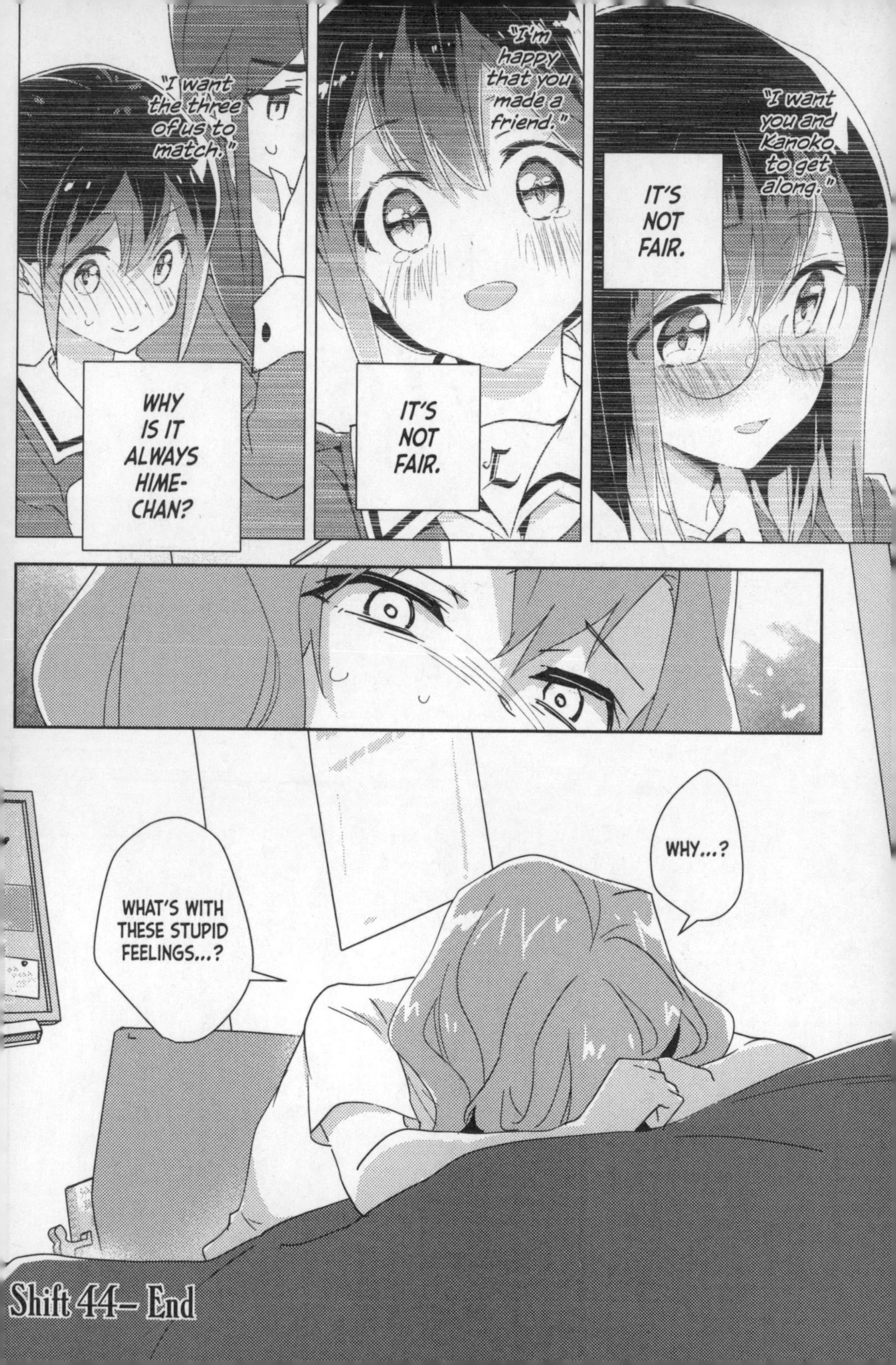
"I want you and Kanoko to get along."
IT'S NOT FAIR.
"I'm happy that you made a friend."
IT'S NOT FAIR.
"I want the three of us to match."
WHY IS IT ALWAYS HIME-CHAN?
WHY...?
WHAT'S WITH THESE STUPID FEELINGS...?
Shift 44– End

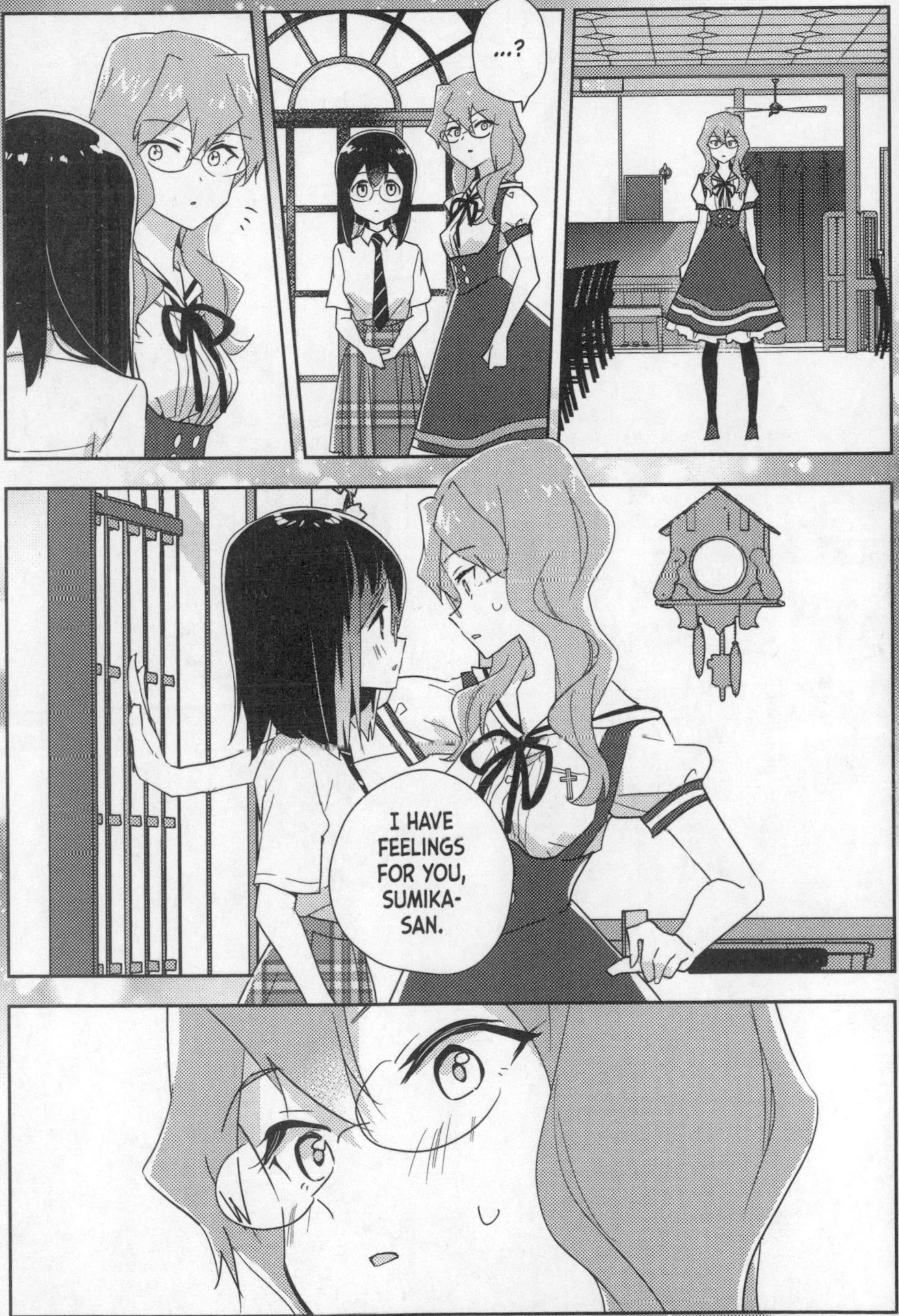
...?
I HAVE FEELINGS FOR YOU, SUMIKA-SAN.

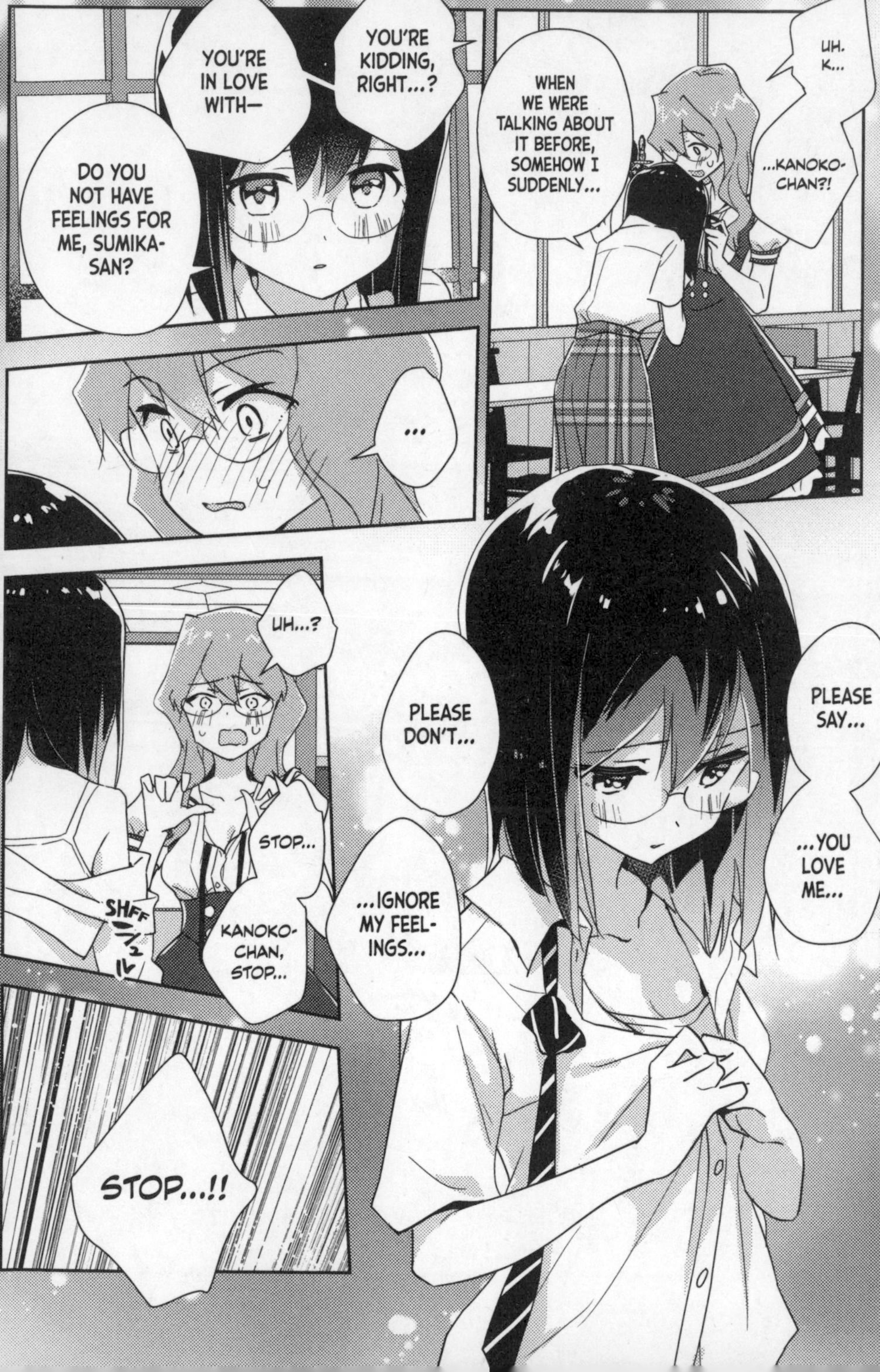
UH. K...
WHEN WE WERE TALKING ABOUT IT BEFORE, SOMEHOW I SUDDENLY...
...KANOKO-CHAN?!
YOU'RE KIDDING, RIGHT...?
YOU'RE IN LOVE WITH—
DO YOU NOT HAVE FEELINGS FOR ME, SUMIKA-SAN?
...
PLEASE SAY...
...YOU LOVE ME...
PLEASE DON'T...
...IGNORE MY FEEL-INGS...
UH...?
STOP...
KANOKO-CHAN, STOP...
SHFF
STOP...!!

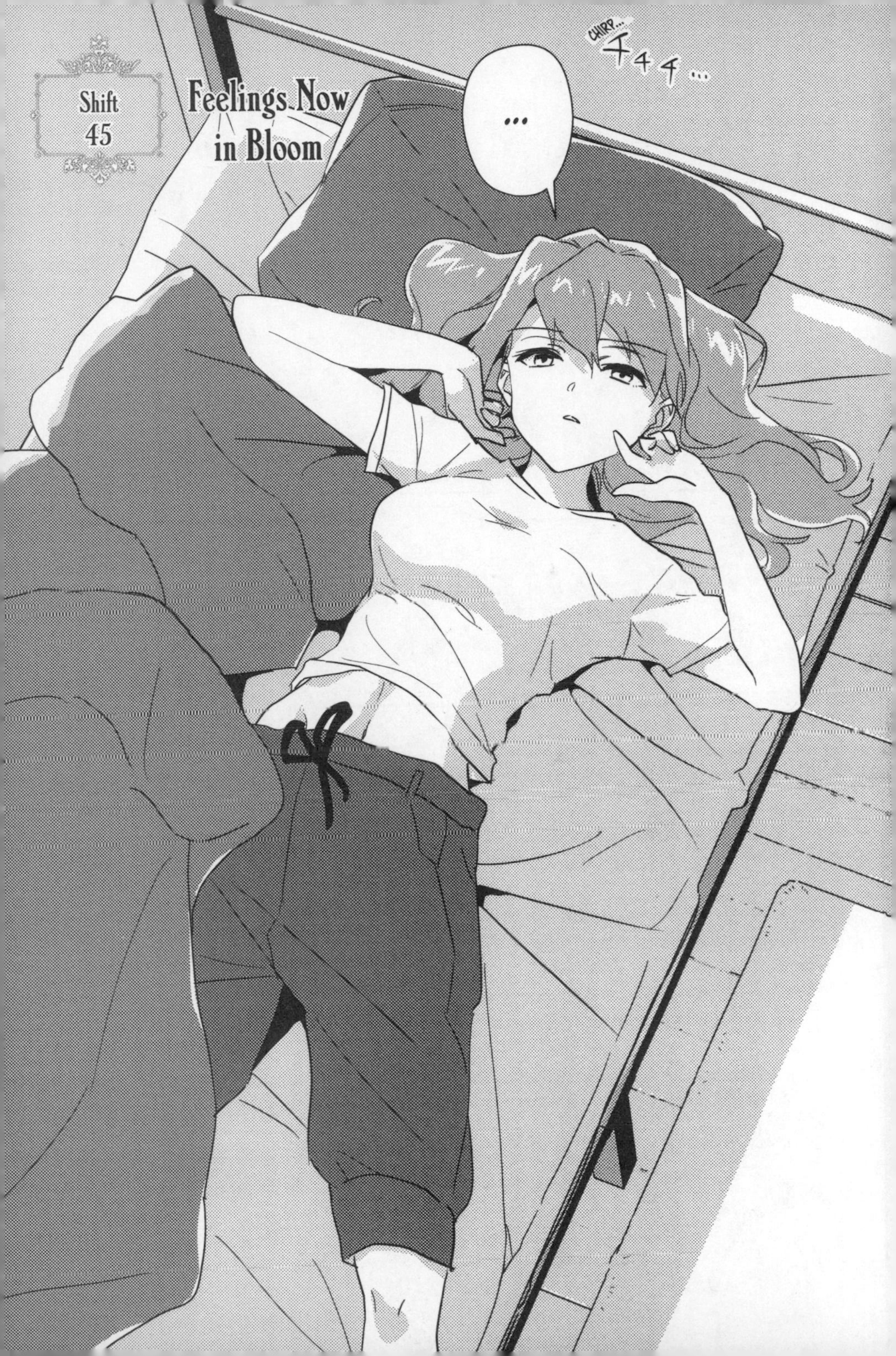
Shift 45
Feelings Now in Bloom
CHIRP... チィィ...
...

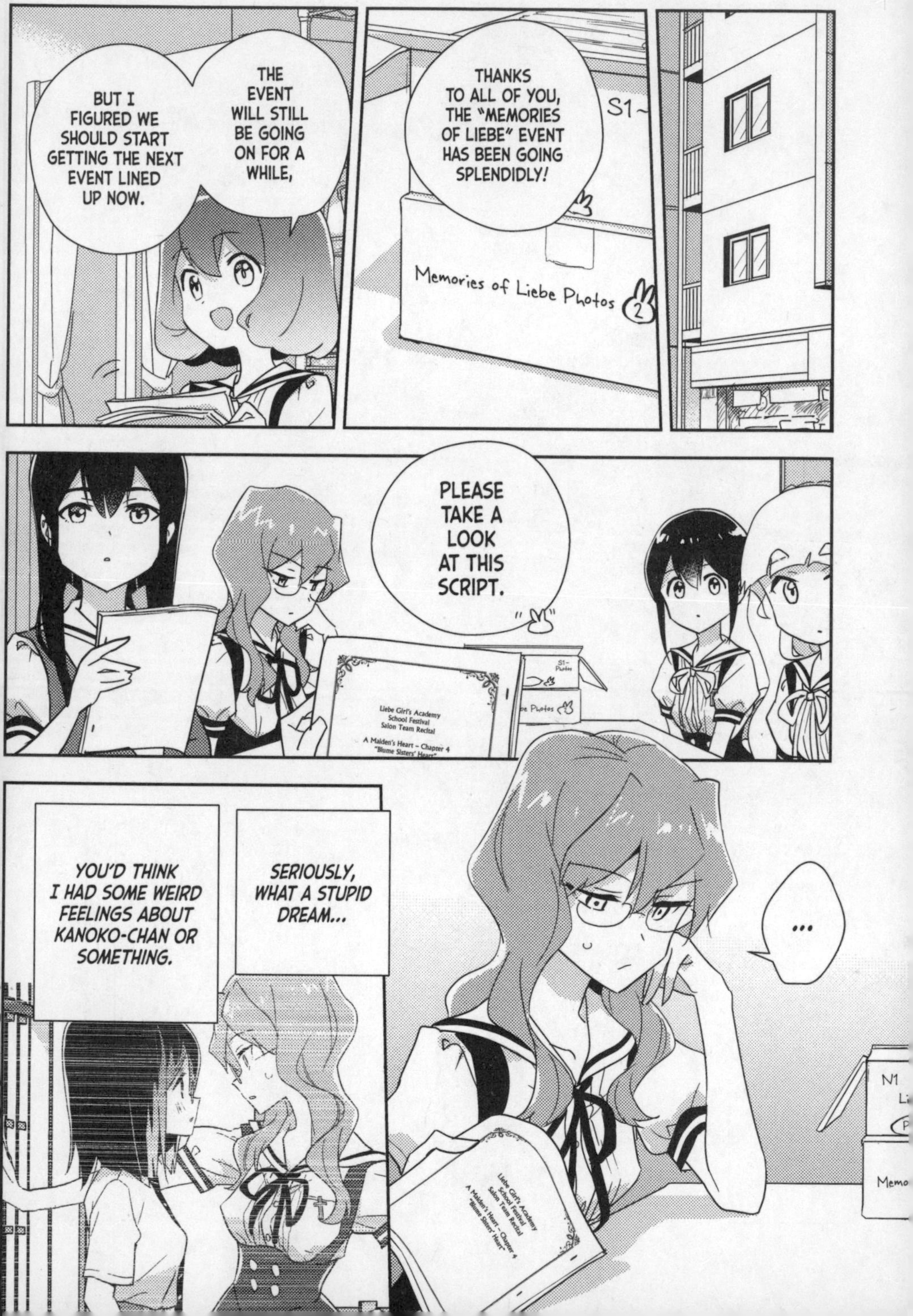
THANKS TO ALL OF YOU, THE "MEMORIES OF LIEBE" EVENT HAS BEEN GOING SPLENDIDLY!
S1~
Memories of Liebe Photos 2
THE EVENT WILL STILL BE GOING ON FOR A WHILE,
BUT I FIGURED WE SHOULD START GETTING THE NEXT EVENT LINED UP NOW.
PLEASE TAKE A LOOK AT THIS SCRIPT.
Liebe Girl's Academy School Festival Salon Team Recital
A Maiden's Heart – Chapter 4 "Blume Sisters' Heart"
...
SERIOUSLY, WHAT A STUPID DREAM...
YOU'D THINK I HAD SOME WEIRD FEELINGS ABOUT KANOKO-CHAN OR SOMETHING.

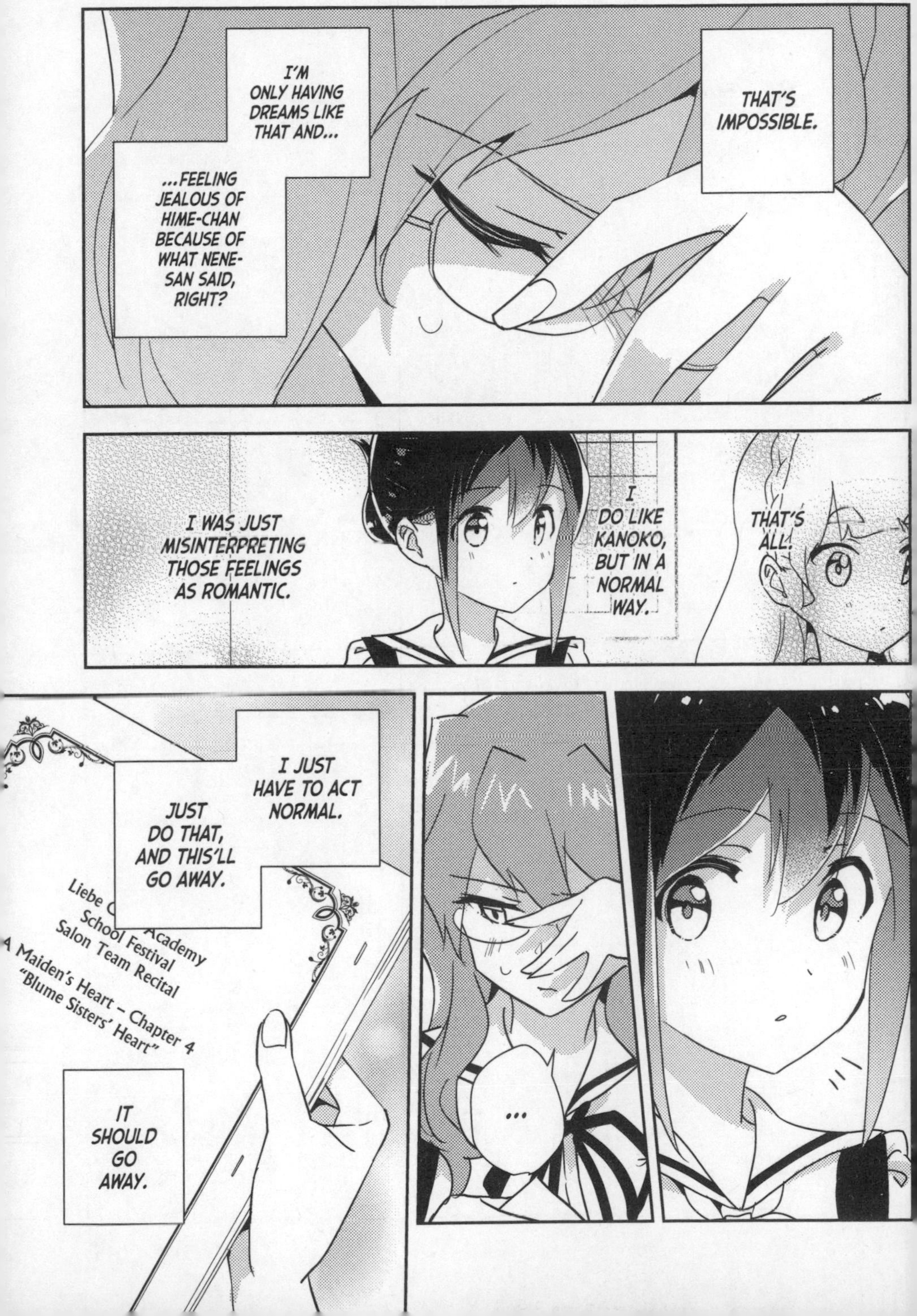

THAT'S IMPOSSIBLE.
I'M ONLY HAVING DREAMS LIKE THAT AND...
...FEELING JEALOUS OF HIME-CHAN BECAUSE OF WHAT NENE-SAN SAID, RIGHT?
THAT'S ALL!
I DO LIKE KANOKO, BUT IN A NORMAL WAY.
I WAS JUST MISINTERPRETING THOSE FEELINGS AS ROMANTIC.
...
I JUST HAVE TO ACT NORMAL.
JUST DO THAT, AND THIS'LL GO AWAY.
Liebe Academy
School Festival
Salon Team Recital
A Maiden's Heart – Chapter 4
"Blume Sisters' Heart"
IT SHOULD GO AWAY.

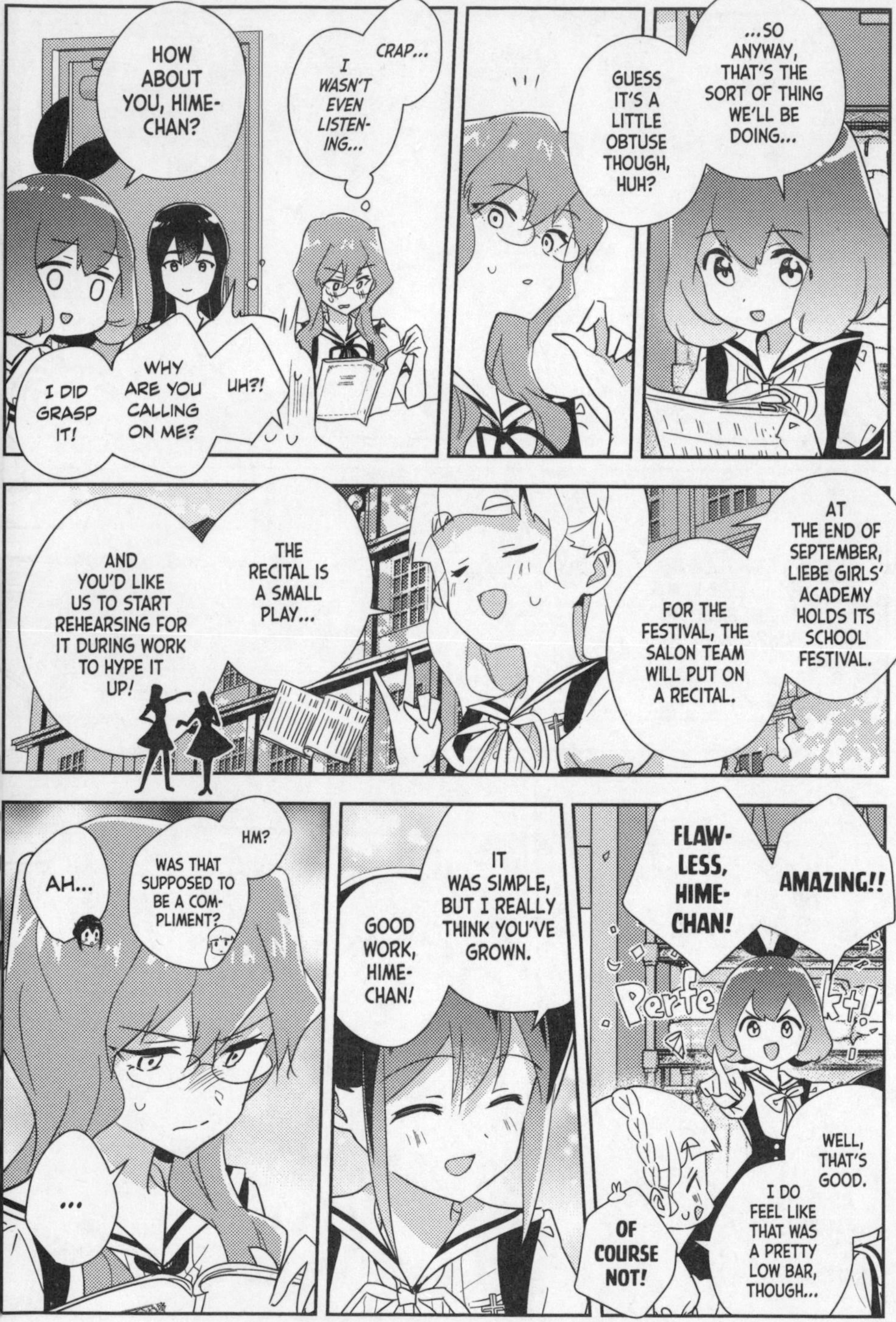
...SO ANYWAY, THAT'S THE SORT OF THING WE'LL BE DOING...
GUESS IT'S A LITTLE OBTUSE THOUGH, HUH?
HOW ABOUT YOU, HIME-CHAN?
CRAP... I WASN'T EVEN LISTENING...
UH?!
WHY ARE YOU CALLING ON ME?
I DID GRASP IT!
AT THE END OF SEPTEMBER, LIEBE GIRLS' ACADEMY HOLDS ITS SCHOOL FESTIVAL.
FOR THE FESTIVAL, THE SALON TEAM WILL PUT ON A RECITAL.
THE RECITAL IS A SMALL PLAY...
AND YOU'D LIKE US TO START REHEARSING FOR IT DURING WORK TO HYPE IT UP!
AMAZING!!
FLAWLESS, HIME-CHAN!
WELL, THAT'S GOOD.
I DO FEEL LIKE THAT WAS A PRETTY LOW BAR, THOUGH...
OF COURSE NOT!
IT WAS SIMPLE, BUT I REALLY THINK YOU'VE GROWN.
GOOD WORK, HIME-CHAN!
HM?
WAS THAT SUPPOSED TO BE A COMPLIMENT?
AH...
...

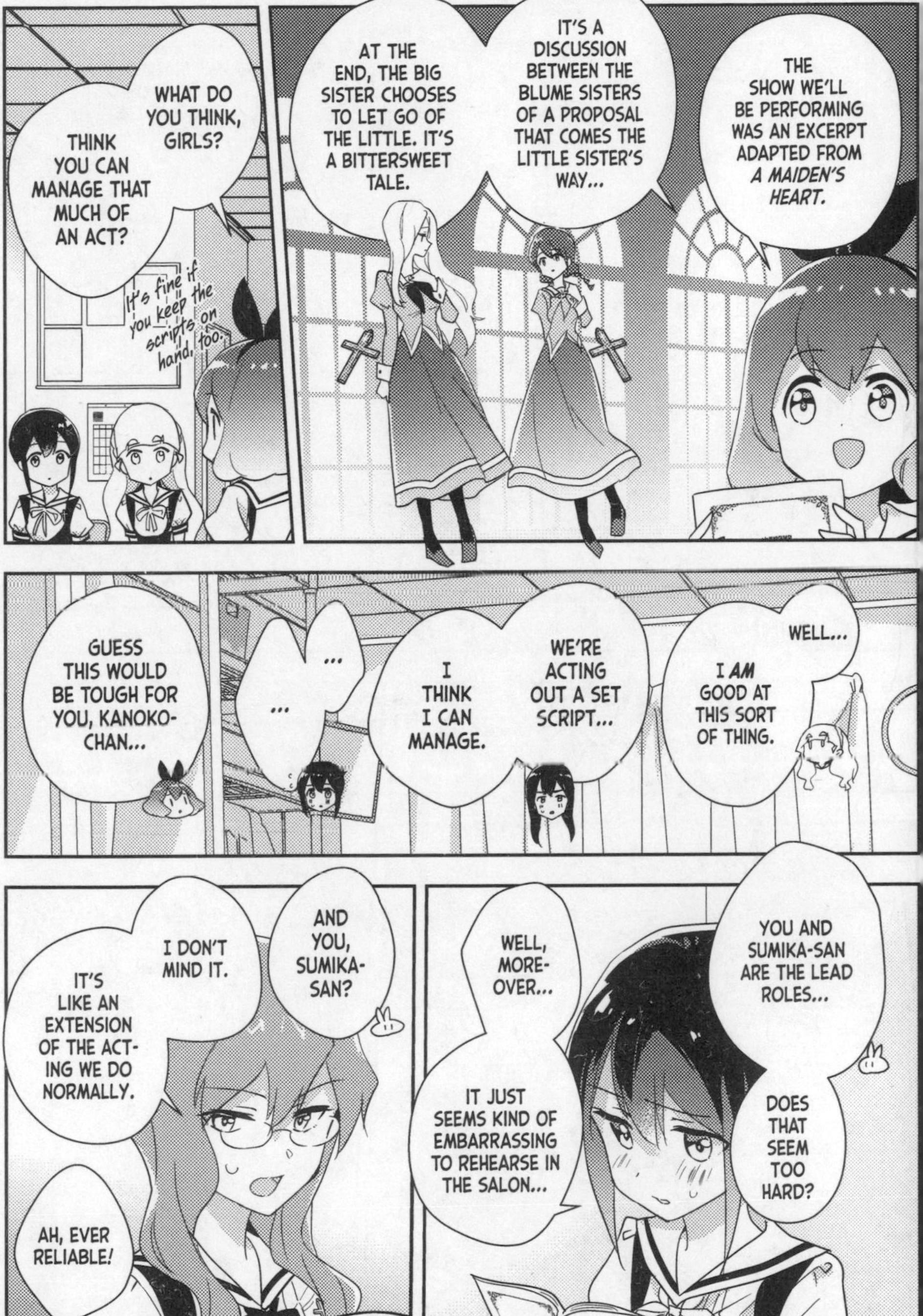
THE SHOW WE'LL BE PERFORMING WAS AN EXCERPT ADAPTED FROM *A MAIDEN'S HEART.*
IT'S A DISCUSSION BETWEEN THE BLUME SISTERS OF A PROPOSAL THAT COMES THE LITTLE SISTER'S WAY...
AT THE END, THE BIG SISTER CHOOSES TO LET GO OF THE LITTLE. IT'S A BITTERSWEET TALE.
WHAT DO YOU THINK, GIRLS?
THINK YOU CAN MANAGE THAT MUCH OF AN ACT?
It's fine if you keep the scripts on hand, too.
WELL...
I *AM* GOOD AT THIS SORT OF THING.
WE'RE ACTING OUT A SET SCRIPT...
I THINK I CAN MANAGE.
...
...
GUESS THIS WOULD BE TOUGH FOR YOU, KANOKO-CHAN...
YOU AND SUMIKA-SAN ARE THE LEAD ROLES...
DOES THAT SEEM TOO HARD?
WELL, MORE-OVER...
IT JUST SEEMS KIND OF EMBARRASSING TO REHEARSE IN THE SALON...
AND YOU, SUMIKA-SAN?
I DON'T MIND IT.
IT'S LIKE AN EXTENSION OF THE ACT-ING WE DO NORMALLY.
AH, EVER RELIABLE!

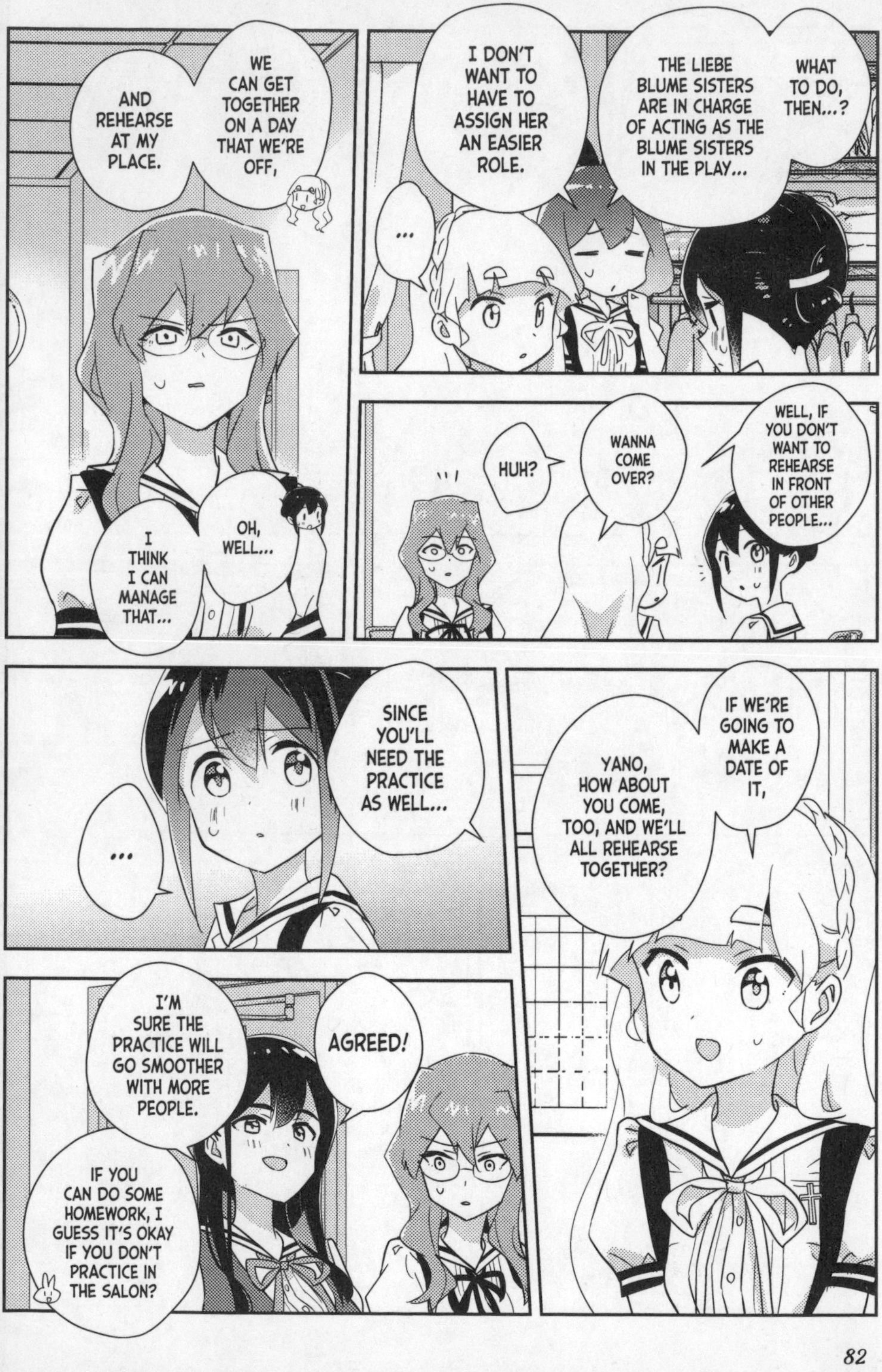
WHAT TO DO, THEN...?
THE LIEBE BLUME SISTERS ARE IN CHARGE OF ACTING AS THE BLUME SISTERS IN THE PLAY...
I DON'T WANT TO HAVE TO ASSIGN HER AN EASIER ROLE.
...
WELL, IF YOU DON'T WANT TO REHEARSE IN FRONT OF OTHER PEOPLE...
WANNA COME OVER?
HUH?
WE CAN GET TOGETHER ON A DAY THAT WE'RE OFF,
AND REHEARSE AT MY PLACE.
OH, WELL...
I THINK I CAN MANAGE THAT...
IF WE'RE GOING TO MAKE A DATE OF IT,
YANO, HOW ABOUT YOU COME, TOO, AND WE'LL ALL REHEARSE TOGETHER?
SINCE YOU'LL NEED THE PRACTICE AS WELL...
...
AGREED!
I'M SURE THE PRACTICE WILL GO SMOOTHER WITH MORE PEOPLE.
IF YOU CAN DO SOME HOMEWORK, I GUESS IT'S OKAY IF YOU DON'T PRACTICE IN THE SALON?

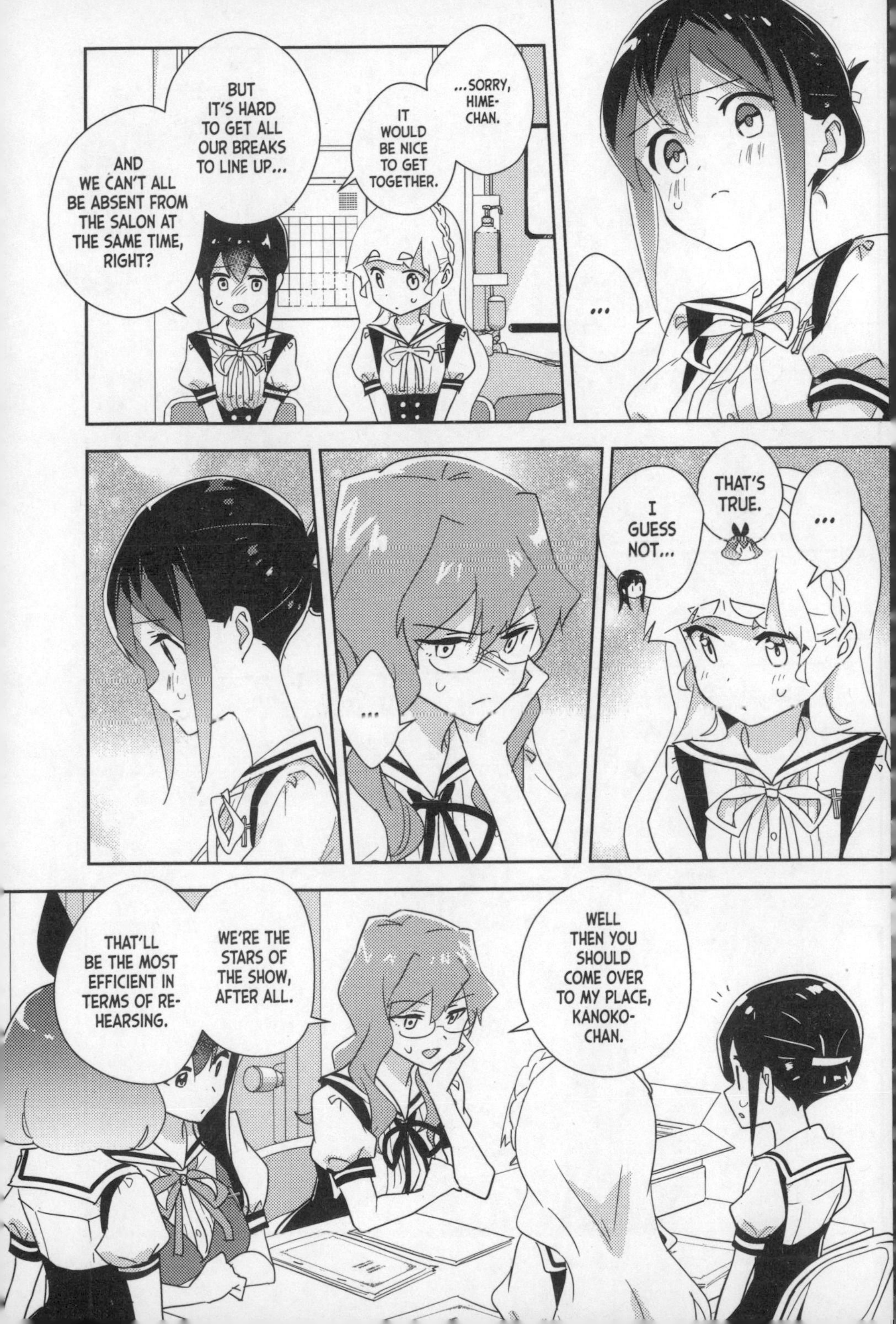
...
...SORRY, HIME-CHAN.
IT WOULD BE NICE TO GET TOGETHER.
BUT IT'S HARD TO GET ALL OUR BREAKS TO LINE UP...
AND WE CAN'T ALL BE ABSENT FROM THE SALON AT THE SAME TIME, RIGHT?
...
THAT'S TRUE.
I GUESS NOT...
...
WELL THEN YOU SHOULD COME OVER TO MY PLACE, KANOKO-CHAN.
WE'RE THE STARS OF THE SHOW, AFTER ALL.
THAT'LL BE THE MOST EFFICIENT IN TERMS OF RE-HEARSING.

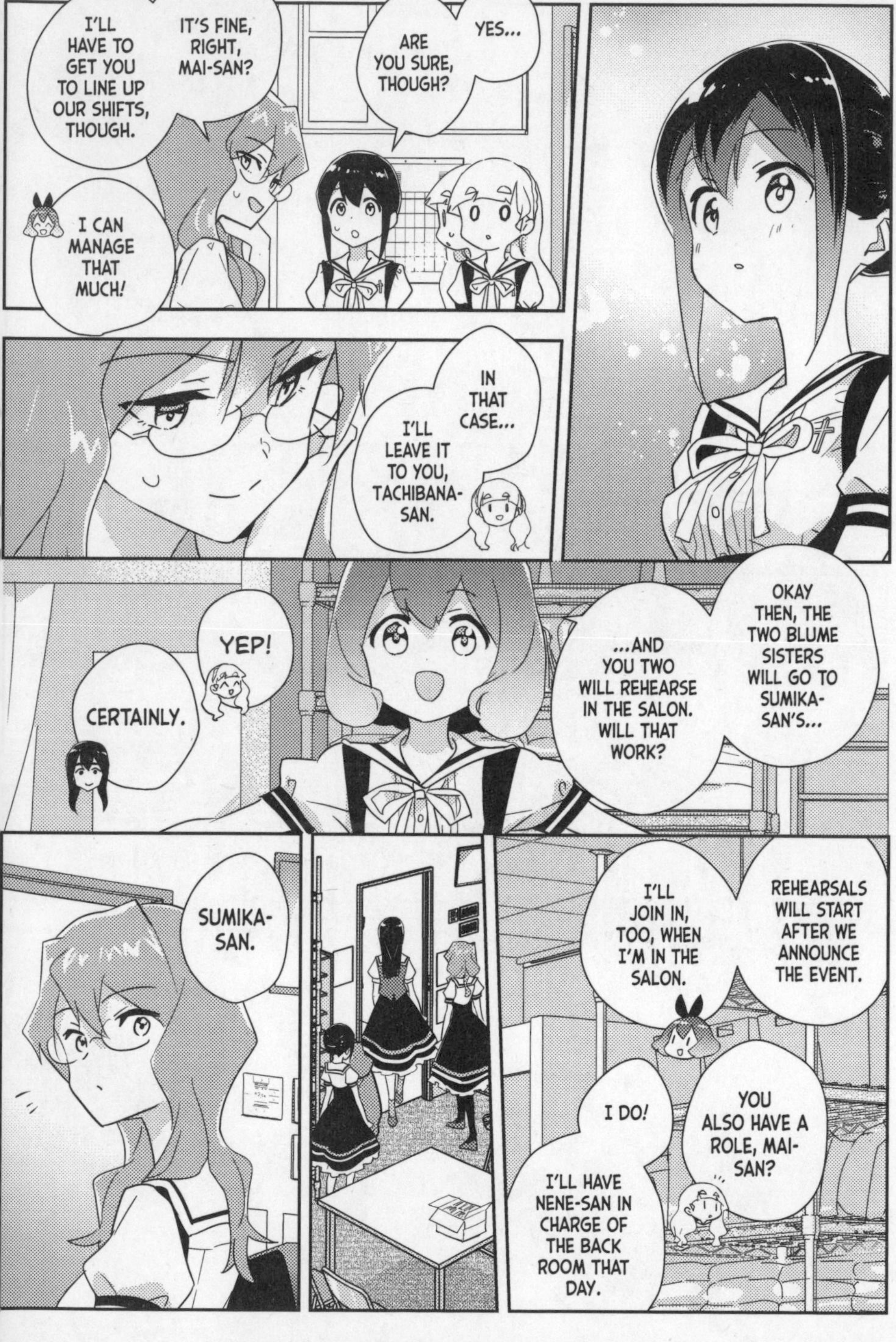
YES...
ARE YOU SURE, THOUGH?
IT'S FINE, RIGHT, MAI-SAN?
I'LL HAVE TO GET YOU TO LINE UP OUR SHIFTS, THOUGH.
I CAN MANAGE THAT MUCH!
IN THAT CASE...
I'LL LEAVE IT TO YOU, TACHIBANA-SAN.
OKAY THEN, THE TWO BLUME SISTERS WILL GO TO SUMIKA-SAN'S...
...AND YOU TWO WILL REHEARSE IN THE SALON. WILL THAT WORK?
YEP!
CERTAINLY.
REHEARSALS WILL START AFTER WE ANNOUNCE THE EVENT.
I'LL JOIN IN, TOO, WHEN I'M IN THE SALON.
YOU ALSO HAVE A ROLE, MAI-SAN?
I DO!
I'LL HAVE NENE-SAN IN CHARGE OF THE BACK ROOM THAT DAY.
SUMIKA-SAN.

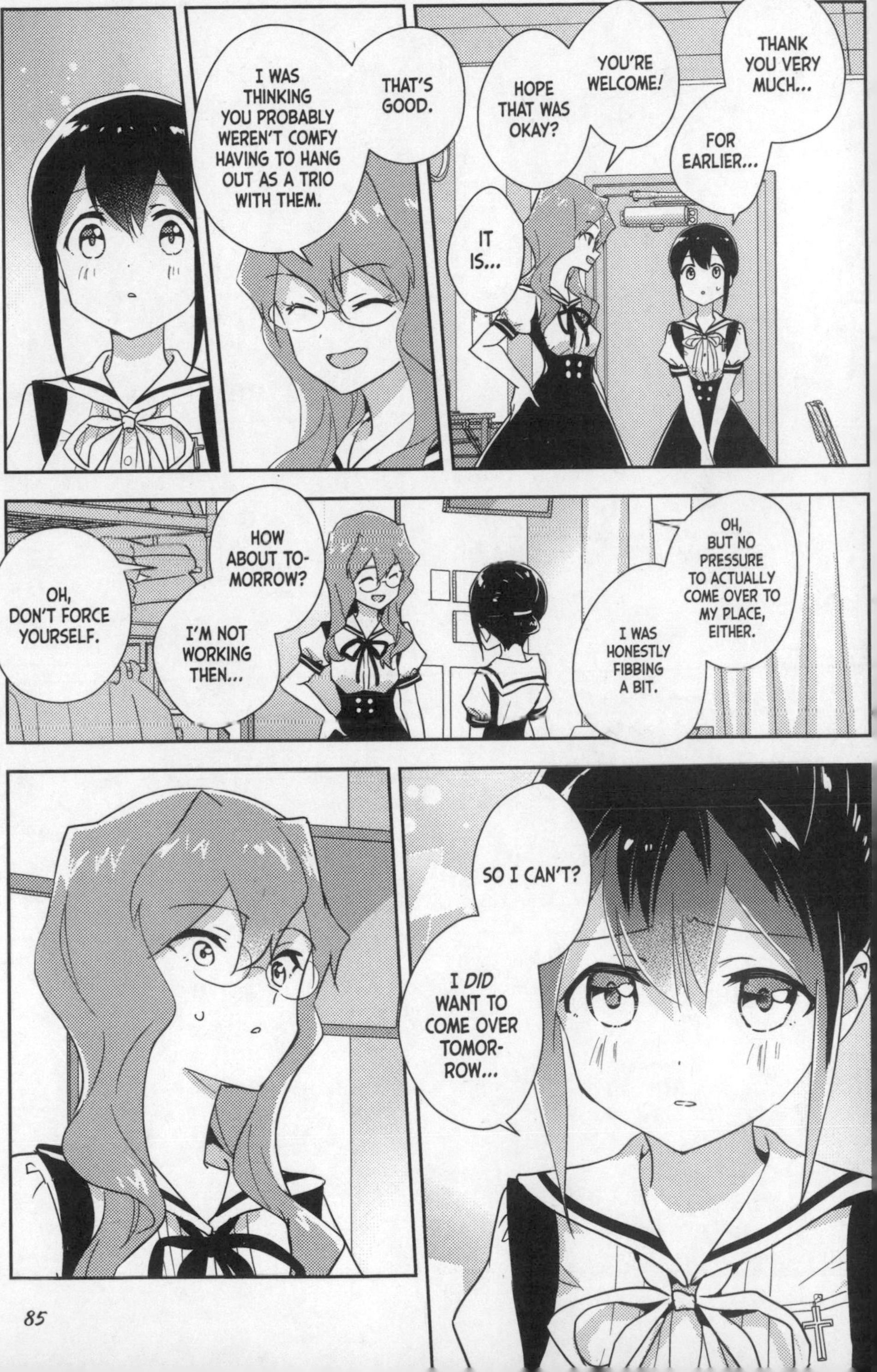
THANK YOU VERY MUCH...
FOR EARLIER...
YOU'RE WELCOME!
HOPE THAT WAS OKAY?
IT IS...
THAT'S GOOD.
I WAS THINKING YOU PROBABLY WEREN'T COMFY HAVING TO HANG OUT AS A TRIO WITH THEM.
OH, BUT NO PRESSURE TO ACTUALLY COME OVER TO MY PLACE, EITHER.
I WAS HONESTLY FIBBING A BIT.
HOW ABOUT TO-MORROW?
I'M NOT WORKING THEN...
OH, DON'T FORCE YOURSELF.
SO I CAN'T?
I *DID* WANT TO COME OVER TOMOR-ROW...

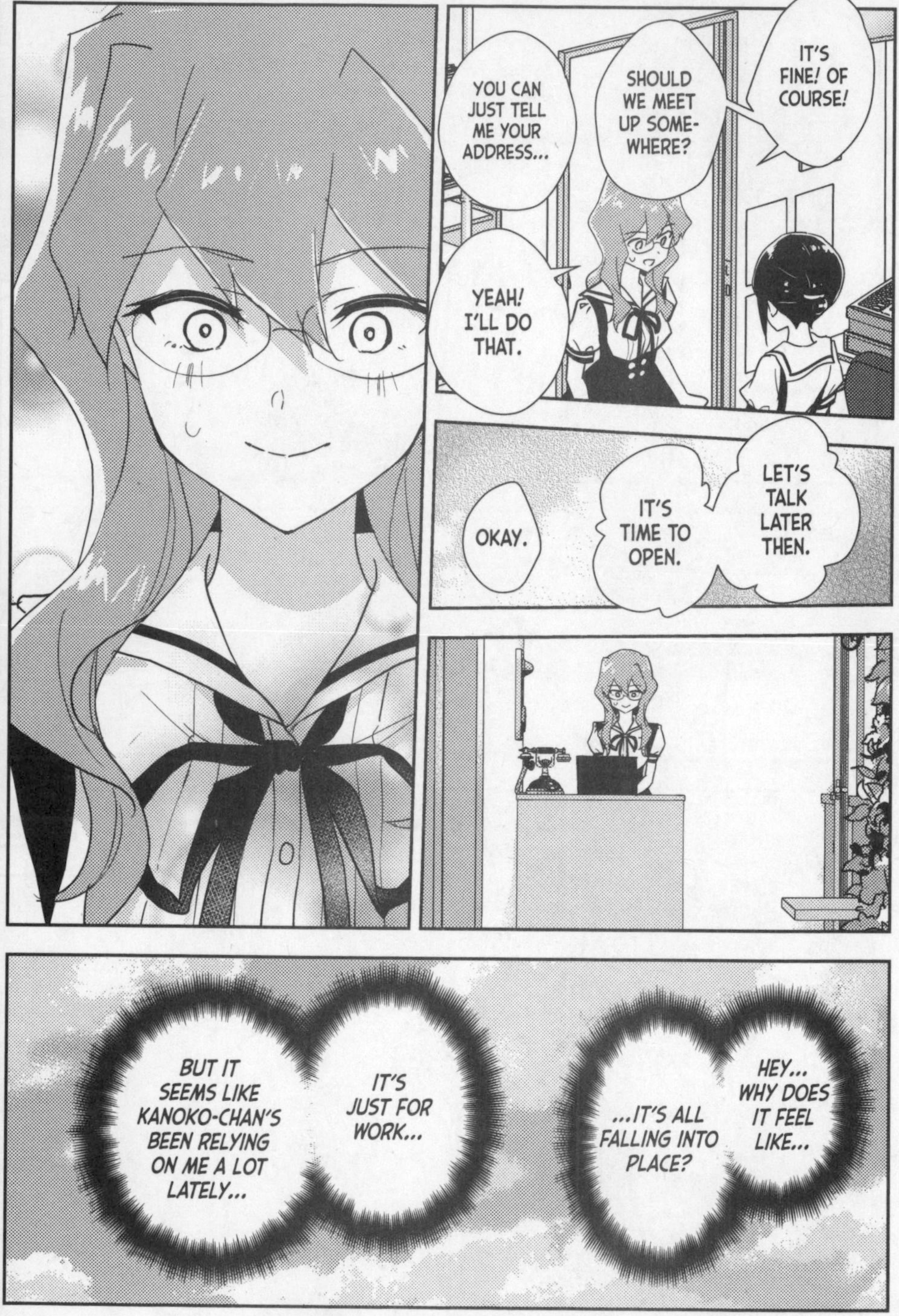
IT'S FINE! OF COURSE!
SHOULD WE MEET UP SOME-WHERE?
YOU CAN JUST TELL ME YOUR ADDRESS...
YEAH! I'LL DO THAT.
LET'S TALK LATER THEN.
IT'S TIME TO OPEN.
OKAY.
HEY... WHY DOES IT FEEL LIKE...
...IT'S ALL FALLING INTO PLACE?
IT'S JUST FOR WORK...
BUT IT SEEMS LIKE KANOKO-CHAN'S BEEN RELYING ON ME A LOT LATELY...

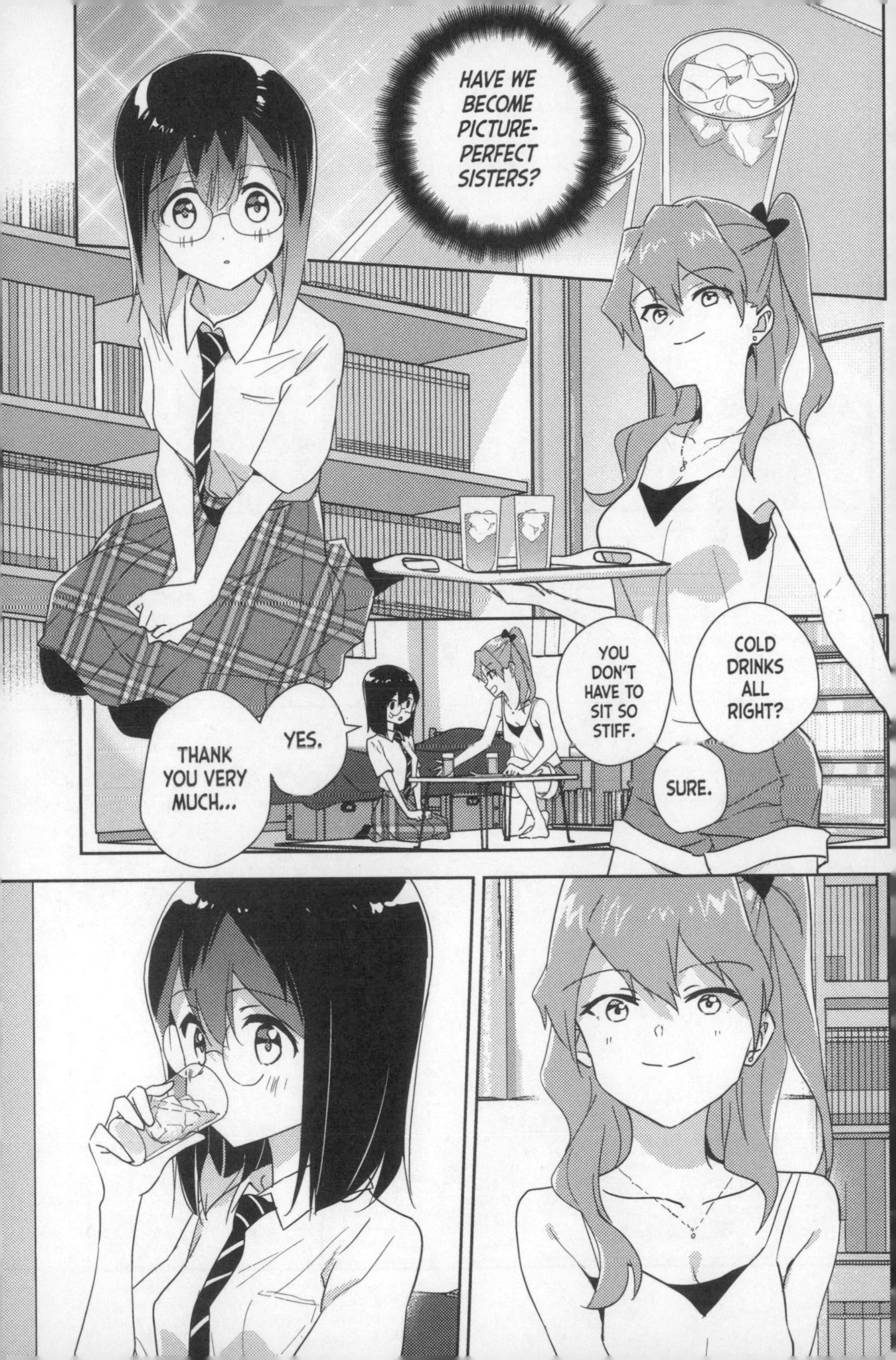
HAVE WE BECOME PICTURE-PERFECT SISTERS?
COLD DRINKS ALL RIGHT?
SURE.
YOU DON'T HAVE TO SIT SO STIFF.
YES.
THANK YOU VERY MUCH...

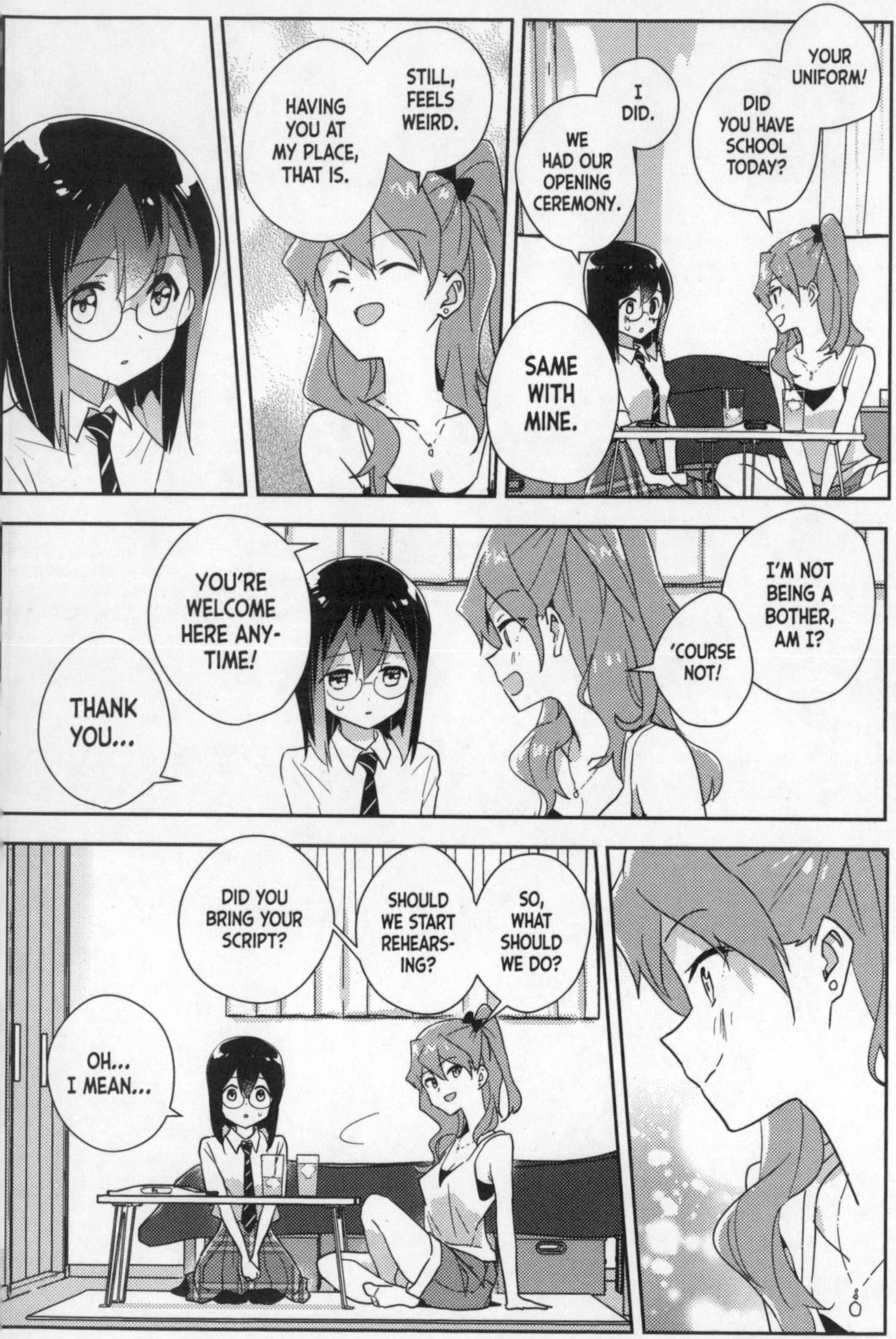
YOUR UNIFORM!
DID YOU HAVE SCHOOL TODAY?
I DID.
WE HAD OUR OPENING CEREMONY.
SAME WITH MINE.
STILL, FEELS WEIRD.
HAVING YOU AT MY PLACE, THAT IS.
I'M NOT BEING A BOTHER, AM I?
'COURSE NOT!
YOU'RE WELCOME HERE ANY-TIME!
THANK YOU...
SO, WHAT SHOULD WE DO?
SHOULD WE START REHEARS-ING?
DID YOU BRING YOUR SCRIPT?
OH... I MEAN...

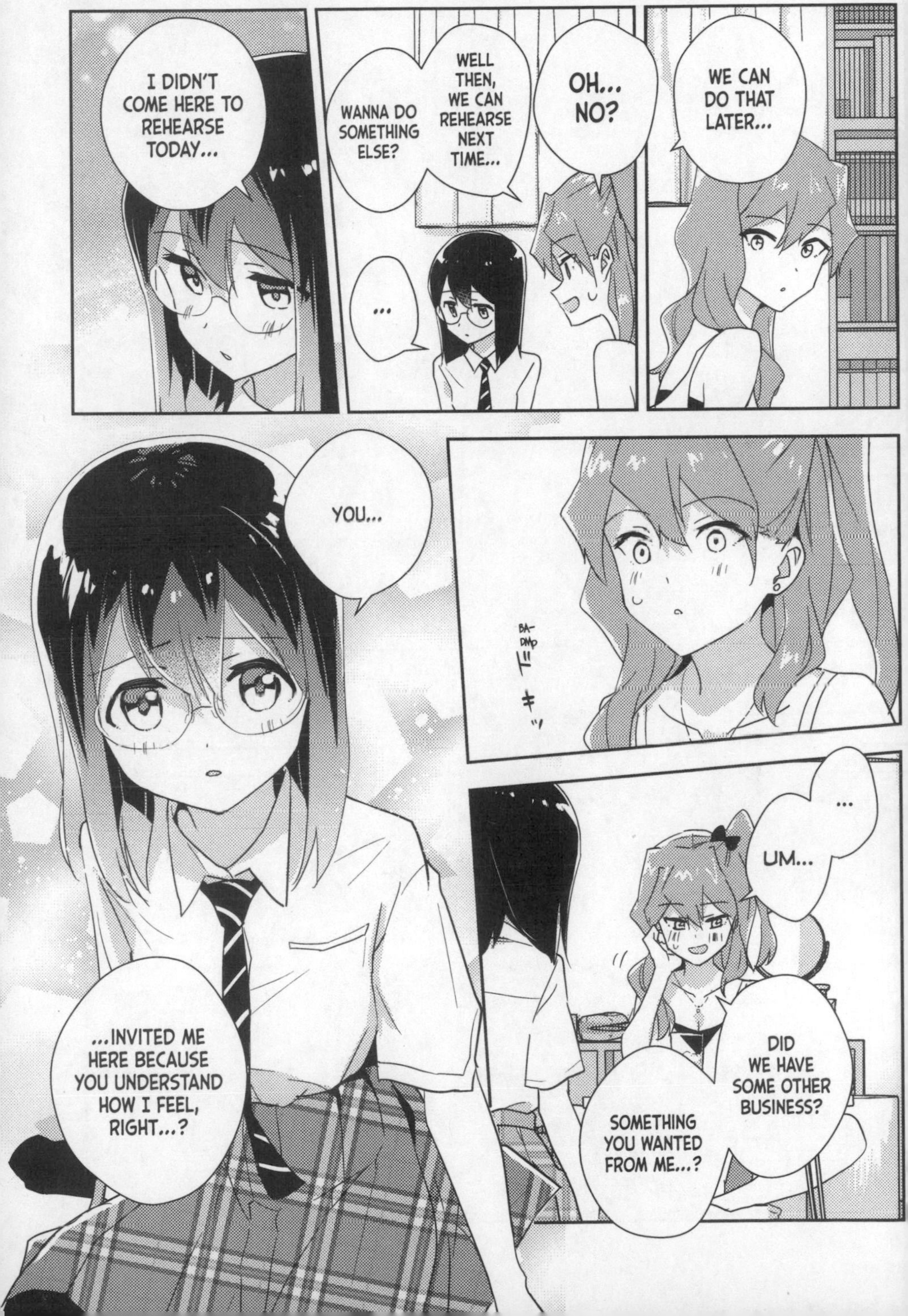
WE CAN DO THAT LATER...
OH... NO?
WELL THEN, WE CAN REHEARSE NEXT TIME...
WANNA DO SOMETHING ELSE?
...
I DIDN'T COME HERE TO REHEARSE TODAY...
BA-DMP
...
UM...
DID WE HAVE SOME OTHER BUSINESS?
SOMETHING YOU WANTED FROM ME...?
YOU...
...INVITED ME HERE BECAUSE YOU UNDERSTAND HOW I FEEL, RIGHT...?

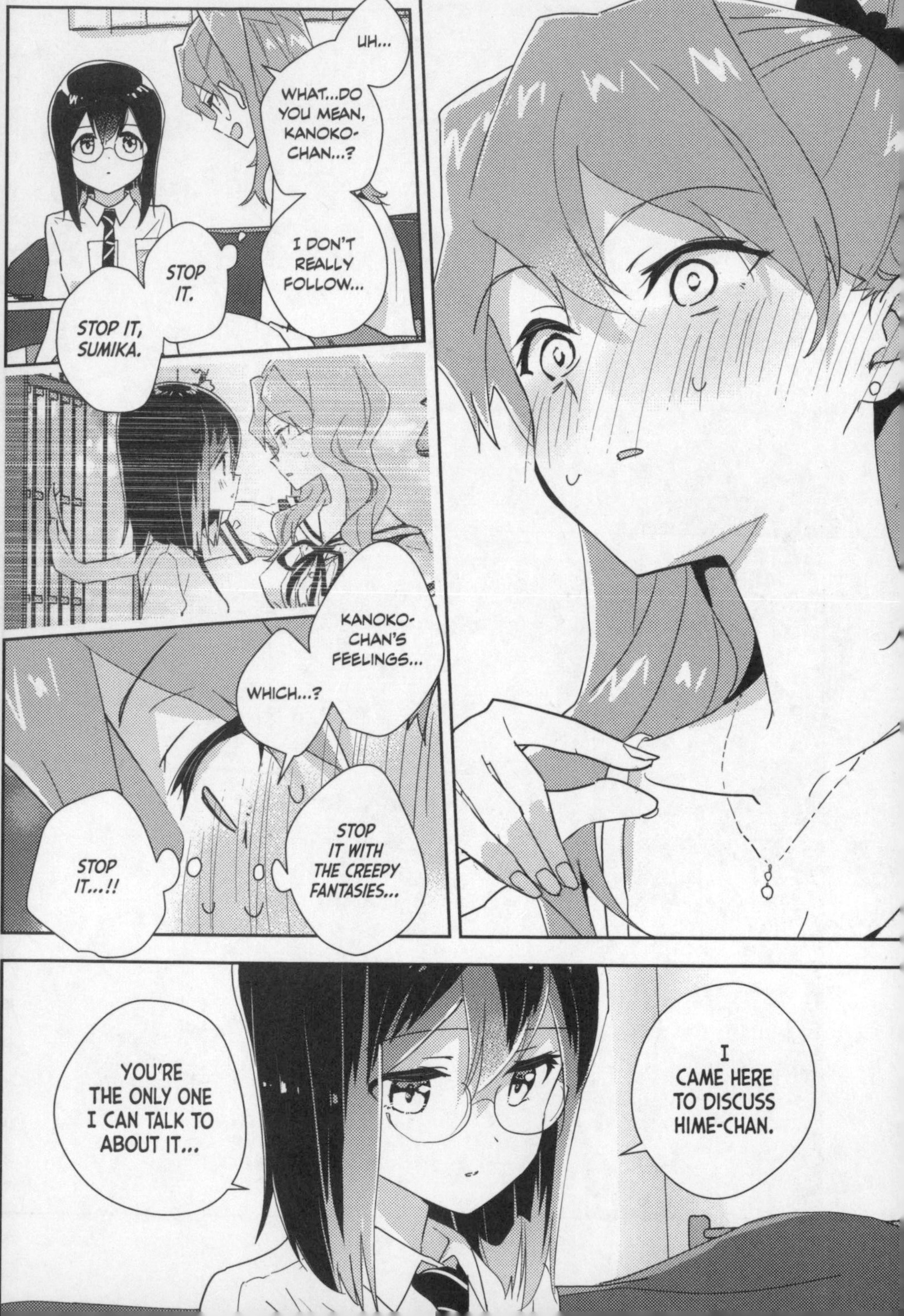
UH...
WHAT...DO YOU MEAN, KANOKO-CHAN...?
I DON'T REALLY FOLLOW...
STOP IT.
STOP IT, SUMIKA.
KANOKO-CHAN'S FEELINGS...
WHICH...?
STOP IT WITH THE CREEPY FANTASIES...
STOP IT...!!
I CAME HERE TO DISCUSS HIME-CHAN.
YOU'RE THE ONLY ONE I CAN TALK TO ABOUT IT...

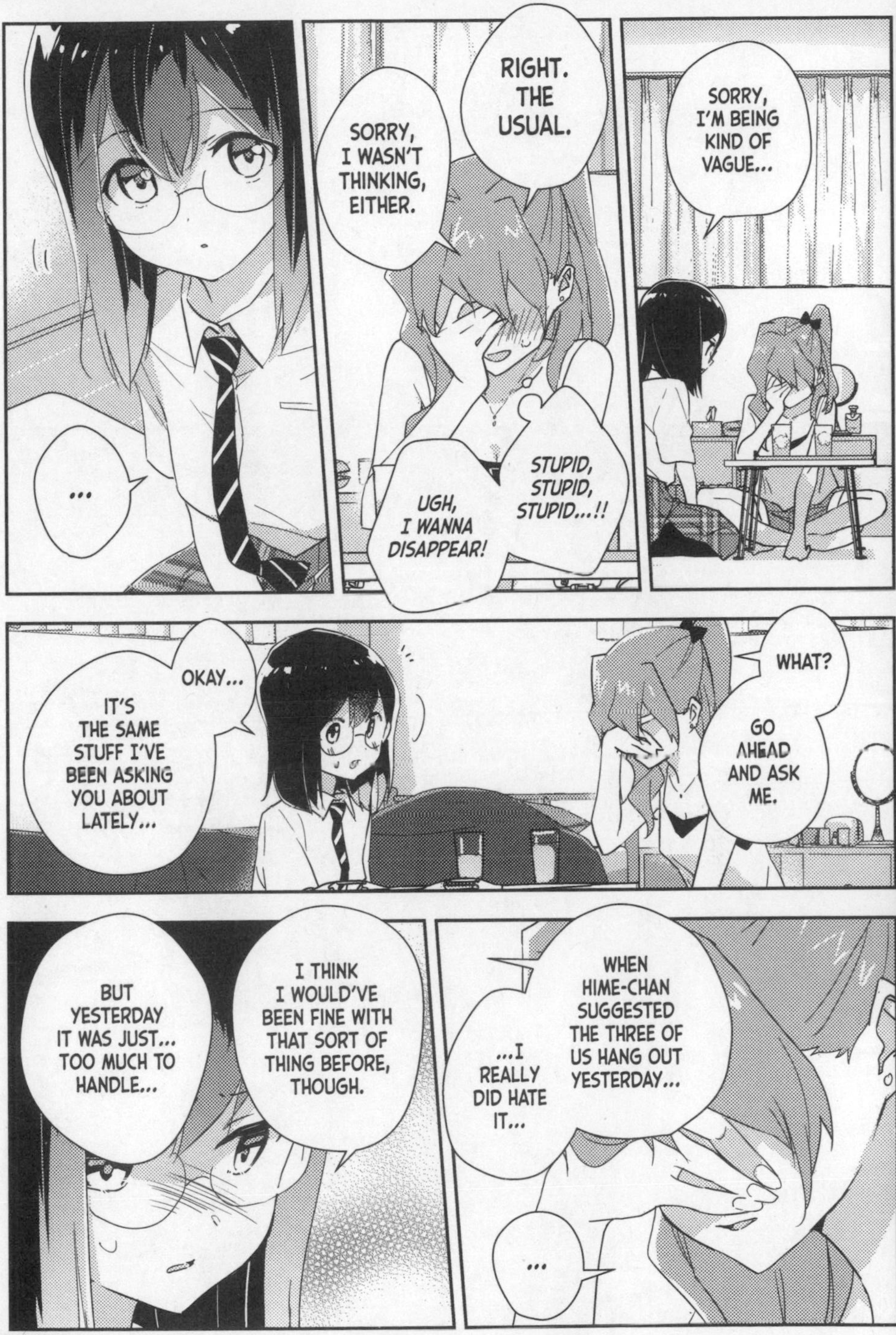
SORRY, I'M BEING KIND OF VAGUE...
RIGHT. THE USUAL.
SORRY, I WASN'T THINKING, EITHER.
STUPID, STUPID, STUPID...!!
UGH, I WANNA DISAPPEAR!
...
WHAT?
GO AHEAD AND ASK ME.
OKAY...
IT'S THE SAME STUFF I'VE BEEN ASKING YOU ABOUT LATELY...
WHEN HIME-CHAN SUGGESTED THE THREE OF US HANG OUT YESTERDAY...
...I REALLY DID HATE IT...
...
I THINK I WOULD'VE BEEN FINE WITH THAT SORT OF THING BEFORE, THOUGH.
BUT YESTERDAY IT WAS JUST... TOO MUCH TO HANDLE...

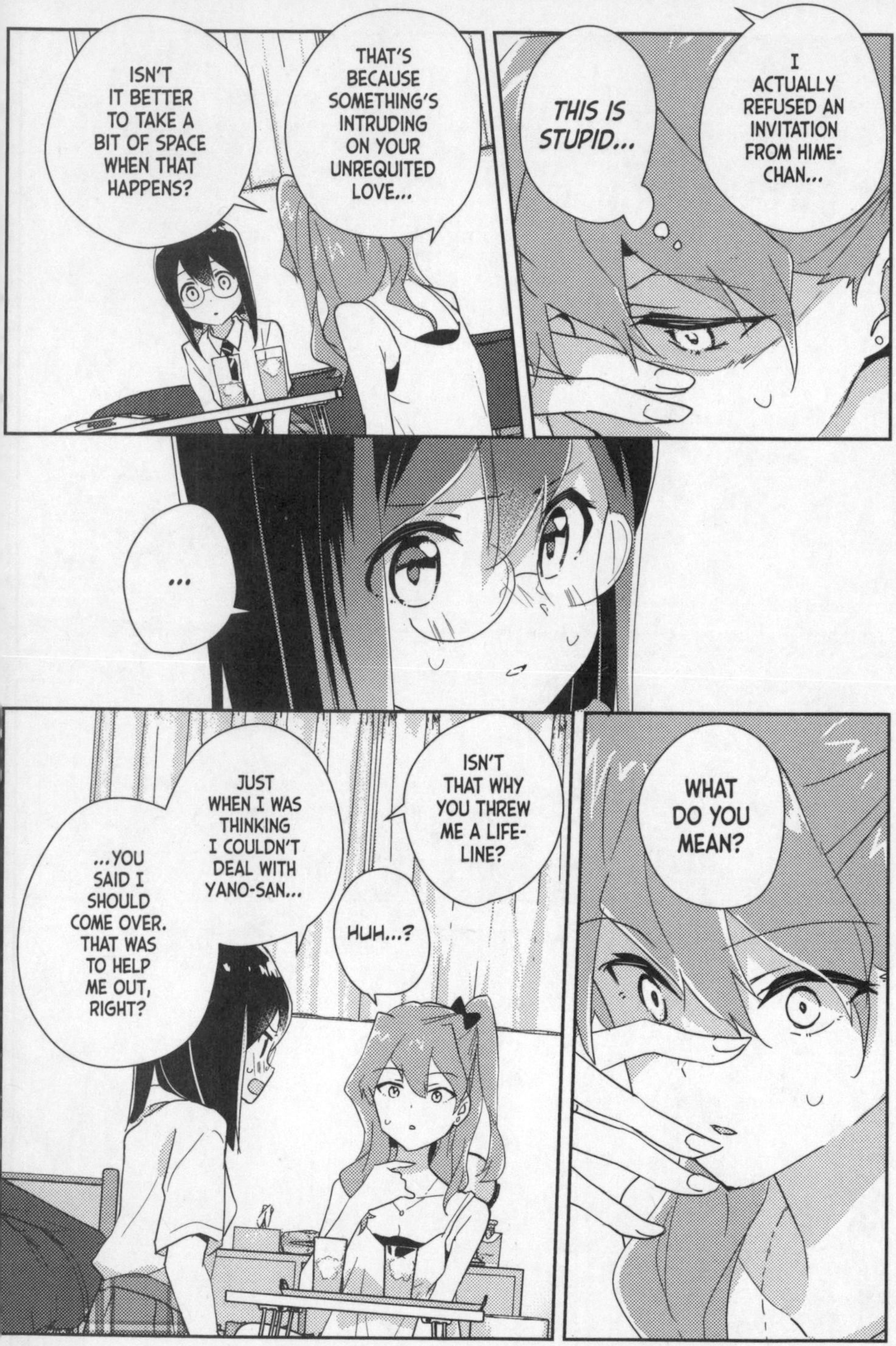
I ACTUALLY REFUSED AN INVITATION FROM HIME-CHAN...
THIS IS STUPID...
THAT'S BECAUSE SOMETHING'S INTRUDING ON YOUR UNREQUITED LOVE...
ISN'T IT BETTER TO TAKE A BIT OF SPACE WHEN THAT HAPPENS?
...
WHAT DO YOU MEAN?
ISN'T THAT WHY YOU THREW ME A LIFE-LINE?
HUH...?
JUST WHEN I WAS THINKING I COULDN'T DEAL WITH YANO-SAN...
...YOU SAID I SHOULD COME OVER. THAT WAS TO HELP ME OUT, RIGHT?

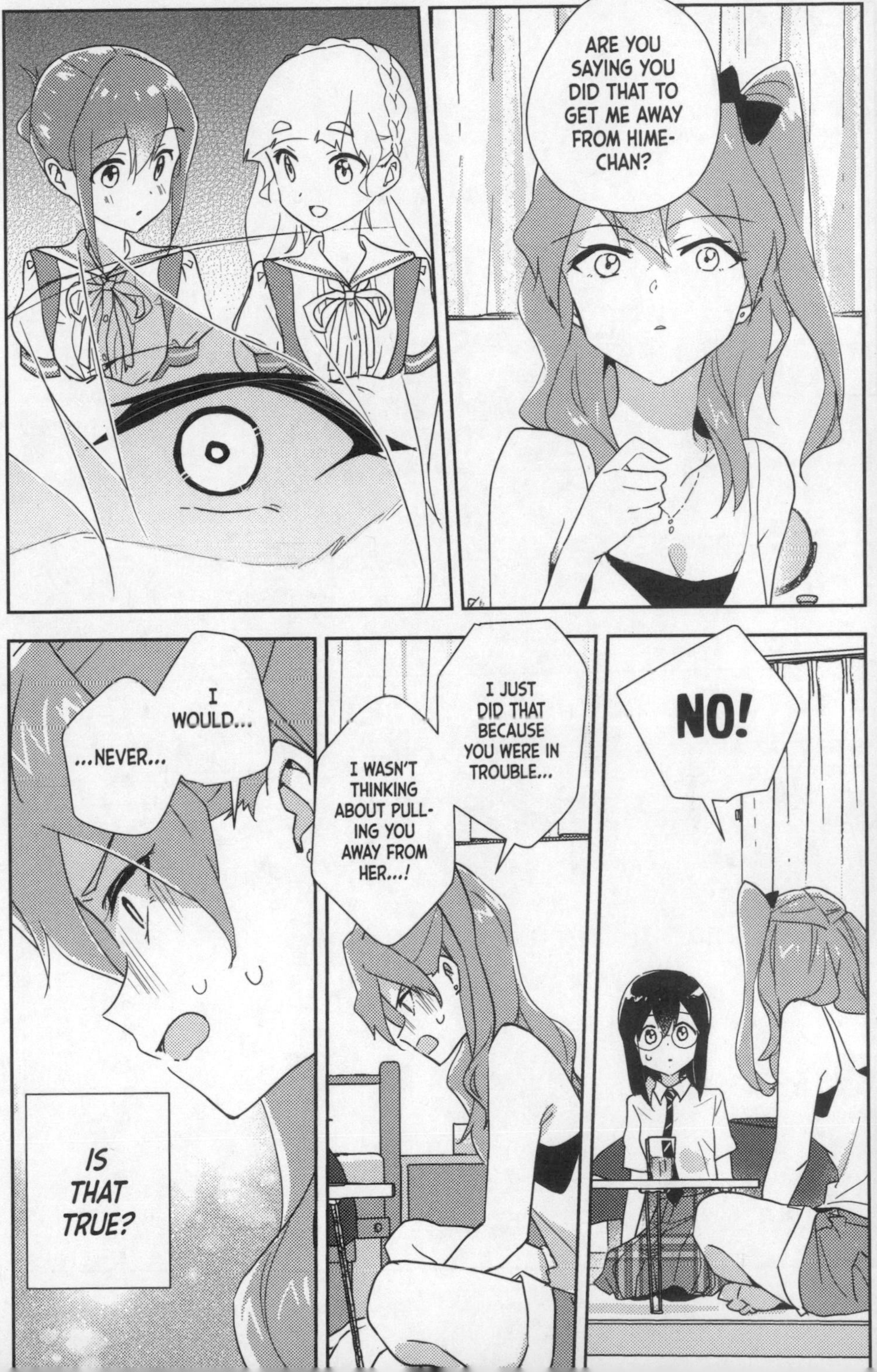
ARE YOU SAYING YOU DID THAT TO GET ME AWAY FROM HIME-CHAN?
NO!
I JUST DID THAT BECAUSE YOU WERE IN TROUBLE...
I WASN'T THINKING ABOUT PULL-ING YOU AWAY FROM HER...!
I WOULD...
...NEVER...
IS THAT TRUE?

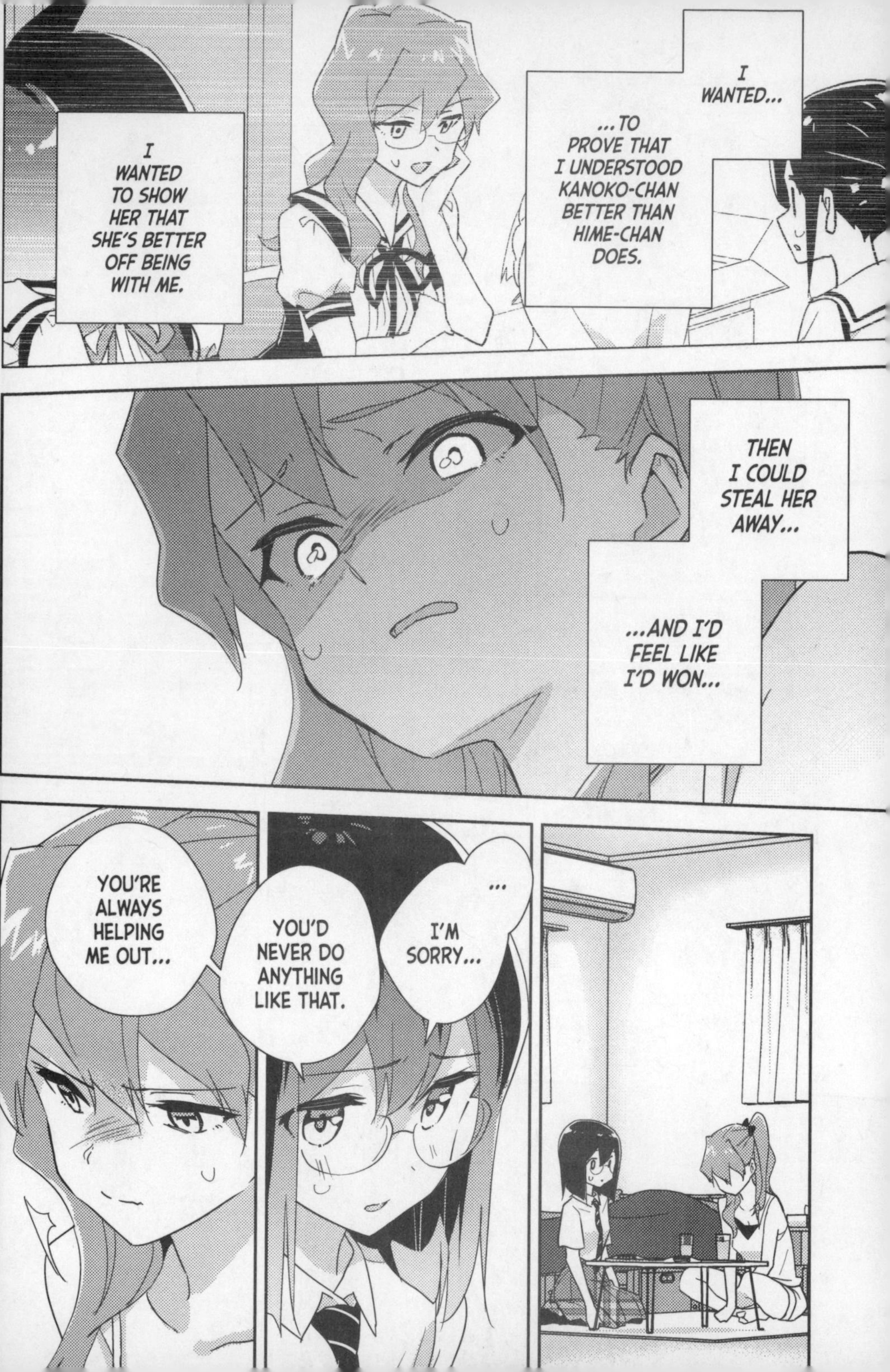
I WANTED...
...TO PROVE THAT I UNDERSTOOD KANOKO-CHAN BETTER THAN HIME-CHAN DOES.
I WANTED TO SHOW HER THAT SHE'S BETTER OFF BEING WITH ME.
THEN I COULD STEAL HER AWAY...
...AND I'D FEEL LIKE I'D WON...
...
I'M SORRY...
YOU'D NEVER DO ANYTHING LIKE THAT.
YOU'RE ALWAYS HELPING ME OUT...

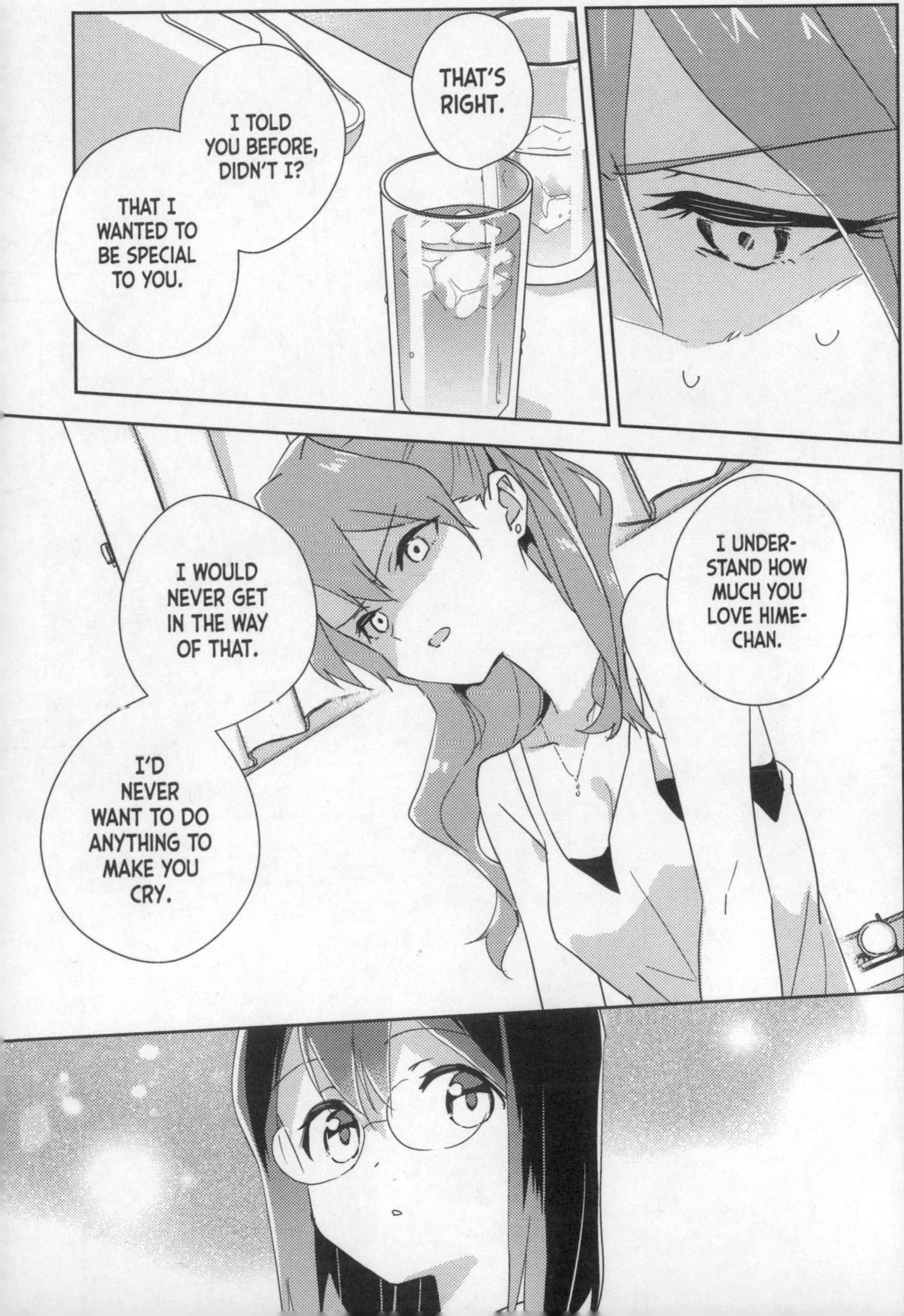
THAT'S RIGHT.
I TOLD YOU BEFORE, DIDN'T I?
THAT I WANTED TO BE SPECIAL TO YOU.
I UNDER-STAND HOW MUCH YOU LOVE HIME-CHAN.
I WOULD NEVER GET IN THE WAY OF THAT.
I'D NEVER WANT TO DO ANYTHING TO MAKE YOU CRY.

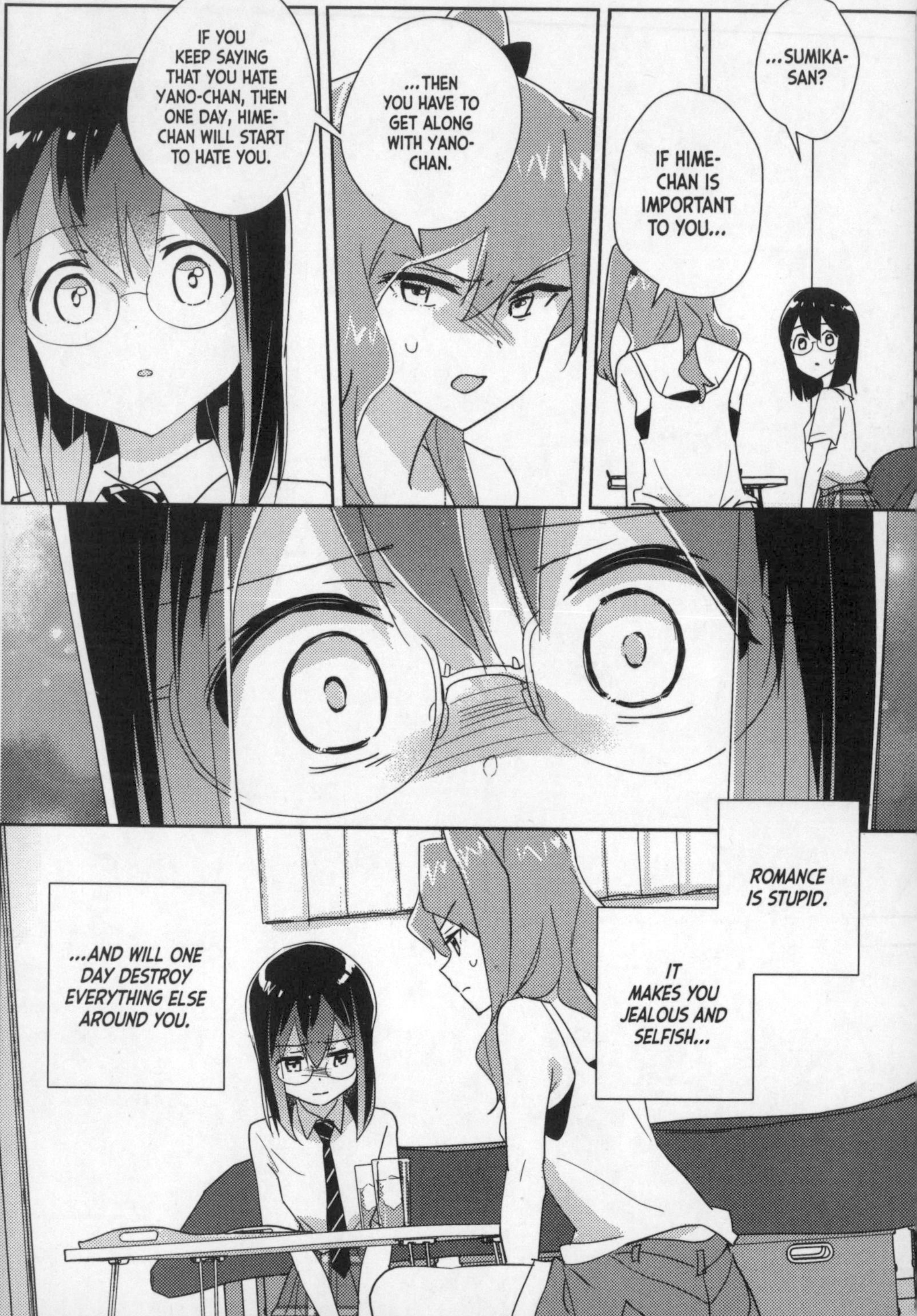
...SUMIKA-SAN?
IF HIME-CHAN IS IMPORTANT TO YOU...
...THEN YOU HAVE TO GET ALONG WITH YANO-CHAN.
IF YOU KEEP SAYING THAT YOU HATE YANO-CHAN, THEN ONE DAY, HIME-CHAN WILL START TO HATE YOU.
ROMANCE IS STUPID.
IT MAKES YOU JEALOUS AND SELFISH...
...AND WILL ONE DAY DESTROY EVERYTHING ELSE AROUND YOU.

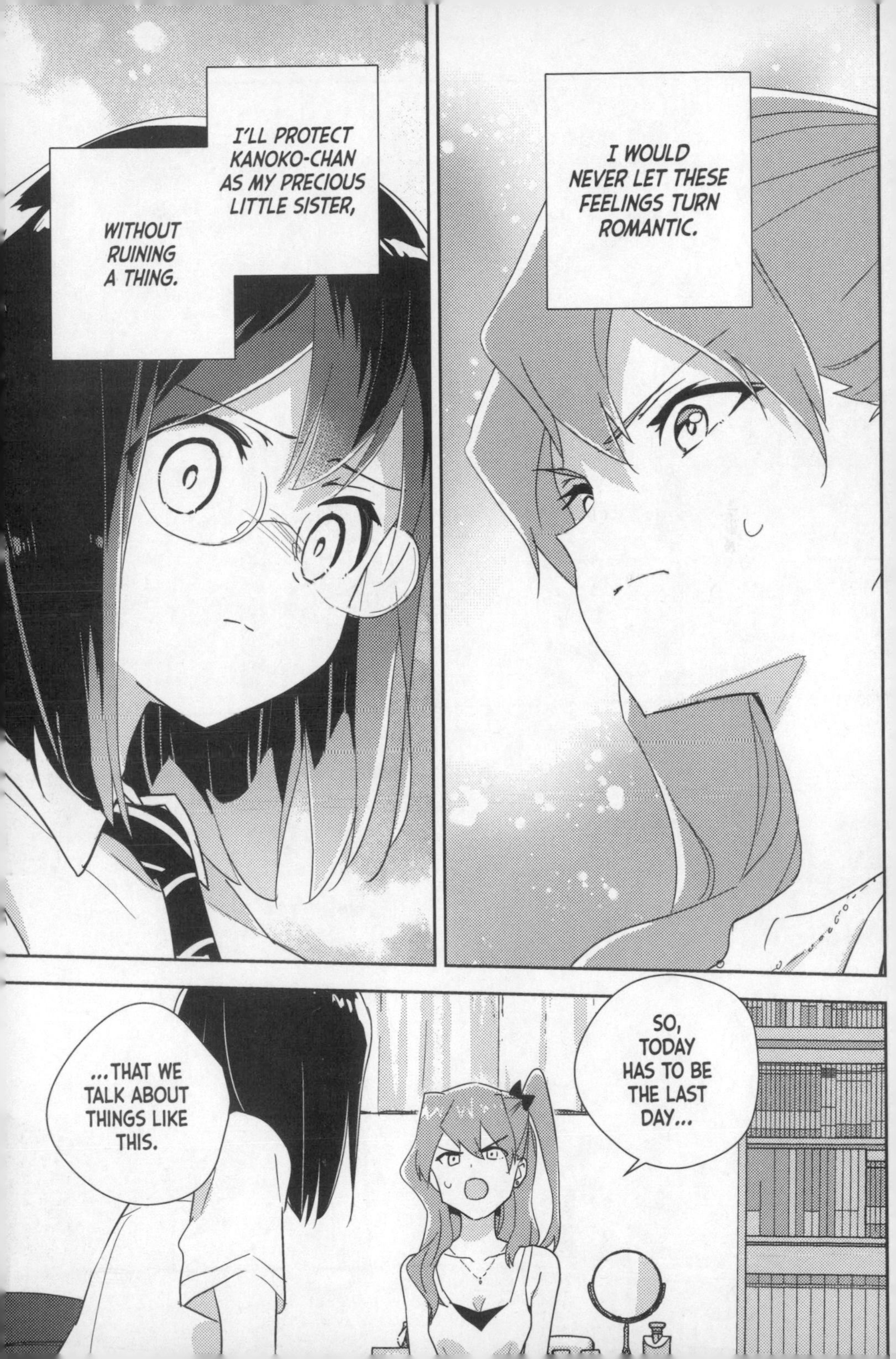
I WOULD NEVER LET THESE FEELINGS TURN ROMANTIC.
I'LL PROTECT KANOKO-CHAN AS MY PRECIOUS LITTLE SISTER,
WITHOUT RUINING A THING.
SO, TODAY HAS TO BE THE LAST DAY...
...THAT WE TALK ABOUT THINGS LIKE THIS.

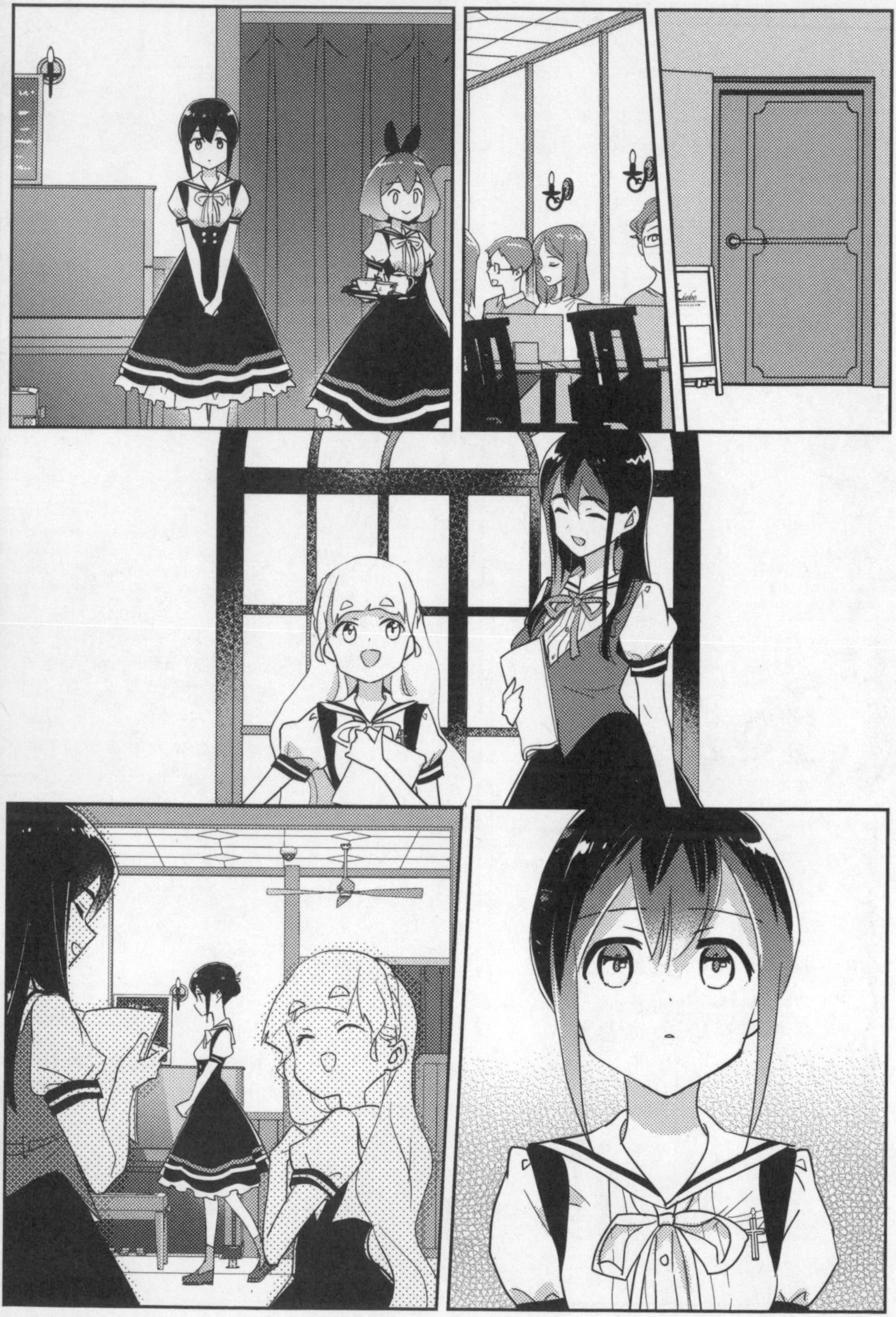
Liebe

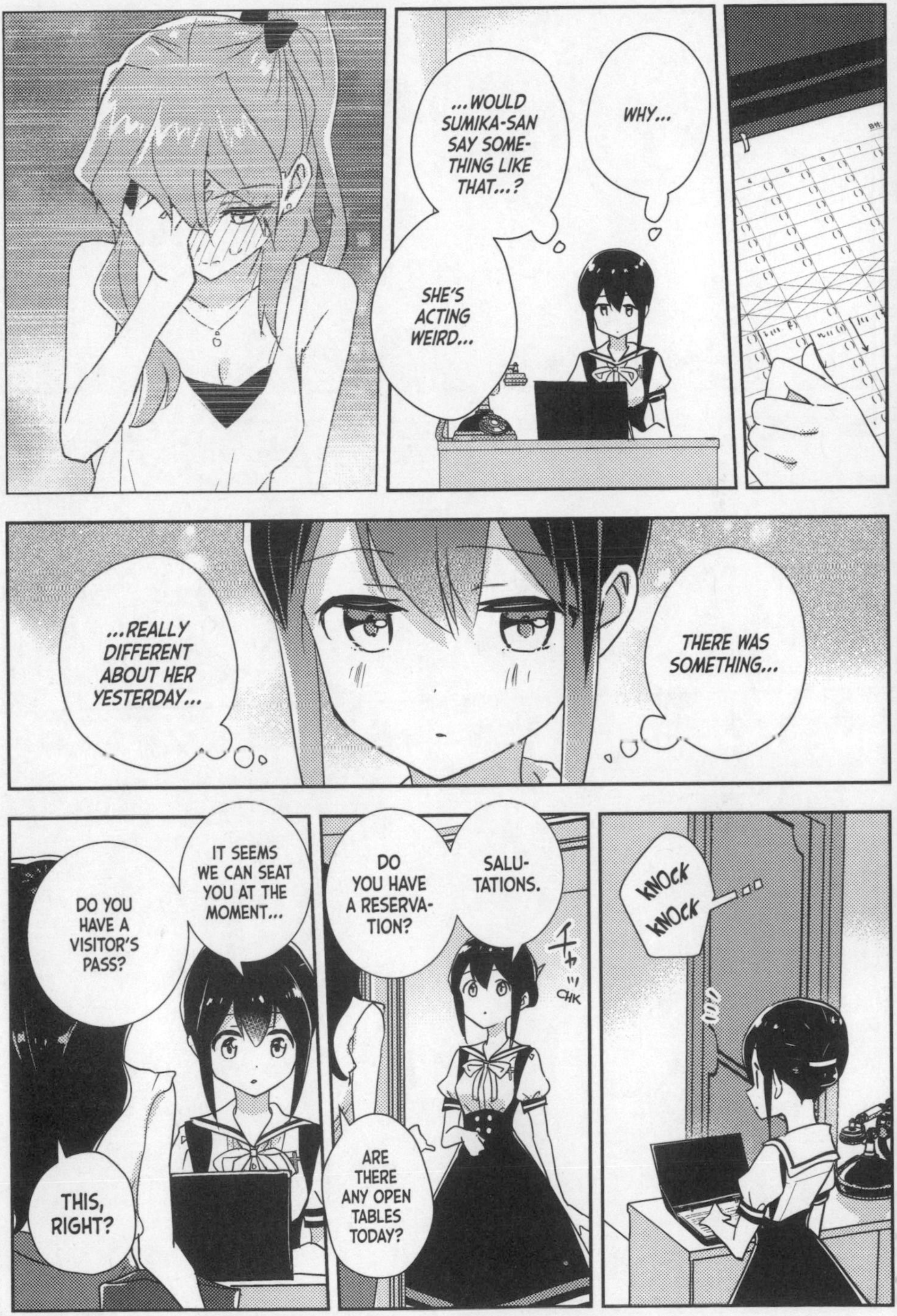
WHY...
...WOULD SUMIKA-SAN SAY SOME-THING LIKE THAT...?
SHE'S ACTING WEIRD...
THERE WAS SOMETHING...
...REALLY DIFFERENT ABOUT HER YESTERDAY...
KNOCK KNOCK
SALU-TATIONS.
DO YOU HAVE A RESERVA-TION?
チャッ
CHK
ARE THERE ANY OPEN TABLES TODAY?
IT SEEMS WE CAN SEAT YOU AT THE MOMENT...
DO YOU HAVE A VISITOR'S PASS?
THIS, RIGHT?

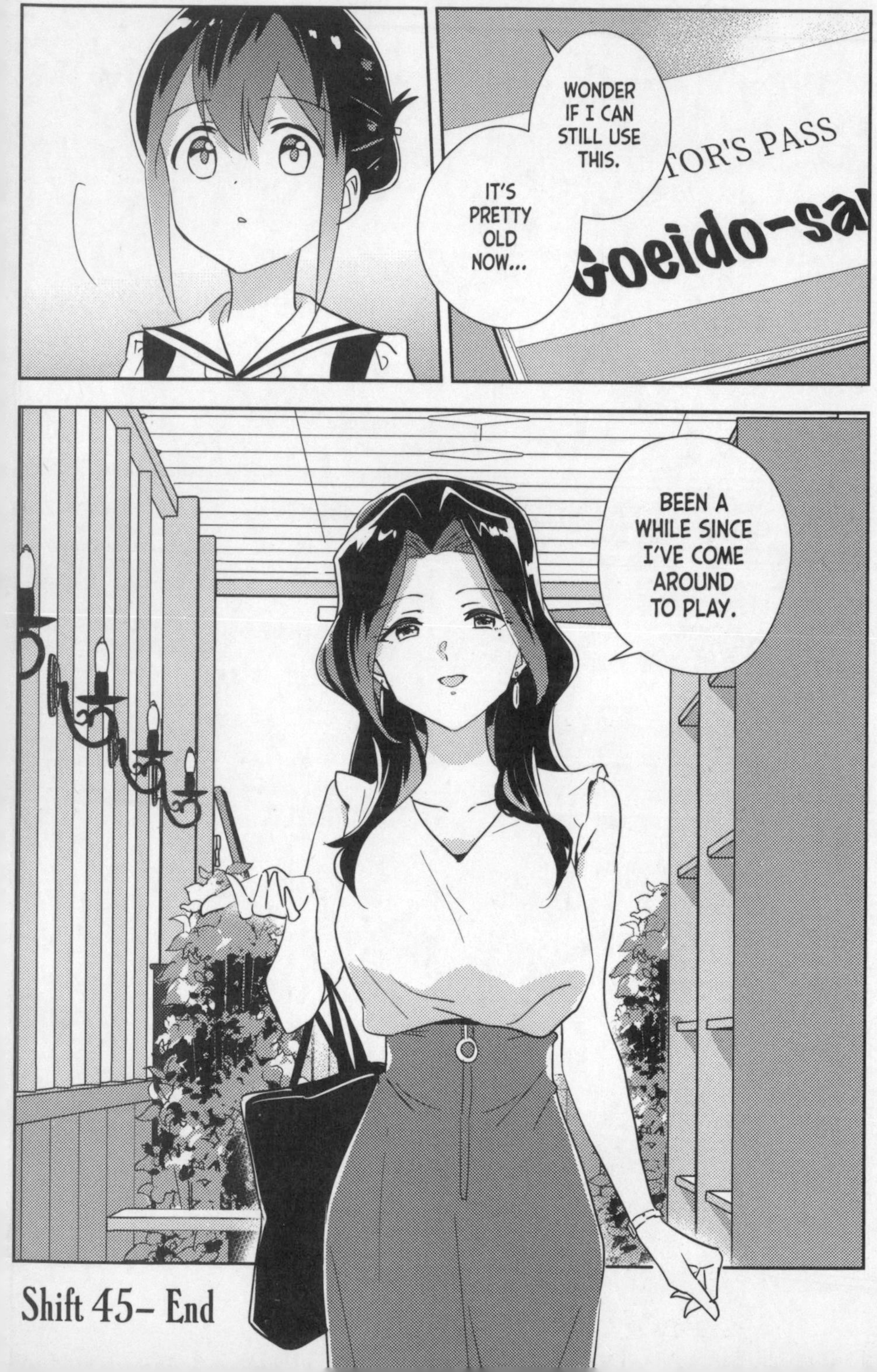
WONDER IF I CAN STILL USE THIS.
IT'S PRETTY OLD NOW...
TOR'S PASS
Goeido-sa
BEEN A WHILE SINCE I'VE COME AROUND TO PLAY.

Shift 45– End

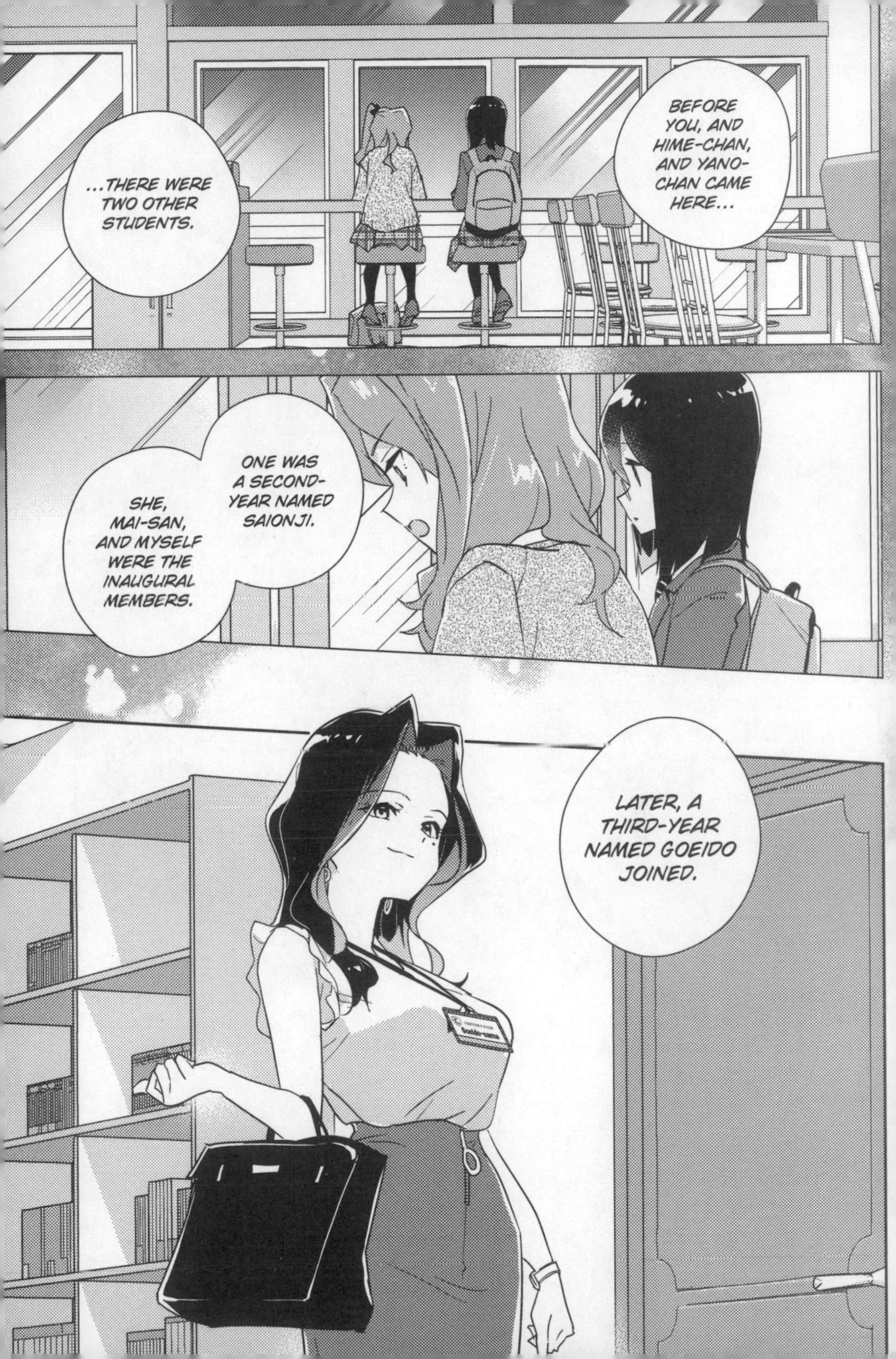
BEFORE YOU, AND HIME-CHAN, AND YANO-CHAN CAME HERE...
...THERE WERE TWO OTHER STUDENTS.
ONE WAS A SECOND-YEAR NAMED SAIONJI.
SHE, MAI-SAN, AND MYSELF WERE THE INAUGURAL MEMBERS.
LATER, A THIRD-YEAR NAMED GOEIDO JOINED.

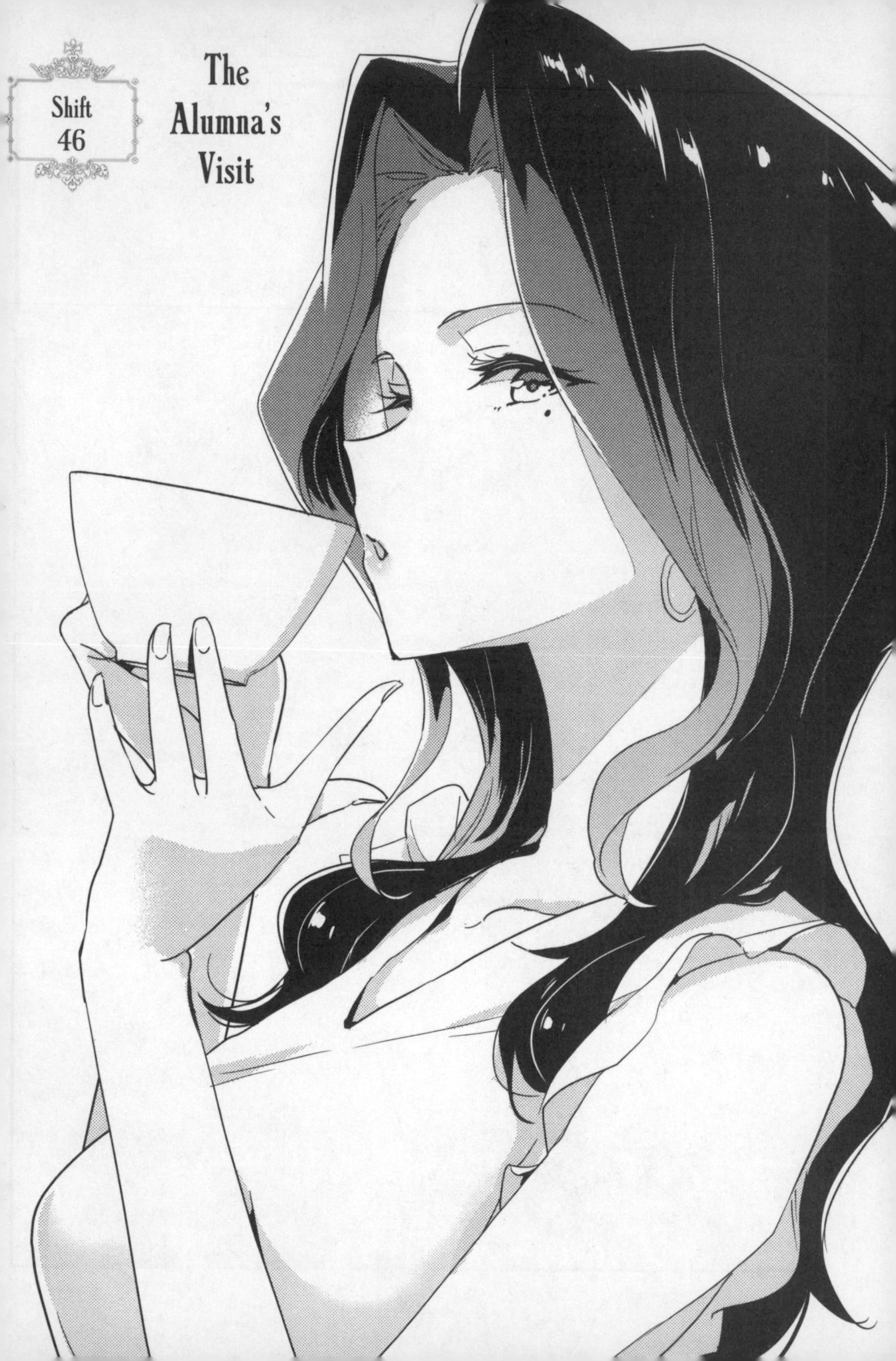
Shift 46
The Alumna's Visit

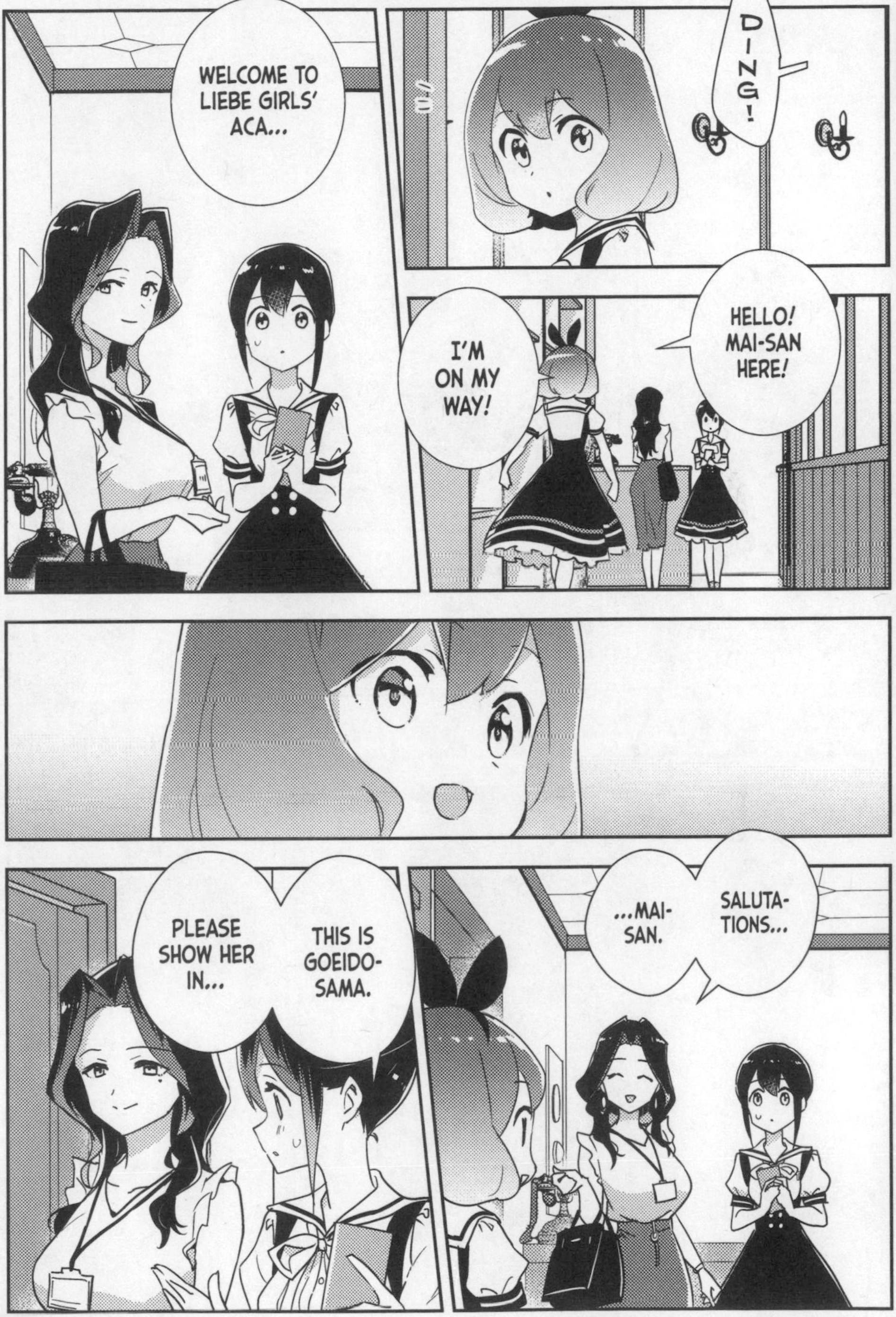
DING!
HELLO! MAI-SAN HERE!
I'M ON MY WAY!
WELCOME TO LIEBE GIRLS' ACA...
SALUTATIONS...
...MAI-SAN.
THIS IS GOEIDO-SAMA.
PLEASE SHOW HER IN...

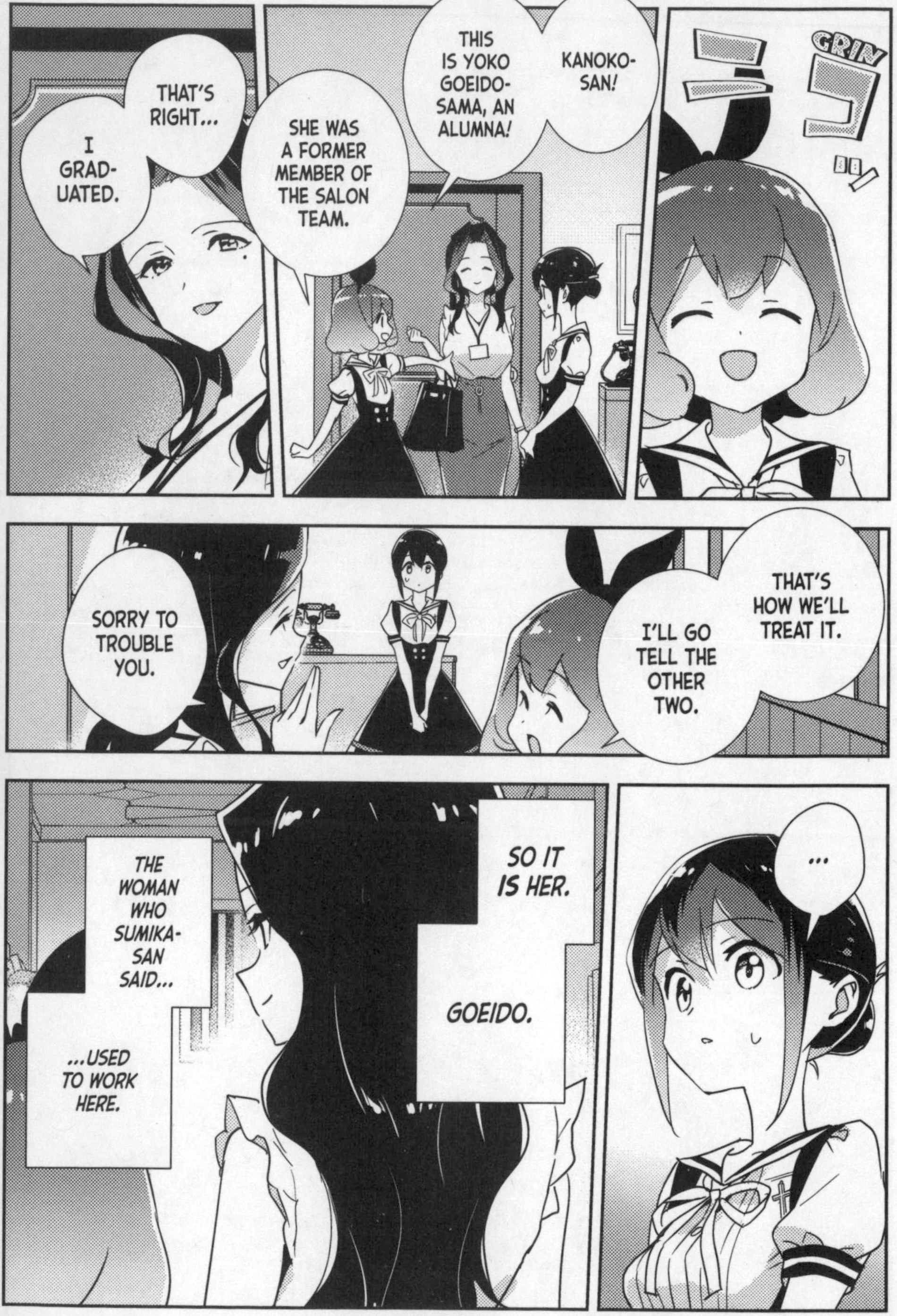
GRIN
KANOKO-SAN!
THIS IS YOKO GOEIDO-SAMA, AN ALUMNA!
SHE WAS A FORMER MEMBER OF THE SALON TEAM.
THAT'S RIGHT...
I GRAD-UATED.
THAT'S HOW WE'LL TREAT IT.
I'LL GO TELL THE OTHER TWO.
SORRY TO TROUBLE YOU.
...
SO IT IS HER.
GOEIDO.
THE WOMAN WHO SUMIKA-SAN SAID...
...USED TO WORK HERE.

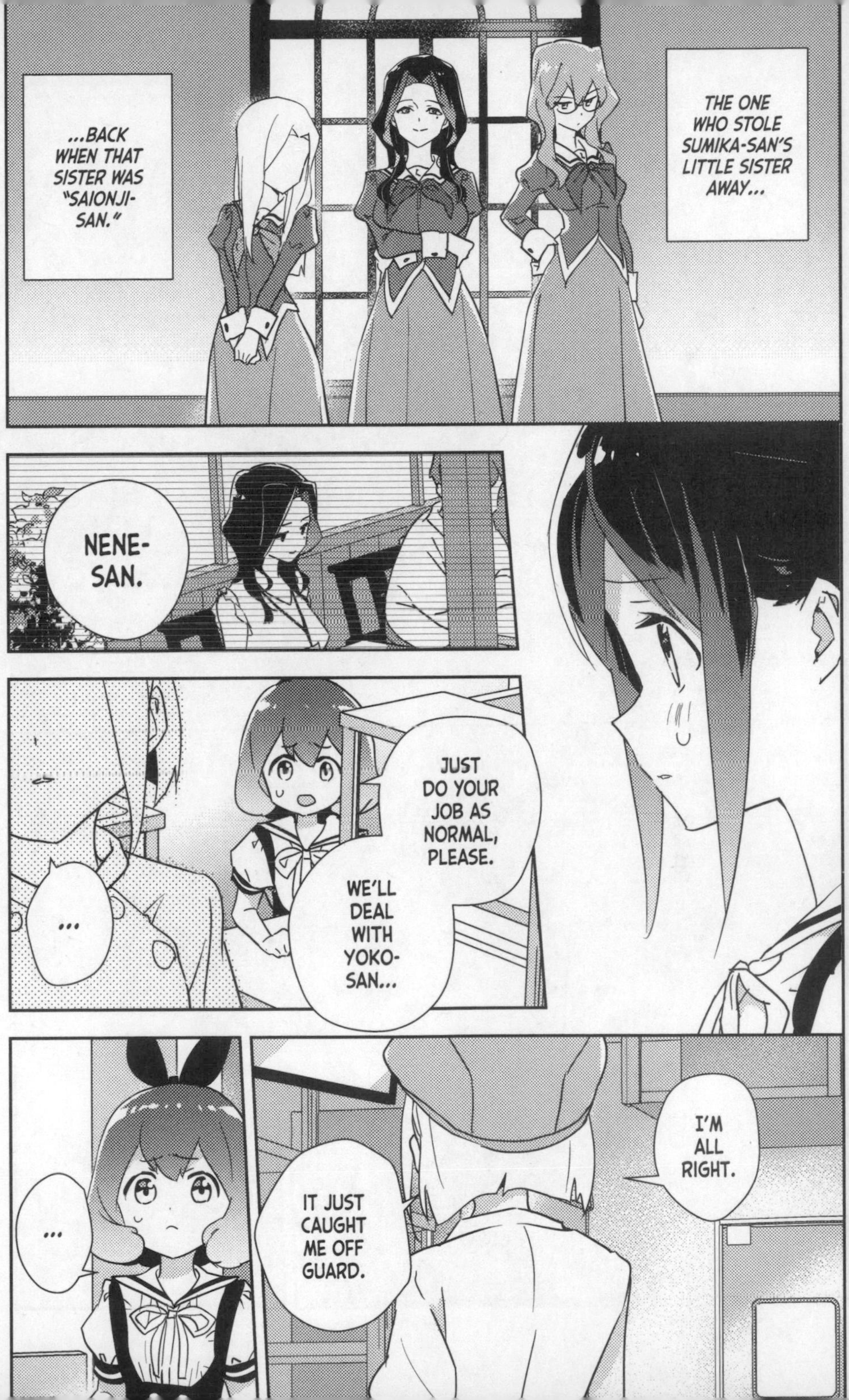
THE ONE WHO STOLE SUMIKA-SAN'S LITTLE SISTER AWAY...
...BACK WHEN THAT SISTER WAS "SAIONJI-SAN."
NENE-SAN.
JUST DO YOUR JOB AS NORMAL, PLEASE.
WE'LL DEAL WITH YOKO-SAN...
...
I'M ALL RIGHT.
IT JUST CAUGHT ME OFF GUARD.
...

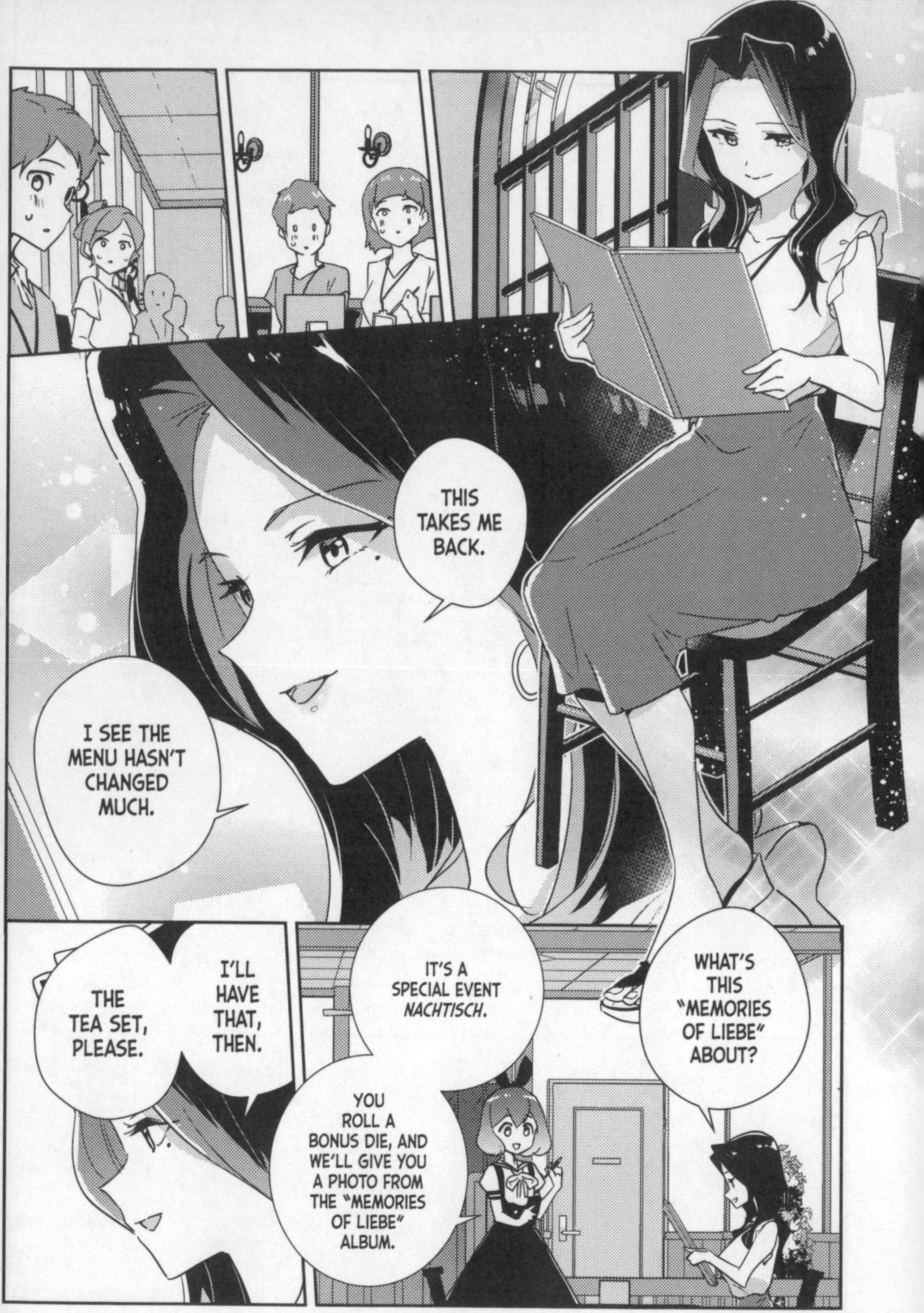
THIS TAKES ME BACK.
I SEE THE MENU HASN'T CHANGED MUCH.
WHAT'S THIS "MEMORIES OF LIEBE" ABOUT?
IT'S A SPECIAL EVENT *NACHTISCH*.
YOU ROLL A BONUS DIE, AND WE'LL GIVE YOU A PHOTO FROM THE "MEMORIES OF LIEBE" ALBUM.
I'LL HAVE THAT, THEN.
THE TEA SET, PLEASE.

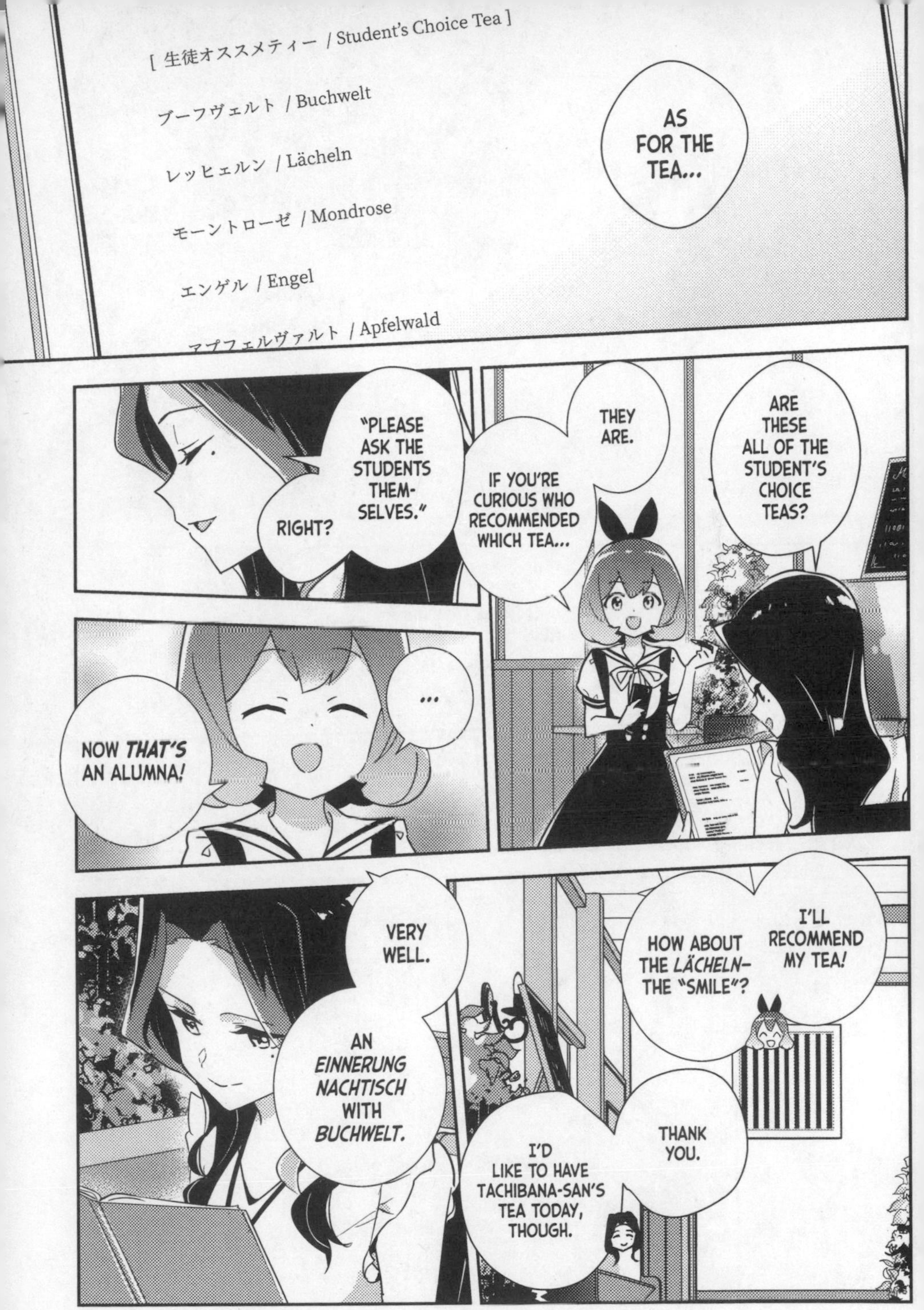
AS FOR THE TEA...
[生徒オススメティー / Student's Choice Tea]
ブーフヴェルト / Buchwelt
レッヒェルン / Lächeln
モーントローゼ / Mondrose
エンゲル / Engel
アプフェルヴァルト / Apfelwald
ARE THESE ALL OF THE STUDENT'S CHOICE TEAS?
THEY ARE.
IF YOU'RE CURIOUS WHO RECOMMENDED WHICH TEA...
"PLEASE ASK THE STUDENTS THEM-SELVES."
RIGHT?
...
NOW *THAT'S* AN ALUMNA!
I'LL RECOMMEND MY TEA!
HOW ABOUT THE *LÄCHELN*—THE "SMILE"?
THANK YOU.
I'D LIKE TO HAVE TACHIBANA-SAN'S TEA TODAY, THOUGH.
VERY WELL.
AN *EINNERUNG NACHTISCH* WITH *BUCHWELT.*

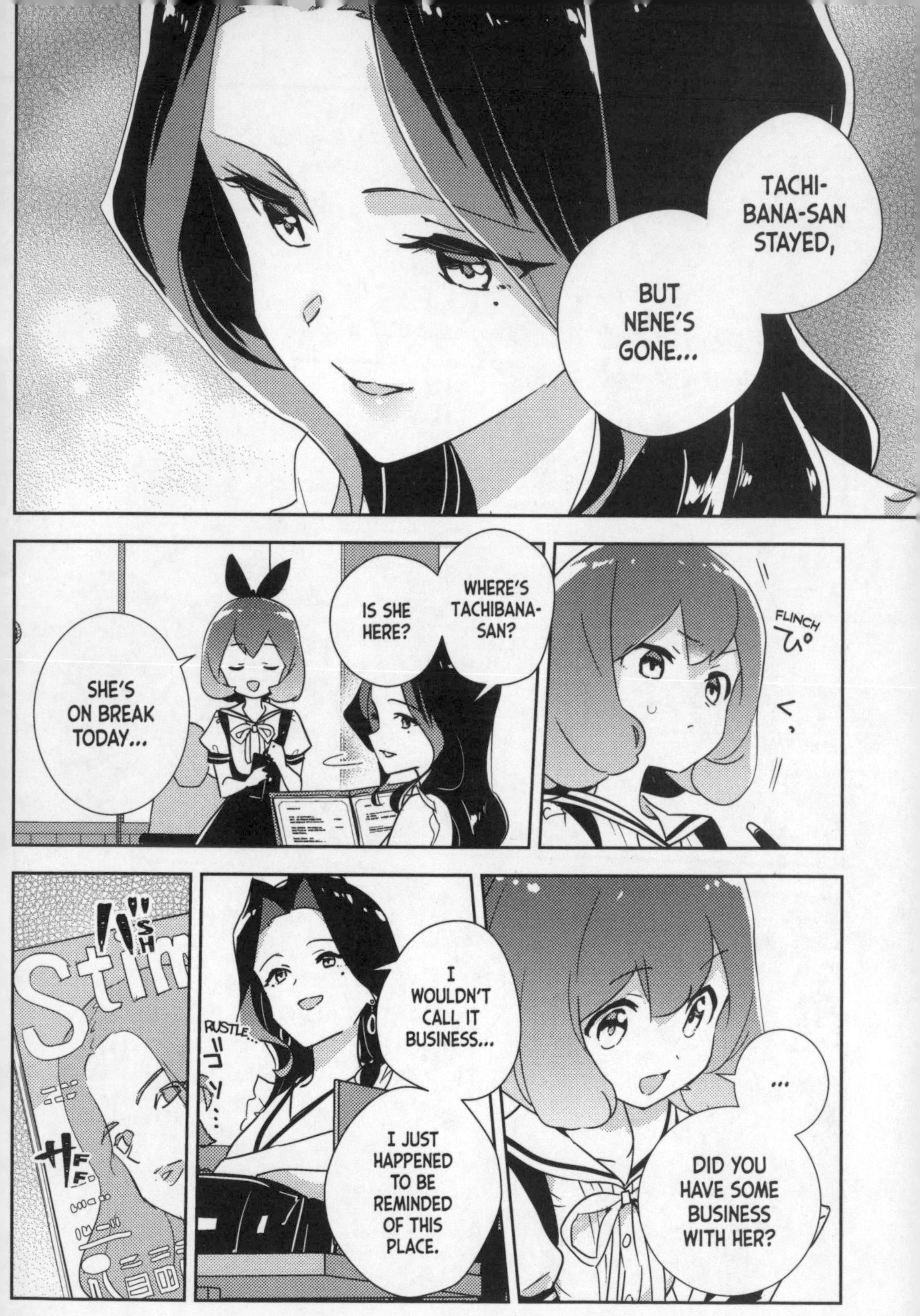
TACHI-BANA-SAN STAYED,
BUT NENE'S GONE...
FLINCH
WHERE'S TACHIBANA-SAN?
IS SHE HERE?
SHE'S ON BREAK TODAY...
...
DID YOU HAVE SOME BUSINESS WITH HER?
I WOULDN'T CALL IT BUSINESS...
I JUST HAPPENED TO BE REMINDED OF THIS PLACE.
RUSTLE...
SH
Stim
HFF

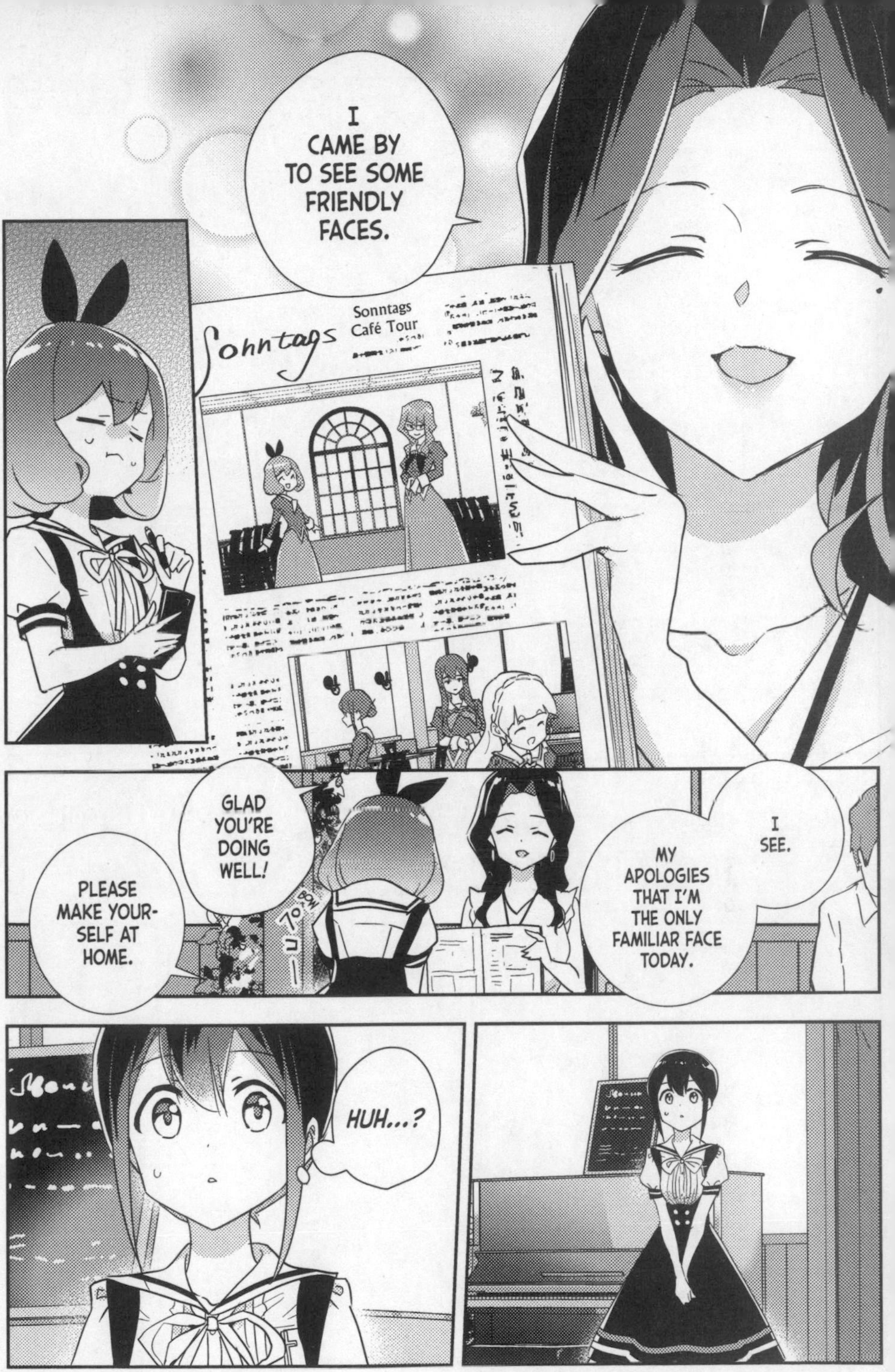
I CAME BY TO SEE SOME FRIENDLY FACES.
Sonntags
Café Tour
Sonntags
I SEE.
MY APOLOGIES THAT I'M THE ONLY FAMILIAR FACE TODAY.
BOW
GLAD YOU'RE DOING WELL!
PLEASE MAKE YOUR-SELF AT HOME.
HUH...?

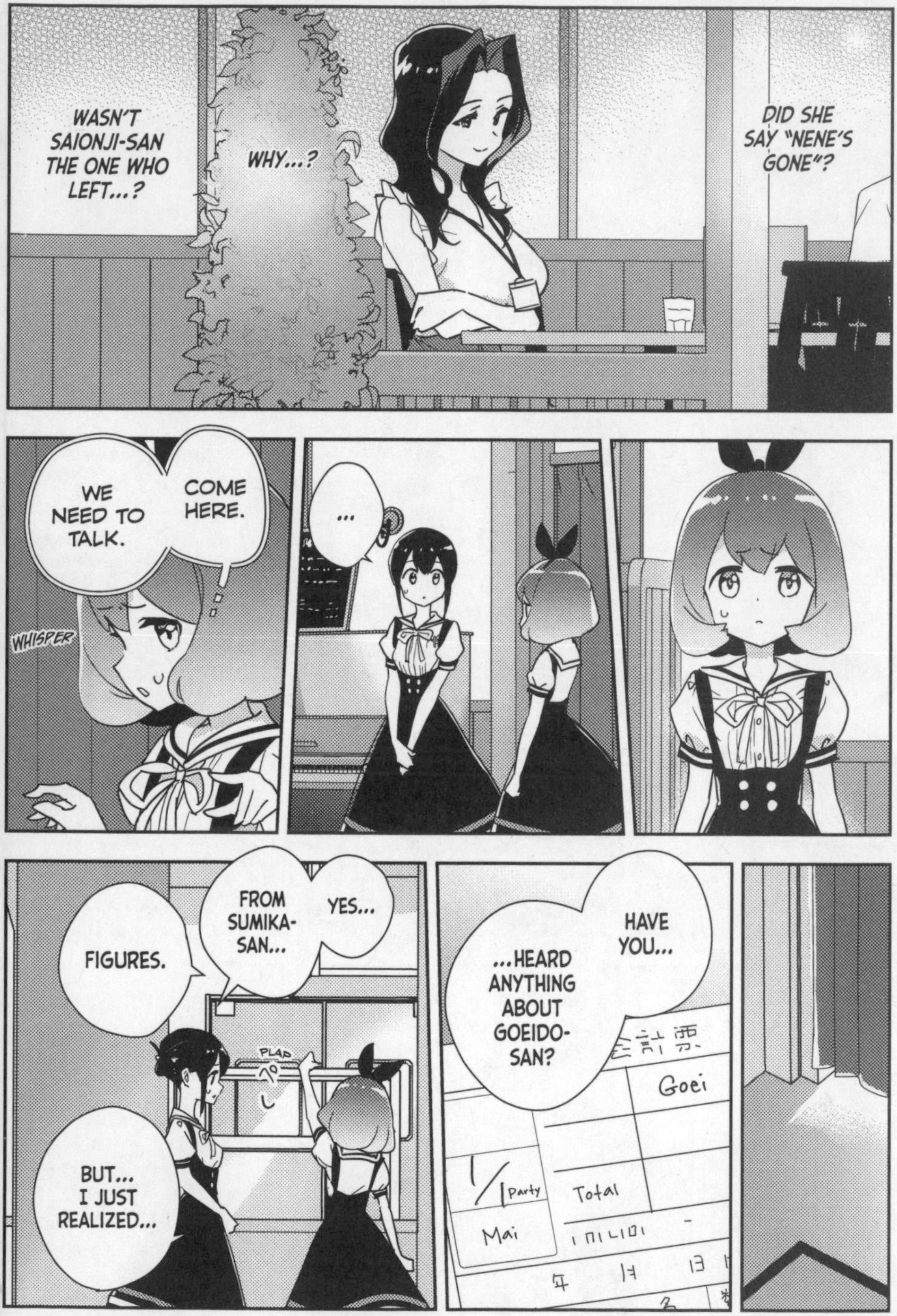
DID SHE SAY "NENE'S GONE"?
WHY...?
WASN'T SAIONJI-SAN THE ONE WHO LEFT...?
...
COME HERE.
WE NEED TO TALK.
WHISPER
HAVE YOU...
...HEARD ANYTHING ABOUT GOEIDO-SAN?
会計票
Goei
1/1 Party
Total
Mai
YES...
FROM SUMIKA-SAN...
FIGURES.
PLAP
ぺし
BUT... I JUST REALIZED...

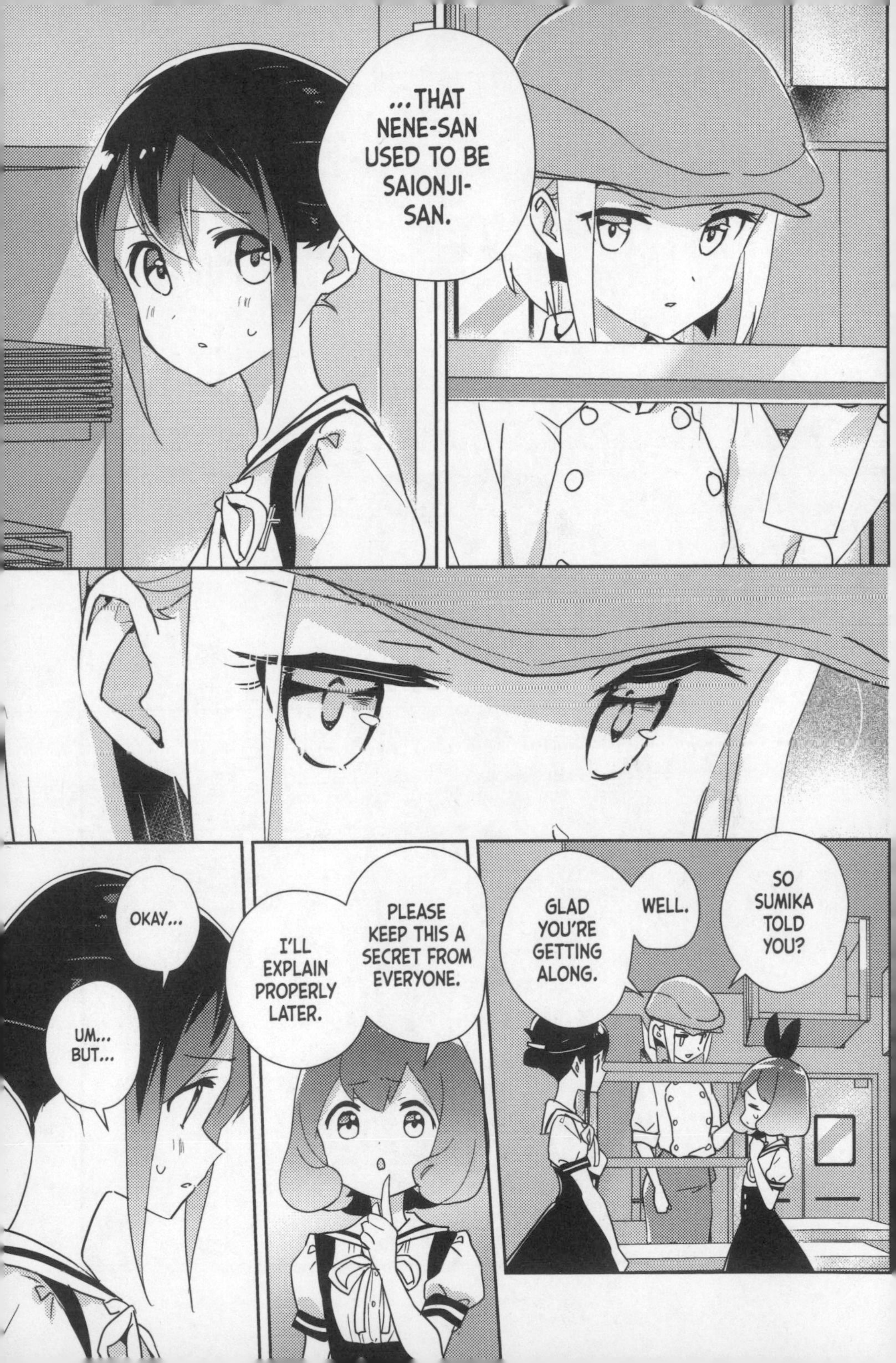
...THAT NENE-SAN USED TO BE SAIONJI-SAN.
SO SUMIKA TOLD YOU?
WELL.
GLAD YOU'RE GETTING ALONG.
PLEASE KEEP THIS A SECRET FROM EVERYONE.
I'LL EXPLAIN PROPERLY LATER.
OKAY...
UM... BUT...

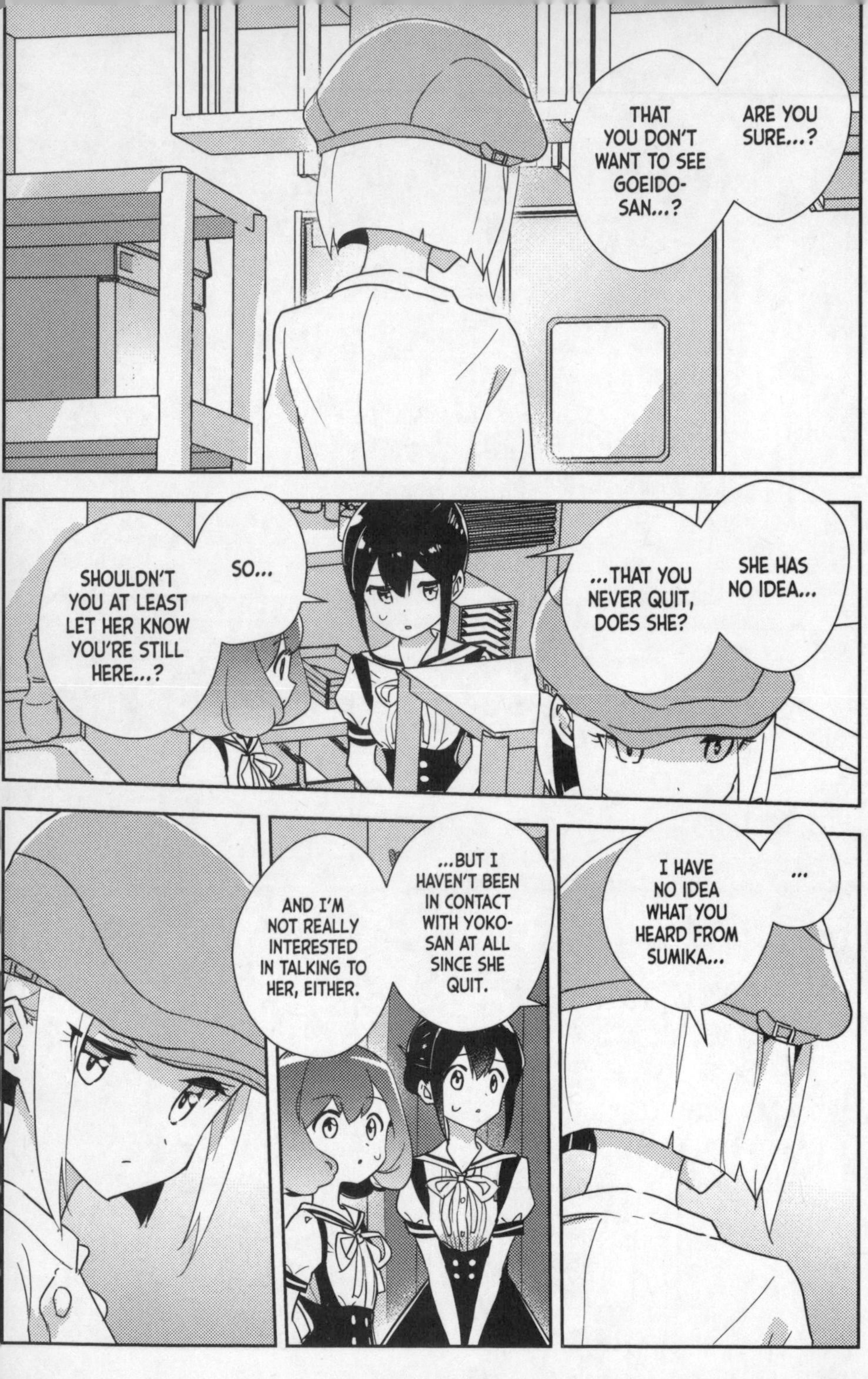
ARE YOU SURE...?
THAT YOU DON'T WANT TO SEE GOEIDO-SAN...?
SHE HAS NO IDEA...
...THAT YOU NEVER QUIT, DOES SHE?
SO...
SHOULDN'T YOU AT LEAST LET HER KNOW YOU'RE STILL HERE...?
...
I HAVE NO IDEA WHAT YOU HEARD FROM SUMIKA...
...BUT I HAVEN'T BEEN IN CONTACT WITH YOKO-SAN AT ALL SINCE SHE QUIT.
AND I'M NOT REALLY INTERESTED IN TALKING TO HER, EITHER.

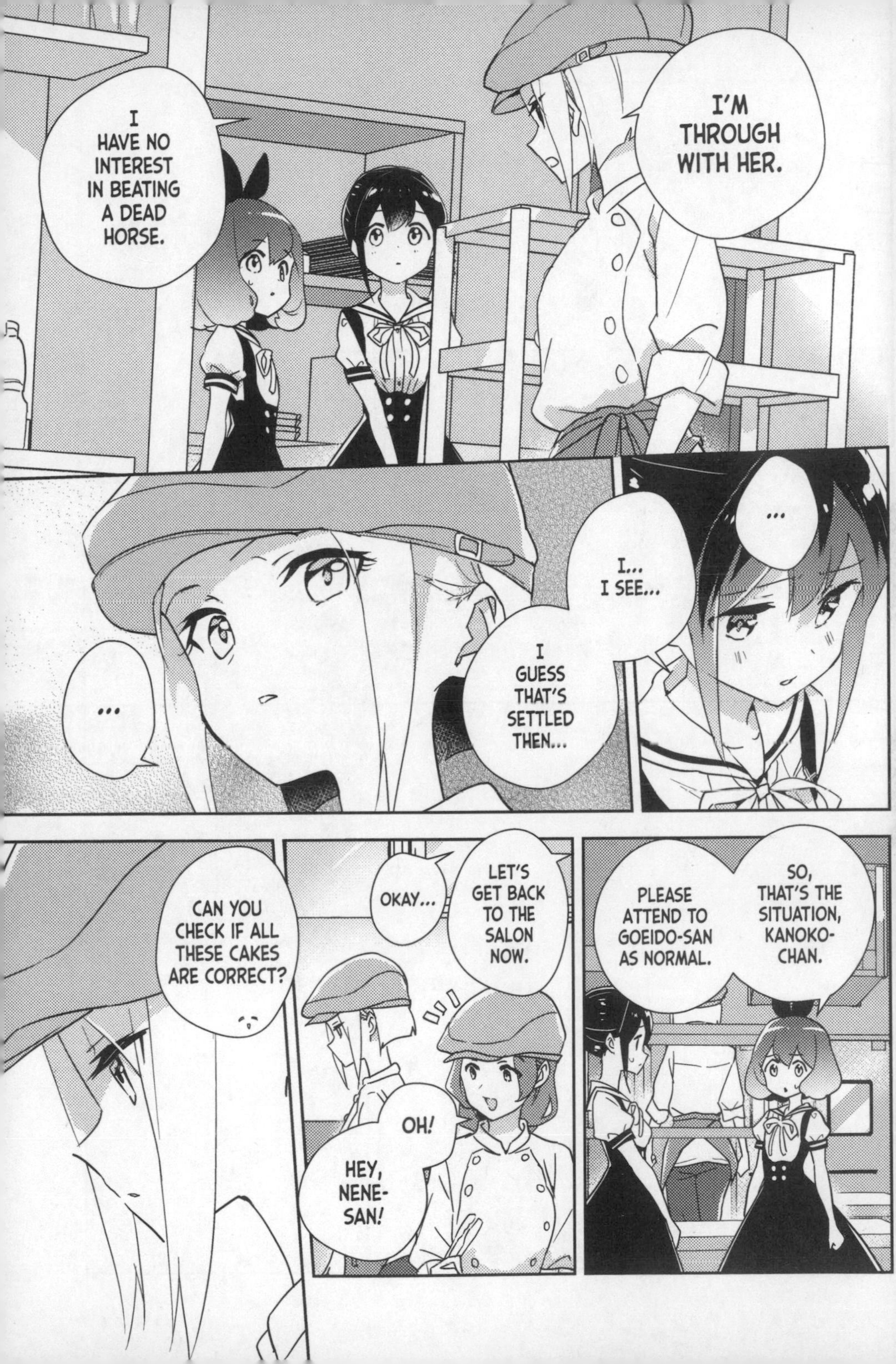
I'M THROUGH WITH HER.
I HAVE NO INTEREST IN BEATING A DEAD HORSE.
...
I... I SEE...
I GUESS THAT'S SETTLED THEN...
...
SO, THAT'S THE SITUATION, KANOKO-CHAN.
PLEASE ATTEND TO GOEIDO-SAN AS NORMAL.
LET'S GET BACK TO THE SALON NOW.
OKAY...
OH!
HEY, NENE-SAN!
CAN YOU CHECK IF ALL THESE CAKES ARE CORRECT?

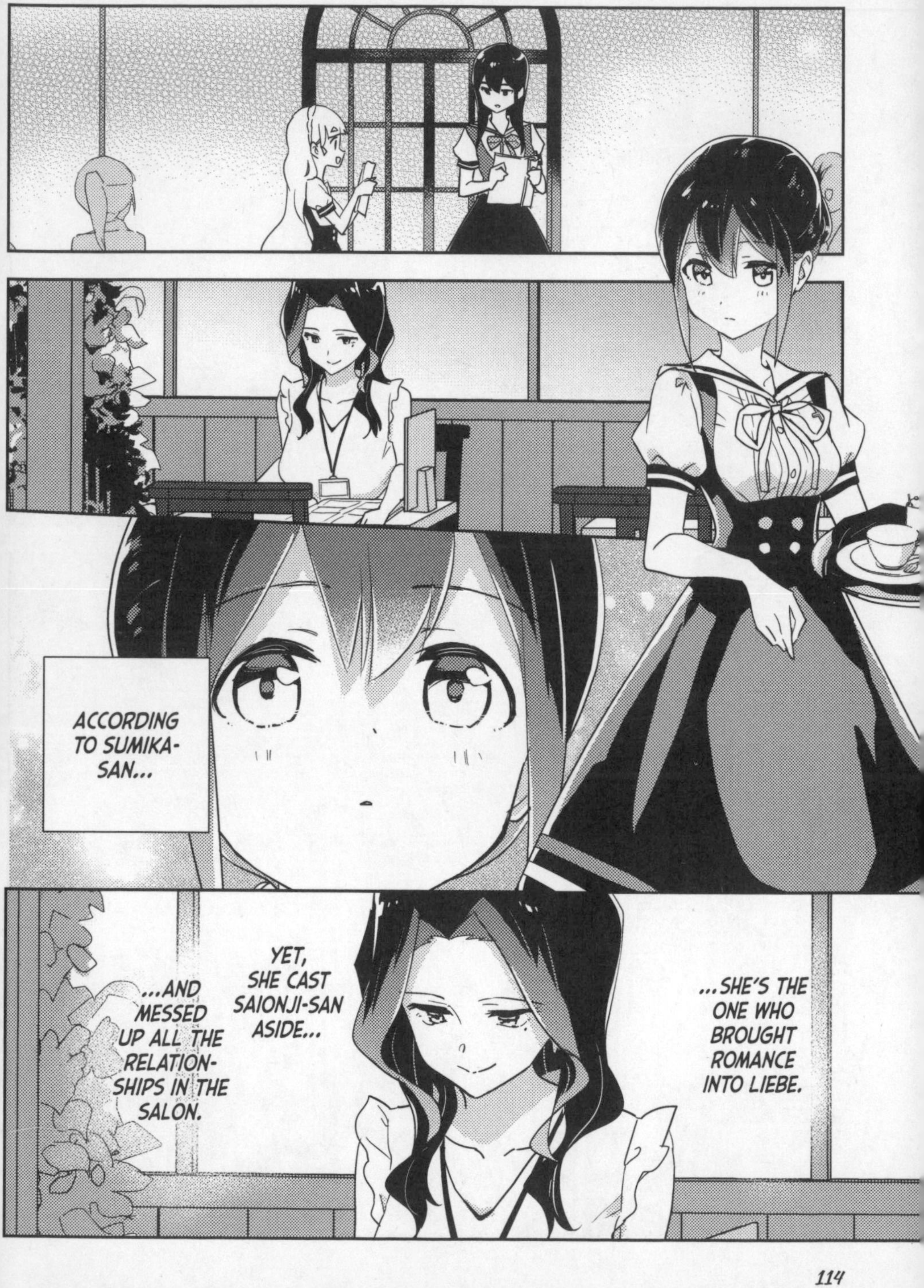
ACCORDING TO SUMIKA-SAN...
...SHE'S THE ONE WHO BROUGHT ROMANCE INTO LIEBE.
YET, SHE CAST SAIONJI-SAN ASIDE...
...AND MESSED UP ALL THE RELATION-SHIPS IN THE SALON.

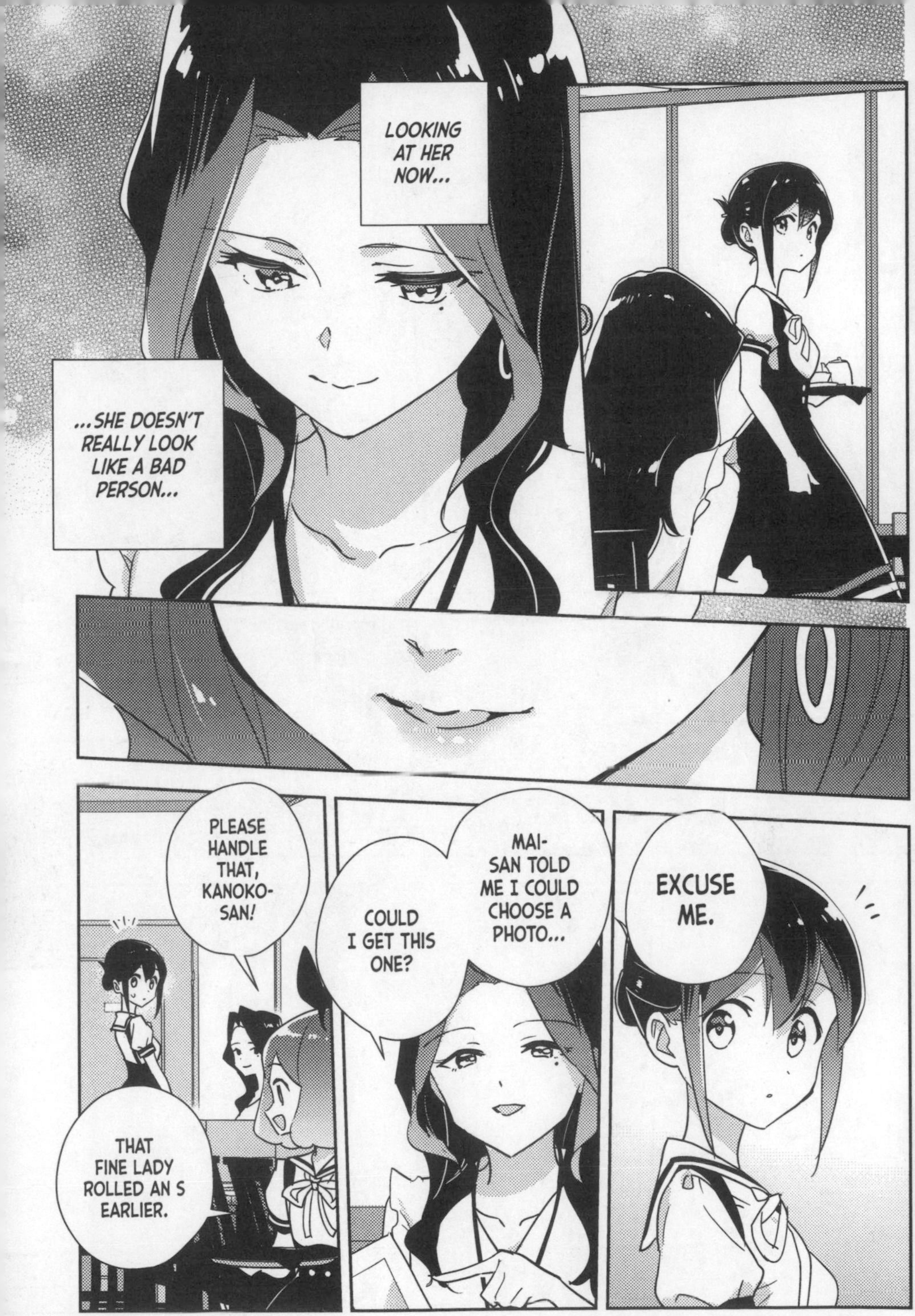
LOOKING AT HER NOW...
...SHE DOESN'T REALLY LOOK LIKE A BAD PERSON...
EXCUSE ME.
MAI-SAN TOLD ME I COULD CHOOSE A PHOTO...
COULD I GET THIS ONE?
PLEASE HANDLE THAT, KANOKO-SAN!
THAT FINE LADY ROLLED AN S EARLIER.

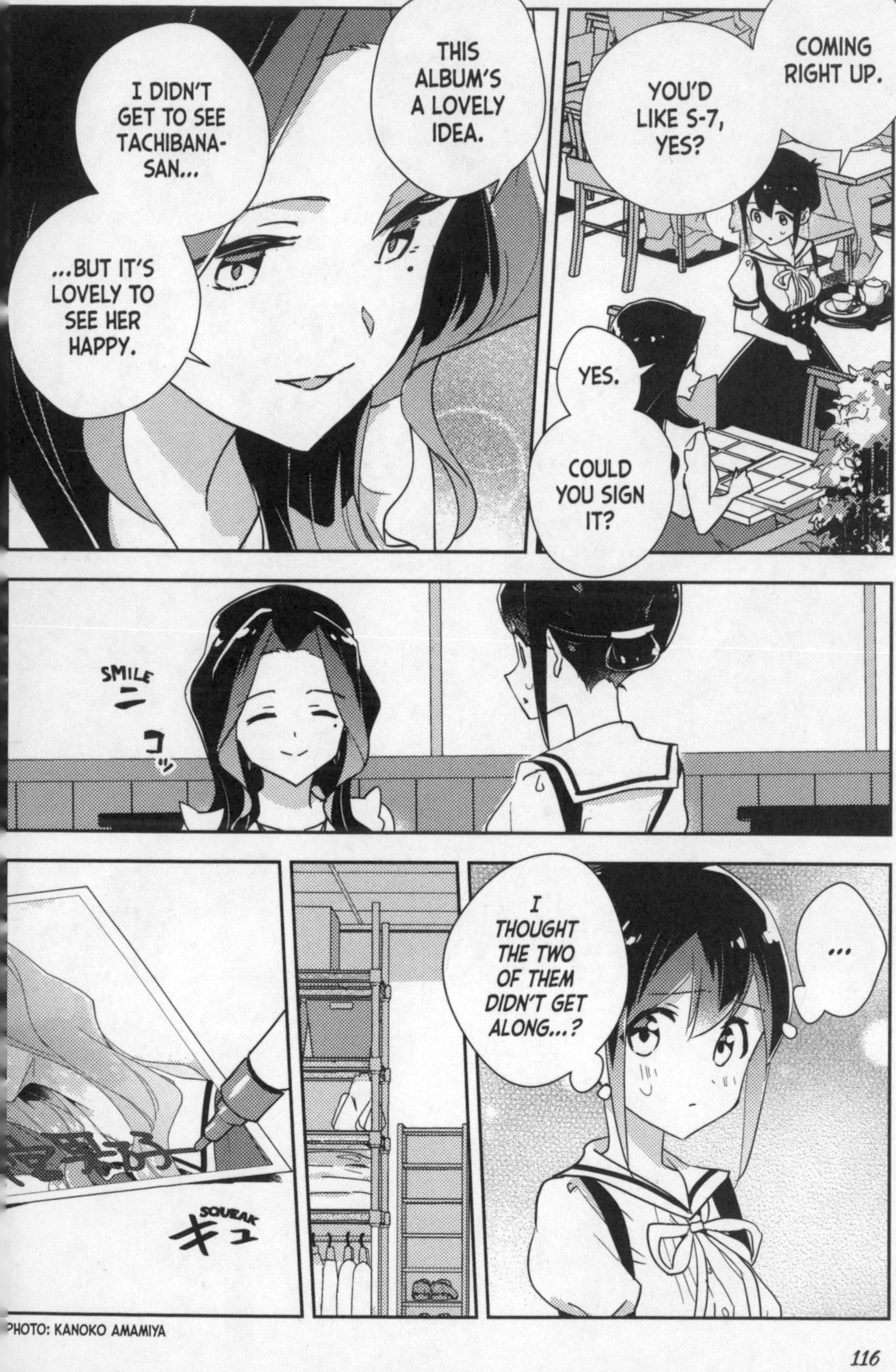
COMING RIGHT UP.
YOU'D LIKE S-7, YES?
YES.
COULD YOU SIGN IT?
THIS ALBUM'S A LOVELY IDEA.
I DIDN'T GET TO SEE TACHIBANA-SAN...
...BUT IT'S LOVELY TO SEE HER HAPPY.
SMILE
ニコッ
...
I THOUGHT THE TWO OF THEM DIDN'T GET ALONG...?
SQUEAK
キュ

PHOTO: KANOKO AMAMIYA

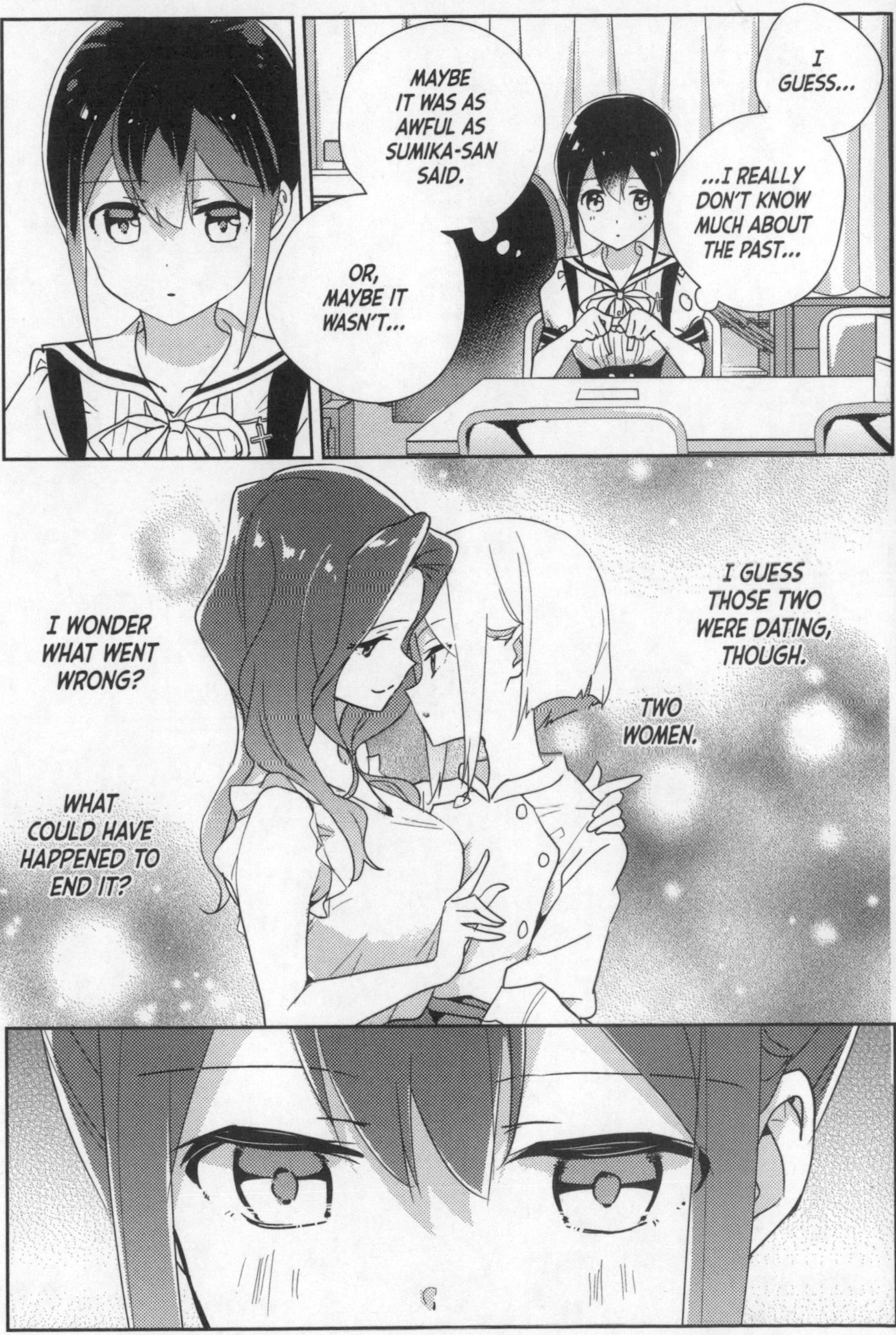
I GUESS...
...I REALLY DON'T KNOW MUCH ABOUT THE PAST...
MAYBE IT WAS AS AWFUL AS SUMIKA-SAN SAID.
OR, MAYBE IT WASN'T...
I GUESS THOSE TWO WERE DATING, THOUGH.
TWO WOMEN.
I WONDER WHAT WENT WRONG?
WHAT COULD HAVE HAPPENED TO END IT?

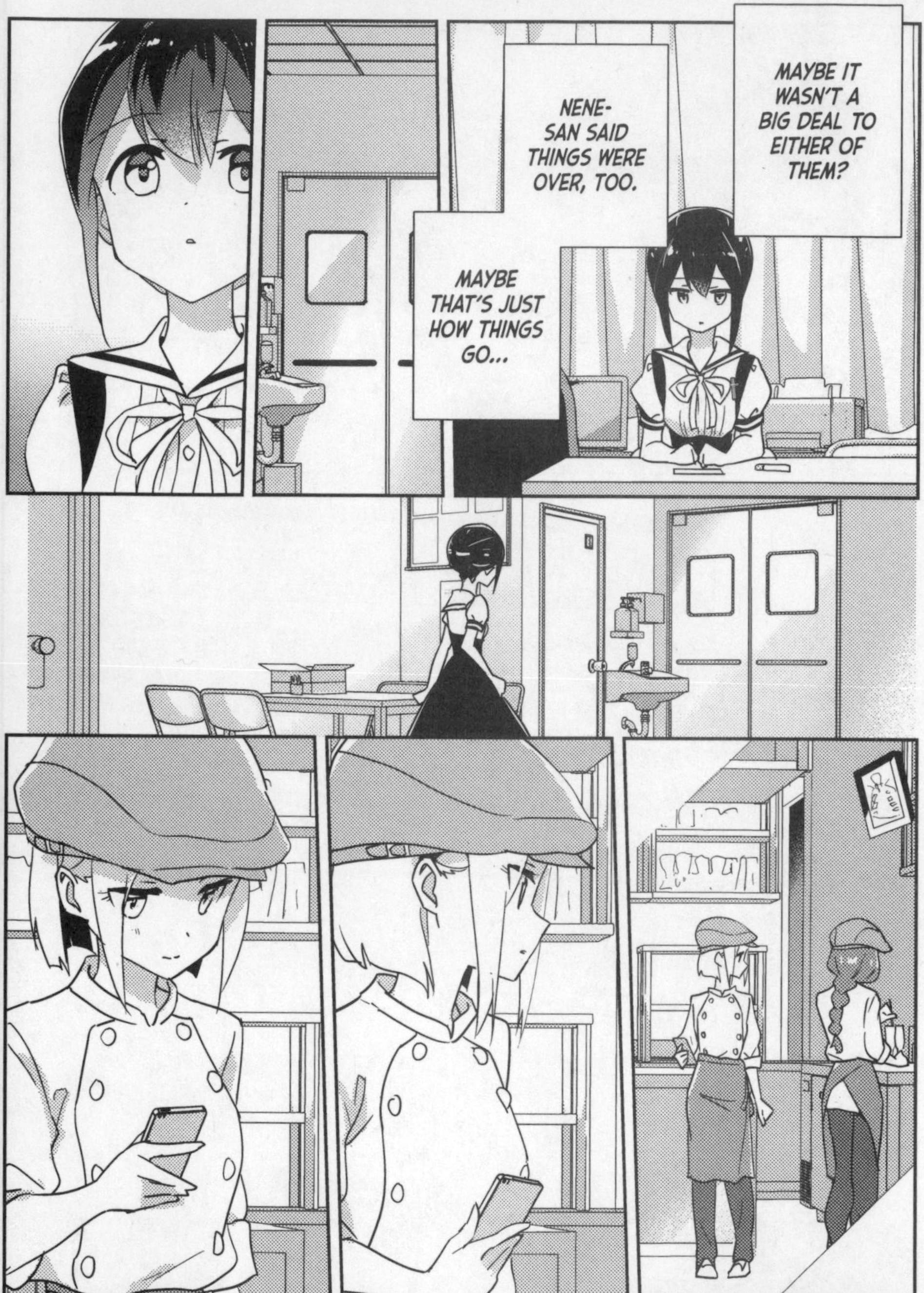
MAYBE IT WASN'T A BIG DEAL TO EITHER OF THEM?
NENE-SAN SAID THINGS WERE OVER, TOO.
MAYBE THAT'S JUST HOW THINGS GO...

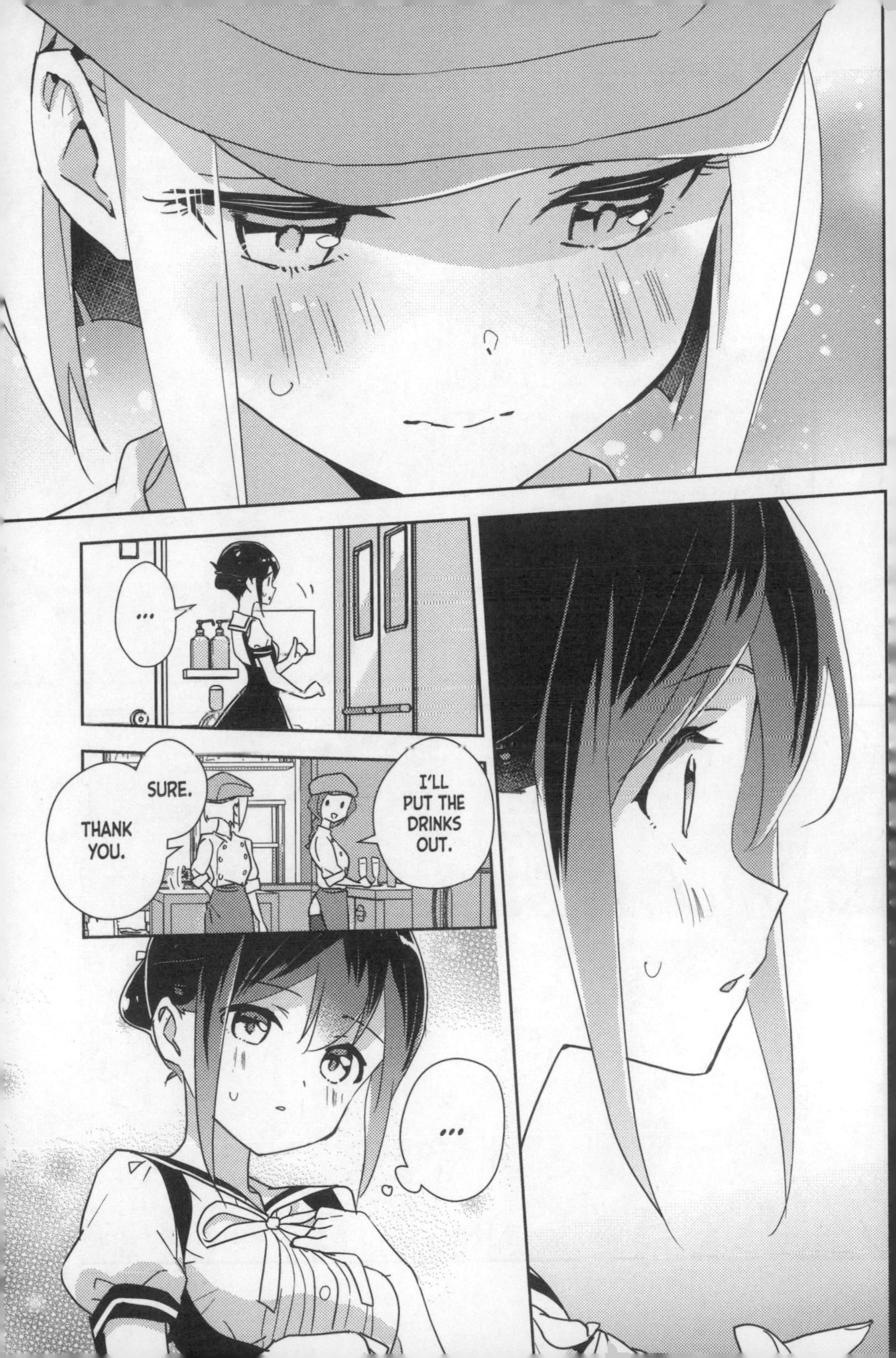
...
I'LL PUT THE DRINKS OUT.
SURE.
THANK YOU.
...

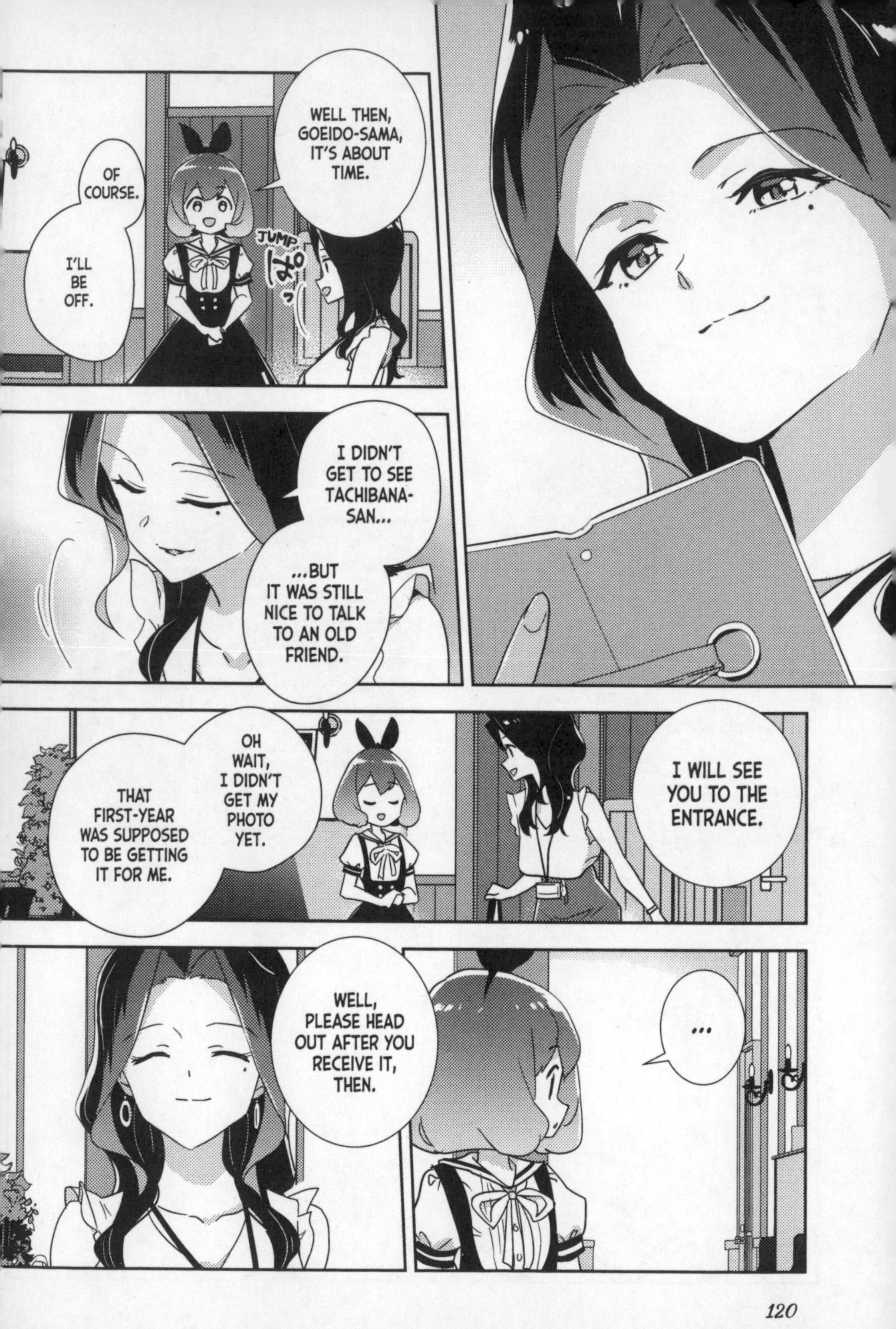
WELL THEN, GOEIDO-SAMA, IT'S ABOUT TIME.
JUMP
ぱっ
OF COURSE.
I'LL BE OFF.
I DIDN'T GET TO SEE TACHIBANA-SAN...
...BUT IT WAS STILL NICE TO TALK TO AN OLD FRIEND.
I WILL SEE YOU TO THE ENTRANCE.
OH WAIT, I DIDN'T GET MY PHOTO YET.
THAT FIRST-YEAR WAS SUPPOSED TO BE GETTING IT FOR ME.
...
WELL, PLEASE HEAD OUT AFTER YOU RECEIVE IT, THEN.

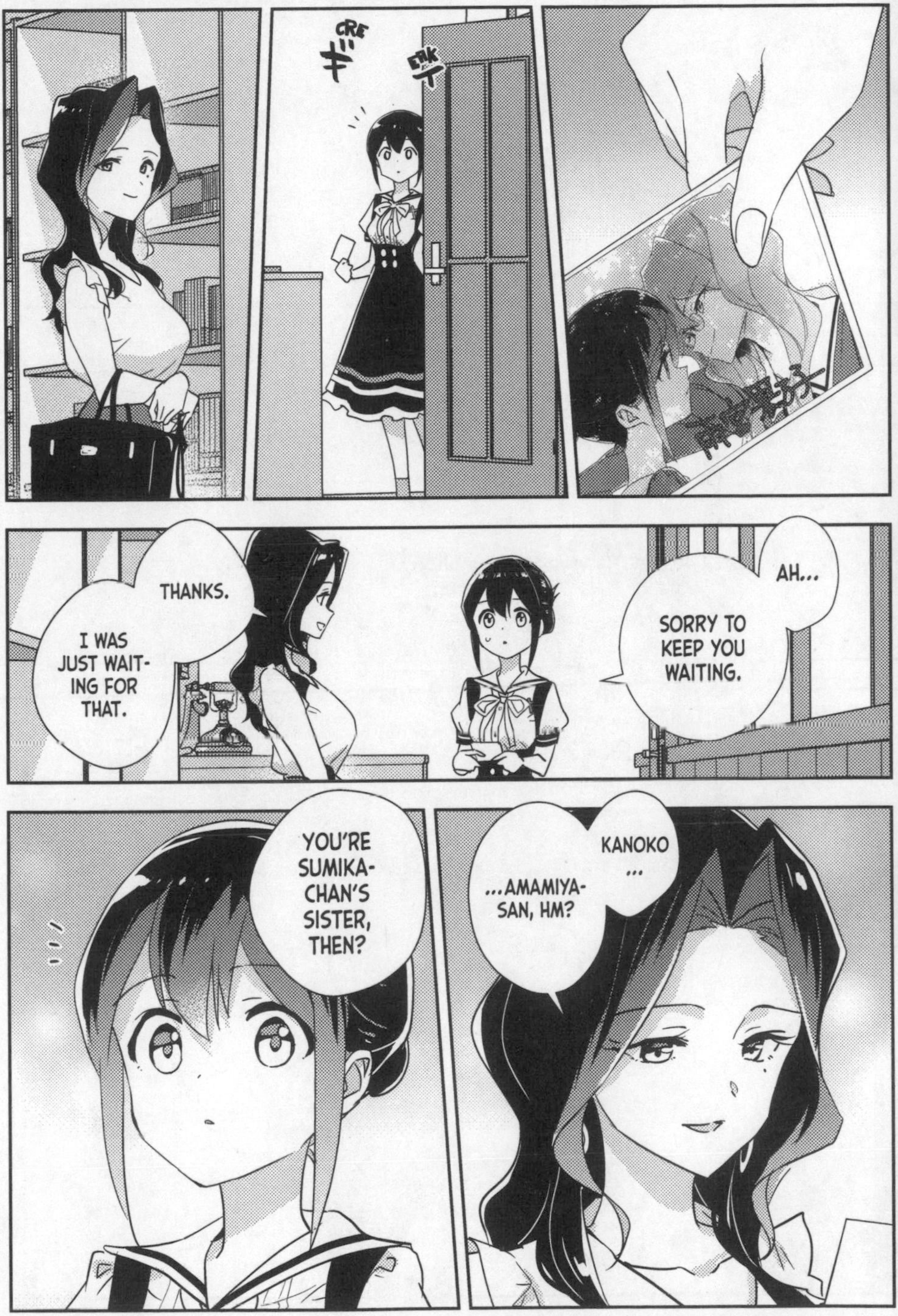
CRE
EAK
AH...
SORRY TO KEEP YOU WAITING.
THANKS.
I WAS JUST WAITING FOR THAT.
KANOKO ...
...AMAMIYA-SAN, HM?
YOU'RE SUMIKA-CHAN'S SISTER, THEN?

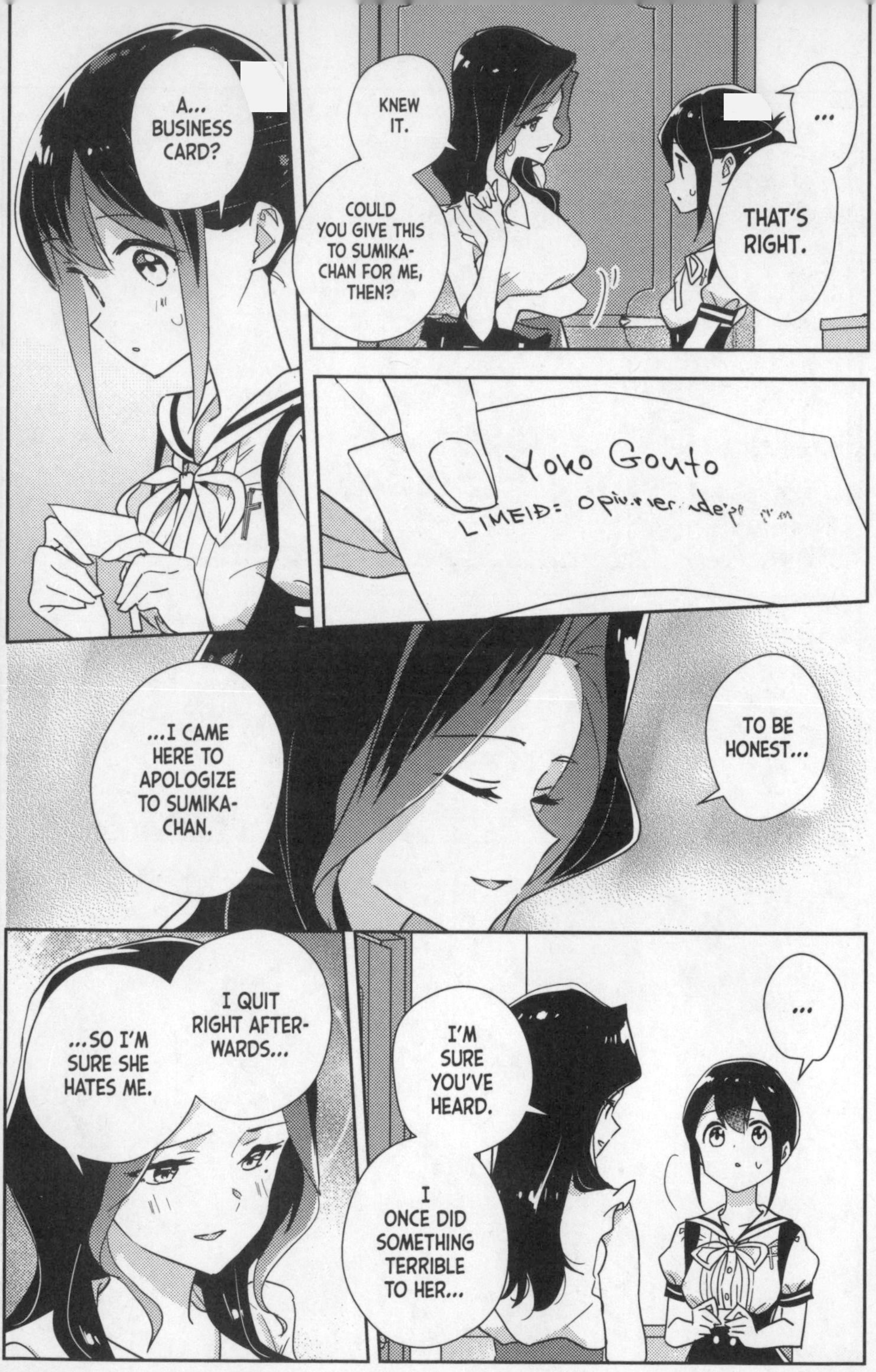
...
THAT'S RIGHT.
KNEW IT.
COULD YOU GIVE THIS TO SUMIKA-CHAN FOR ME, THEN?
Yoko Gouto
LIMEID:
A... BUSINESS CARD?
TO BE HONEST...
...I CAME HERE TO APOLOGIZE TO SUMIKA-CHAN.
...
I'M SURE YOU'VE HEARD.
I ONCE DID SOMETHING TERRIBLE TO HER...
I QUIT RIGHT AFTERWARDS...
...SO I'M SURE SHE HATES ME.

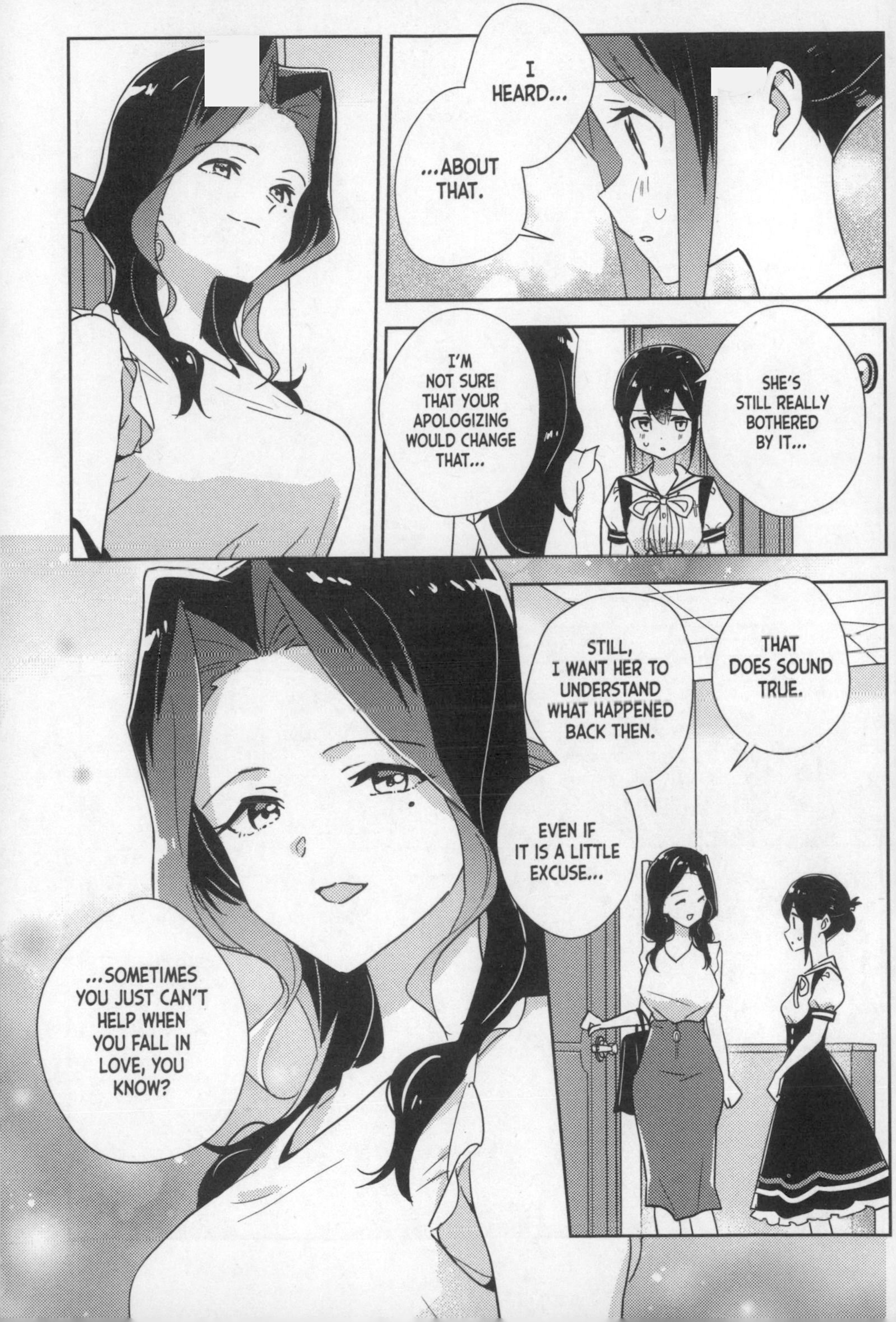
I HEARD...
...ABOUT THAT.
SHE'S STILL REALLY BOTHERED BY IT...
I'M NOT SURE THAT YOUR APOLOGIZING WOULD CHANGE THAT...
THAT DOES SOUND TRUE.
STILL, I WANT HER TO UNDERSTAND WHAT HAPPENED BACK THEN.
EVEN IF IT IS A LITTLE EXCUSE...
...SOMETIMES YOU JUST CAN'T HELP WHEN YOU FALL IN LOVE, YOU KNOW?

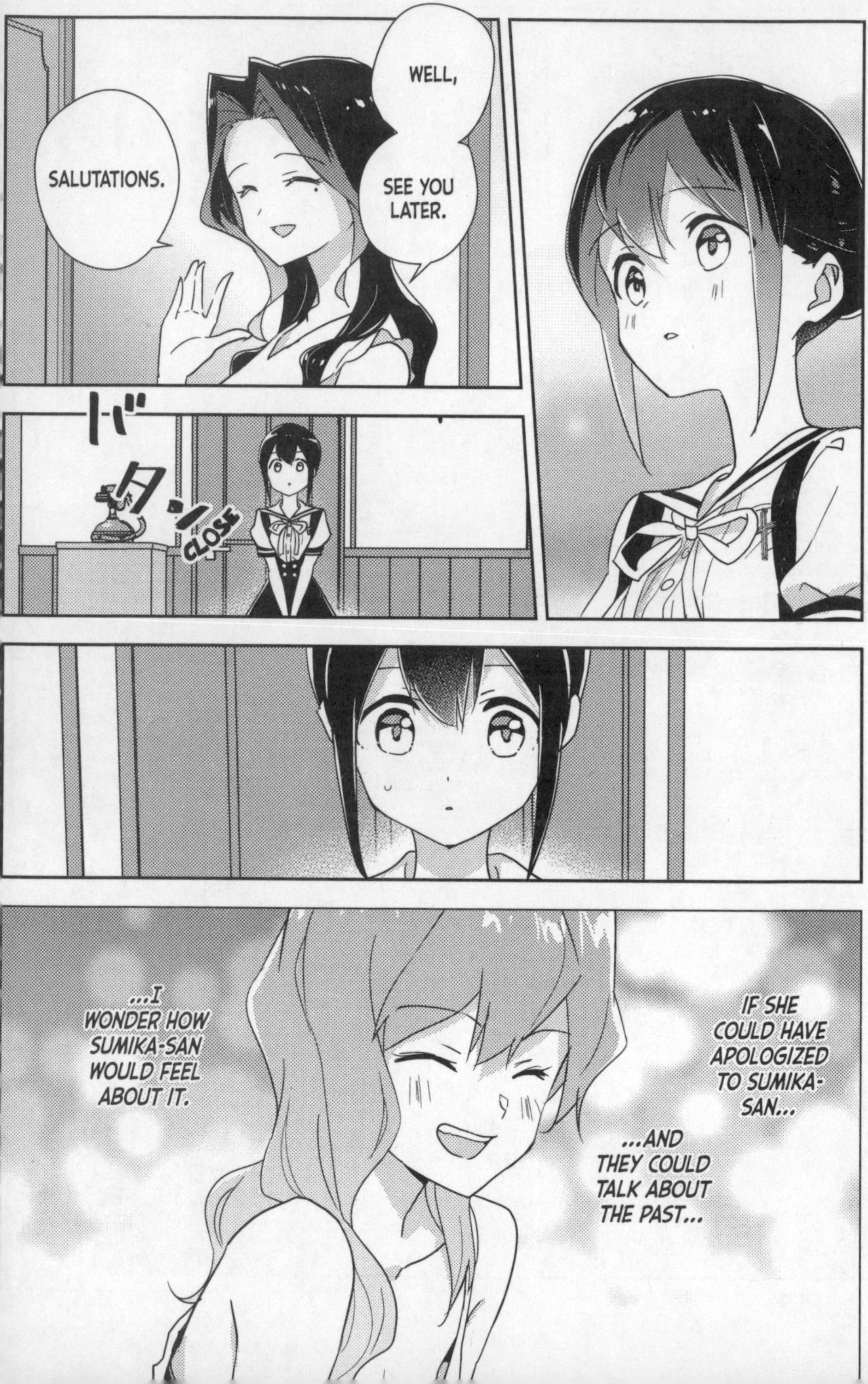
WELL,
SEE YOU LATER.
SALUTATIONS.
バタン
CLOSE
IF SHE COULD HAVE APOLOGIZED TO SUMIKA-SAN...
...AND THEY COULD TALK ABOUT THE PAST...
...I WONDER HOW SUMIKA-SAN WOULD FEEL ABOUT IT.

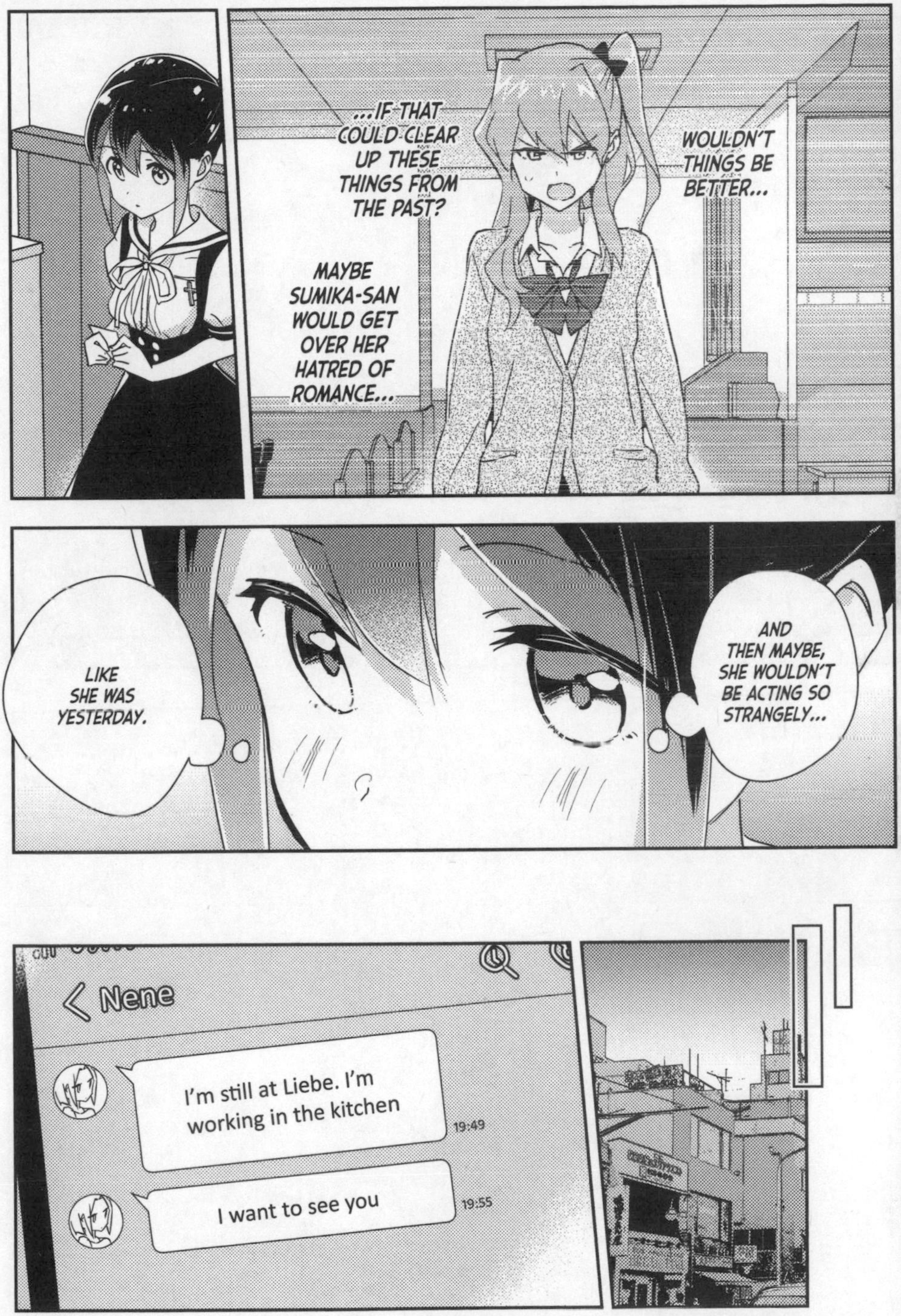
WOULDN'T THINGS BE BETTER...
...IF THAT COULD CLEAR UP THESE THINGS FROM THE PAST?
MAYBE SUMIKA-SAN WOULD GET OVER HER HATRED OF ROMANCE...
AND THEN MAYBE, SHE WOULDN'T BE ACTING SO STRANGELY...
LIKE SHE WAS YESTERDAY.
Nene
I'm still at Liebe. I'm working in the kitchen
19:49
I want to see you
19:55

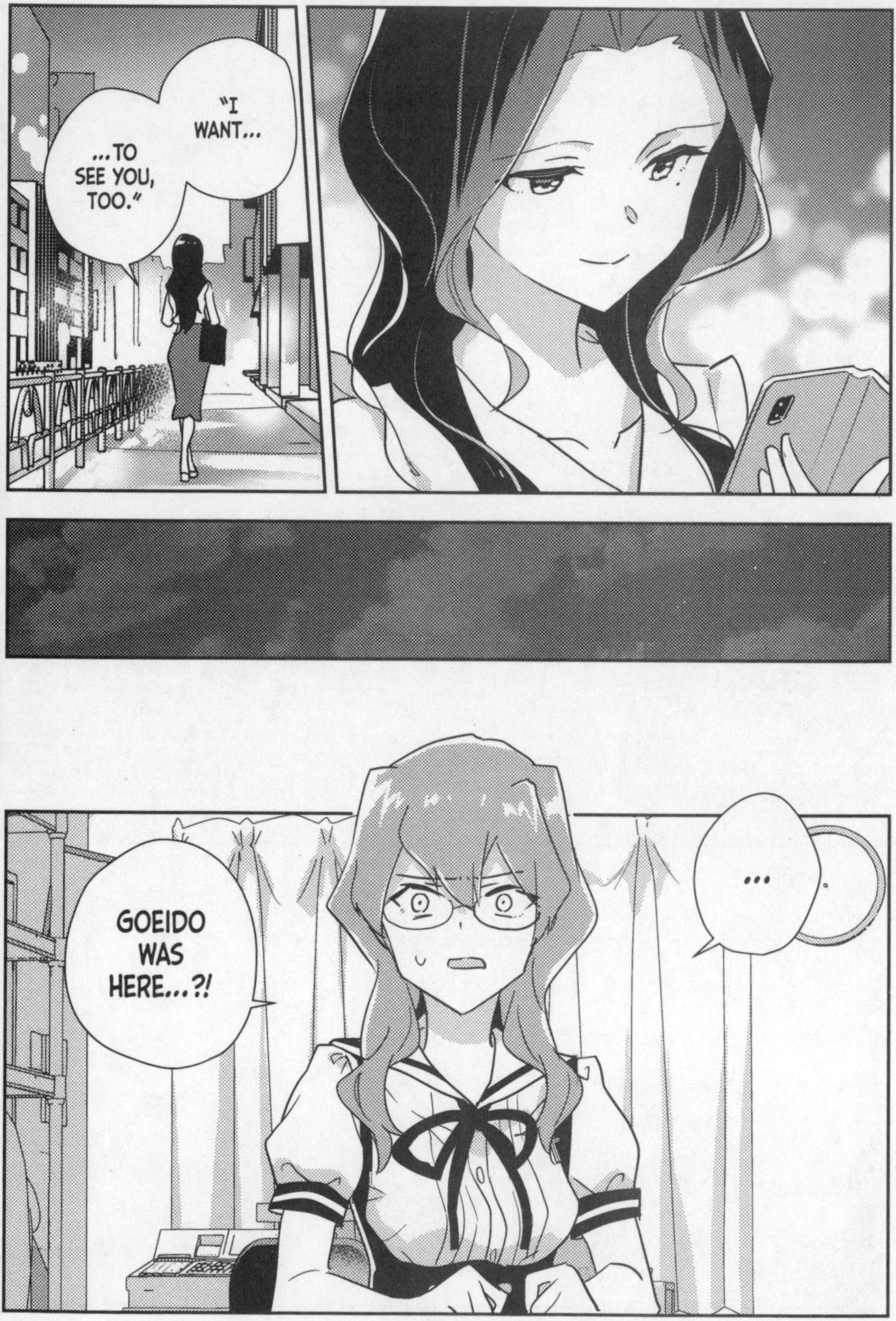
“I WANT...
...TO SEE YOU, TOO.”
...
GOEIDO WAS HERE...?!

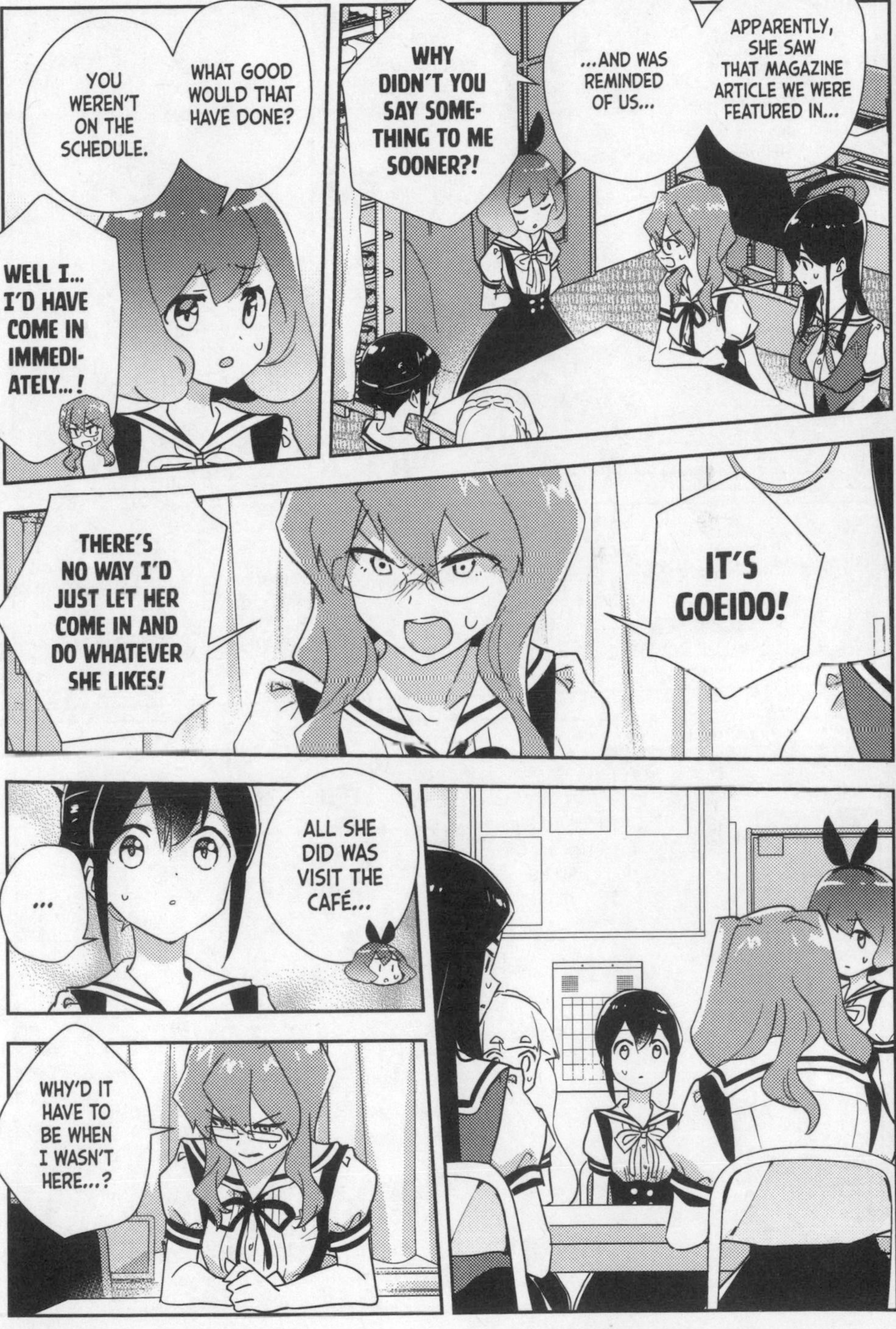
APPARENTLY, SHE SAW THAT MAGAZINE ARTICLE WE WERE FEATURED IN...
...AND WAS REMINDED OF US...
WHY DIDN'T YOU SAY SOME-THING TO ME SOONER?!
WHAT GOOD WOULD THAT HAVE DONE?
YOU WEREN'T ON THE SCHEDULE.
WELL I... I'D HAVE COME IN IMMEDI-ATELY...!
IT'S GOEIDO!
THERE'S NO WAY I'D JUST LET HER COME IN AND DO WHATEVER SHE LIKES!
ALL SHE DID WAS VISIT THE CAFÉ...
...
WHY'D IT HAVE TO BE WHEN I WASN'T HERE...?

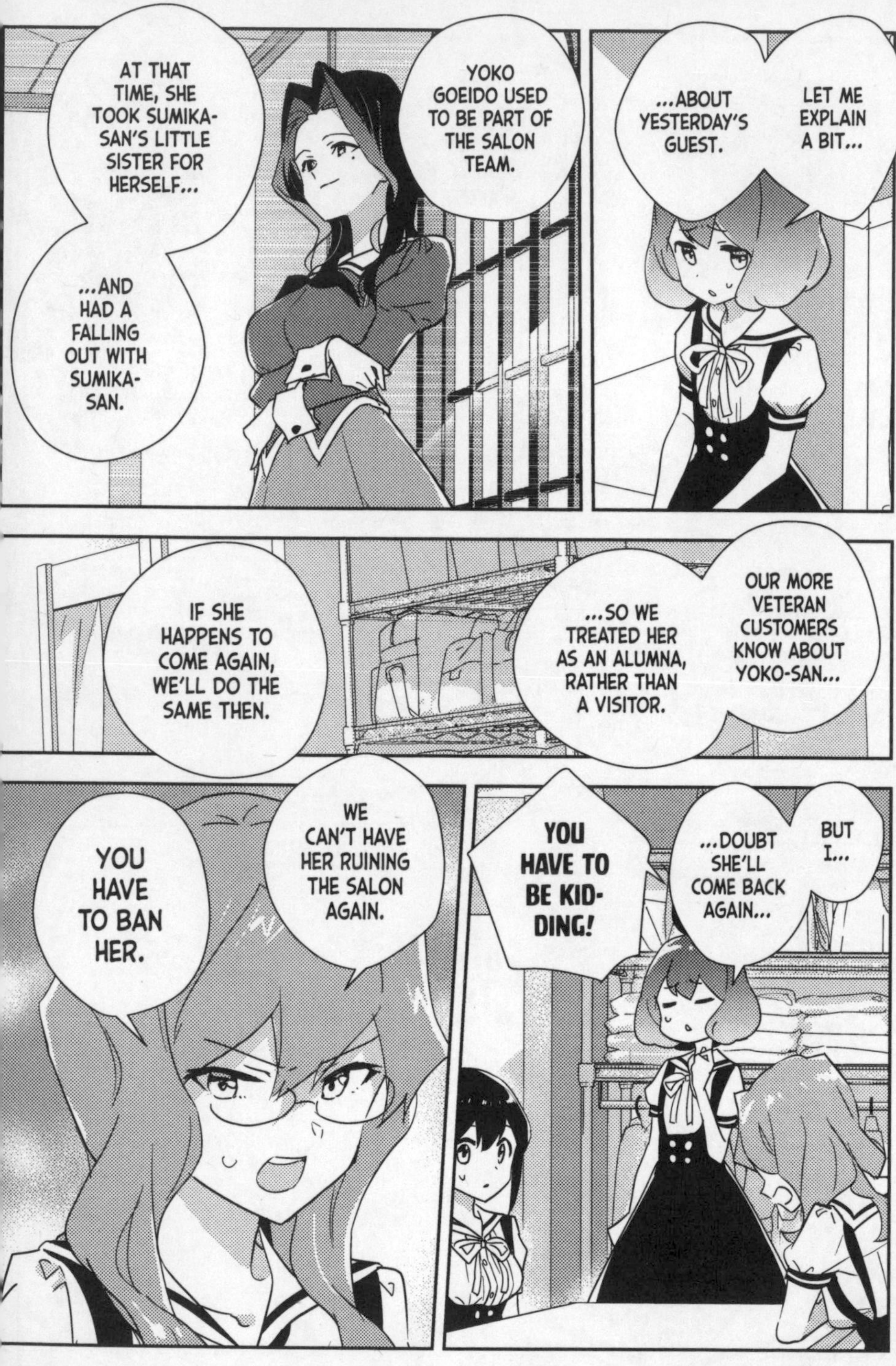
LET ME EXPLAIN A BIT...
...ABOUT YESTERDAY'S GUEST.
YOKO GOEIDO USED TO BE PART OF THE SALON TEAM.
AT THAT TIME, SHE TOOK SUMIKA-SAN'S LITTLE SISTER FOR HERSELF...
...AND HAD A FALLING OUT WITH SUMIKA-SAN.
OUR MORE VETERAN CUSTOMERS KNOW ABOUT YOKO-SAN...
...SO WE TREATED HER AS AN ALUMNA, RATHER THAN A VISITOR.
IF SHE HAPPENS TO COME AGAIN, WE'LL DO THE SAME THEN.
BUT I...
...DOUBT SHE'LL COME BACK AGAIN...
YOU HAVE TO BE KID-DING!
WE CAN'T HAVE HER RUINING THE SALON AGAIN.
YOU HAVE TO BAN HER.

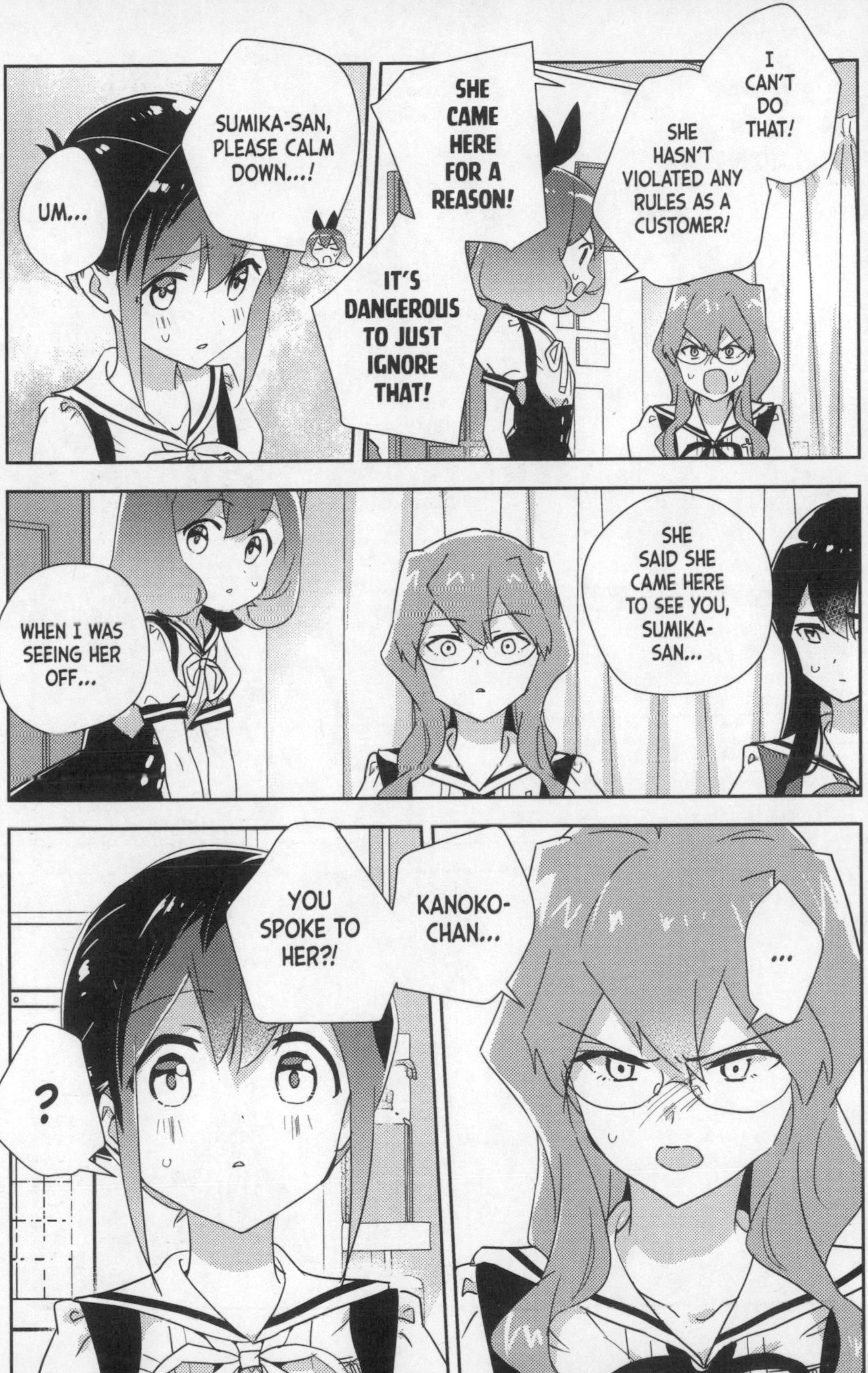
I CAN'T DO THAT!
SHE HASN'T VIOLATED ANY RULES AS A CUSTOMER!
SHE CAME HERE FOR A REASON!
IT'S DANGEROUS TO JUST IGNORE THAT!
SUMIKA-SAN, PLEASE CALM DOWN...!
UM...
SHE SAID SHE CAME HERE TO SEE YOU, SUMIKA-SAN...
WHEN I WAS SEEING HER OFF...
...
KANOKO-CHAN...
YOU SPOKE TO HER?!
?

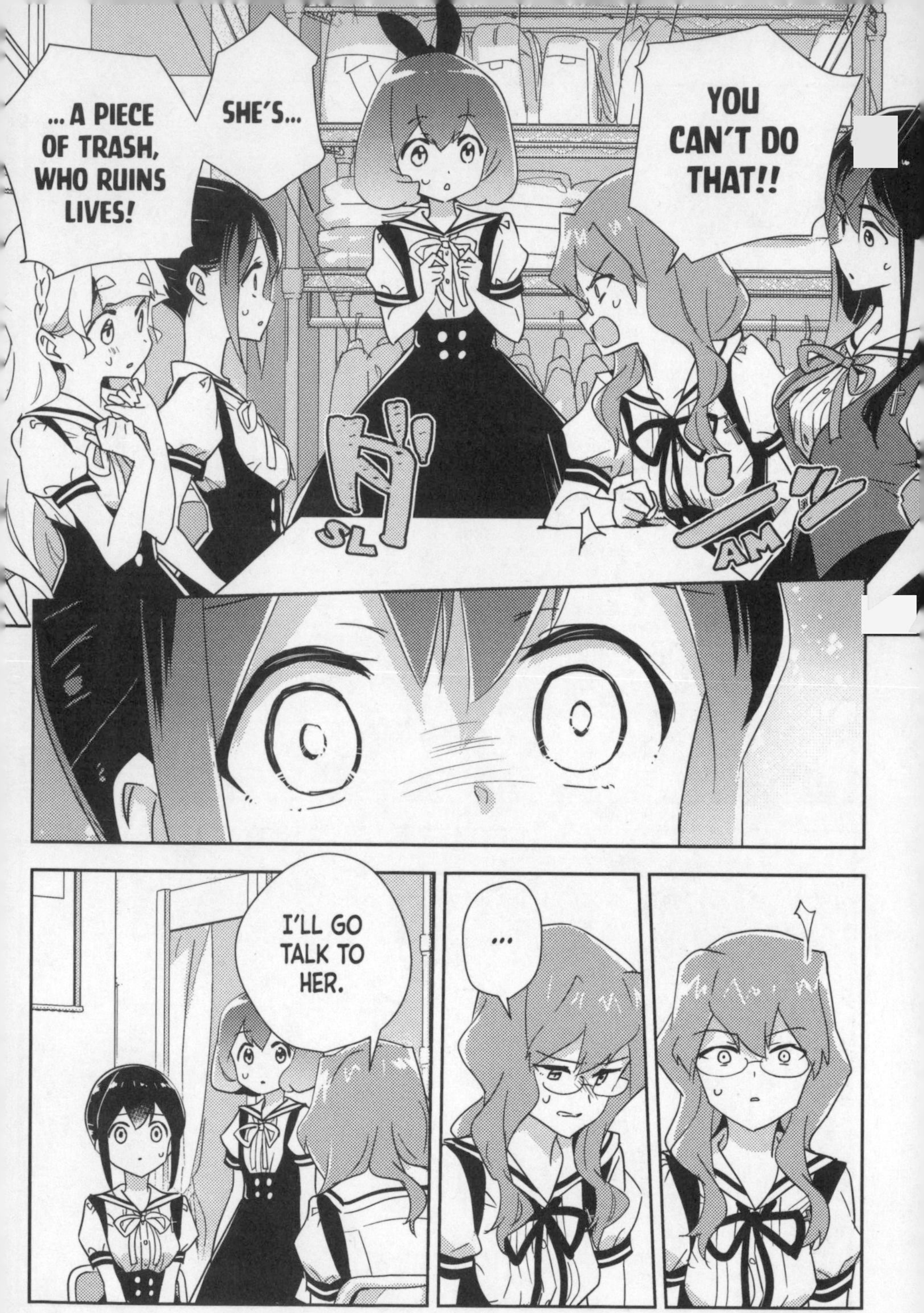
YOU CAN'T DO THAT!!
SHE'S...
...A PIECE OF TRASH, WHO RUINS LIVES!
SL
AM
...
I'LL GO TALK TO HER.

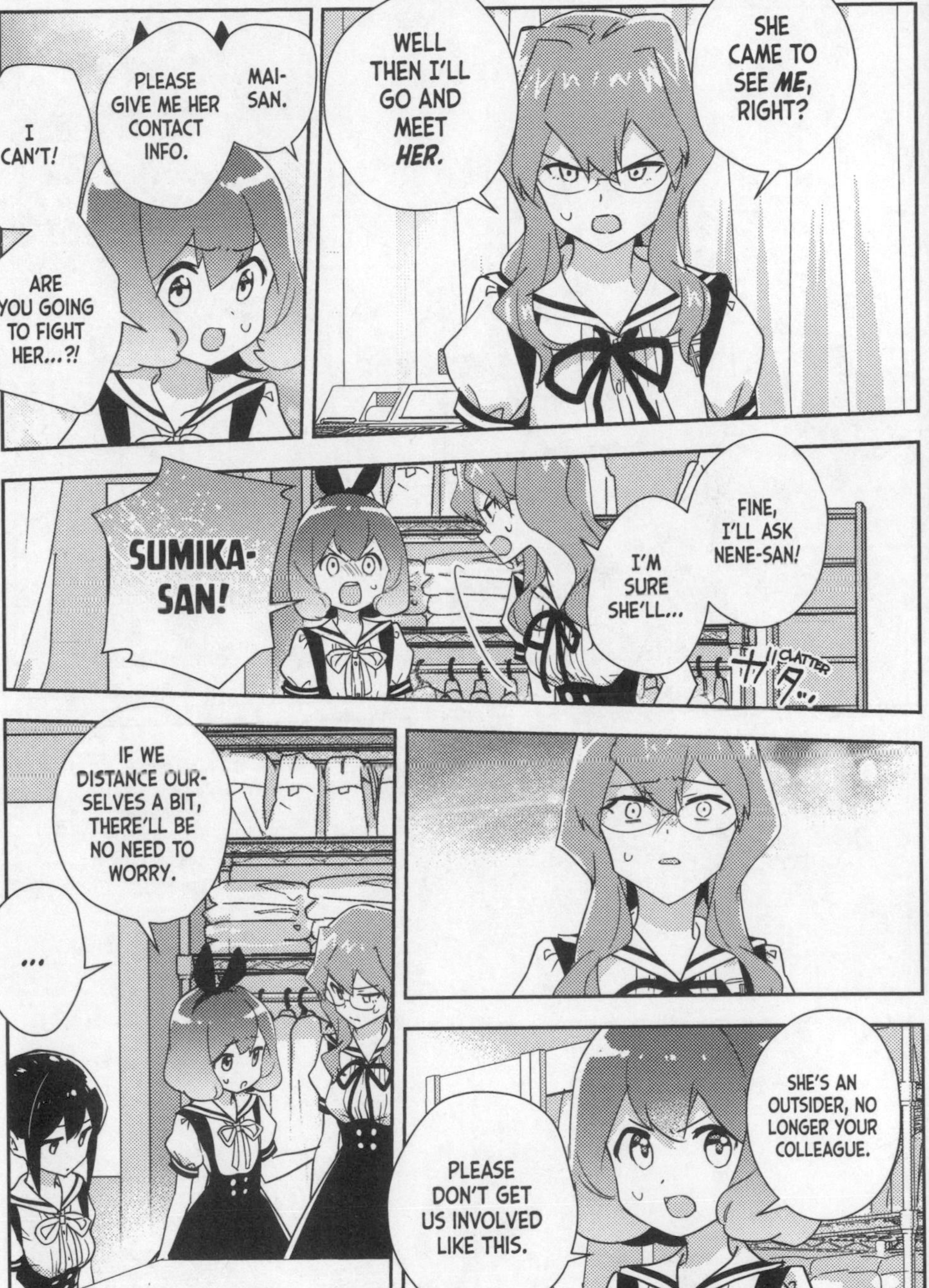
SHE CAME TO SEE *ME*, RIGHT?
WELL THEN I'LL GO AND MEET *HER.*
MAI-SAN.
PLEASE GIVE ME HER CONTACT INFO.
I CAN'T!
ARE YOU GOING TO FIGHT HER...?!
FINE, I'LL ASK NENE-SAN!
I'M SURE SHE'LL...
CLATTER
SUMIKA-SAN!
SHE'S AN OUTSIDER, NO LONGER YOUR COLLEAGUE.
PLEASE DON'T GET US INVOLVED LIKE THIS.
IF WE DISTANCE OURSELVES A BIT, THERE'LL BE NO NEED TO WORRY.
...

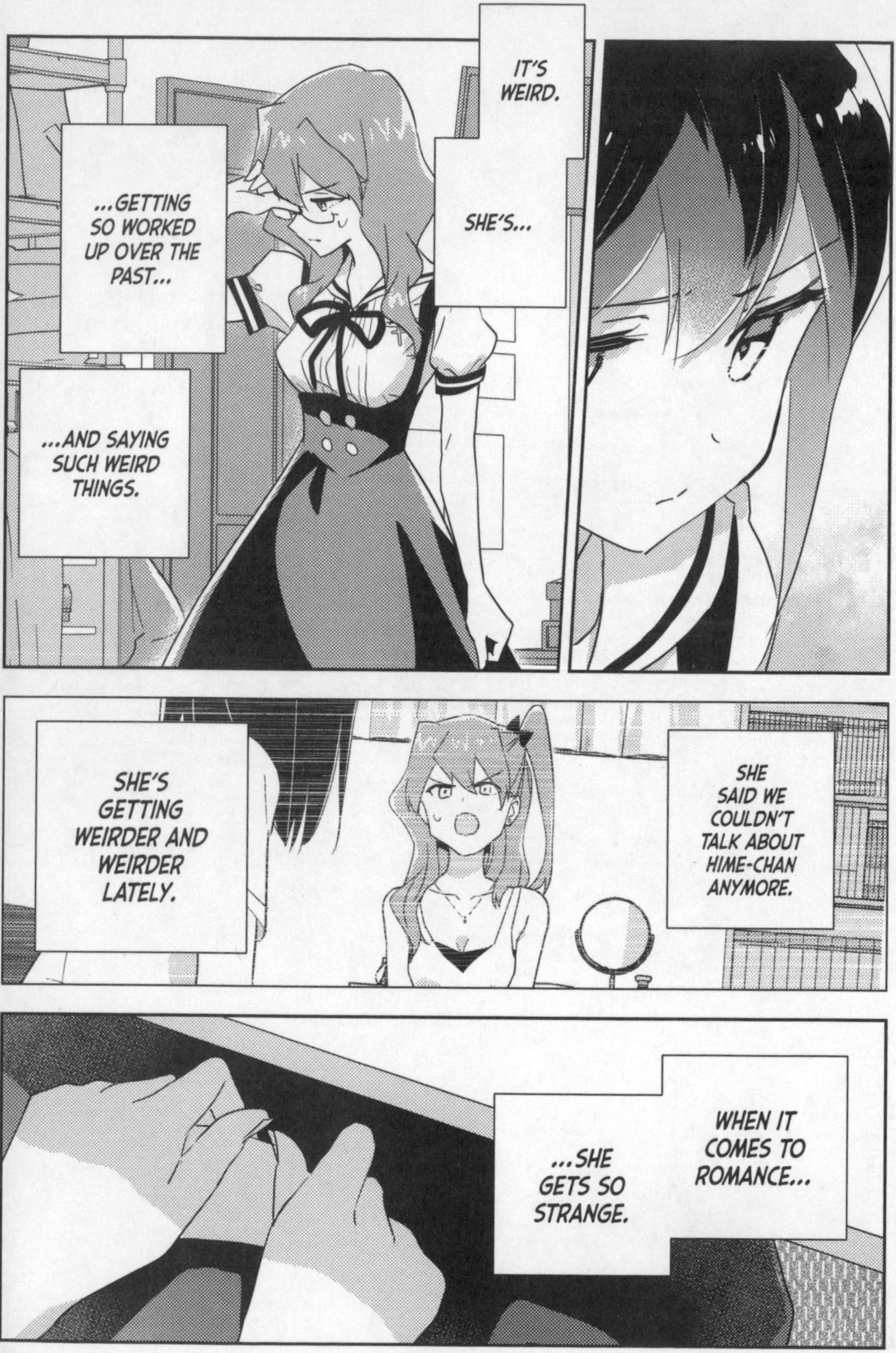
IT'S WEIRD.
SHE'S...
...GETTING SO WORKED UP OVER THE PAST...
...AND SAYING SUCH WEIRD THINGS.
SHE SAID WE COULDN'T TALK ABOUT HIME-CHAN ANYMORE.
SHE'S GETTING WEIRDER AND WEIRDER LATELY.
WHEN IT COMES TO ROMANCE...
...SHE GETS SO STRANGE.

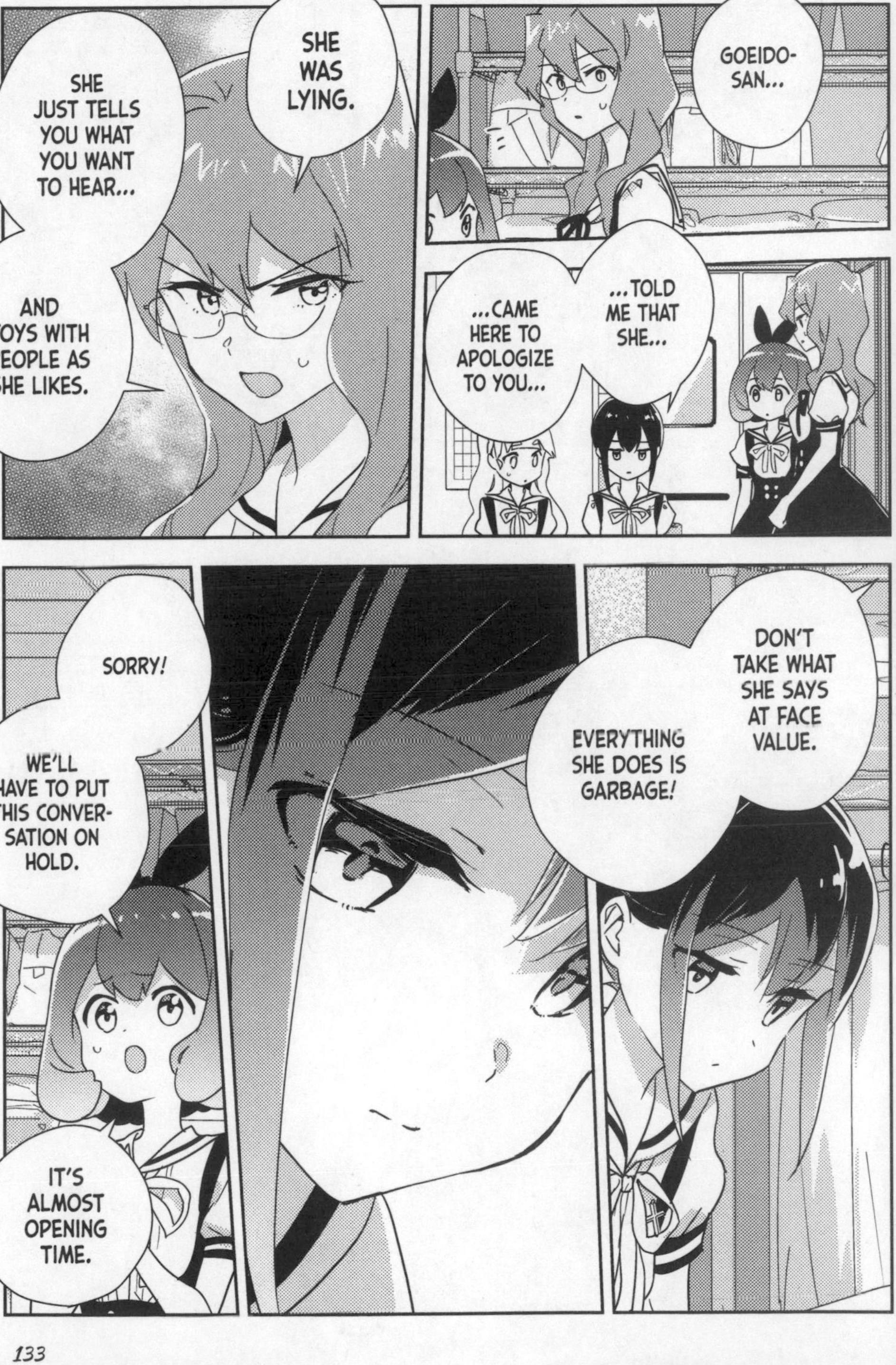
GOEIDO-SAN...
...TOLD ME THAT SHE...
...CAME HERE TO APOLOGIZE TO YOU...
SHE WAS LYING.
SHE JUST TELLS YOU WHAT YOU WANT TO HEAR...
AND TOYS WITH PEOPLE AS SHE LIKES.
DON'T TAKE WHAT SHE SAYS AT FACE VALUE.
EVERYTHING SHE DOES IS GARBAGE!
SORRY!
WE'LL HAVE TO PUT THIS CONVER-SATION ON HOLD.
IT'S ALMOST OPENING TIME.

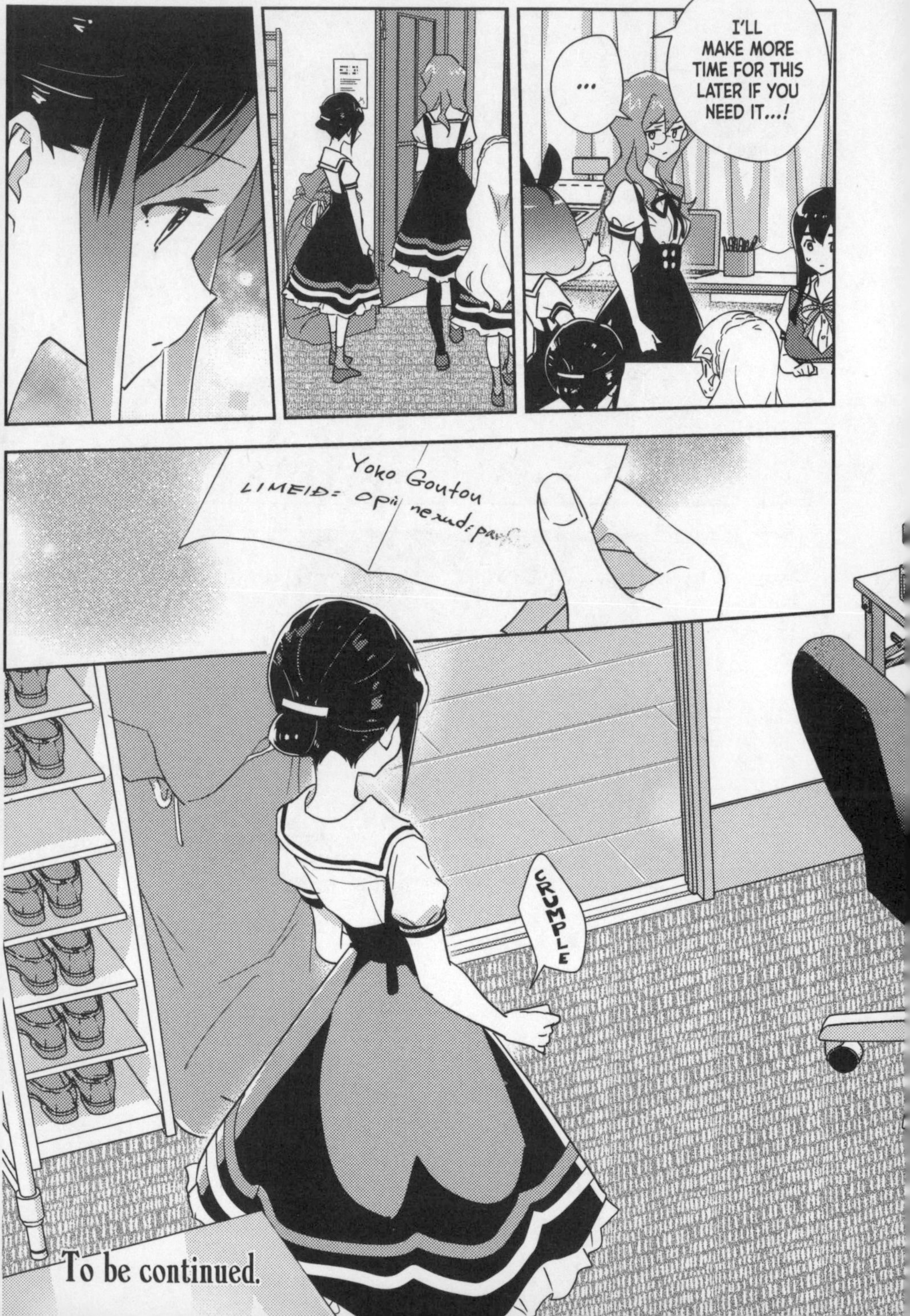
I'LL MAKE MORE TIME FOR THIS LATER IF YOU NEED IT...!
...
Yoko Goutou
CRUMPLE
To be continued.

Yuri Is My Job!

Shift 46.5 Asking Questions Is Shinooka-san's Job!

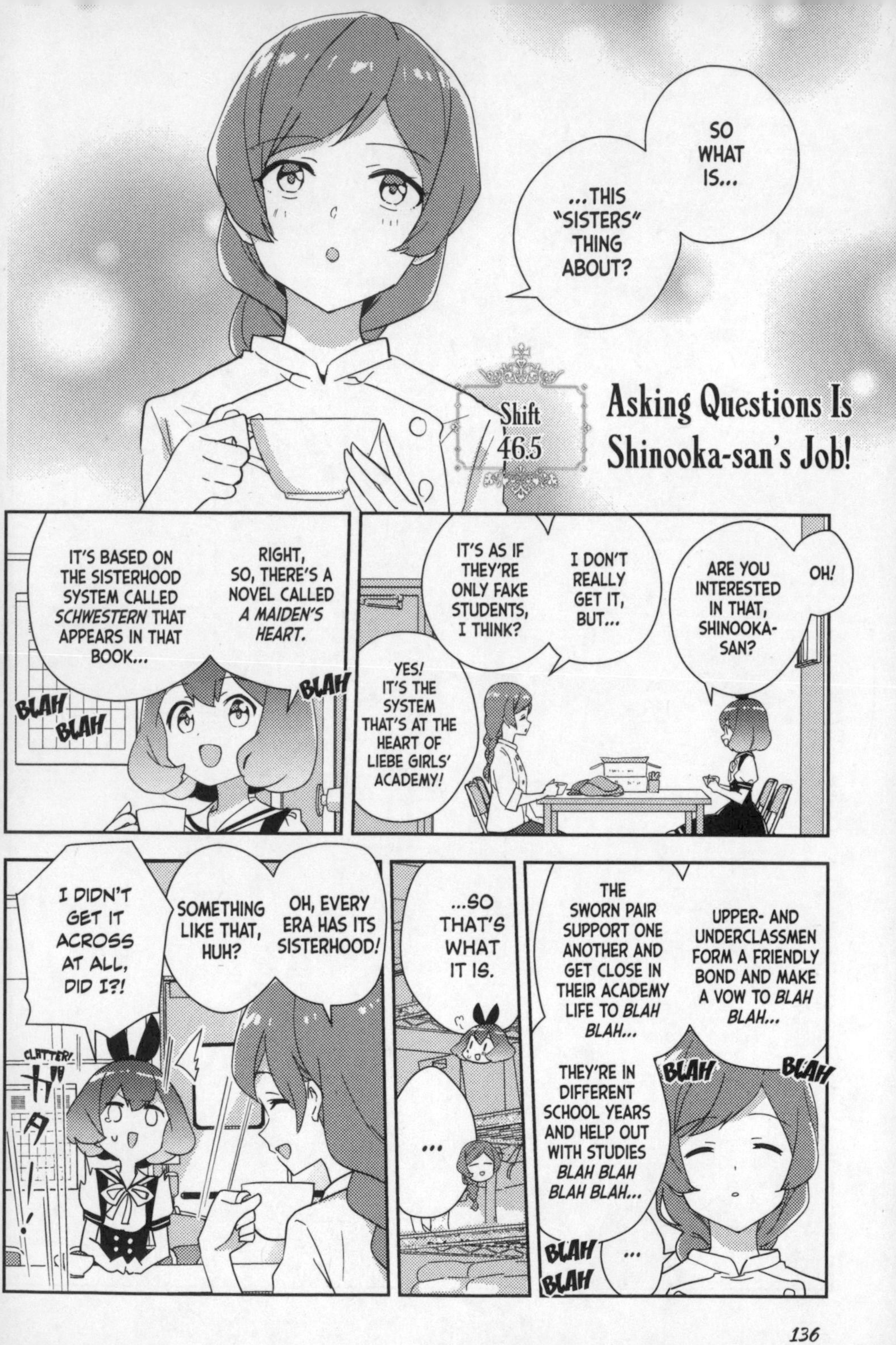
SO WHAT IS...
...THIS "SISTERS" THING ABOUT?
OH!
ARE YOU INTERESTED IN THAT, SHINOOKA-SAN?
I DON'T REALLY GET IT, BUT...
IT'S AS IF THEY'RE ONLY FAKE STUDENTS, I THINK?
YES! IT'S THE SYSTEM THAT'S AT THE HEART OF LIEBE GIRLS' ACADEMY!
RIGHT, SO, THERE'S A NOVEL CALLED *A MAIDEN'S HEART.*
IT'S BASED ON THE SISTERHOOD SYSTEM CALLED *SCHWESTERN* THAT APPEARS IN THAT BOOK...
BLAH
BLAH
BLAH
UPPER- AND UNDERCLASSMEN FORM A FRIENDLY BOND AND MAKE A VOW TO *BLAH BLAH...*
THE SWORN PAIR SUPPORT ONE ANOTHER AND GET CLOSE IN THEIR ACADEMY LIFE TO *BLAH BLAH...*
BLAH
BLAH
THEY'RE IN DIFFERENT SCHOOL YEARS AND HELP OUT WITH STUDIES *BLAH BLAH BLAH BLAH...*
...
BLAH
BLAH
...SO THAT'S WHAT IT IS.
...
OH, EVERY ERA HAS ITS SISTERHOOD!
SOMETHING LIKE THAT, HUH?
I DIDN'T GET IT ACROSS AT ALL, DID I?!
CLATTER!

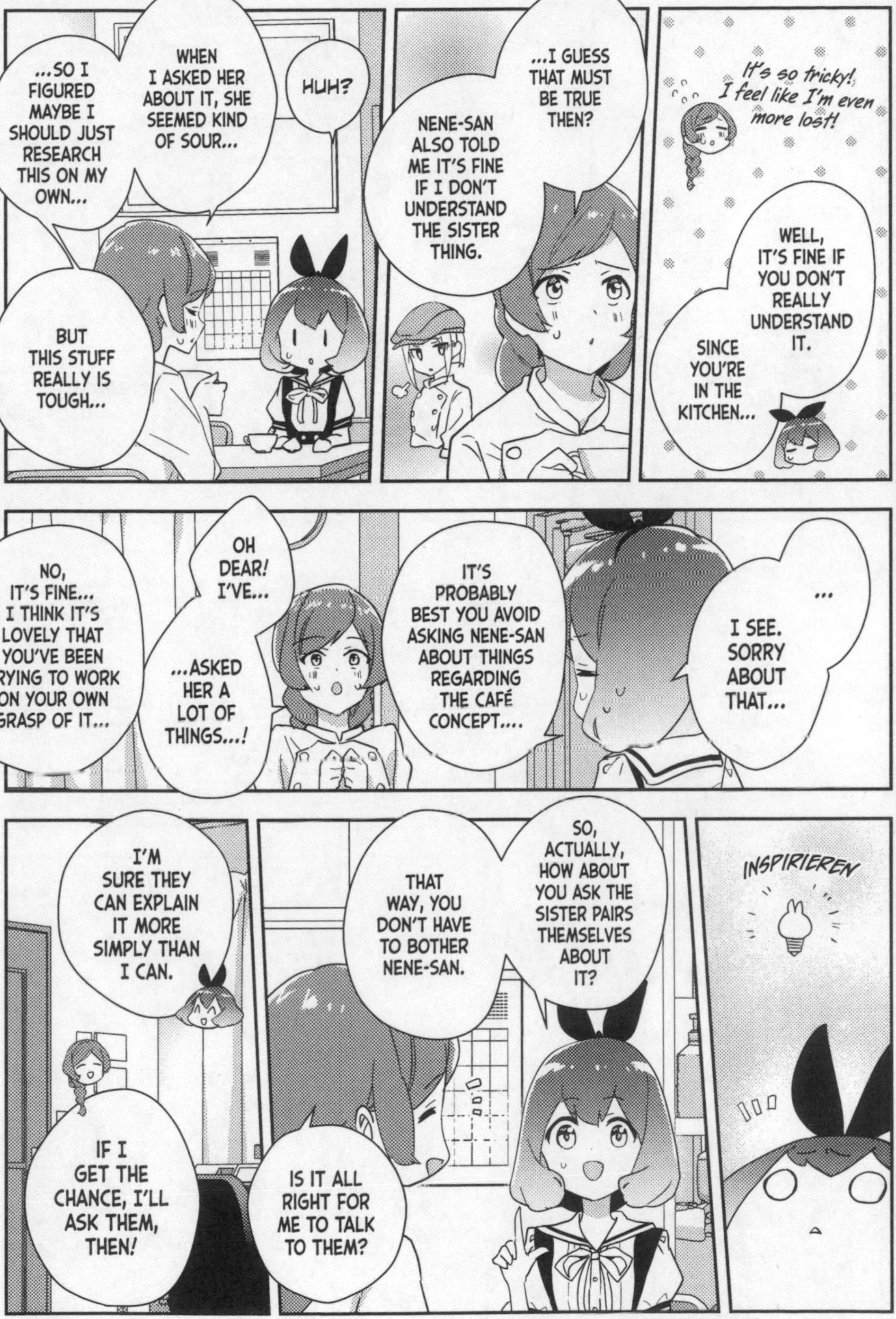
It's so tricky! I feel like I'm even more lost!
WELL, IT'S FINE IF YOU DON'T REALLY UNDERSTAND IT.
SINCE YOU'RE IN THE KITCHEN...
...I GUESS THAT MUST BE TRUE THEN?
NENE-SAN ALSO TOLD ME IT'S FINE IF I DON'T UNDERSTAND THE SISTER THING.
HUH?
WHEN I ASKED HER ABOUT IT, SHE SEEMED KIND OF SOUR...
...SO I FIGURED MAYBE I SHOULD JUST RESEARCH THIS ON MY OWN...
BUT THIS STUFF REALLY IS TOUGH...
...
I SEE. SORRY ABOUT THAT...
IT'S PROBABLY BEST YOU AVOID ASKING NENE-SAN ABOUT THINGS REGARDING THE CAFÉ CONCEPT....
OH DEAR! I'VE...
...ASKED HER A LOT OF THINGS...!
NO, IT'S FINE... I THINK IT'S LOVELY THAT YOU'VE BEEN TRYING TO WORK ON YOUR OWN GRASP OF IT...
INSPIRIEREN
SO, ACTUALLY, HOW ABOUT YOU ASK THE SISTER PAIRS THEMSELVES ABOUT IT?
THAT WAY, YOU DON'T HAVE TO BOTHER NENE-SAN.
IS IT ALL RIGHT FOR ME TO TALK TO THEM?
I'M SURE THEY CAN EXPLAIN IT MORE SIMPLY THAN I CAN.
IF I GET THE CHANCE, I'LL ASK THEM, THEN!

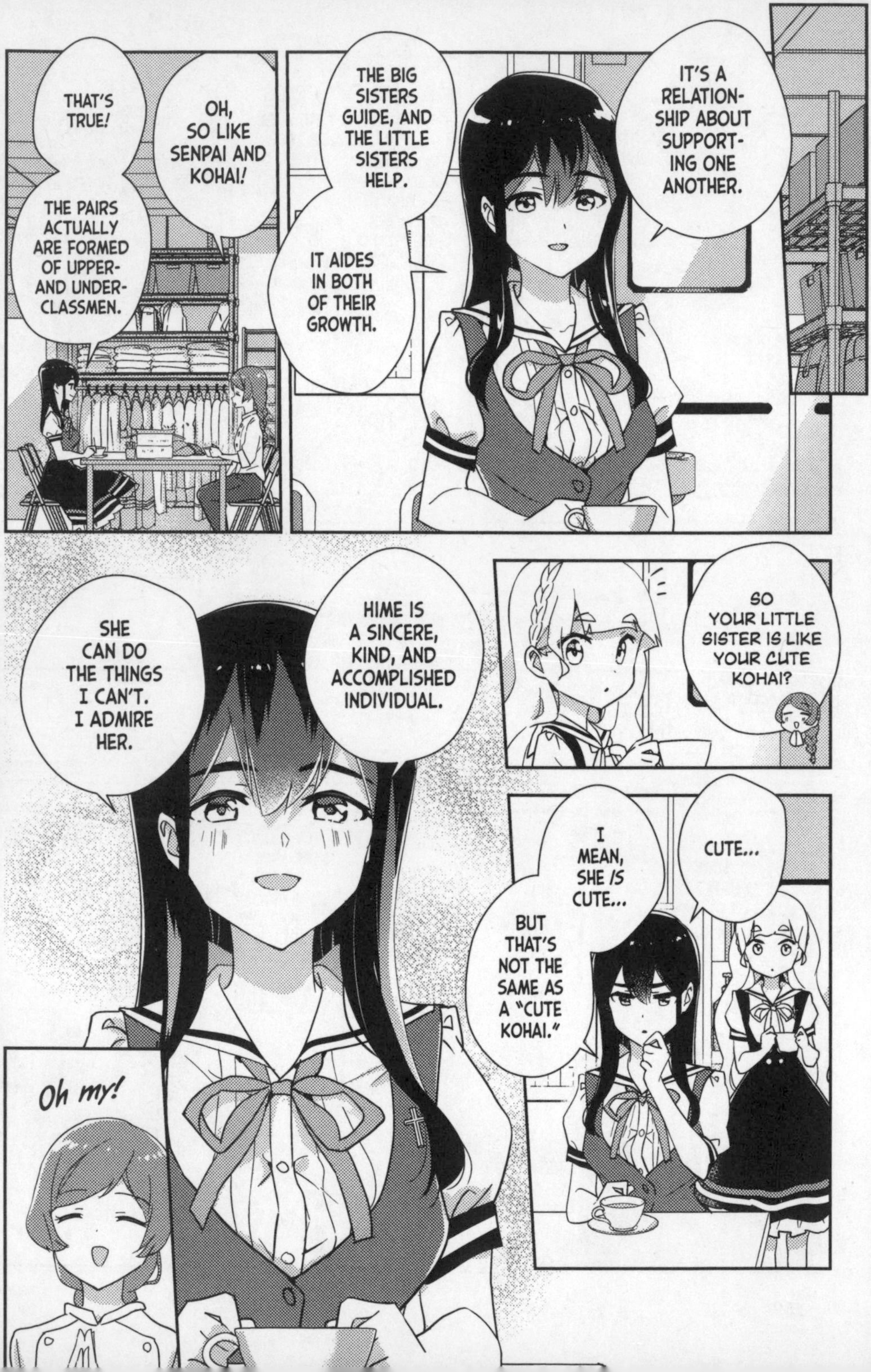
IT'S A RELATIONSHIP ABOUT SUPPORTING ONE ANOTHER.
THE BIG SISTERS GUIDE, AND THE LITTLE SISTERS HELP.
IT AIDES IN BOTH OF THEIR GROWTH.
OH, SO LIKE SENPAI AND KOHAI!
THAT'S TRUE!
THE PAIRS ACTUALLY ARE FORMED OF UPPER- AND UNDER-CLASSMEN.
SO YOUR LITTLE SISTER IS LIKE YOUR CUTE KOHAI?
CUTE...
I MEAN, SHE *IS* CUTE...
BUT THAT'S NOT THE SAME AS A "CUTE KOHAI."
HIME IS A SINCERE, KIND, AND ACCOMPLISHED INDIVIDUAL.
SHE CAN DO THE THINGS I CAN'T. I ADMIRE HER.
Oh my!

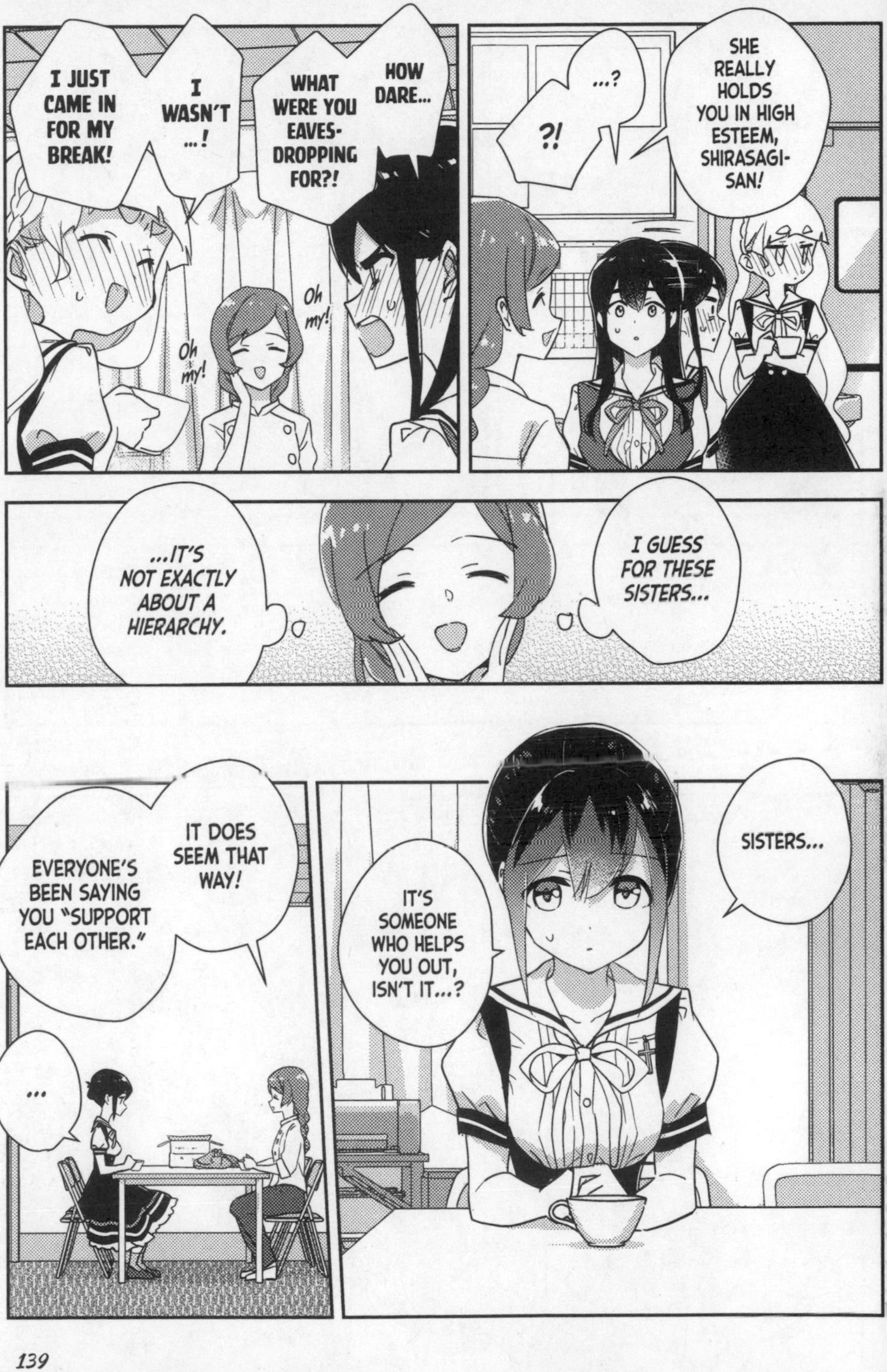
SHE REALLY HOLDS YOU IN HIGH ESTEEM, SHIRASAGI-SAN!
...?
?!
HOW DARE...
WHAT WERE YOU EAVES-DROPPING FOR?!
Oh my!
I WASN'T ...!
I JUST CAME IN FOR MY BREAK!
Oh my!
I GUESS FOR THESE SISTERS...
...IT'S NOT EXACTLY ABOUT A HIERARCHY.
SISTERS...
IT'S SOMEONE WHO HELPS YOU OUT, ISN'T IT...?
IT DOES SEEM THAT WAY!
EVERYONE'S BEEN SAYING YOU "SUPPORT EACH OTHER."
...

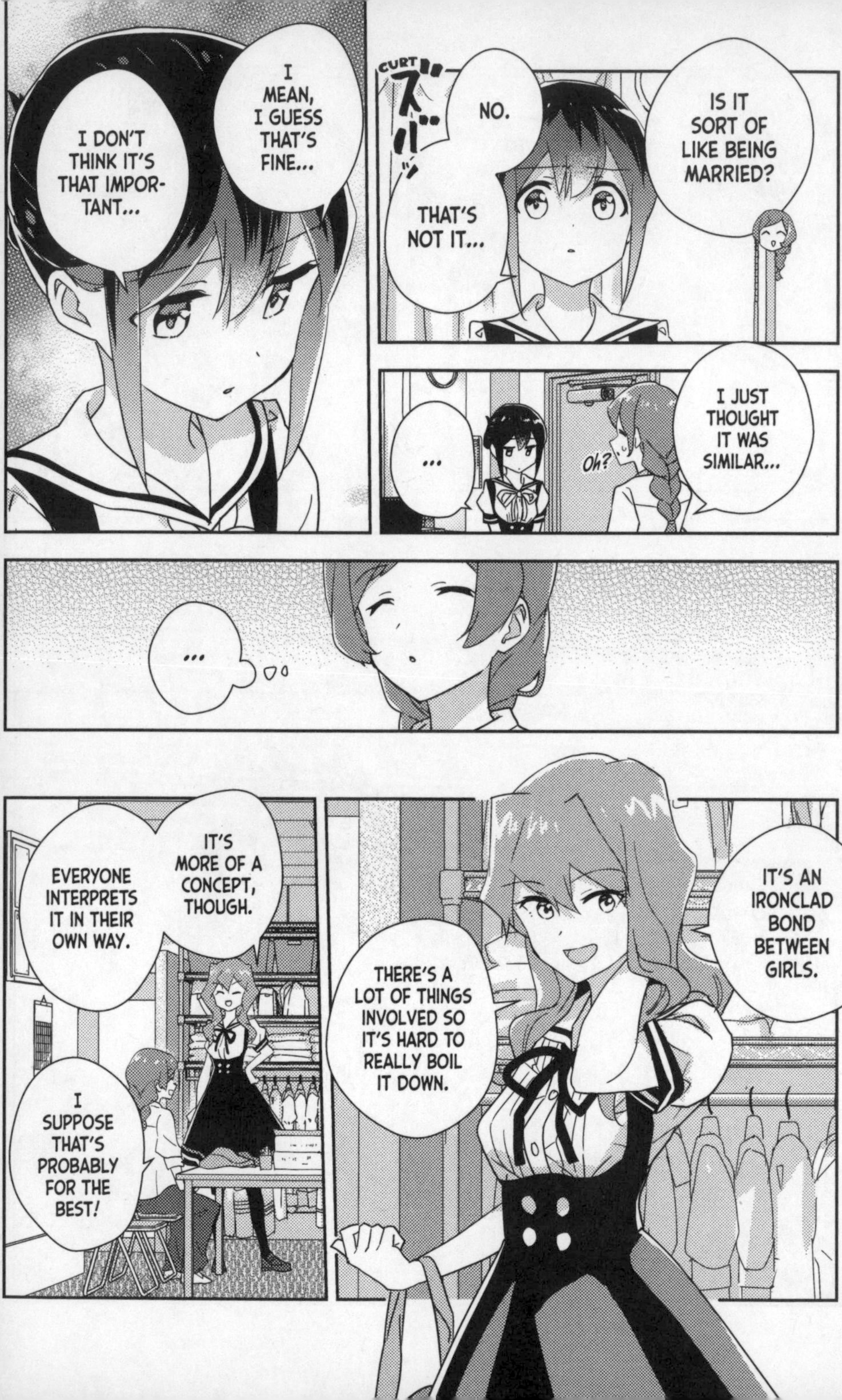
IS IT SORT OF LIKE BEING MARRIED?
CURT ズバッ
NO.
THAT'S NOT IT...
I JUST THOUGHT IT WAS SIMILAR...
Oh?
...
I MEAN, I GUESS THAT'S FINE...
I DON'T THINK IT'S THAT IMPORTANT...
...
IT'S AN IRONCLAD BOND BETWEEN GIRLS.
THERE'S A LOT OF THINGS INVOLVED SO IT'S HARD TO REALLY BOIL IT DOWN.
IT'S MORE OF A CONCEPT, THOUGH.
EVERYONE INTERPRETS IT IN THEIR OWN WAY.
I SUPPOSE THAT'S PROBABLY FOR THE BEST!

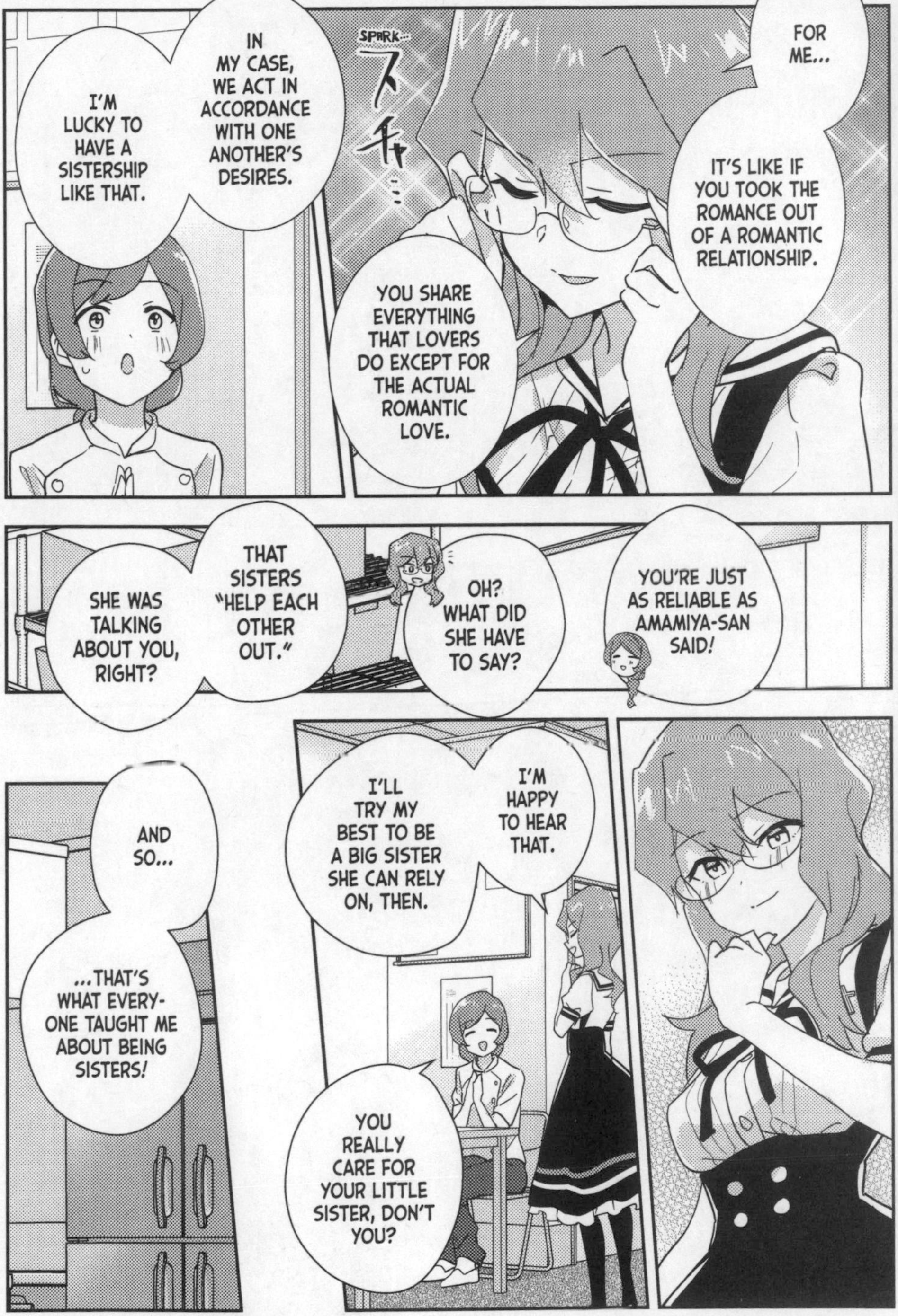
FOR ME...
IT'S LIKE IF YOU TOOK THE ROMANCE OUT OF A ROMANTIC RELATIONSHIP.
SPARK... スチャ...
YOU SHARE EVERYTHING THAT LOVERS DO EXCEPT FOR THE ACTUAL ROMANTIC LOVE.
IN MY CASE, WE ACT IN ACCORDANCE WITH ONE ANOTHER'S DESIRES.
I'M LUCKY TO HAVE A SISTERSHIP LIKE THAT.
YOU'RE JUST AS RELIABLE AS AMAMIYA-SAN SAID!
OH? WHAT DID SHE HAVE TO SAY?
THAT SISTERS "HELP EACH OTHER OUT."
SHE WAS TALKING ABOUT YOU, RIGHT?
I'M HAPPY TO HEAR THAT.
I'LL TRY MY BEST TO BE A BIG SISTER SHE CAN RELY ON, THEN.
YOU REALLY CARE FOR YOUR LITTLE SISTER, DON'T YOU?
AND SO...
...THAT'S WHAT EVERY-ONE TAUGHT ME ABOUT BEING SISTERS!

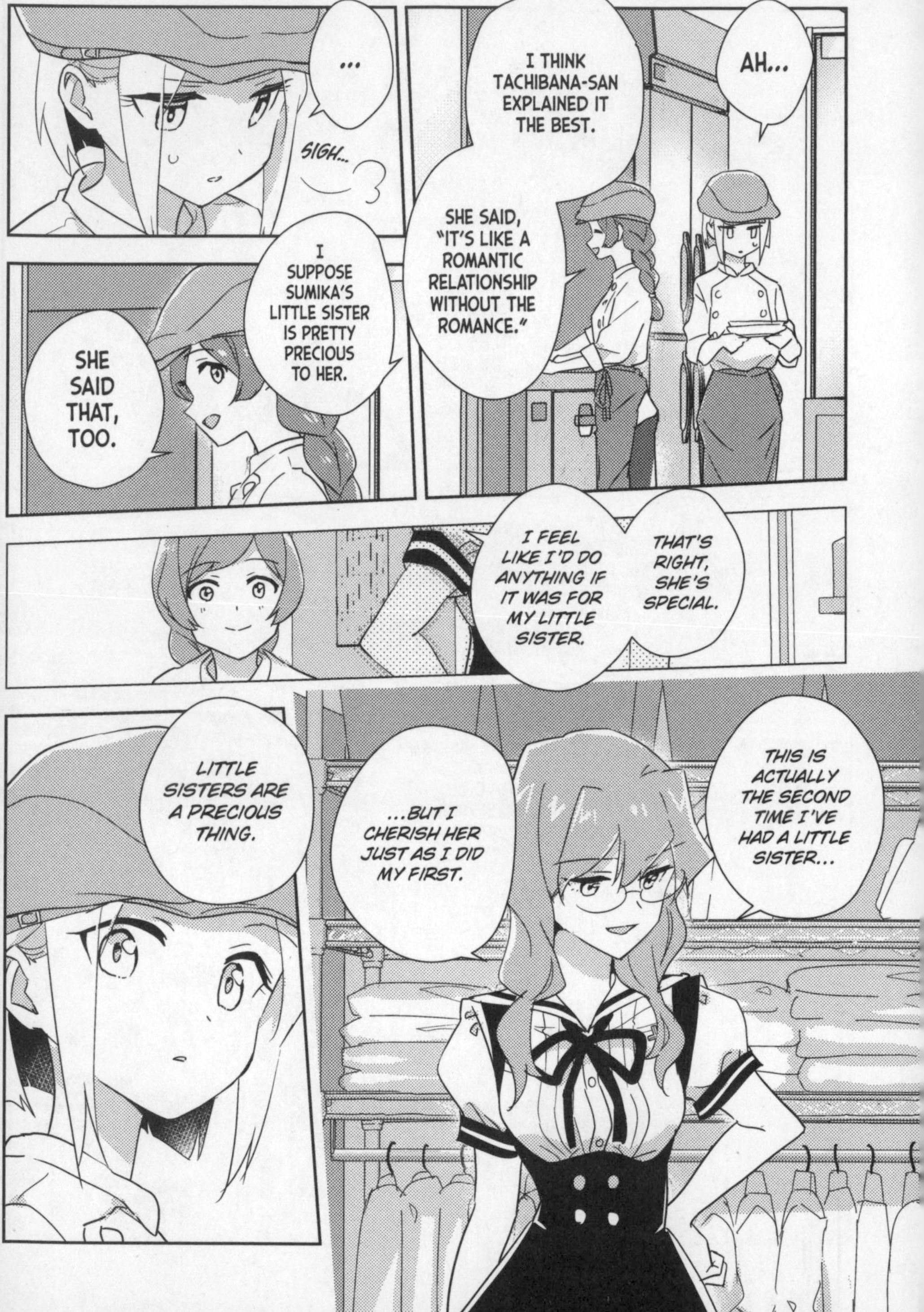
AH...
I THINK TACHIBANA-SAN EXPLAINED IT THE BEST.
SHE SAID, "IT'S LIKE A ROMANTIC RELATIONSHIP WITHOUT THE ROMANCE."
...
SIGH...
I SUPPOSE SUMIKA'S LITTLE SISTER IS PRETTY PRECIOUS TO HER.
SHE SAID THAT, TOO.
THAT'S RIGHT, SHE'S SPECIAL.
I FEEL LIKE I'D DO ANYTHING IF IT WAS FOR MY LITTLE SISTER.
THIS IS ACTUALLY THE SECOND TIME I'VE HAD A LITTLE SISTER...
...BUT I CHERISH HER JUST AS I DID MY FIRST.
LITTLE SISTERS ARE A PRECIOUS THING.

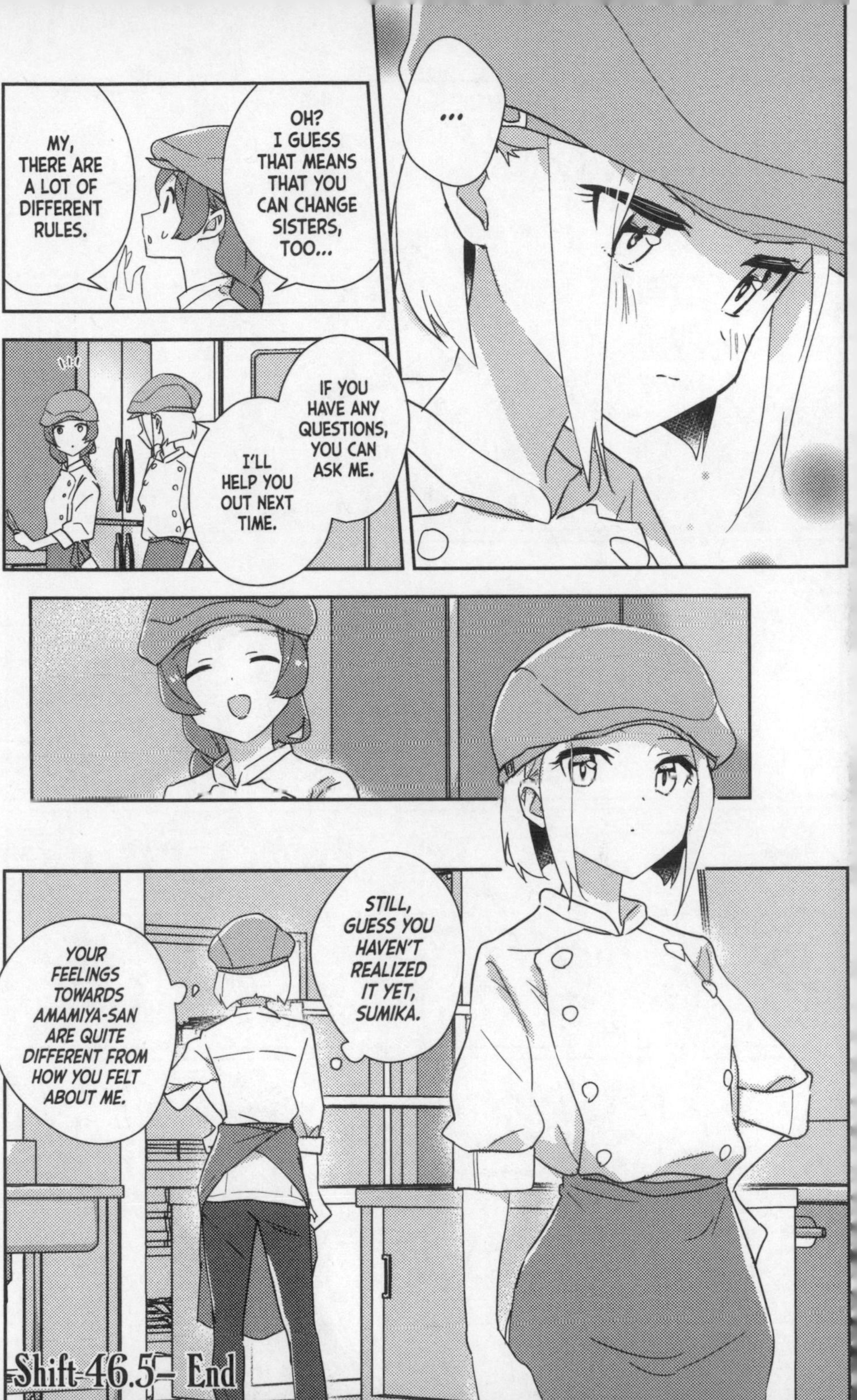
...
OH? I GUESS THAT MEANS THAT YOU CAN CHANGE SISTERS, TOO...
MY, THERE ARE A LOT OF DIFFERENT RULES.
IF YOU HAVE ANY QUESTIONS, YOU CAN ASK ME.
I'LL HELP YOU OUT NEXT TIME.
STILL, GUESS YOU HAVEN'T REALIZED IT YET, SUMIKA.
YOUR FEELINGS TOWARDS AMAMIYA-SAN ARE QUITE DIFFERENT FROM HOW YOU FELT ABOUT ME.
-Shift-46.5- End

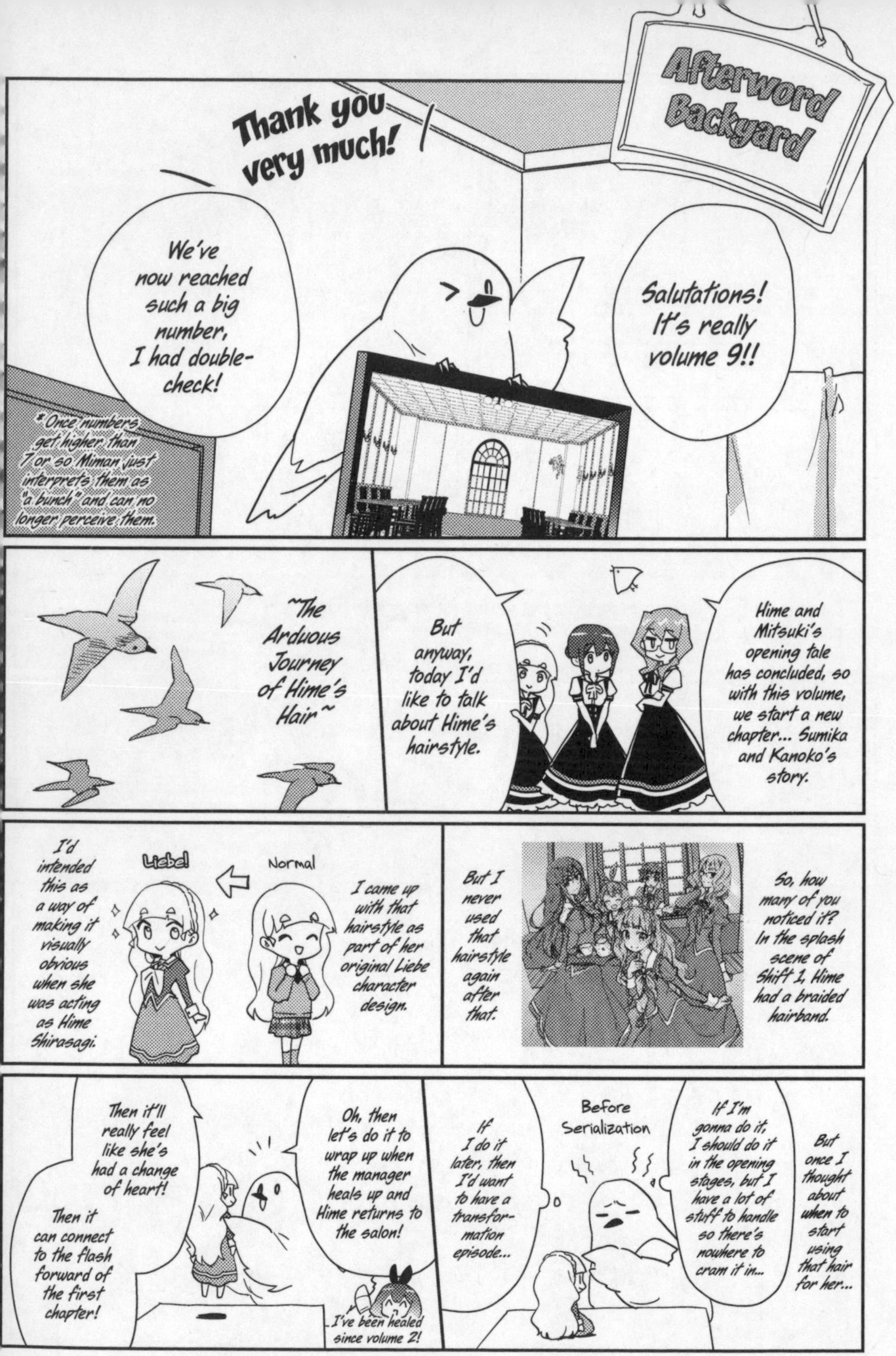
Afterword Backyard!
Salutations! It's really volume 9!!
Thank you very much!
We've now reached such a big number, I had double-check!
*Once numbers get higher than 7 or so Miman just interprets them as "a bunch" and can no longer perceive them.
Hime and Mitsuki's opening tale has concluded, so with this volume, we start a new chapter... Sumika and Kanoko's story.
But anyway, today I'd like to talk about Hime's hairstyle.
~The Arduous Journey of Hime's Hair~
So, how many of you noticed it? In the splash scene of Shift 1, Hime had a braided hairband.
But I never used that hairstyle again after that.
I came up with that hairstyle as part of her original Liebe character design.
Normal
Liebe!
I'd intended this as a way of making it visually obvious when she was acting as Hime Shirasagi.
But once I thought about when to start using that hair for her...
If I'm gonna do it, I should do it in the opening stages, but I have a lot of stuff to handle so there's nowhere to cram it in...
Before Serialization
If I do it later, then I'd want to have a transformation episode...
Oh, then let's do it to wrap up when the manager heals up and Hime returns to the salon!
I've been healed since volume 2!
Then it'll really feel like she's had a change of heart!
Then it can connect to the flash forward of the first chapter!

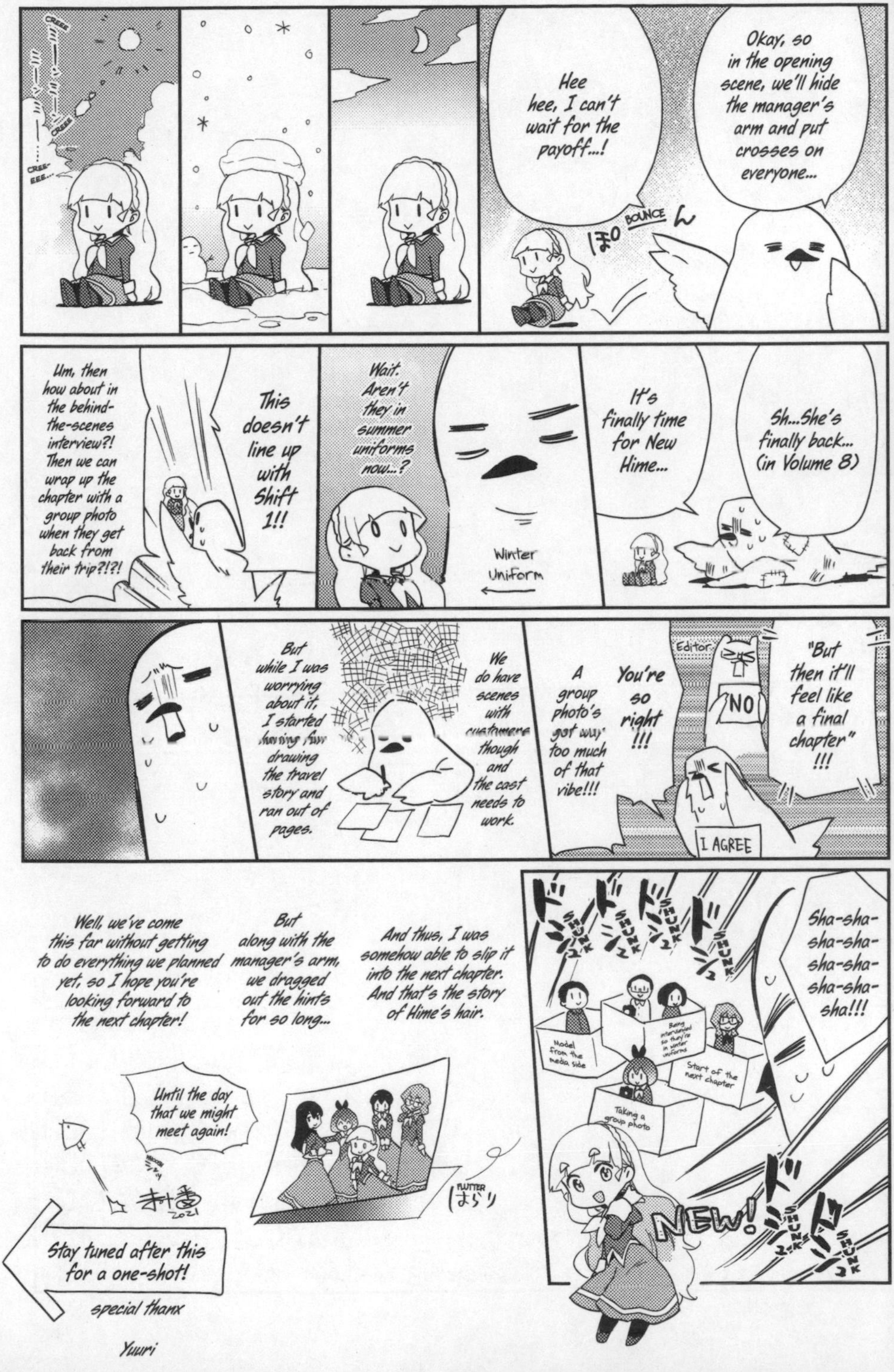

Okay, so in the opening scene, we'll hide the manager's arm and put crosses on everyone...
Hee hee, I can't wait for the payoff...!
BOUNCE
CREEE
CREEE
CREE-EEE...
Sh...She's finally back... (in Volume 8)
It's finally time for New Hime...
Winter Uniform
Wait. Aren't they in summer uniforms now...?
This doesn't line up with Shift 1!!
Um, then how about in the behind-the-scenes interview?! Then we can wrap up the chapter with a group photo when they get back from their trip?!?!
"But then it'll feel like a final chapter"!!!
Editor
NO
I AGREE
You're so right!!!
A group photo's got way too much of that vibe!!!
We do have scenes with customers though and the cast needs to work.
But while I was worrying about it, I started having fun drawing the travel story and ran out of pages.
Sha-sha-sha-sha-sha-sha-sha-sha-sha!!!
SHUNK
SHUNK
SHUNK
SHUNK
Being interviewed so they're in winter uniforms
Model from the media side
Start of the next chapter
Taking a group photo
NEW!
SHUNK
SHUNK
And thus, I was somehow able to slip it into the next chapter. And that's the story of Hime's hair.
But along with the manager's arm, we dragged out the hints for so long...
Well, we've come this far without getting to do everything we planned yet, so I hope you're looking forward to the next chapter!
FLUTTER
Until the day that we might meet again!
2021
Stay tuned after this for a one-shot!
special thanx
Yuuri

First Printing
Shift 42 "Comics Yurihime" June 2021 Edition
Shift 43 "Comics Yurihime" July 2021 Edition
Shift 44 "Comics Yurihime" August 2021 Edition
Shift 45 "Comics Yurihime" October 2021 Edition
Shift 46 "Comics Yurihime" November 2021 Edition
Shift 46.5 "Comics Yurihime" Bonus Story
I Am Your Destiny "Éclair bleue Anata ni Hibiku Yuri Anthology" (KADOKAWA)

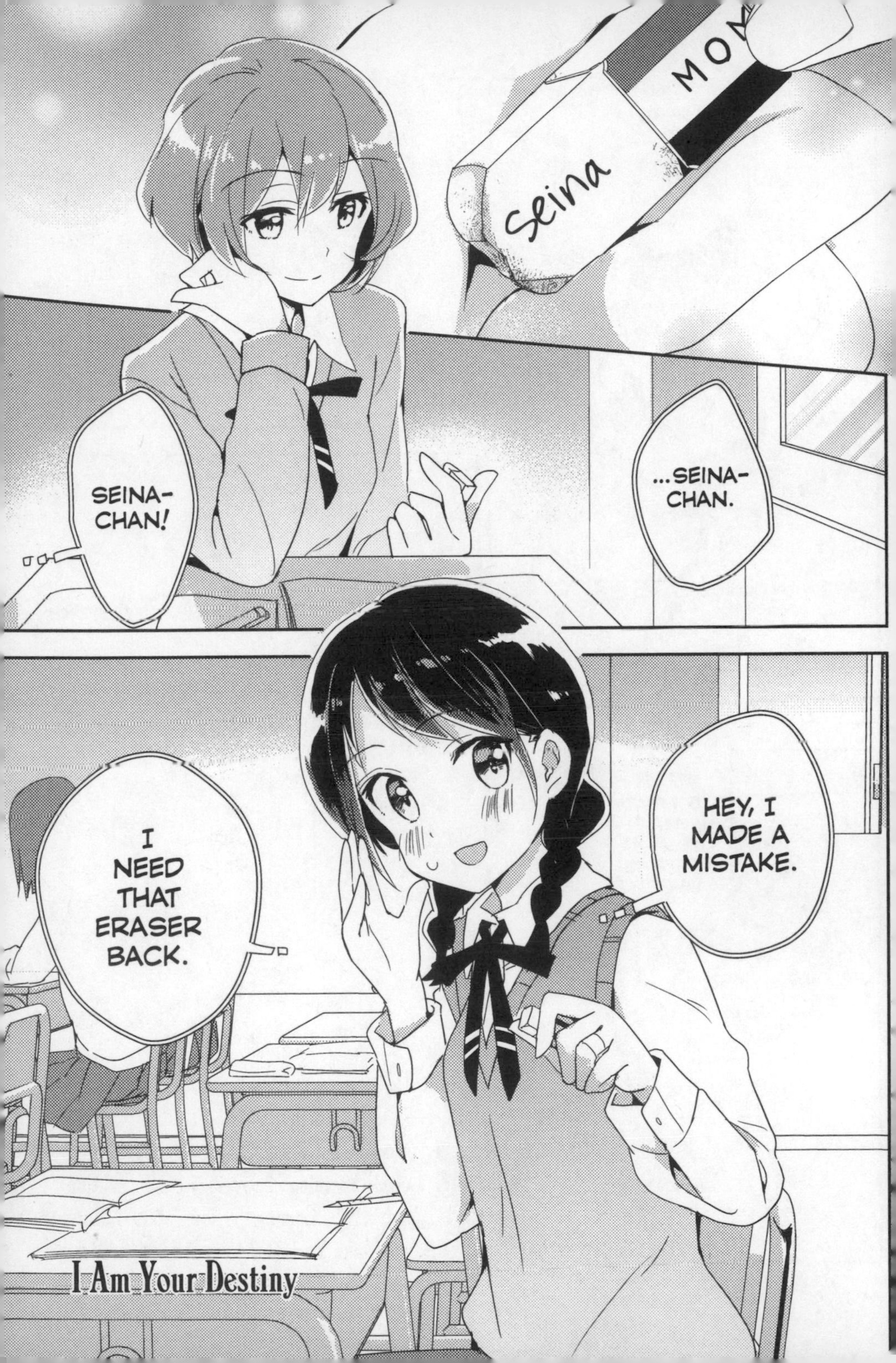

MOM
Seina
...SEINA-CHAN.
SEINA-CHAN!
HEY, I MADE A MISTAKE.
I NEED THAT ERASER BACK.
I Am Your Destiny

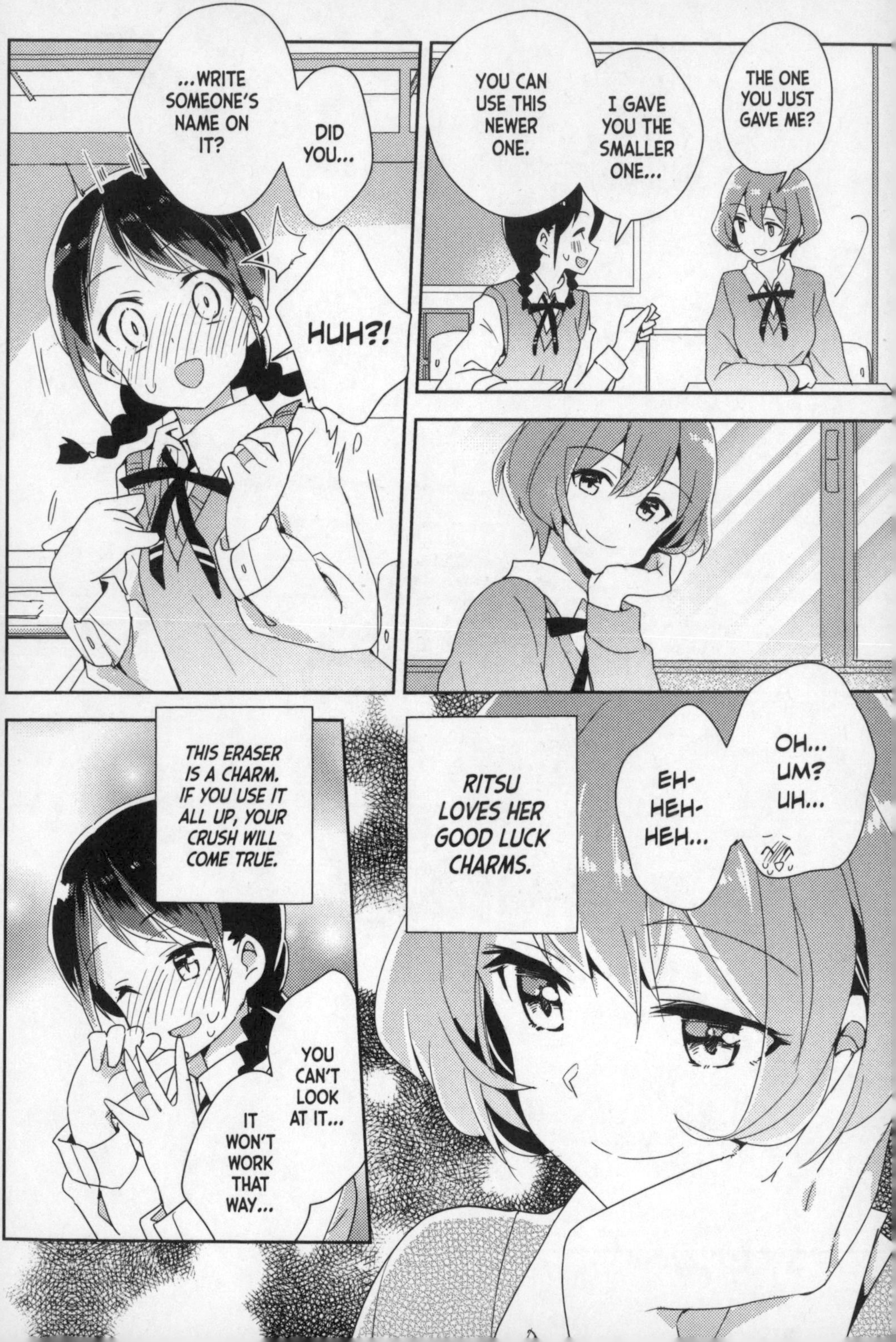
THE ONE YOU JUST GAVE ME?
I GAVE YOU THE SMALLER ONE...
YOU CAN USE THIS NEWER ONE.
DID YOU...
...WRITE SOMEONE'S NAME ON IT?
HUH?!
OH... UM? UH...
EH-HEH-HEH...
RITSU LOVES HER GOOD LUCK CHARMS.
THIS ERASER IS A CHARM. IF YOU USE IT ALL UP, YOUR CRUSH WILL COME TRUE.
YOU CAN'T LOOK AT IT...
IT WON'T WORK THAT WAY...

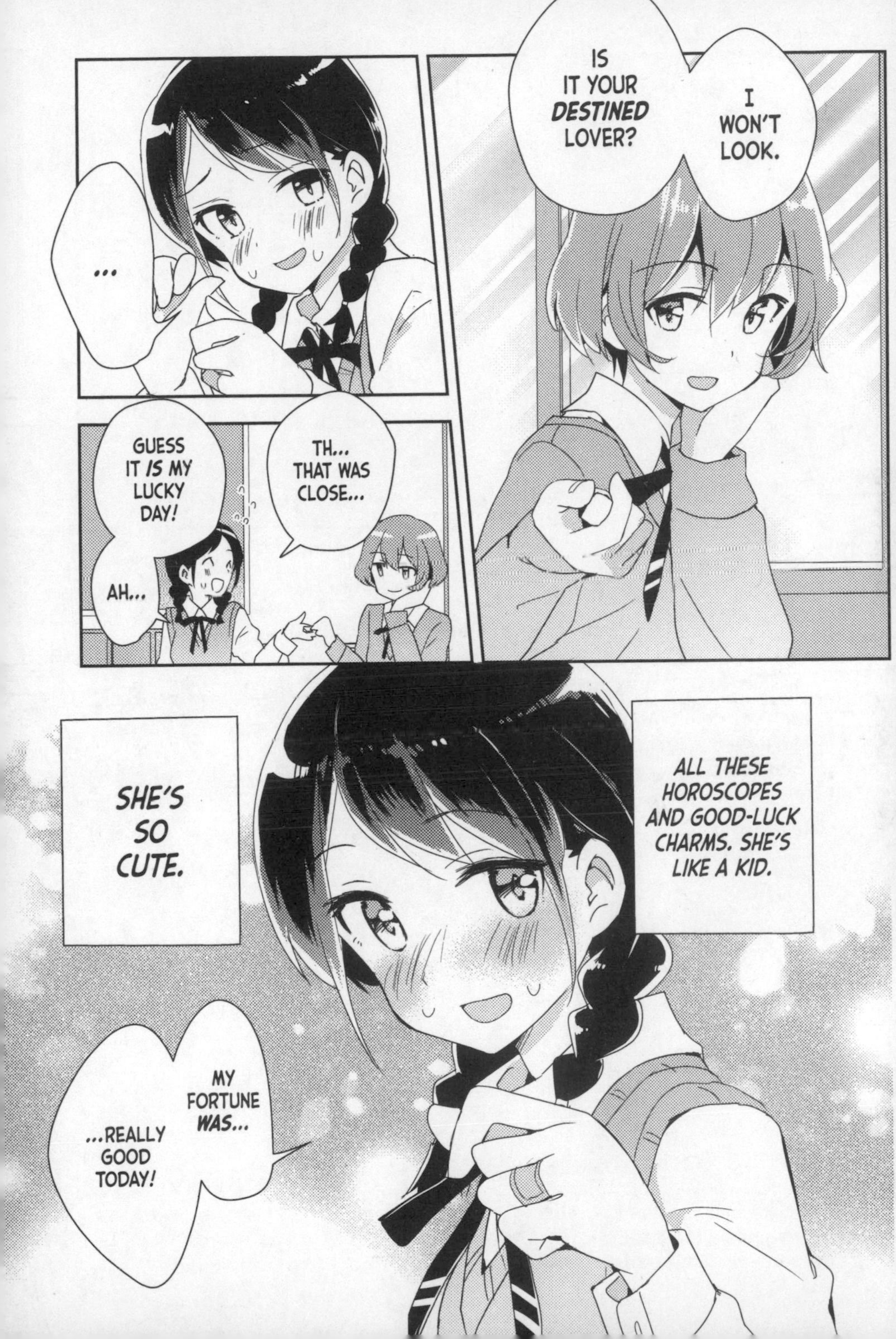
I WON'T LOOK.
IS IT YOUR *DESTINED* LOVER?
...
TH... THAT WAS CLOSE...
GUESS IT *IS* MY LUCKY DAY!
AH...
ALL THESE HOROSCOPES AND GOOD-LUCK CHARMS. SHE'S LIKE A KID.
SHE'S SO CUTE.
MY FORTUNE *WAS*...
...REALLY GOOD TODAY!

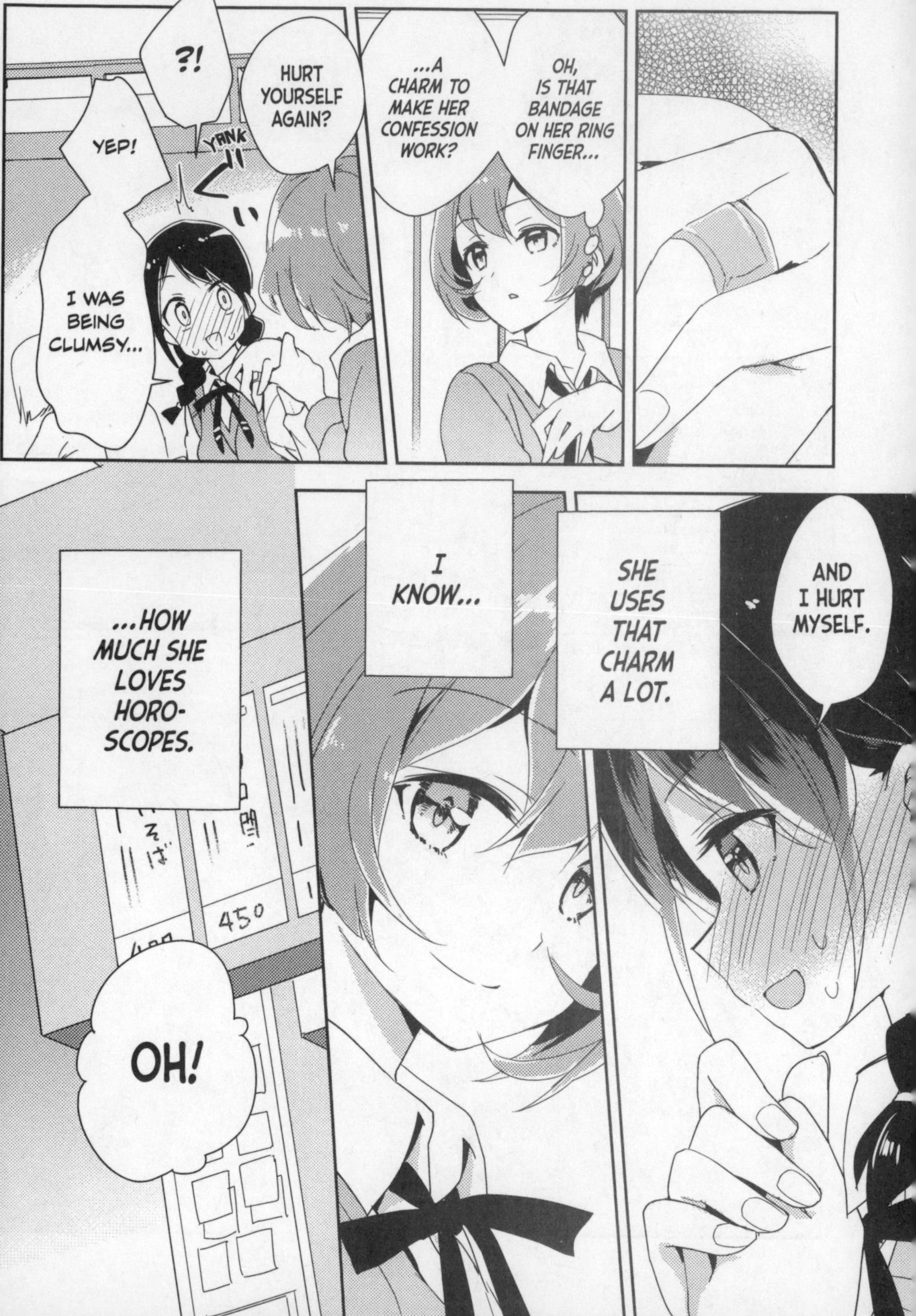
OH, IS THAT BANDAGE ON HER RING FINGER...
...A CHARM TO MAKE HER CONFESSION WORK?
HURT YOURSELF AGAIN?
?!
YANK
YEP!
I WAS BEING CLUMSY...
AND I HURT MYSELF.
SHE USES THAT CHARM A LOT.
I KNOW...
...HOW MUCH SHE LOVES HORO-SCOPES.
450
OH!

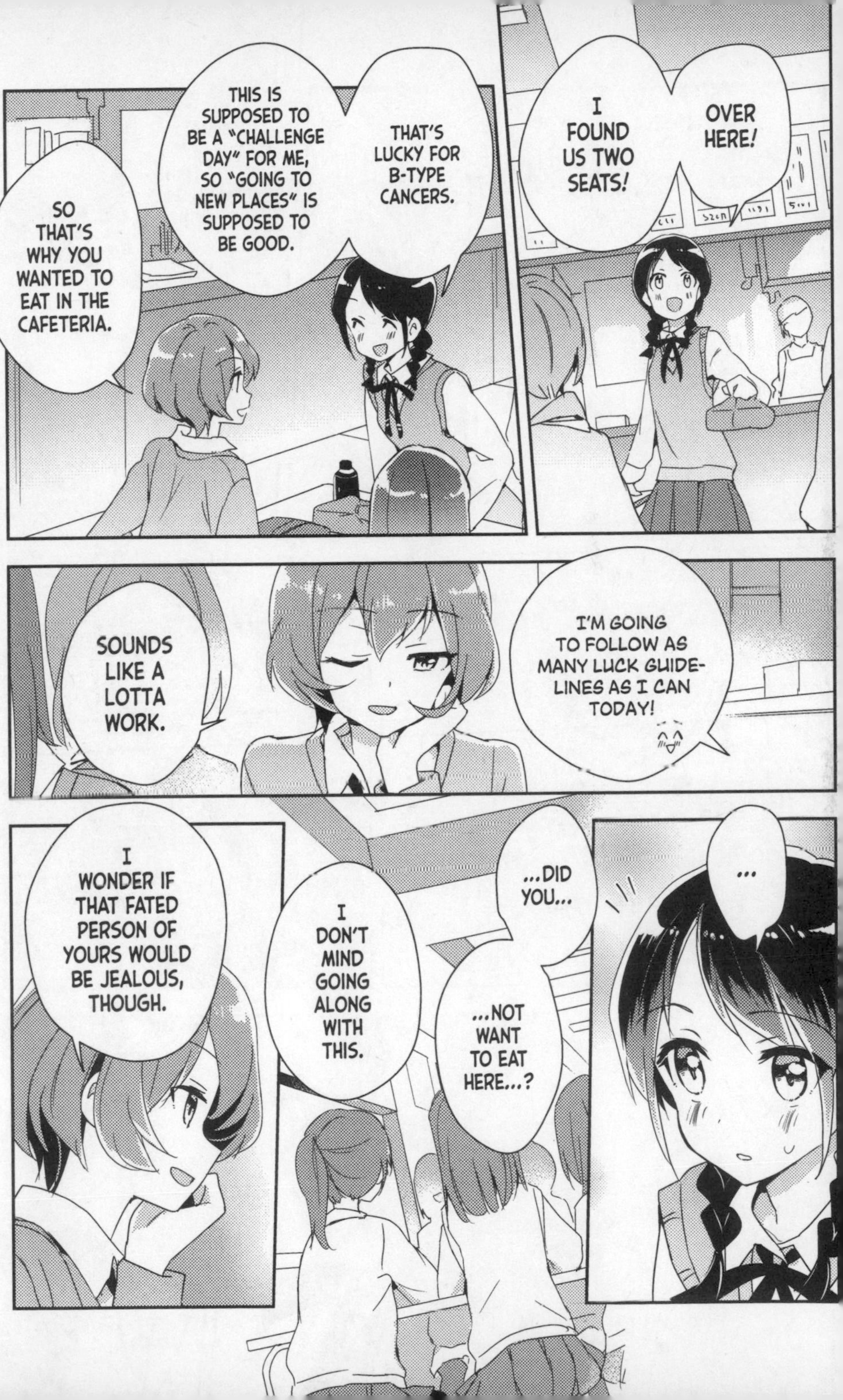
OVER HERE!
I FOUND US TWO SEATS!
THAT'S LUCKY FOR B-TYPE CANCERS.
THIS IS SUPPOSED TO BE A "CHALLENGE DAY" FOR ME, SO "GOING TO NEW PLACES" IS SUPPOSED TO BE GOOD.
SO THAT'S WHY YOU WANTED TO EAT IN THE CAFETERIA.
I'M GOING TO FOLLOW AS MANY LUCK GUIDE-LINES AS I CAN TODAY!
SOUNDS LIKE A LOTTA WORK.
...
...DID YOU...
...NOT WANT TO EAT HERE...?
I DON'T MIND GOING ALONG WITH THIS.
I WONDER IF THAT FATED PERSON OF YOURS WOULD BE JEALOUS, THOUGH.

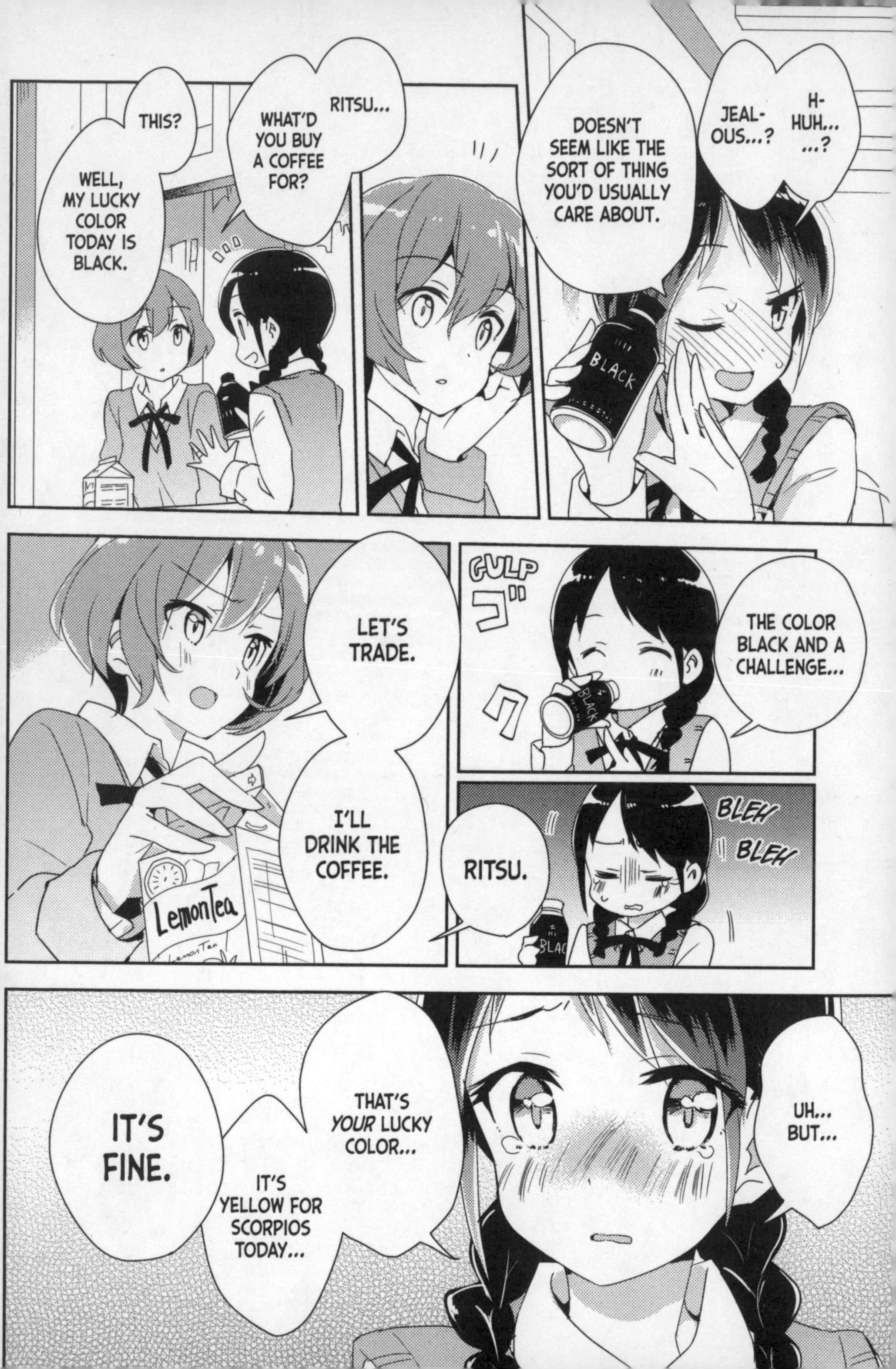
H-HUH... ...?
JEAL-OUS...?
DOESN'T SEEM LIKE THE SORT OF THING YOU'D USUALLY CARE ABOUT.
RITSU... WHAT'D YOU BUY A COFFEE FOR?
THIS?
WELL, MY LUCKY COLOR TODAY IS BLACK.
BLACK
GULP
THE COLOR BLACK AND A CHALLENGE...
BLACK
BLEH BLEH
RITSU.
LET'S TRADE.
I'LL DRINK THE COFFEE.
LemonTea
UH... BUT...
THAT'S *YOUR* LUCKY COLOR...
IT'S YELLOW FOR SCORPIOS TODAY...
IT'S FINE.

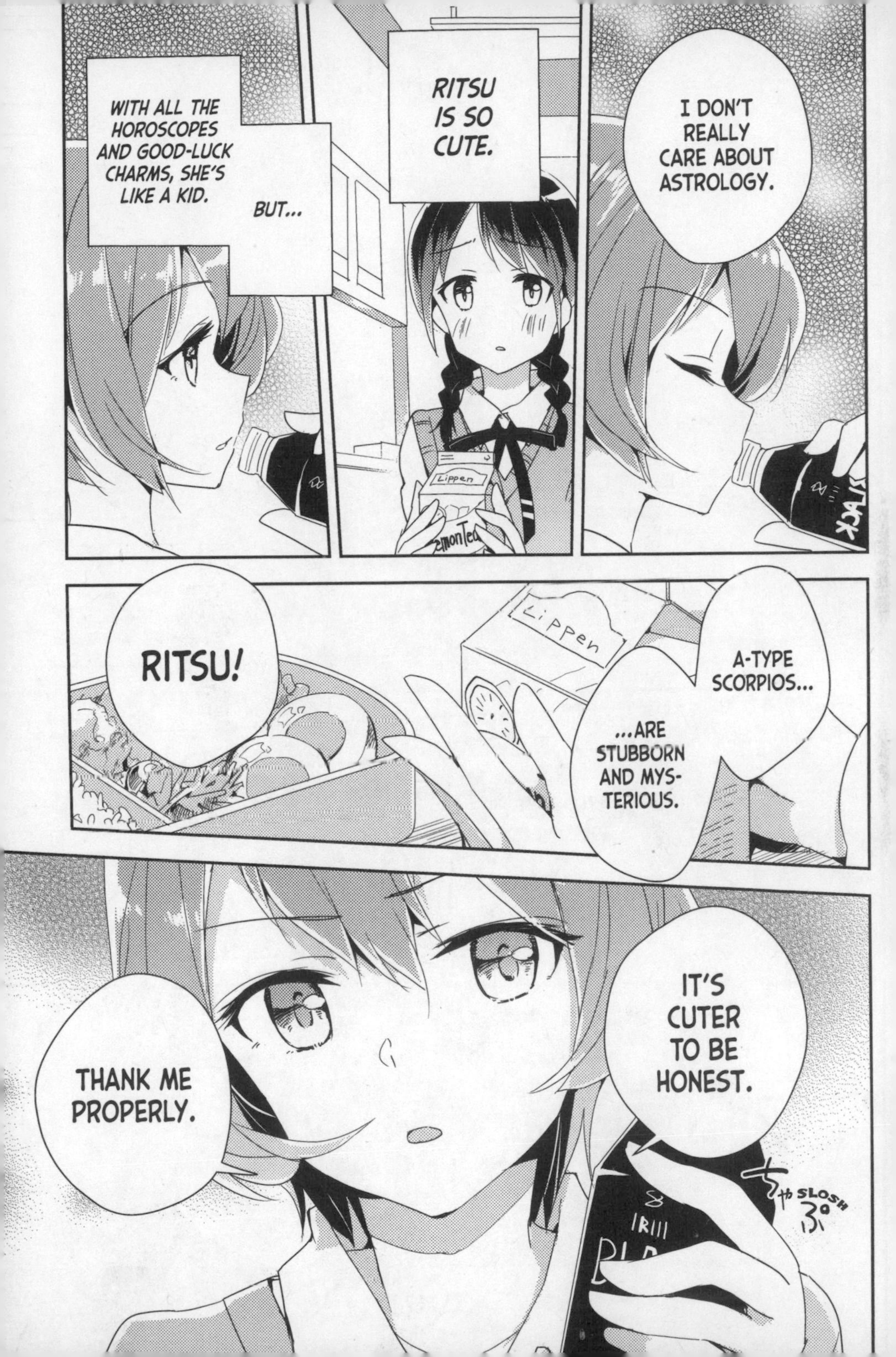
I DON'T REALLY CARE ABOUT ASTROLOGY.
RITSU IS SO CUTE.
WITH ALL THE HOROSCOPES AND GOOD-LUCK CHARMS, SHE'S LIKE A KID.
BUT...
Lippen
A-TYPE SCORPIOS...
...ARE STUBBORN AND MYS-TERIOUS.
RITSU!
Lippen
IT'S CUTER TO BE HONEST.
THANK ME PROPERLY.
SLOSH

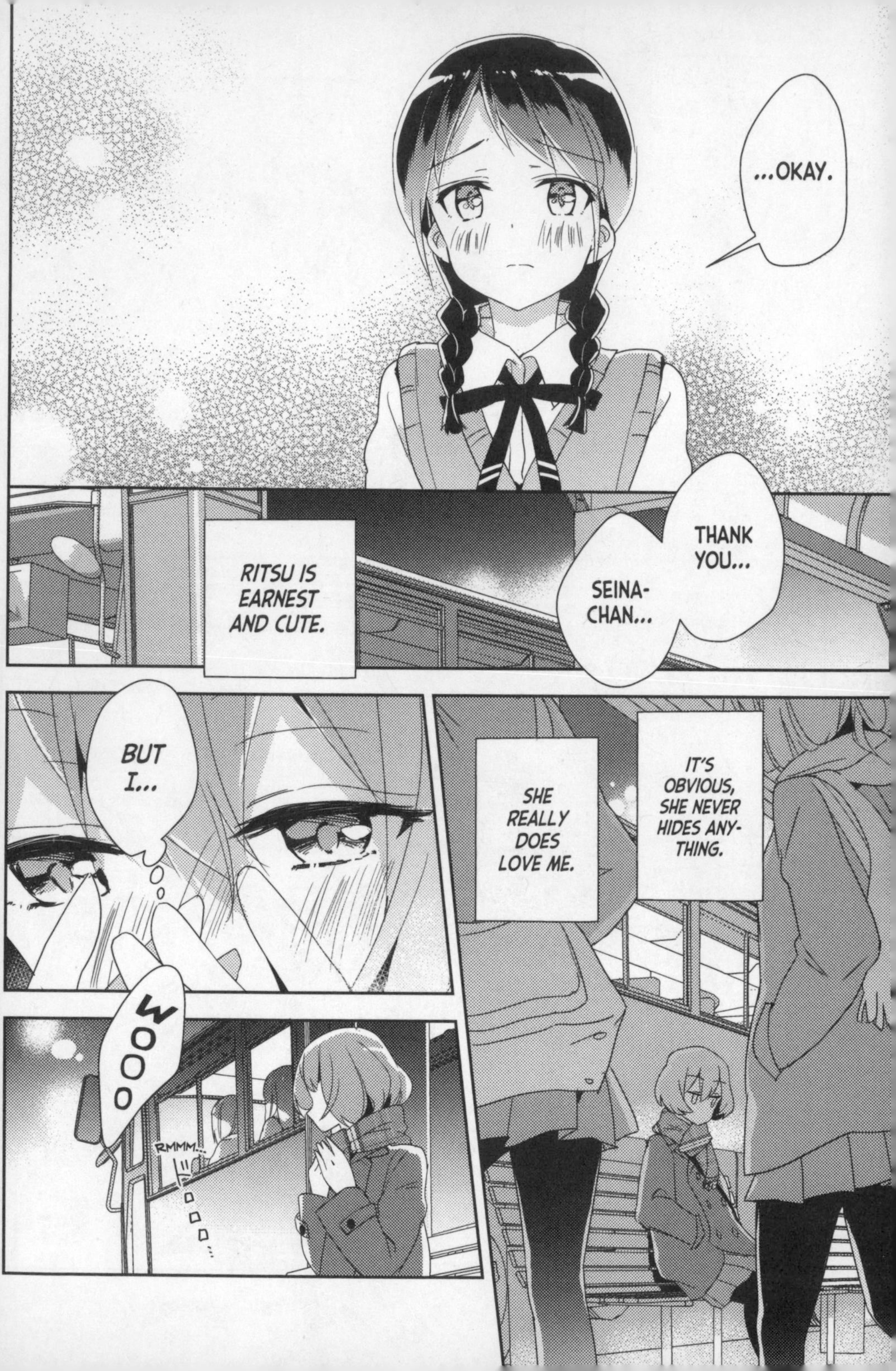
...OKAY.
THANK YOU... SEINA-CHAN...
RITSU IS EARNEST AND CUTE.
IT'S OBVIOUS, SHE NEVER HIDES ANY-THING.
SHE REALLY DOES LOVE ME.
BUT I...
WOOO
RMMM...

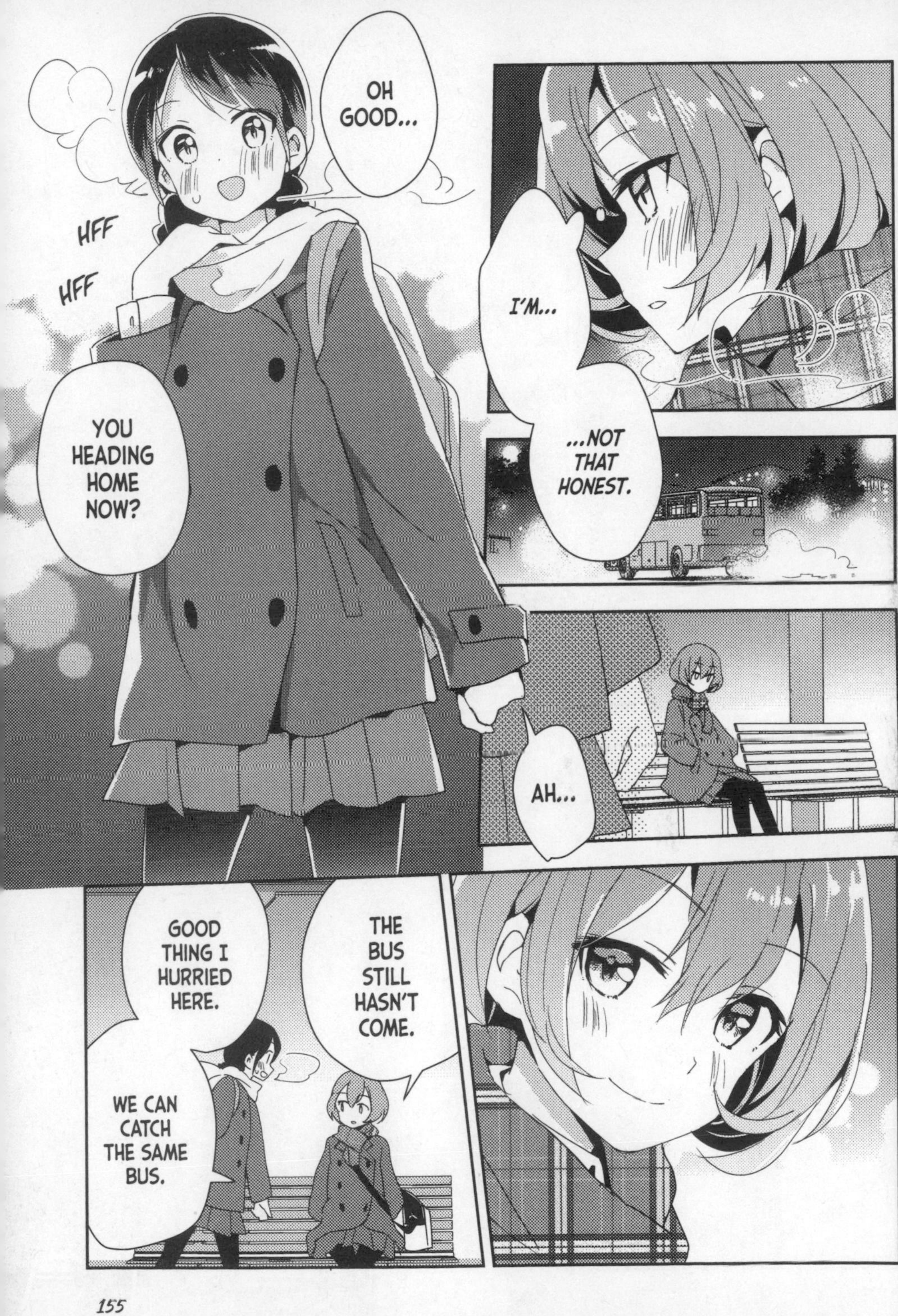
I'M...
...NOT THAT HONEST.
AH...
OH GOOD...
HFF
HFF
YOU HEADING HOME NOW?
THE BUS STILL HASN'T COME.
GOOD THING I HURRIED HERE.
WE CAN CATCH THE SAME BUS.

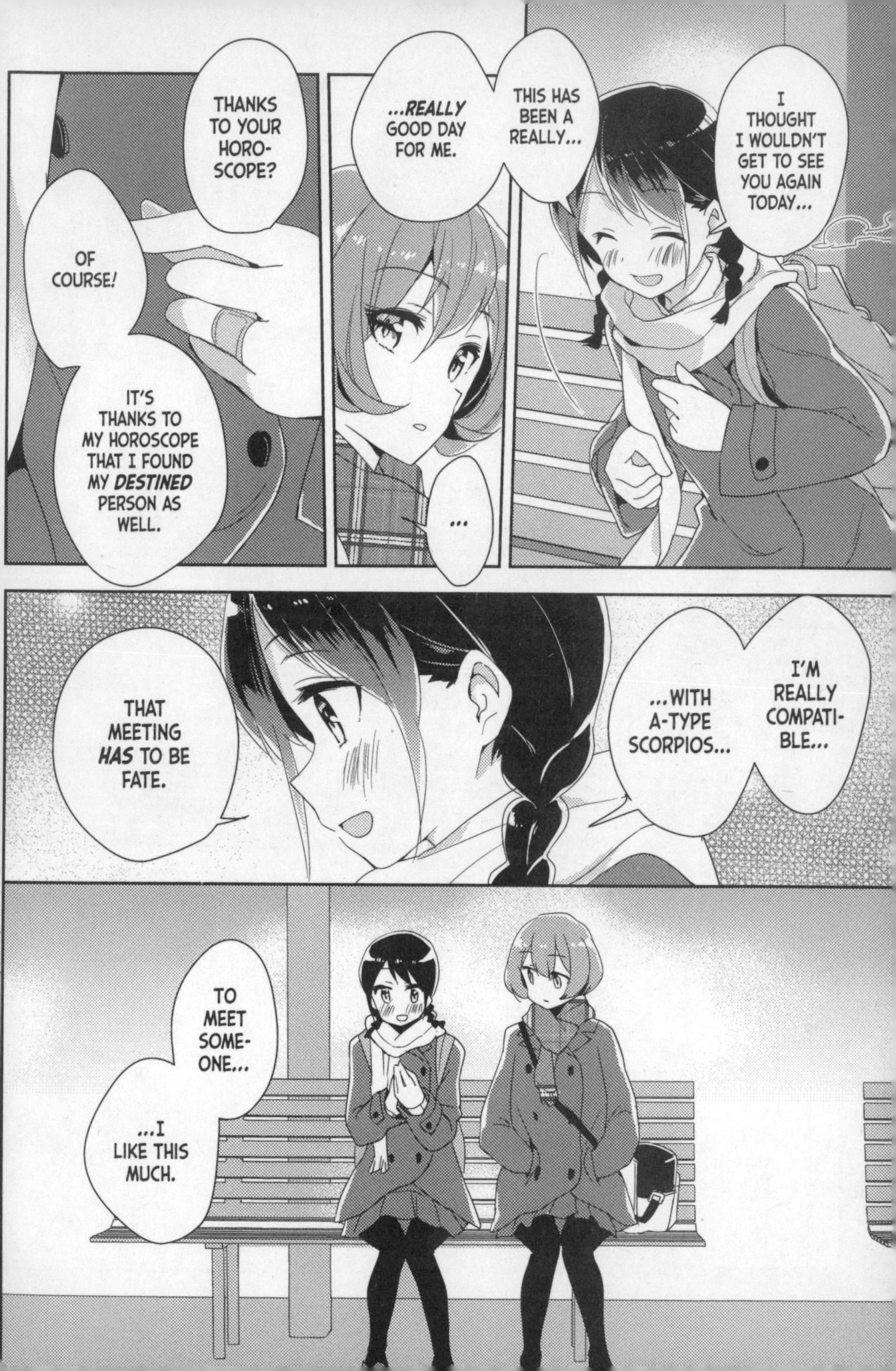
I THOUGHT I WOULDN'T GET TO SEE YOU AGAIN TODAY...
THIS HAS BEEN A REALLY...
...REALLY GOOD DAY FOR ME.
...
THANKS TO YOUR HORO-SCOPE?
OF COURSE!
IT'S THANKS TO MY HOROSCOPE THAT I FOUND MY DESTINED PERSON AS WELL.
I'M REALLY COMPATI-BLE...
...WITH A-TYPE SCORPIOS...
THAT MEETING HAS TO BE FATE.
TO MEET SOME-ONE...
...I LIKE THIS MUCH.

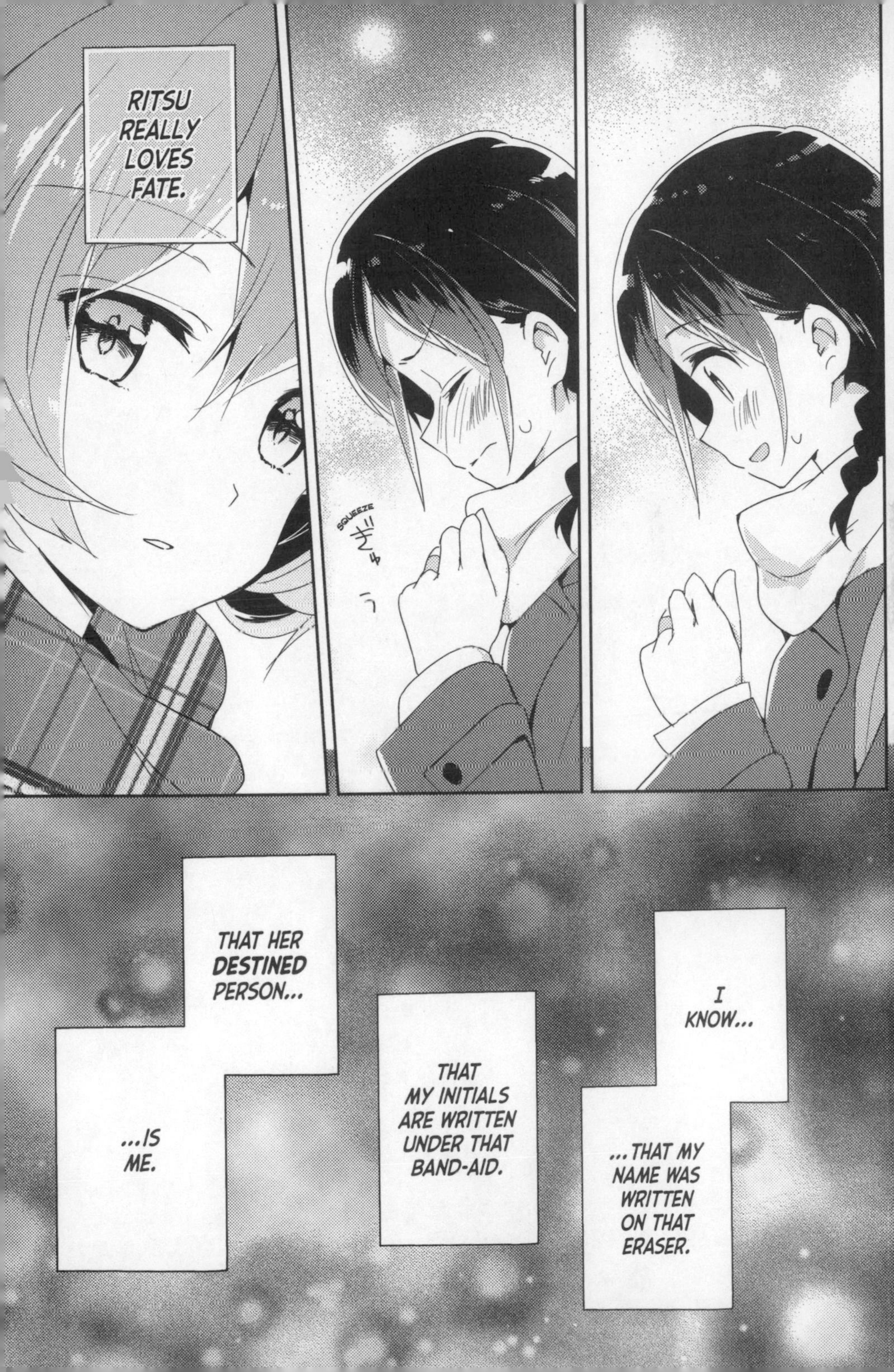
SQUEEZE
RITSU REALLY LOVES FATE.
I KNOW...
...THAT MY NAME WAS WRITTEN ON THAT ERASER.
THAT MY INITIALS ARE WRITTEN UNDER THAT BAND-AID.
THAT HER DESTINED PERSON...
...IS ME.

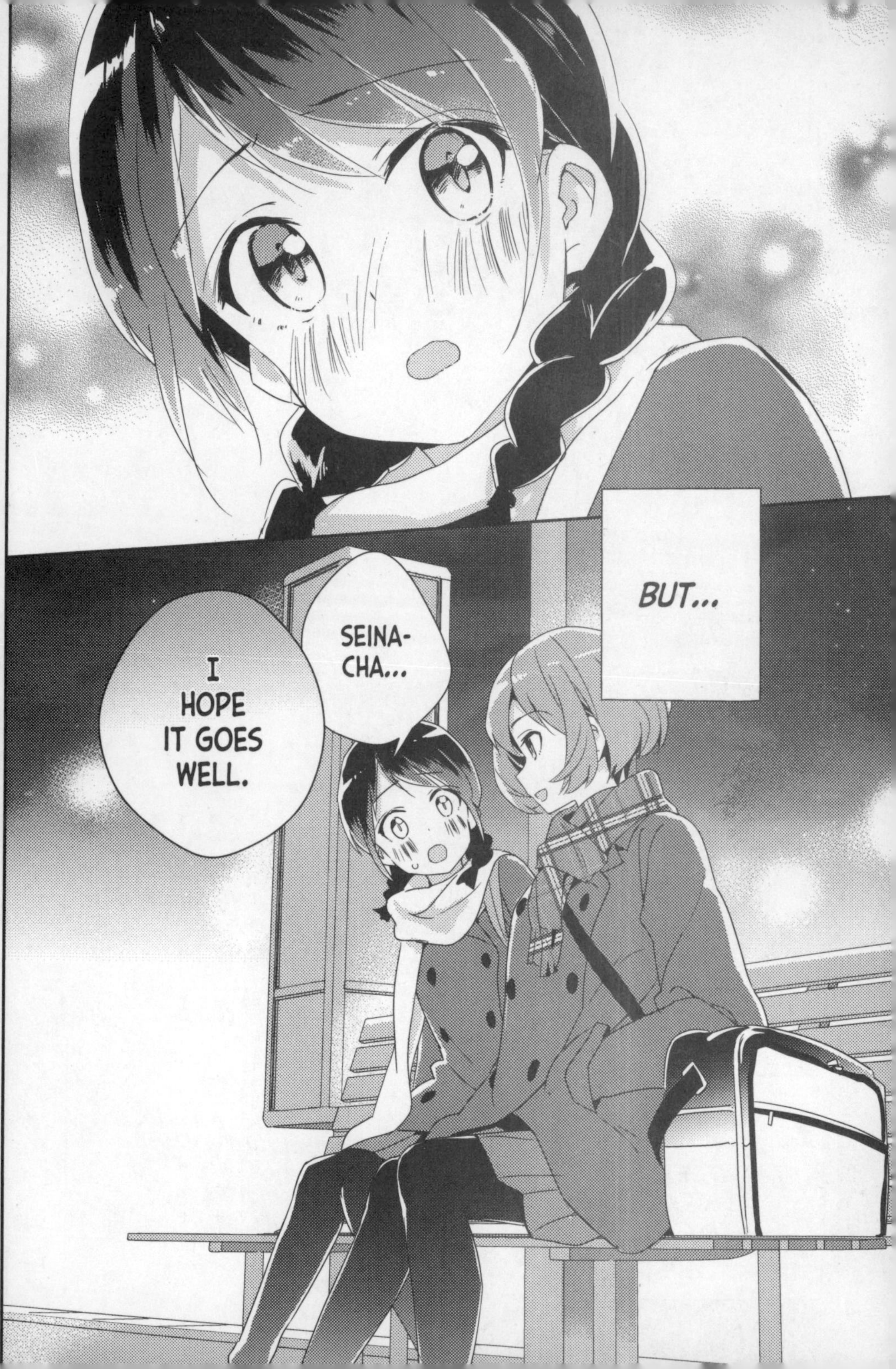
BUT...
SEINA-CHA...
I HOPE IT GOES WELL.

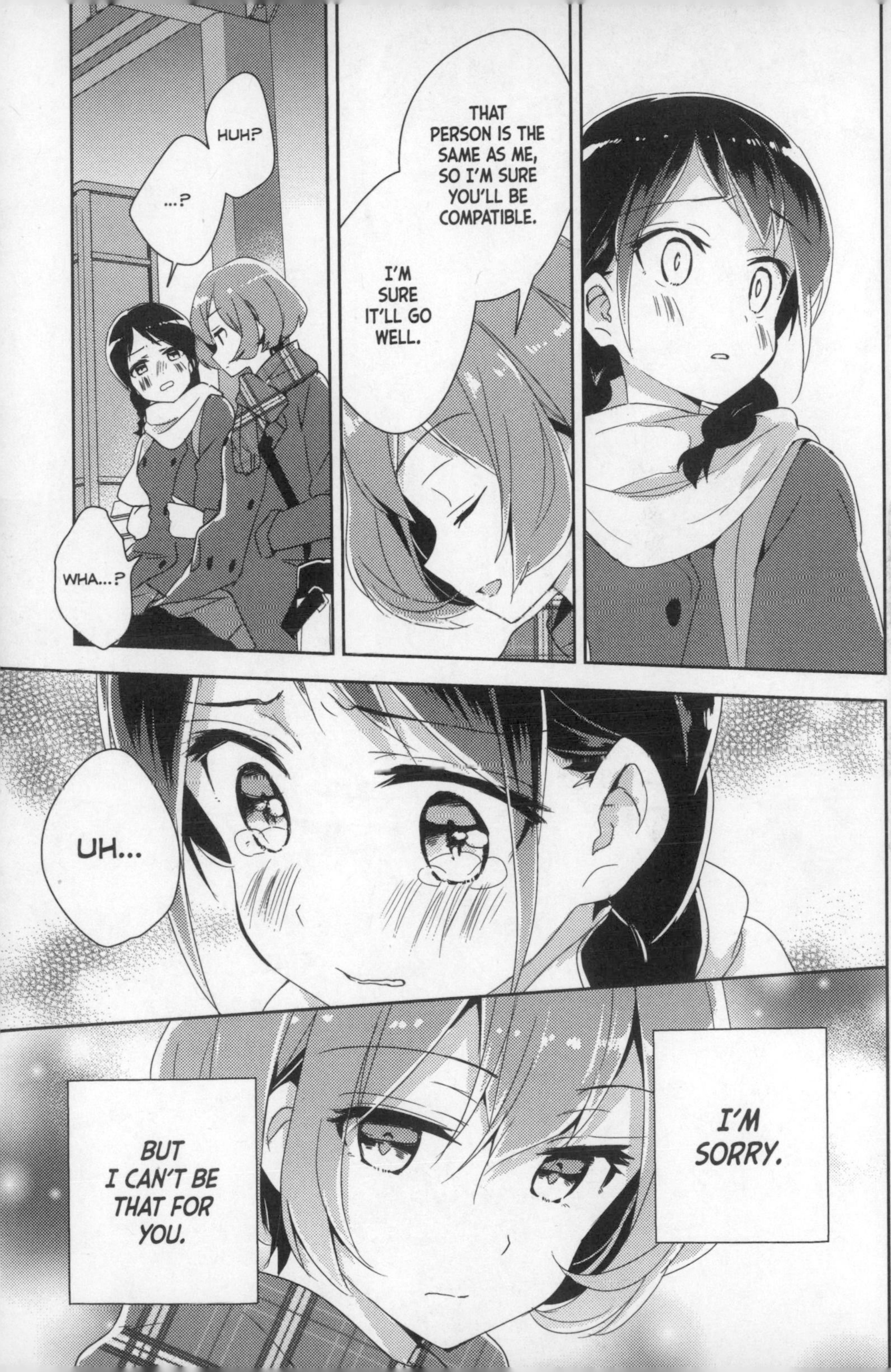
THAT PERSON IS THE SAME AS ME, SO I'M SURE YOU'LL BE COMPATIBLE.
I'M SURE IT'LL GO WELL.
HUH?
...?
WHA...?
UH...
I'M SORRY.
BUT I CAN'T BE THAT FOR YOU.

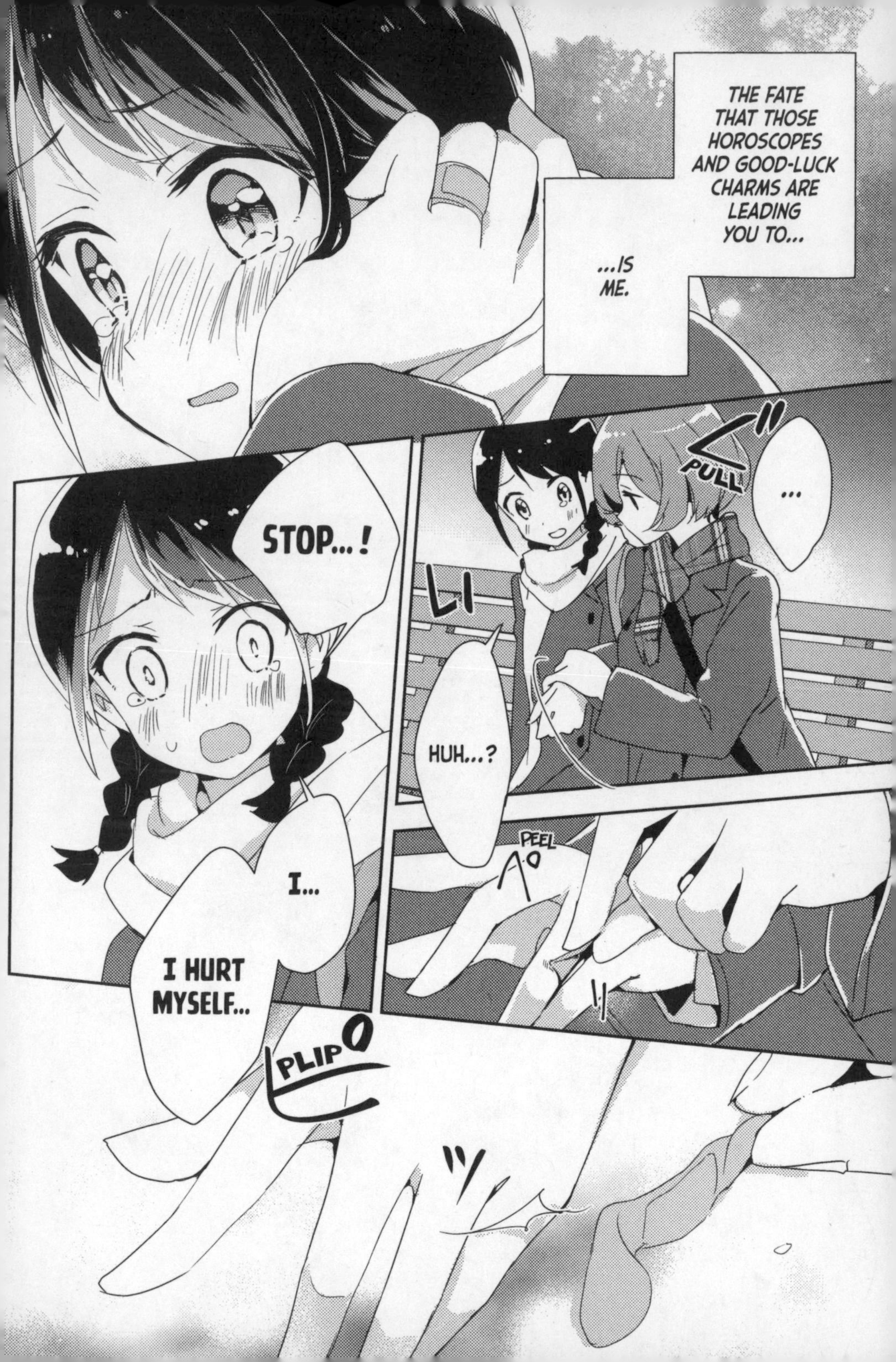
THE FATE THAT THOSE HOROSCOPES AND GOOD-LUCK CHARMS ARE LEADING YOU TO...
...IS ME.
PULL
...
HUH...?
PEEL
STOP...!
I...
I HURT MYSELF...
PLIP

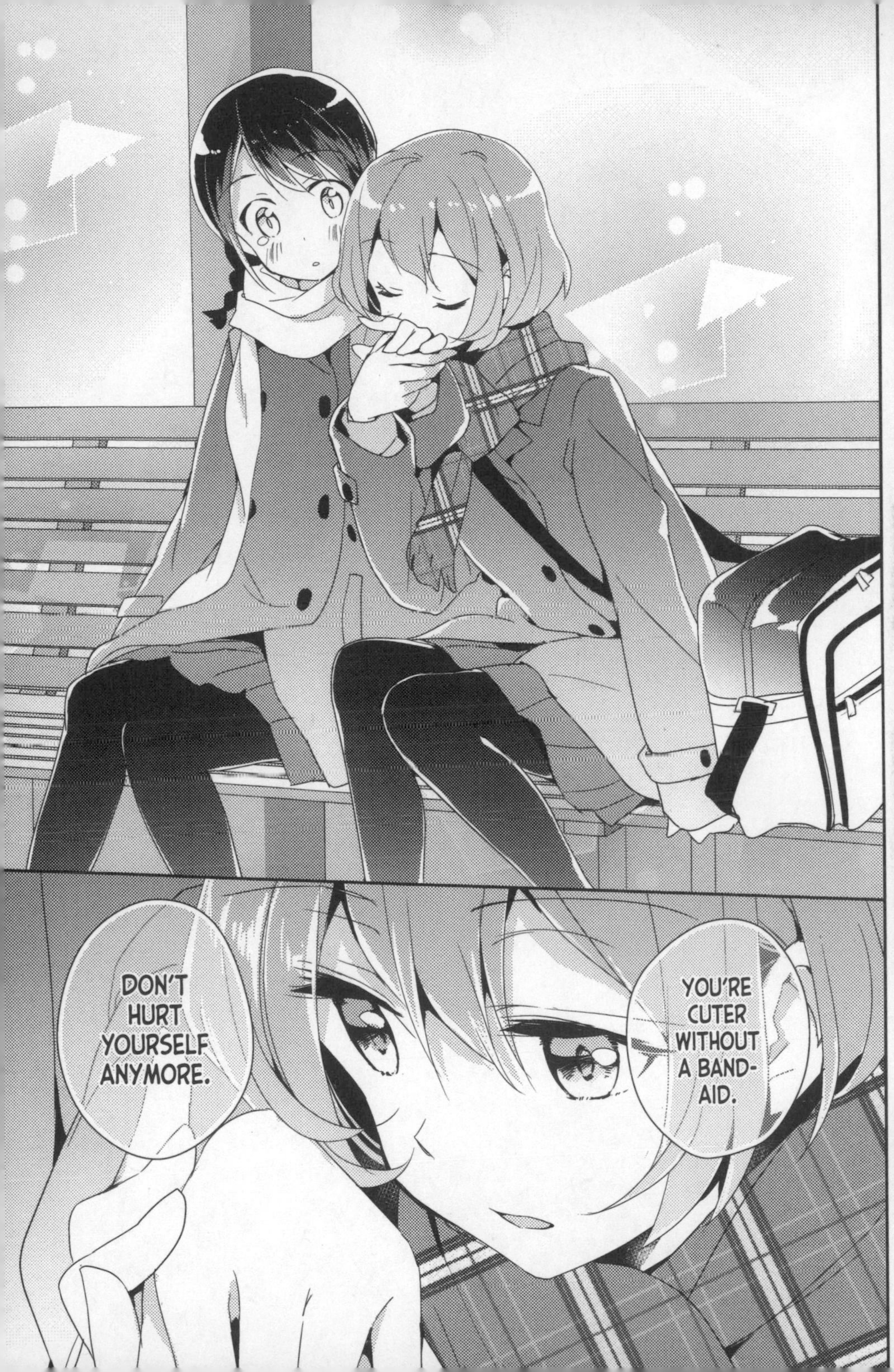
YOU'RE CUTER WITHOUT A BAND-AID.
DON'T HURT YOURSELF ANYMORE.

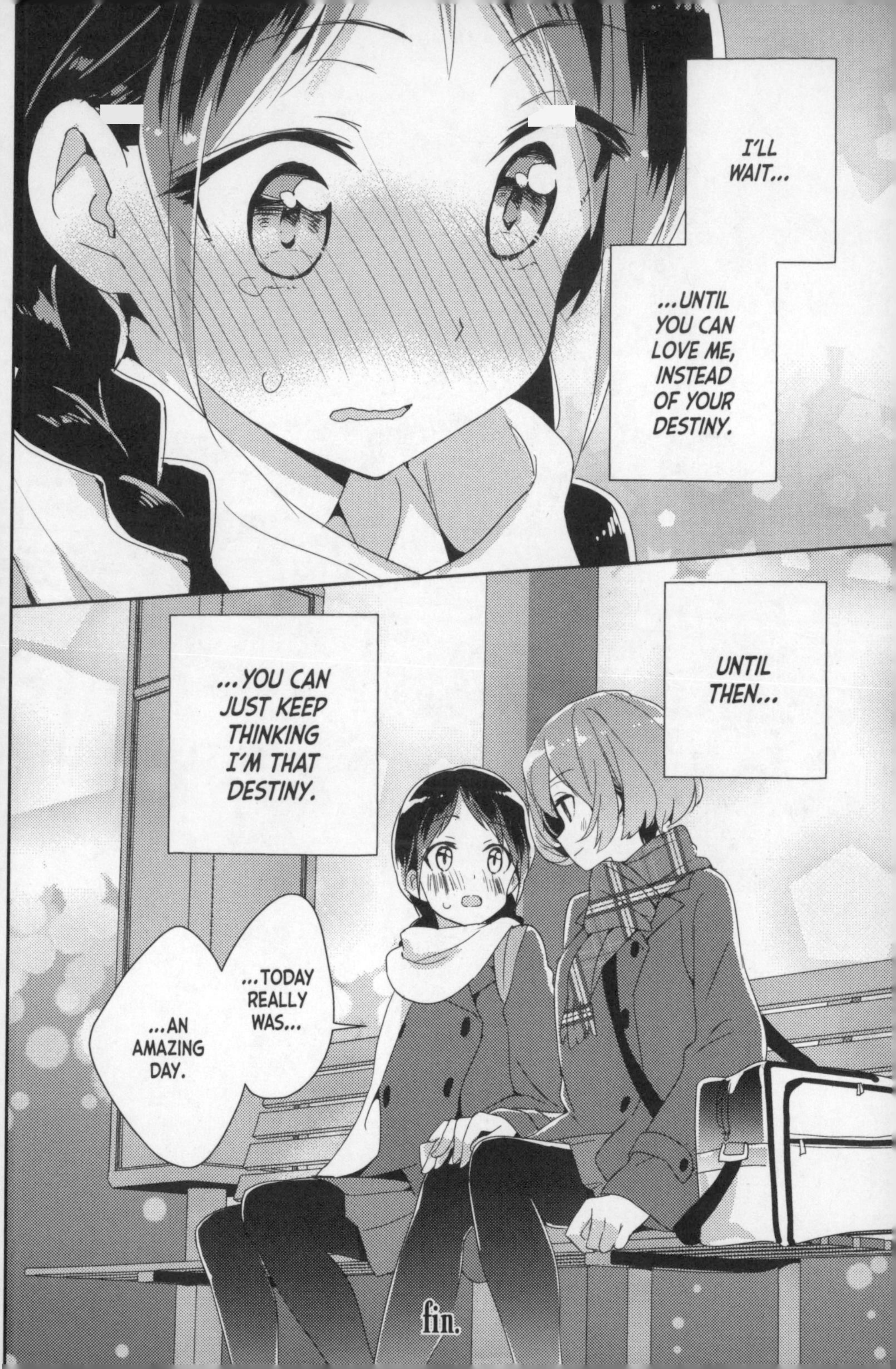
I'LL WAIT...
...UNTIL YOU CAN LOVE ME, INSTEAD OF YOUR DESTINY.
UNTIL THEN...
...YOU CAN JUST KEEP THINKING I'M THAT DESTINY.
...TODAY REALLY WAS...
...AN AMAZING DAY.
fin.

Thank you very much!

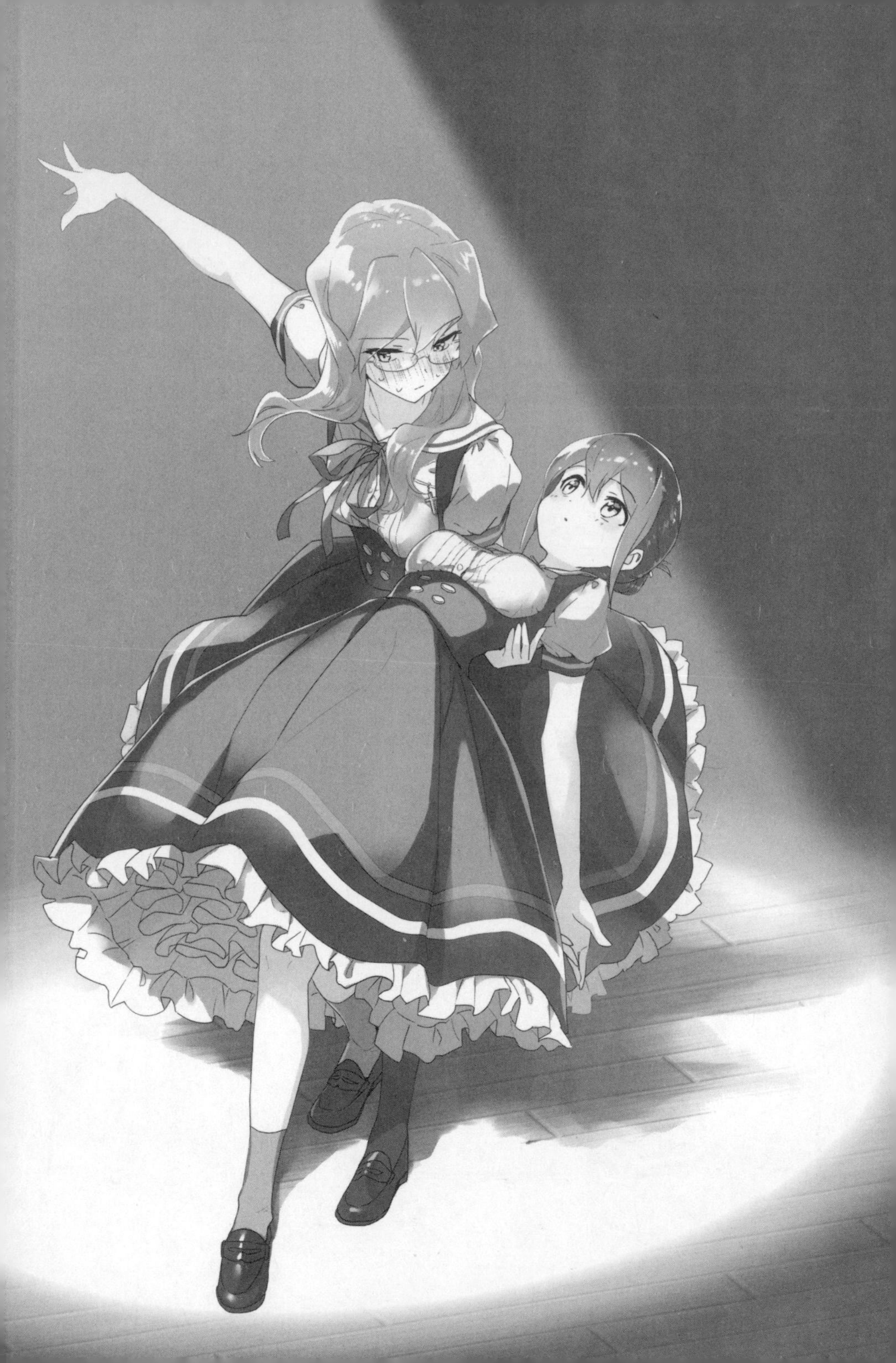

Kanoko-chan's

Review!
Café Liebe Operation Manual

Handling Former Employees

Cast members who have resigned are to be treated as "students who quit the Salon team," with the premise being that they have left the Salon but they still attend the Academy, so we see them from time to time.

The Salon team is made up of students chosen by the academy chairperson, so naturally, sometimes they also quit, based on the chairperson's judgement, as well as the student's circumstances. Thus, if asked about their reason for quitting, it's fine to say, "I'm not sure." The guests are fully aware that leaving the Salon team means resignation, so they usually don't broach the subject much.

Nene Saionji-san is also recognized as a student who quit the Salon team, so guests probably assume that she resigned from the café as well. They probably have no idea that she still works in the kitchen.

Yoko Goeido-san was a third-year, and very sophisticated, so instead, the premise is that she graduated from the Academy. Sumika-san was supposed to be in the same year, so this created a bit of a discrepancy, but...thankfully the guests don't broach that topic either.

❧ miman ❧

Salutations.

Here unfolds a new chapter.

Sumika desires peace for Liebe,

and Kanoko has her own yearnings.

Can the two maintain the status quo...?

Yuri Is My Job!

KC
KODANSHA
COMICS

The prince in his dark days

By **Hico Yamanaka**

A drunkard for a father, a household of poverty... For 17-year-old Atsuko, misfortune is all she knows and believes in. Until one day, a chance encounter with Itaru—the wealthy heir of a huge corporation—changes everything. The two look identical, uncannily so. When Itaru curiously goes missing, Atsuko is roped into being his stand-in. There, in his shoes, Atsuko must parade like a prince in a palace. She encounters many new experiences, but at what cost...?

SAINT ☆ YOUNG MEN

A LONG AWAITED ARRIVAL IN PREMIUM 2-IN-1 HARDCOVER

After centuries of hard work, Jesus and Buddha take a break from their heavenly duties to relax among the people of Japan, and their adventures in this lighthearted buddy comedy are sure to bring mirth and merriment to all!

PERFECT WORLD

Rie Aruga

A TOUCHING NEW SERIES ABOUT LOVE AND COPING WITH DISABILITY

An office party reunites Tsugumi with her high school crush Itsuki. He's realized his dream of becoming an architect, but along the way, he experienced a spinal injury that put him in a wheelchair. Now Tsugumi's rekindled feelings will butt up against prejudices she never considered — and Itsuki will have to decide if he's ready to let someone into his heart...

"Depicts with great delicacy and courage the difficulties some with disabilities experience getting involved in romantic relationships... Rie Aruga refuses to romanticize, pushing her heroine to face the reality of disability. She invites her readers to the same tasks of empathy, knowledge and recognition."
—Slate.fr

"An important entry [in manga romance]... The emotional core of both plot and characters indicates thoughtfulness... [Aruga's] research is readily apparent in the text and artwork, making this feel like a real story."
—Anime News Network

KC KODANSHA COMICS

The art-deco cyberpunk classic from the creators of *xxxHOLiC* and *Cardcaptor Sakura*!

"Starred Review. This experimental sci-fi work from CLAMP reads like a romantic version of *AKIRA*."
—Publishers Weekly

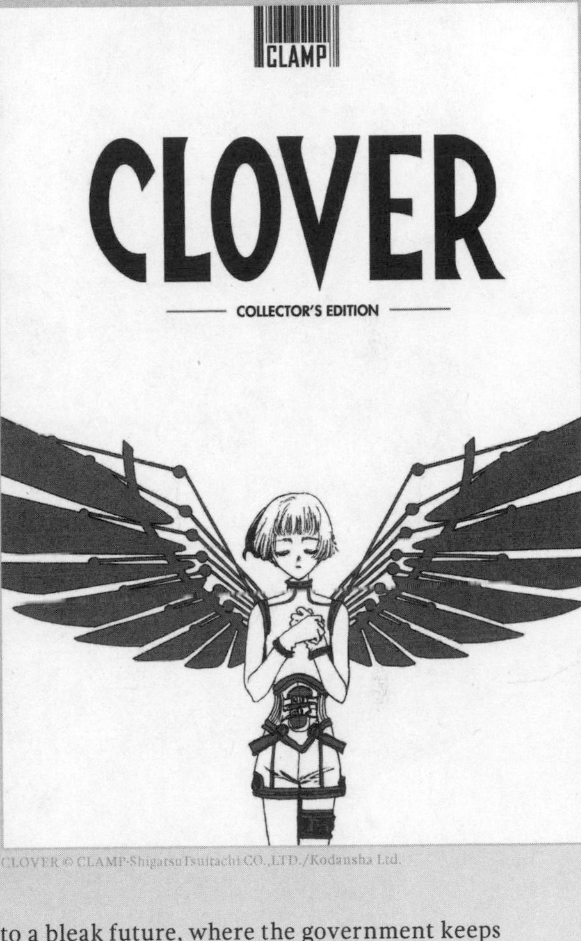
CLAMP
CLOVER
COLLECTOR'S EDITION

CLOVER © CLAMP-ShigatsuTsuitachi CO.,LTD./Kodansha Ltd.

Su was born into a bleak future, where the government keeps tight control over children with magical powers—codenamed "Clovers." With Su being the only "four-leaf" Clover in the world, she has been kept isolated nearly her whole life. Can ex-military agent Kazuhiko deliver her to the happiness she seeks? Experience the complete series in this hardcover edition, which also includes over twenty pages of ravishing color art!

KC KODANSHA COMICS

THE SWEET SCENT OF LOVE IS IN THE AIR! FOR FANS OF OFFBEAT ROMANCES LIKE *WOTAKOI*

Sweet and Soap © Kintetsu Yamada / Kodansha Ltd.

In an office romance, there's a fine line between sexy and awkward... and that line is where Asako — a woman who sweats copiously — meets Koutarou — a perfume developer who can't get enough of Asako's, er, scent. Don't miss a romcom manga like no other!

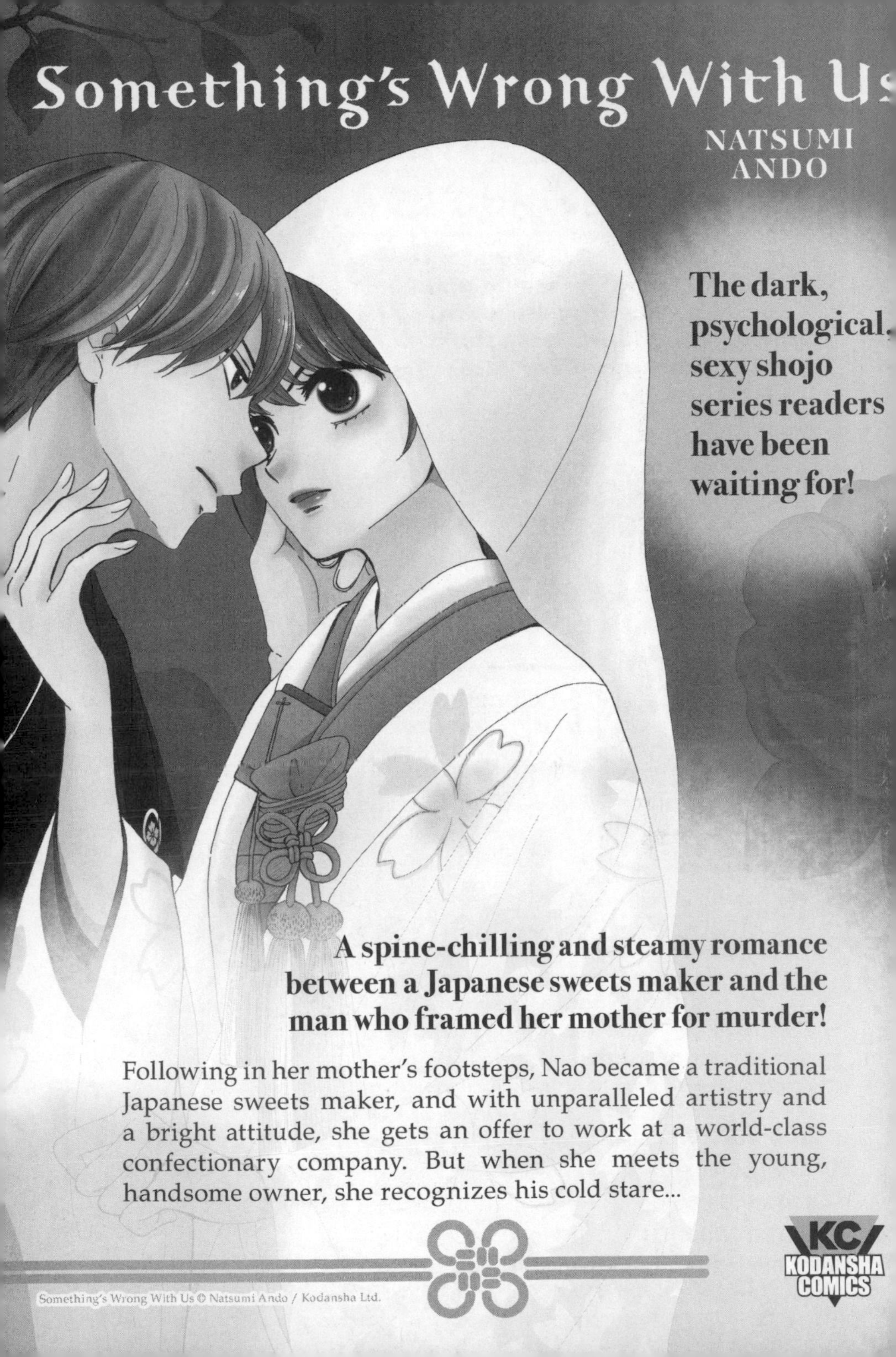
Something's Wrong With Us
NATSUMI ANDO
The dark, psychological, sexy shojo series readers have been waiting for!
A spine-chilling and steamy romance between a Japanese sweets maker and the man who framed her mother for murder!
Following in her mother's footsteps, Nao became a traditional Japanese sweets maker, and with unparalleled artistry and a bright attitude, she gets an offer to work at a world-class confectionary company. But when she meets the young, handsome owner, she recognizes his cold stare...
KC KODANSHA COMICS

WAITING FOR SPRING

A sweet romantic story of a soft-spoken high school freshman and her quest to make friends. For fans of earnest, fun, and dramatic shojo like *Kimi ni Todoke* and *Say I Love You*.

KISS ME AT THE STROKE OF MIDNIGHT

An all-new Cinderella comedy perfect for fans of *My Little Monster* and *Say I Love You!*

LOVE AND LIES

Love is forbidden. When you turn 16, the government will assign you your marriage partner. This dystopian manga about teen love and defiance is a sexy, funny, and dramatic new hit! Anime now streaming on Anime Strike!

KC KODANSHA COMICS

A SMART, NEW ROMANTIC COMEDY FOR FANS OF *SHORTCAKE CAKE* AND *TERRACE HOUSE*!

A romance manga starring high school girl Meeko, who learns to live on her own in a boarding house whose living room is home to the odd (but handsome) Matsunaga-san. She begins to adjust to her new life away from her parents, but Meeko soon learns that no matter how far away from home she is, she's still a young girl at heart — especially when she finds herself falling for Matsunaga-san.

Young characters and steampunk setting, like *Howl's Moving Castle* and *Battle Angel Alita*

Beyond the Clouds © 2018 Nicke / Ki-oon

A boy with a talent for machines and a mysterious girl whose wings he's fixed will take you beyond the clouds! In the tradition of the high-flying, resonant adventure stories of Studio Ghibli comes a gorgeous tale about the longing of young hearts for adventure and friendship!

The adorable new odd-couple cat comedy manga from the creator of the beloved *Chi's Sweet Home*, in full color!

Sue & Tai-chan

Konami Kanata

Sue is an aging housecat who's looking forward to living out her life in peace... but her plans change when the mischievous black tomcat Tai-chan enters the picture! Hey! Sue never signed up to be a catsitter! *Sue & Tai-chan* is the latest from the reigning meow-narch of cute kitty comics, Konami Kanata.

A Kodansha Comics Trade Paperback Original
Yuri Is My Job! 9 copyright © 2021 miman
English translation copyright © 2022 miman

All rights reserved.

Published in the United States by Kodansha Comics, an imprint of Kodansha USA Publishing, LLC, New York.

Publication rights for this English edition arranged through Kodansha Ltd., Tokyo.

First published in Japan in 2021 by Ichijinsha Inc., Tokyo as *Watashi no Yuri wa Oshigotodesu!*, volume 9.

ISBN 978-1-64651-417-5

Printed in the United States of America.

www.kodansha.us

1st Printing
Translation: Diana Taylor
Lettering: Jennifer Skarupa
Editing: Haruko Hashimoto
Kodansha Comics edition cover design by Phil Balsman

Publisher: Kiichiro Sugawara

Director of publishing services: Ben Applegate
Director of publishing operations: Dave Barrett
Associate director, publishing operations: Stephen Pakula
Publishing services managing editor: Madison Salters, Alanna Ruse
Production managers: Emi Lotto, Angela Zurlo